TEACHING FOR EFFECTIVE LEARNING IN HIGHER EDUCATION

TEACHING FOR EFFECTIVE LEARNING IN HIGHER EDUCATION

by

Nira Hativa

Tel Aviv University,
Tel Aviv,
Israel

KLUWER ACADEMIC PUBLISHERS

DORDRECHT / BOSTON / LONDON

A C.I.P. Catalogue record for this book is available from the Library of Congress.

ISBN 0-7923-6843-6

Published by Kluwer Academic Publishers,
P.O. Box 17, 3300 AA Dordrecht, The Netherlands.

Sold and distributed in North, Central and South America
by Kluwer Academic Publishers,
101 Philip Drive, Norwell, MA 02061, U.S.A.

In all other countries, sold and distributed
by Kluwer Academic Publishers,
P.O. Box 322, 3300 AH Dordrecht, The Netherlands.

Printed on acid-free paper

Printed in the Netherlands.

To my family: Devorah, Moshe, Uri, Sigal, Izchak, Tamir, Alon, Ortal and Liron

CONTENTS

Creating a Positive Classroom Environment

FOREWORD BY DOUGLAS M. OSHEROFF

Stanford University,

1996 Nobel Laureate in Physics

It perhaps can be said that I have a natural talent as a research physicist. I was 'born' with a silver spoon in my mouth, in that my Ph.D. thesis work represented a major discovery in physics. The same cannot be said for my talent as a teacher, although with a great deal of effort I am able to keep from embarrassing myself. After graduate school I spent my first fifteen years at the AT&T Bell Laboratories doing almost nothing but research. One of the few things I did beside research, however, was to tour New Jersey giving demonstration lectures on low temperature physics to K-12 student groups. My wife thus believed that I had a natural interest in teaching, and encouraged me to become a university professor. That did not happen until I was already a member of the National Academy of Sciences, and the recipient of three prestigious research awards.

I was petrified when I began teaching my first large lecture course. Stanford at that time provided virtually no training for faculty in classroom teaching, and very few guidelines of any sort. My first class had almost 300 students, divided into two sections. I gave each lecture twice, one at 9am and the second at 10am. Between lectures my head teaching assistant would come down from the audience and tell me what I had done wrong the first hour. I am still amazed that I would have been so desperate as to accept criticism from an ex-student who had never given a single lecture. Such, however, was my classroom training.

I did enjoy teaching, however, even though it took a large commitment in time for me to do a decent job. Perhaps I worked too hard, for in 1991 Stanford awarded me one of their prizes in recognition of a novel laboratory course I had been teaching. I also enjoyed teaching the large lecture courses, however, and liked the idea that I was able to influence the way so many bright Stanford students thought about physics. In addition, I felt that good teaching had special rewards, such as when a student decided to major in physics because I had awakened in him a love for the subject, or when ex-students introduced me to their parents on graduation weekend.

My first contact with Nira Hativa occurred when she sent a questionnaire to members of the Stanford Physics Faculty regarding their teaching attitudes and practices. While teaching is taken very seriously in the department, physicists as a rule do not believe that specialists in education can possibly understand the complexities of teaching physics, particularly to undergraduates. As a result, I was a member of a very small group that completed and returned that questionnaire. Perhaps I should say attempted to complete the questionnaire, for there were a number of questions about whose meaning I could only speculate.

Several months later Nira wrote me indicating that she would soon be visiting Stanford, and wanted to interview me regarding my responses to her questionnaire. At this moment I began to question my decision to return the form in the first place, but agreed to meet with her one Saturday morning. In that interview Nira asked me why I had failed to answer certain questions. I replied that I had no idea what she was asking. For example, what did she mean by asking "Do you regard physics as a hierarchical subject?" To this complaint she replied: "Do you regard physics as a subject for which an understanding of more advanced concepts requires a firm understanding of more basic ones?" I think it was at that moment that I believed that Nira might understand the process by which one teaches physics better than I did, and our discussion went on for almost two hours.

My next contact with Nira occurred a few years later, when she asked if she could spend part of her sabbatical working with members of the Stanford Physics Faculty in order to improve their teaching. I was at that time chair of the department, and recognized all too well the shortcomings of some of our illustrious faculty members in the classroom, and the advantages that a good reputation in teaching had in dealing with the Dean's Office. Ultimately I arranged for Nira to come, and soon after her arrival 'Hativa' became a verb describing the unpleasant process by which Nira made my faculty aware of their classroom shortcomings. Even I was not left in blissful ignorance, as her zeal to improve our teaching effectiveness became a consuming passion.

At the end of Nira's stay, I suppose that my first reaction was one of relief that I had not been forced to step down from being chair by an irate faculty. Indeed, many of those professors who worked with Nira indicated that they had found their interactions with her to have been quite constructive. In addition, Nira provided Stanford with two new teaching resources. The first was a computerized mid-course student evaluation form. This form provided much more immediate and thus useful feedback on teaching effectiveness than did the University form which is filled out at the end of the course, and not returned to the individual instructors until near the end of the next teaching term. Later Nira's form served as a template when the University form was revised. The second was a series of videotapes featuring some of the best classroom teachers at Stanford in the sciences and engineering. Completion of this video series required a second visit by Nira.

This book provides a wealth of information for those who wish to improve their teaching style. The book is well written, and organized in a manner that makes it possible for the reader to use only those chapters that are of interest. I think that Part I should be of interest to everyone, however, and deserves to be read thoroughly. Part II should be read by everyone who is unable to motivate a class. I found Part III particularly useful for those teaching technical subjects, and I intend to adopt several of the teaching strategies suggested there. I also found Part IV to be of particular interest to me. Although I use several of the strategies suggested there, I agreed with the analysis, and found ways in which I can more efficiently use my class time.

I very much enjoyed the discussion of testing and grading in Chapter 19, as I do write my own exams, and my own philosophy on what a good exam should contain and what a good average score should be has evolved over the years. For the first midterm exam I ever gave, the mean was only 41%. This was devastating both to me and to the students. I think that such a disaster can easily happen to someone who has been away from teaching for so long. This was a class for sophomores; however some freshmen with advanced placement credit would also enroll. I distinctly remember a freshman woman coming into my office to complain that the exam was too hard. She had probably never received less than 90% on any exam in her life. I asked what her grade was, and she replied 43%. To this I responded "Oh, you beat the mean. That's not so bad," at which point she burst into tears. I am now quite good at writing exams that will yield a mean within a desired range, but have adopted an effective strategy for motivating those students who do poorly on my first midterm exams: I track how each student does relative to the mean on each exam. If students do better on the later exams than the first, the program automatically gives back half the points they would have had were they to have done as well on the first exam as the later exams. Not only does this give poor early performers hope, but also an incentive to work harder.

Good teaching obviously requires a firm understanding of the material to be covered in the course, as well as enough beyond that so as to answer the questions of interested students. Yet subject knowledge alone is not enough. Professors usually consider their lecture styles to be highly developed, and well suited to their personalities and the subject matter. I believe that the few hours needed to read this book will provide enough new ideas and insights for most instructors, however, that their investment in time will be richly rewarded.

FOREWORD BY WILBERT M. MCKEACHIE

The University of Michigan,

Past president of the American Psychological Association (APA) and the American Association for Higher Education (AAHE)

Those who know my book, *Teaching Tips*, (1oth ed., 1999) may wonder why I would write a foreword for a book that seems to be a competitor. There are at least three reasons:

1. This is an excellent book.
2. Nira Hativa is my friend.
3. I believe that *Teaching for Effective Learning* and *Teaching Tips* complement one another. True, our books cover many of the same topics, but we approach them in different ways. I like Nira's surveys of faculty and students and her use of bar graphs to communicate the results.

I like the many quotations of student comments that add color and richness to her descriptions of good and poor teachers. I have put many Post-its on pages where there are points I want to remember or where there are practical suggestions I want to try out in my own class this fall.

I was particularly pleased that Nira emphasizes the intrinsic rewards in teaching as illustrated in Figure 1.3 and continuing throughout the book to the very last paragraph where she reports that one outcome of a program for evaluating and improving teaching is enthusiasm. Faculty members who use this book will gain greater intrinsic satisfaction both because of a deeper understanding of teaching and learning and from an increased repertoire of teaching strategies.

The book begins with a good discussion of the question, "What is good teaching?" which goes beyond our typical statement that good instruction brings about the achievement of the goals it is intended to achieve. Nira reports surveys of faculty members' ratings of the importance of differing educational goals and of student preferences for teacher characteristics and behaviors. This leads nicely into her discussion of instructor beliefs and approaches to teaching.

This in turn is logically followed by the remaining chapters discussing a variety of strategies for effective instruction and the concluding chapter on ways to improve. Certainly one important tool for improvement is *Teaching for Effective Learning*. Here, too, Nira makes a unique contribution. She links teacher thinking and beliefs to their teaching and discusses barriers to active learning in lectures and discussion. A particularly interesting chapter "Avoiding 'Noise' in Teaching". All in all a fine book.

Introduction

The Book, Its Aim and Content

TEACHING FOR EFFECTIVE LEARNING

> The ultimate outcome of instructional practice is effective student learning (Donald, 2000, p. 2).

> Good teaching encourages high quality student learning (Ramsden, 1992, p. 86).

The paramount aim of teaching is that students learn. Thus, the ultimate criterion of effective teaching is effective and successful learning. There is substantial research evidence that good teaching does make a difference in student learning so that students who are well taught learn more than students who are poorly taught. We also know that there are some characteristics and methods that are consistently associated with good university[1] teaching (Cross, 1993). This book identifies these characteristics and methods for the reader and presents them within a theoretical framework that explains how they affect student learning. Because students' learning depends substantially on their behavior, the book perceives good teaching as "an evocative process that aims to involve students actively in their own learning and to elicit from them their best learning performance" (ibid., p. 12).

Although the book's main themes relate to classroom instruction, it also discusses other teacher activities so as to cover the entire act of teaching, which consists of "vision, design, enactment, outcomes, and analysis" (Shulman, 1998, p. 6). To further elaborate:

---

[1] In this book, the term "university" represents all types of universities and colleges.

Teaching refers to the design and implementation of activities to promote student learning. It certainly goes beyond what teachers do in the classroom. It includes course design and the development of instructional materials, the out-of-class interactions between faculty members and students, as well as the formative and summative assessment of student learning (Smith, Forthcoming, p. 1).

Therefore, this book presents also topics other than classroom teaching, such as planning the course and the lesson, assigning homework, and assessing student learning.

TEACHING AS SCHOLARLY WORK[2]

In the last decade, we have seen a growing tendency to perceive university teaching as scholarly work and as scholarship. To illustrate, the March-April 1991 issue of the Stanford Observer published on its front page an item entitled "Teaching Initiative Gets Teeth," which reports that the university's president:

...announced in March $7 million in new programs to improve teaching of undergraduate students. Included are economic incentives to reward faculty for outstanding classroom instruction. He also proposed modifications in the faculty appointment and promotion process that would give greater attention to teaching and other forms of scholarship, apart from research. The proposed changes in promotion and hiring processes include limiting the number of research papers to be considered, broadening the definition of scholarship to include materials used in teaching, e.g., textbooks and original computer courseware for undergraduate courses, and establishing regular systems of post-tenure evaluation of teaching using peer review as a complement to student evaluations.

According to this approach, the status of teaching in the university should be raised to the same level as that of research, in contrast with the current situation where teaching does not count much in the faculty reward system, particularly in research universities. Teaching is usually perceived by faculty as a routine task rather than as an aspect of professional scholarly work, an act of intellectual invention deserving their time and attention (Shulman & Hutchings, 1997). Shulman advocates that the faculty's view of teaching change from "simply a matter of methods and techniques" to an activity "of selecting, organizing, and transforming one's field so that it can be engaged and understood at a deep level by students" (ibid., p. 7).

This book suggests for the first step in promoting the perception of teaching as scholarly intellectual work to change faculty's perception of teaching as "simply a matter of methods and techniques", a random collection of "do's and don'ts," or an aggregation of teaching techniques that

[2] See also Chapter 1: Scholarly Teaching and the Scholarship of Teaching.

one should remember and use. The book does so by presenting teaching as a logical structure of interconnected teaching behaviors whose contribution to student learning is based on theory and research.

THE BOOK'S AUDIENCE

College and university teachers are one of the three main audiences of the book. They are expected to teach well, and their teaching performance is judged for important matters such as tenure, promotion, and salary. However, as discussed in Chapter 1, most faculty members in higher education have not received any formal, systematic pedagogical preparation to guide them in effective teaching. This book aims to help faculty obtain this knowledge—to provide the framework and tools for understanding and improving their teaching practices and processes. The book presents pedagogical knowledge that goes beyond any specific subject matter; thus, it addresses faculty of all academic disciplines.

The book also aims to benefit *faculty developers* who may wish to deepen their understanding of teaching processes, get some ideas for their practical work, prepare transparencies from the charts in this book to use in workshops for faculty, and use the book for assigning reading to their clients. The model that the book presents may contribute to their work in promoting faculty's understanding of the theoretical framework for effective teaching.

Lastly, the book addresses *researchers* in that it provides a substantive research literature regarding all aspects of effective teaching. However, because the book also approaches practitioners, the studies are reported here mainly in terms of their conclusions rather than their methods and critical analyses. The value for researchers is thus primarily in the identification and overview of a very extensive related literature.

THE BOOK'S KNOWLEDGE BASE

The theoretical knowledge presented here is based on the research literature in the domains of *education, communication, sociology,* and *educational psychology.* An additional source is the literature published by teaching centers in universities all over the US and Canada. In addition, the book is based on substantial practical wisdom contributed by students and teachers.

This book puts forth the voice of the students—the clients of university instruction—regarding all aspects of teaching that they experience. Their voice is represented by authentic comments that they wrote in thousands of instructor-evaluation forms that I have collected over many years. One survey (File, 1984) found that *the major problem that first year university students experienced in understanding class instruction was their lecturers' inability to communicate their knowledge to them.* Students' comments, in most of the chapters, reflect their frustration with problematic teacher communication, as well as their satisfaction with teachers who have good communication skills.

The book is also based on the classroom practices of university teachers that I have identified through observing many classes in a variety of schools and departments; analyzing dozens of videotaped classes of award-winning teachers; and interviewing many faculty members—those regarded by their students as either good or poor teachers.

STRUCTURE OF THE BOOK

The book consists of four parts. It starts (Part I, Chapters 1-4) with the notion of good/effective teaching; then it promotes the motivation of college and university faculty to invest in providing good teaching, and presents research results describing faculty's perceptions of teaching, learning and students. Findings about students' learning styles and characteristics, and their preferences for teacher characteristics are reported as well. Part II (Chapters 5-7) describes theory and research related to a variety of methods and styles of teaching that may be applied in colleges and universities, with a special emphasis on those designed for active learning. Part III (Chapters 8-17) presents a structured model for effective teaching, consisting of teaching dimensions that have been identified as most crucial in effective teaching. These are: making the presentation organized, clear, and interesting/ engaging, and maintaining a pleasant classroom climate. Each of these main dimensions is broken down into intermediate dimensions, which are further broken down into classroom strategies/behaviors that contribute to the main dimensions. Part IV (Chapters 18-19) discusses several important issues related to teaching courses in higher education: course and lesson planning, testing and grading, and readings and other homework assignments. The last part (V) (Chapter 20) suggests ways to improve teaching. The book ends with an appendix that leads teachers through the lesson planning process by using a layout for planning that incorporates pedagogical considerations. By doing so, the appendix ties all the chapters on effective teaching dimensions and strategies together.

The chapters on teaching dimensions and strategies present theory as well as practical applications. The theory includes related research and many illuminating comments by students. The practical applications suggest teaching strategies to use in class.

The best way to use this book for improving teaching[3] is not to read the whole book at once, as you would read a novel, but to refer to it as a professional text for educators, or as a handbook of ideas. Thus, start by reading the first four chapters that provide the theoretical basis for the teaching methods and strategies that follow in the other chapters. It is very important that teachers understand the theoretical basis for the instructional strategies they use. Then concentrate on each of the following chapters separately, or only on those that relate to topics you feel you need to improve on. Read each chapter carefully, while going from the theory to the suggestions for practice. However, a person looking exclusively for practical advice can read only the practical suggestions in each chapter, which are placed in a shaded box, and thus can be easily identified. When you read these suggestions record any teaching strategy that seems relevant and possible for you to perform and that fits your personality and your students.

I hope the book is found to be insightful and beneficial by all readers.

---

[3] See also Chapter 20: Improving Teaching for Effective Learning.

PART I

EFFECTIVE TEACHING AND LEARNING

Chapter 1

What Makes Good Teaching

SCHOLARLY TEACHING AND THE SCHOLARSHIP OF TEACHING

In the Introduction, we learned about the current tendency to perceive teaching as scholarly intellectual work, or as scholarship. What do these two notions mean? There is some confusion and overlapping in their definition.

Glassick, Huber, and Maeroff (1997, p. 25) suggest that all forms of *scholarly work*, including teaching, should be characterized and assessed by these standards: clear goals, adequate preparation, appropriate methods, significant results, effective presentation, and reflective critique. Shulman and Hutchings (1997) suggest the following guidelines for viewing *teaching as scholarly work*:

- Seeing teaching as a process of ongoing inquiry and reflection. This view of teaching can lead to better faculty understanding of their students' learning and what they, as teachers, can do to make that learning more powerful.
- Seeing faculty as responsible for the quality of their professional work as teachers. They must play a central role in ensuring and improving the quality of their teaching.

In a later publication Shulman (2000, p. 50) defines *scholarly teaching* as "teaching that is well grounded in the sources and resources appropriate to the field. It reflects a thoughtful selection and integration of ideas and examples, and well-designed strategies of course design, development, transmission, interaction and assessment."

9

Shulman adds that for teaching to be perceived as *scholarship* (beyond being *scholarly teaching*) it should also be perceived as community property. Teaching, like research, must be situated within the scholarly community from which it comes and through which it must be valued, reviewed, and evaluated. It needs collegial exchange and "publicness". Faculty should be aware that, as for other scholarship, knowledge of teaching is cummulative and contributes to practice beyond one's own so that members of the community can build on each other's work. Thus, there are three conditions for seeing teaching as community property—that it is (a) public; (b) peer-reviewed and critiqued; and (c) exchanged with other members of the professional communities, so they, in turn, can build each on the others' work

In a Delphi study aimed to define the *"scholarship of teaching"* using experts—academics who enjoyed an excellent reputation for their scholarly work on postsecondary teaching, learning, and faculty evaluation, and who have published explicitly on the scholarship of teaching (Kreber, Forthcoming)—the following characteristics of "those that practice the scholarship of teaching" won the strongest endorsement and the highest consensus among the panelists:

- They examine, interpret, and share learning about teaching, thereby contributing to the scholarly community of their discipline.
- They have an understanding of how students learn, and they know what practices are most effective.
- Their scholarship of teaching includes discovery, integration, and application.
- They learn both about the knowledge in their field and how to make connections with students.
- They know that people learn in diverse ways; hence, they know that instruction should be diversified as well.
- They constantly reflect on the processes and outcomes of teaching and learning and acknowledge the contextual nature of teaching.
- They conduct research on teaching and learning; They gather evidence, interpret it, share the results, and change their practice.
- They develop their practice through a cycle of action, reflection and improvement.
- They share their experiences with others (they act as mentors, communicators, faculty developers, etc.).

As can be seen, these characteristics that fall under the notion of the *scholarship of teaching* belong to Shulman's two definitions—of the *scholarship of teaching* and of *scholarly teaching*. However, in spite of the lack of agreement on clear and concise definitions of these two notions, we may connect both to *effective teaching*. We saw above that one of the characteristics of any scholarly work, including *scholarly teaching*, is effective presentation, and that to practice the *scholarship of teaching*, faculty should understand how students learn and should gain knowledge of what teaching practices are most effective in promoting student learning. Thus, we may conclude that *effective teaching*, as defined next, is an important aspect of *scholarly teaching* and, accordingly to some definitions, of *the scholarship of teaching* as well.

EFFECTIVE TEACHING

What do we mean by "effective teaching"? We define[4] it here roughly as *teaching that brings about effective and successful student learning that is deep and meaningful.* Successful teaching entails "the positive changes produced in students in relevant academic domains including the cognitive, affective, and occasionally the psychomotor ones" (Abrami, d'Apollonia, & Rosenfield, 1997, p. 324). The cognitive category includes both specific and general cognitive skills. The affective category involves attitudes and interests toward the subject matter in particular, and interpersonal skills related to learning and working in a social context (ibid.).

What, then, do we mean by "successful and meaningful student learning"? The American Psychological Association (APA) suggests 14 principles for defining this concept. Two of these suggest that learning be achieved through a continuous process of students' linking new knowledge to their own experiences and existing knowledge base. The new knowledge becomes integrated with the learner's prior knowledge and understanding so that it can be used most effectively in new tasks, and transferred most readily to new situations (APA, 1997, Principles 1 and 3).[5]

However, classroom teaching is not the only factor that affects students' learning of the course material. An additional major factor is students' learning outside of class:

> We need to remember that the learning environment of our students, however, consists of the entire campus, and with the advent of the Internet, increasingly extends beyond campus. This means that learning experiences are increasingly variable. On campus, students will spend less than three hours per week in any given classroom, and other venues such as the library, laboratory, cafeteria, work or field placements, or the student's own room acquire greater importance as learning settings (Donald, 2000, p. 3).

---

[4] See the first citations and paragraphs in the Introduction.
[5] See Chapter 4: What Makes Effective Learning? Psychological Principles.

Considering the limited time students spend in the classroom, the effective teacher is the one who best uses class time to promote students' successful learning during that time, to provide beneficial background knowledge and assignments for learning outside class, and to motivate and guide students in their learning.

The largest contributor to student learning gains at the postsecondary level is the effort they put into their work (Pace, 1988). Other factors that affect students' learning of the course material relate to students' diverse preparation for independent learning, perceptions of their responsibility for learning (ibid.), aptitudes for learning, approaches to studying, and preferences for teaching characteristics and styles.[6] The effective teacher is the one who successfully accommodates all these factors while teaching.

However, in this book we neglect the point of view of student efforts and concentrate on the teacher. We start with those aspects of teaching that involve the teacher's actions and behavior in the classroom.

Gage (1963) suggested that any research on teaching should investigate the following three questions: How do teachers behave? Why do they behave as they do? And what are the effects of their behavior? Following Gage, to understand teaching that positively affects student learning, we need to examine the first two questions. They are discussed in this chapter and in Chapters 2 and 3. Students' effective and meaningful learning is discussed in Chapter 4. We start with a discussion of the second question.

WHY DO TEACHERS BEHAVE AS THEY DO?
TEACHERS' BACKGROUND CHARACTERISTICS

The background characteristics of teachers that were found to affect their classroom teaching behavior may be divided into four categories: (a) their personal characteristics that affect instruction; (b) their knowledge base for teaching; (c) their motivation for teaching; and (d) their thinking about and perceptions of teaching, learning, and students. Indeed, the main reasons for low student ratings of faculty members that I have identified are a lack of teaching aptitudes, a lack of the proper knowledge needed for teaching, low motivation, and damaging perceptions and beliefs regarding teaching and students (Hativa, Forthcoming). Therefore, the widely accepted notion that "everybody can teach well," provided he or she puts sufficient time into lesson preparation, is definitely a myth (Hativa, 1995). Teaching, like any

---

[6] See Chapter 4: Diversity In Students' Aptitudes for Learning

other profession, is successfully developed through the integration of appropriate thinking, motivation, knowledge, aptitudes, and skills.

The first two categories of teacher background characteristics as listed above—teaching aptitudes and the knowledge base for teaching—are discussed next, whereas the third category (motivation for teaching) is presented in Chapter 2 and the fourth (teachers' thinking and beliefs) in Chapter 3.

Personal Characteristics That Affect Instruction—Teaching Aptitudes

In most universities, particularly in research universities, new faculty members are selected primarily on the basis of proven research abilities, although there is an increasing tendency to consider some evidence of teaching quality. The aptitudes and skills for excellence in research are very different from those required for excellence in teaching. To illustrate, a person with unclear diction, stammering, or a heavy foreign accent can be a high research performer, but with low ability to come across in a lecture.

This role of personal characteristics in promoting or reducing teaching effectiveness has been little covered in the teaching effectiveness literature, in spite of its potentially crucial effect on classroom instruction. Feldman (1986) revealed significant correlations between 11 of 14 clusters of instructors' personality traits, as rated by either peers or students (e.g., having positive self-regard, self-esteem, energy, enthusiasm, positive view of others, being sociable, gregarious, friendly, and agreeable), and the ratings of the same instructors on overall teaching effectiveness. In other words, certain personal characteristics of the instructor seem to be highly related to the positive or negative global evaluations made by students. Murray, Ruston, and Paunonen (1990) showed that specific personality traits make differential contributions to teaching effectiveness in different types of courses (e.g., introductory, general, required honors, graduate courses). The personality traits that they examined were leadership, extraversion/introversion, liberalism, supportiveness, intellectual curiosity, endurance, and others. They concluded that university teachers tend to be differentially suited to different types of courses rather than uniformly effective or ineffective in all courses, and that teachers' compatibility with courses is determined in part by personality characteristics. Following are a few examples of personal characteristics that may negatively affect teaching effectiveness.

Speech and language problems. A person's problematic oral delivery may diminish listeners' ability to attend to or understand the material conveyed. The main problems in oral delivery are manifested in speech anxiety (e.g., stammering); unclear diction (e.g., swallowing words or other speech pathologies, heavy foreign accent); monotonousness; overly rapid speaking rate; or unpleasant tone. Several studies (e.g., Land, 1981; Land & Smith, 1981; Smith & Land, 1980b) have indicated that the use of vague terms or mazes (defined as false starts or halts in speech, redundancy, and semantically nonsensical word combinations) significantly diminish student ability to understand what is taught. (Murray, 1997) showed that speech quality (measured by occurrences of voice fades in mid-sentence, stutters, mumbles, or slurred words) negatively correlated with student ratings on overall teaching effectiveness. On the basis of all these disruptive speech problems, Dick and Robinson (1994) suggested requiring all instructional teaching assistants (TAs) in US colleges and universities to satisfy oral English proficiency tests, and providing speech training to all international TAs. In fact, several pre-service teacher education programs do include speech training (Bayless & Moody, 1984; Buzza, 1988).

Empathy with students. A person with a low capacity to empathize with others, to understand how they think and feel, and to correctly interpret both their verbal and nonverbal behavior, is unable to understand students and their difficulties and needs in learning. Teachers who fit this description are incapable of correctly interpreting students' verbal and nonverbal messages and are unaware of when students get bored and inattentive. These teachers, who can be great researchers, cannot adjust their pace and level of teaching to the majority of their students, and thus they often teach "above the students' heads".

"Hyperlink"/associative way of thinking. There are people whose natural way of thinking is associative rather than linearly organized. These people's discourse is characterized by jumping from one idea to another in a sequence whose logic is frequently not manifest to the listener and therefore hard to follow. Although this way of thinking would not reduce a professor's research performance, it is detrimental to the clarity of his/her instruction (Hativa, 1985). Logical progression in material presentation was found to be central to achieving clarity in teaching (Cruickshank, 1985; Evans & Guymon, 1978; Hines, Curickshank, & Kennedy, 1985). Teachers who "jump around" in their presentation confuse students and diminish their ability to learn (Jones, 1979).

Insecure behavior. Students may interpret shyness or insecure behavior as an indication of their teachers' low confidence in their own ability to teach well, in an insufficient command of the material, or in being poorly prepared. Again, this behavior does not reduce a person's research performance.

The second category of teachers' background characteristics—their knowledge base—is presented next and discussed in terms of its impact on classroom teaching behavior.

Knowledge Base for Effective Teaching

Those who can, do; those who understand, teach. (Shulman, 1986, p. 14).[7]

One of the most prevalent beliefs held by university teachers[8] is that what counts in good teaching is the teacher's thorough knowledge of the material. However, knowledge and understanding of the material do not necessarily translate into the ability to teach it to someone else, moreover to teach it to a diverse population of students concurrently. One also needs knowledge of how to convey the material. Shulman (1989) described the good teacher as one who knows how to make his/her knowledge of the material approachable to students by providing examples, analogies and metaphors, and other methods. Such a teacher makes his/her knowledge accessible by connecting the new material to students' knowledge, expecting students to succeed, encouraging them, and demanding the investment of time and effort. The good teacher understands not only the content but also which aspects of the content are crucial for understanding, which are peripheral, and which may be difficult for particular students in class to grasp. Thus, effective teaching requires understanding that builds on a wide knowledge base that consists of several domains, as identified by Shulman and his colleagues (Grossman, 1995; Shulman, 1986):

Subject-matter knowledge: knowledge of the subject matter one is teaching.

Pedagogical content knowledge: specific knowledge of how to teach the particular course content in the particular domain. It concerns teachers' effective representations of the specific subject matter content.

General pedagogical knowledge: general knowledge about teaching—how to organize and manage the classroom, and general methods of effective teaching.

Knowledge of learners and learning: familiarity with learning theories; with the physical, social, psychological, and cognitive development of students; and with motivational theory and practice.

---

[7] A twist of George Bernard Shaw's aphorism: "Those who can, do; those who cannot, teach."

[8] See Chapter 3: Thinking and Beliefs That Damage Teaching Effectiveness—belief (g).

> Good teaching and good learning are linked through the students' experiences of what we do. It follows that we cannot teach better unless we are able to see what we are doing from their point of view (Ramsden, 1992, p. 86).

Curricular knowledge: knowledge both of the processes of curriculum development (e.g., planning a course), and awareness of sources for supporting and enriching the learning of the course material—textbooks, audio-visuals, demonstrations, and so forth.

Knowledge of educational ends: knowledge of educational goals, purposes and values, and their philosophical and historical grounds.

Knowledge of context: grasp of the multiple and embedded situations and settings within which teachers work: the department, the university, the organization of academic peers in the same domain, and so forth.

Knowledge of self: instructors' awareness of their own values, dispositions, strengths and weaknesses, and their educational philosophy, goals for students, and purposes for teaching.

Effects of Deficiencies in Knowledge Base for Teaching

Many university teachers suffer from a deficient knowledge base for teaching because of the insufficient preparation for teaching that they receive, as described in the next section. To illustrate, interviews with over 700 faculty (Freedman et al., 1979) revealed that only a few could define the pedagogical basis for their classroom behavior, and that almost none possessed any model or theory of teaching.

Consequently, even those instructors who do have sound teaching aptitudes may teach poorly when lacking the proper pedagogical knowledge—when they do not know what makes effective teaching and how to convey their knowledge to their students. The following are two comments made by students in a US research university. These and other comments are taken from instructor evaluation forms completed by students. These comments confirm that some teachers do not know how to communicate their knowledge to students, that is, they are deficient in pedagogical knowledge. Excerpts from students' comments will be presented throughout the book, in the print style used below.

- The professor knows his stuff but doesn't clearly convey his knowledge to class.
- He seemed to know the material but was not able to get it across to students very clearly.

Deficiencies in pedagogical knowledge negatively affect all aspects of university teaching. When planning their lessons, most instructors think solely about the content and how to present it. They only seldom consider pedagogical concerns, for example, how to make their presentation clear and interesting, or how to adapt it to the particular students in class (Joan Stark, 1999, personal communication). It also often happens that even when instructors are familiar with particular effective teaching techniques, they do not use in them in their classroom instruction. This is caused by the tension between these new techniques and deeply rooted habits of teaching, or by the lack of knowledge on how to apply the new techniques in practice, or by reluctance to take risks in applying them (Hativa, Forthcoming).

So, how do university instructors gain knowledge for effective teaching?

Gaining the Knowledge Base for Teaching: Learning to Teach

In contrast with schoolteachers who acquire and develop their teaching skills and knowledge over several years of theoretical studies and apprenticeship-based practice, most university instructors do not receive any preparation for their teaching role. The professional training they undergo during their graduate studies concentrates on promoting their research rather than their teaching capabilities (Hativa, 1995). This practice is probably based on two implicit assumptions about how faculty acquired knowledge on how to teach: (a) that they learned from the better teachers whom they observed during the many years that they themselves were students (termed "apprenticeship by observation"), and (b) that they received practical training for classroom teaching in their TA work. However, the substantial proportion of instructors perceived by students as "less than good teachers" indicates that that these two assumptions have no grounding in reality. Apprenticeship by observation is definitely insufficient for acquiring practical teaching knowledge—one cannot learn any practical skill by merely watching, that is, without obtaining any theoretical background or supervised practical training—Can one learn ballet dancing from watching and imitating professional dancers?

To identify how university professors perceive the process by which they have learned to teach, Hativa (1997) presented this question to faculty in a research university, along with 15 possible sources for learning-to-teach as optional answers. The question was formulated in two parts: A: Have you experienced this source for learning how to teach? [Yes/No], and B: If yes, how large/significant was its contribution to your current teaching? [Rated from 1 (smallest) through 5 (largest contribution)]. Results are presented in Figure 1-1, arranged by decreasing proportion of respondents who, in Part B of the question, rated the contribution of the source as either large (4) or very large (5), that is, as making a substantial contribution to their current teaching.

Sources for Learning

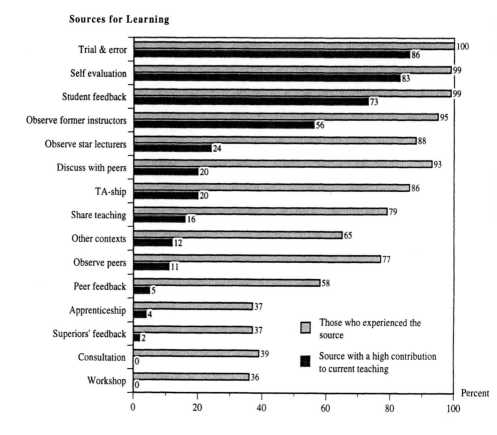

Figure 1-1: Sources for Learning How to Teach in the University

Answers to Part A of the survey question revealed that almost all (95% and more) of the respondents had experienced four of the 15 sources for learning to teach: trial-and-error, self-evaluation, student feedback, and observations of former instructors. More than two thirds of the respondents experienced discussions with peers, observations of star lecturers, teaching assistantship, sharing teaching with other faculty, and observing peers' teaching. Answers to Part B identified three sources that stood out as contributing highly to current teaching: trial-and-error in one's own teaching, self-evaluation of teaching, and to a somewhat lesser extent, student feedback. In fact, these three sources overlap substantially: professors develop their pedagogical knowledge primarily through trial-and-error, which is based on reflection, on student feedback, and on self-evaluation. Interestingly, observation of former instructors, which is in the fourth place, contributed to current teaching for only about one half of the respondents.

The remaining 11 sources contributed considerably less to current teaching, and almost one half (seven) of all the sources were seen as contributing only slightly to faculty members' teaching (these same sources were rated as contributing highly by less than 20% of the respondents). Strikingly, although the large majority of all respondents experienced discussions with peers on matters of teaching, teaching as TAs, sharing teaching a course with peers,[9] observing peers' classes, and teaching in contexts other than the university before becoming professors,[10] only a small proportion of them perceived these experiences to have contributed much to their current teaching practices. Similarly, although almost 40% of the respondents experienced some departmental or university support (e.g., workshops, consultation, superiors' feedback, or apprenticeship), most of them perceived this support to have made only a minor contribution. All in all, in faculty perceptions, most of the sources for learning to teach that are generally regarded as beneficial and that are commonly applied in faculty development programs either by teaching centers or by schools and departments, failed to achieve their aim. This is particularly true for sources of departmental and institutional support, which made the smallest contributions to faculty's teaching among the 15 sources. Interacting with peers and the TA-ing experience were also perceived by faculty in this study as influencing their teaching only marginally. Altogether, this survey suggests that neither of the implicit assumptions about two sources for learning to teach—observations of former instructors and TA-ing experience—indeed contribute substantially to faculty's current teaching practices.

If so, then which sources did contribute most to present teaching? The survey revealed that almost all professors acquired their practical pedagogical knowledge "on the job", through trial-and-error, and by reflecting on their teaching with the aid of student evaluations and feedback. Consequently, until these professors became experts in teaching, generations of students may have suffered from the "error" aspect of these trial-and-error experiences. Moreover, in many cases, this nonsystematic unplanned training is insufficient to generate the appropriate pedagogical knowledge or the ability to apply it in actual classroom teaching. It appears that knowledge thus acquired may just as likely promote university teachers' misperceptions and misconceptions regarding students and teaching, leading to faulty adaptation of teaching to the students.

---

[9] Written comments revealed that these shared courses were divided into units taught by various instructors; however, those instructors who shared teaching in the course usually did not attend one another's lectures.

[10] For example, in pre-college schools, summer camps, army, workshops, tutoring peers or younger students.

There is no reason to believe that the relevance of this discussion is limited to faculty in the single research university in which the data was collected. Instructors with poor preparation for teaching are found in all higher education institutions because they undergo the same teaching-preparation procedures. We may conclude that professors in colleges and universities do not receive adequate preparation for the major role of teaching, and that the main assumptions underlying this policy seem to be largely wrong.

We turn now to the second question that is essential for any research on teaching as suggested by Gage (1963): How do teachers behave in class? We concentrate on outstanding teachers because their behavior may serve as a guide for effective teaching. Hundreds of educational studies have attempted to identify behaviors that are common to successful teachers, as described next.

HOW DO EFFECTIVE TEACHERS BEHAVE IN CLASS? MAIN DIMENSIONS OF EFFECTIVE TEACHING

There is wide agreement that the two main indicators of effective teaching are student achievement and satisfaction from instruction. Achievement is usually measured by the students' success in the course's quizzes and tests, whereas satisfaction from instruction is measured by their ratings of teachers on evaluation forms. The general dimensions as well as the particular classroom strategies and behaviors that contribute to effective teaching are, therefore, most frequently identified by computing the correlation of the ratings made by students on each teaching dimension, strategy or behavior with either (a) the students' grades on a test, or (b) the students' ratings of their instructor on an overall teaching-performance item (Abrami & d'Apollonia, 1990). Two additional methods for identifying effective teaching strategies and behaviors are the use of questionnaires that ask either students or instructors to rate a given list of teaching strategies and behaviors regarding their perceived importance for student learning.

Dozens of studies have been conducted using these four methods for identifying components of effective teaching at the postsecondary level. Two reviews that summarized numerous such studies (Feldman, 1989a; 1997) showed that three teaching dimensions were identified by all four methods to be most related to effective teaching: "preparation-and-organization," "clarity-and-understandableness," and "stimulation of interest in the course and its perceived subject matter." Other teaching strategies found to relate to effective teaching but to a somewhat lower degree were *challenging students intellectually, maintaining good rapport with them, and supporting their learning.* These strategies contribute to creating a *positive classroom climate* that is conducive to learning, considered here to be the fourth dimension of effective teaching.

I propose a model (Figure 1-2) that arranges the dimensions of effective teaching into a hierarchical structure of three levels: high (main dimensions), intermediate, and low:

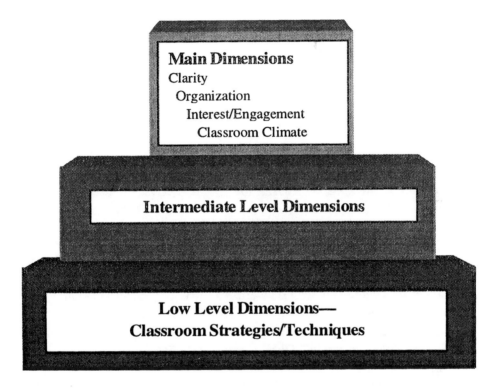

Figure 1-2: The Structure of the Dimensions and Classroom Strategies for Effective Teaching

The uppermost level consists of the main dimensions presented here—clarity, interest, and so on. The lowest level forms a wide foundation consisting of observable classroom strategies and behaviors. The intermediate level consists of one or more layers of dimensions.[11] In this

---

[11] In educational research, behaviors belonging to the upper two levels (e.g., "teacher clarity", or "simplifying the material presented") are entitled "high-inference" teacher behaviors because rating them requires students or observers to make high-inference considerations, whereas behaviors belonging to the lowest level (e.g., "presents questions to students") are entitled "low-inference" because rating them requires students or observers to make only low-inference considerations, such as counting the frequency of their occurrence during the lesson.

model, each teacher behavior at the upper two levels is broken down into one or more additional behaviors. This process, described and illustrated in Part III of this book, proceeds until we reach the classroom teaching strategies that belong to the lowest level. See Figure 10-2 for an illustration of how this model is best used.

Disciplinary Differences in the Main Dimensions of Effective Teaching

There is substantial research evidence that student ratings of teachers   on overall performance differ systematically as a function of the academic domain or discipline. Cashin (1990) for approximately 100,000 US classes, and Murray (Murray & Renaud, 1995) for 400 courses in a Canadian university likewise concluded that, on average, these ratings were highest for arts and humanities teachers, intermediate for social science teachers, and lowest for science, mathematics, and engineering teachers.

Disciplinary differences were identified also in the perceived importance of particular teaching dimensions, such as organization or clarity. In two early studies (Musella & Rusch, 1968; Riley, Ryan, & Lifshits, 1950), several hundreds university students in five academic areas were asked to select three out of ten instructor behaviors that most contributed to learning. In both studies, differences were found between the sciences, where "systematic organization" and "ability to explain clearly" were among the top three qualities, and the arts and the social sciences, where the most frequently selected qualities were "ability to encourage thought," "enthusiastic attitude," and "expert knowledge." Feldman's (1976) review of 72 studies that investigated university students' perceptions of good teaching provides a broader insight into disciplinary differences:

> Certain consistent differences among academic fields also appear in the studies in this area. Students majoring in the fields of natural sciences, physical sciences, and mathematics as well as students describing their preferences for teachers in these fields (whether or not these fields were their majors), put relatively more stress than do other students on the importance of teachers being able to explain clearly.... Moreover, there appears to be greater emphasis in these fields, as well as in the social sciences, on the instructor's preparation and organization of course material.... Finally, emphasis on the ability of the teacher to encourage thought and to be intellectually challenging is more evident in the social sciences, humanities, and fine arts than in other fields (pp. 255-256).

Stark, Lowther, Bentley, and Martens (1990) found that college mathematics instructors showed the least concern with students' needs for growth compared to instructors involved in literature, history, sociology, fine arts, psychology, composition, foreign language, and biology, whereas biology faculty reported the least concern with student preparation and interest. Hativa (1997), surveying research university professors on teaching issues, identified significant differences in thinking on teaching and in classroom behavior between two clusters of academic domains—humanities and social sciences on the one hand, and mathematics, natural sciences and engineering on the other.

We may conclude that systematic differences in students' level of satisfaction from instruction and in the importance attributed to the main dimensions of effective teaching emerge between clusters of disciplines.

SUMMARY

Effective teaching is roughly defined as teaching that brings about effective and meaningful student learning. Successful student learning is achieved through a continuous process of students' linking new knowledge to their experiences and their existing knowledge base. This process fosters the expansion of new knowledge and its integration with learners' prior knowledge and understanding, so that it can be used most effectively in new tasks and transferred more readily to new situations.

Any research on teaching should investigate the following three questions: How do teachers behave? Why do they behave as they do? And what are the effects of their behavior?

The question: "Why do teachers behave as they do?" relates to teachers' background characteristics. Those characteristics may be divided into four categories: (a) teachers' personal characteristics that affect teaching—their teaching aptitudes; (b) their knowledge base for teaching; (c) their motivation for teaching; and (d) their thinking about teaching, learning, and students.

For category (a), instructors who lack teaching aptitudes—such as those who show speech and language problems, have a "hyperlinking" or associative way of thinking, show little empathy with other people, or exhibit insecure behavior in class, often prove to be ineffective teachers. For category (b), effective teaching requires teacher understanding that builds on a wide knowledge base including the following categories: subject-matter knowledge, pedagogical content knowledge, general pedagogical knowledge, knowledge of learners and learning, curricular knowledge, knowledge of educational ends, knowledge of context, and knowledge of self. Deficiencies in pedagogical knowledge negatively affect all aspects of university teaching.

A survey to ascertain how university professors have acquired their practical pedagogical knowledge found that they gained this knowledge as they were teaching, through trial-and-error, and via reflection on their teaching by means of student evaluation and feedback. Consequently, until these professors became experts in teaching, generations of students may have suffered from the "error" aspect of this process. In many cases, this nonsystematic unplanned training is insufficient for generating the appropriate pedagogical knowledge and the teacher's ability to apply it in actual classroom teaching. The knowledge thus acquired may promote misperceptions and misconceptions regarding students and teaching, leading to ineffective teaching. Issues related to the categories (c) and (d) are discussed in Chapters 2 and 3, respectively.

The question "How do effective teachers behave in the classroom?" has been addressed by a profusion of research. Students perceive effective instructors as those who are interesting, clear, and organized; structure the material; challenge students intellectually, maintain good rapport with them, and support their learning. I suggest here a model for the dimensions of effective teaching, perceiving them as arranged in a hierarchical structure of three levels: high/main, intermediate, and low. The lowest level forms a wide foundation consisting of observable classroom behaviors and strategies; the intermediate level consists of one or more layers of intermediate dimensions; and the upper level consists of the main dimensions of effective teaching, identified in research as clarity, interest, organization, and creating a positive classroom climate. In this model, each teacher behavior at the upper two levels is broken down into one or more additional behaviors. The process proceeds until we reach the classroom teaching techniques belonging to the lowest level.

This chapter offers some answers to the question of "why do teachers behave as they do?" by examining teacher personal characteristics and their knowledge base for teaching. To further understand why effective teachers behave as they do, the next chapter discusses teacher motivation to invest in teaching.

Chapter 2

Why Teach Well?

MOTIVATION TO INVEST IN TEACHING

Many professors appear to be interested in the craft of teaching and to be committed to improving their competence as teachers, particularly when their institutions also have a strong commitment to teaching (Blackburn, Lawrence, Bieber, & Trautvetter, 1991). To support this statement, faculty appear to invest a very large amount of time and effort in preparing their lessons, particularly when teaching new courses, and even more so in courses for which they do not use a textbook (Hativa, 1993; 1997).

Figure 2-1 presents the percentage of faculty members in an Ivy league university who gave either "agree" or "strongly agree" responses to eight factors that may motivate them to invest time and effort in their teaching (Hativa, 1997). Intrinsic motivation emerged as the strongest of the factors. Intrinsic motivation stems from internal satisfaction from a job well done and from students' personal feedback. Surprisingly, the use of a measure of teaching performance in tenure, promotion, and salary considerations took only second place in motivating faculty. Another reward that showed high motivational power is the department's encouragement of quality teaching, indicating the significance of departmental support for good teaching. The two standard methods for publicizing the results of teacher evaluations—student ratings and teaching awards—were favored by only a low proportion of the respondents. Most surprising is the low ranking of cash awards, which appeared far below all other motivators. This last result may be explained by the fact that faculty in this prestigious university can obtain consultation jobs that are highly remunerative, far beyond the cash rewards offered by the university.

Motivator

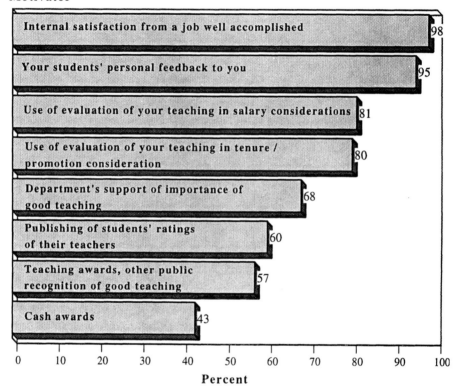

Figure 2-1: Factors That Motivate University Professors to Invest in Teaching

Faculty's high intrinsic motivation to teach well can be explained by the high standards of general excellence that they must have demonstrated throughout their professional career. The long and difficult process that they completed to obtain a doctoral degree and then ascend the steps of the academic promotional ladder screens faculty so that those who survive tend to be very ambitious, persistent, highly motivated, and serious in their aspiration for excellence in all facets of academic work, including teaching.

The main incentives for boosting professors' intrinsic motivation to teach well are that good teaching may positively affect the students, the teacher, and the academic department. In addition, understanding the various benefits of good teaching may provide greater incentives for faculty members to invest efforts in improving their teaching performance, and for administrators to support those efforts by various means.

STUDENT BENEFITS FROM GOOD TEACHING

In one of the math classes (of about 30 students) that I videotaped at a community college in the US, the instructor, well known for his good teaching, stopped teaching 10 minutes before the lesson's end and asked me to conduct an impromptu discussion with the class on teaching-related issues. The following is an accurate transcription of an excerpt from that discussion.

Question: What are the effects of good versus poor teaching on your learning?

Student 1: A good teacher who's well prepared and organized relaxes the class, because if he knows what he's doing, he presents an aura of confidence so we pick that up. A teacher who doesn't know what he's doing is fumbling up there. We don't trust him, so we don't learn from him.

Student 2: Plus, we enjoy the class. If you understand everything, then you enjoy it, and when the teacher doesn't explain himself very well or he's boring, I don't like going to that class and I don't learn anything.

Question: What do you do when you have a teacher from whom you don't learn much?

Many students: Drop the class! (*all laugh*).

Student 3: You struggle when you have a teacher that you don't enjoy. It's much more difficult to learn when you're tense. But when there's joking in the class and everybody is relaxed and is understanding the material it's much easier to learn. Therefore, it becomes easier as we go along.

Student 4: I think one thing that makes this class relaxed is that if you don't understand, there's not a lot of pressure that you're dumb. For example *(regarding an ineffective teacher),* I'm constantly saying: "Wait a minute, wait a minute, I don't understand where you've got that." If we don't get any feedback from a teacher, we get stuck. But this teacher says— let's approach it again: Where is the problem? What don't you understand? And then we'll tackle that and this makes for a very relaxed class.

Student 5: I think good teacher versus bad teacher affects us a lot. This is why I like math and I hate physics. It has direct relationships to the teachers.

The main themes that emerge are great appreciation of a good teacher as compared with negative feelings toward the poor teacher. A good teacher induces a relaxed and enjoyable atmosphere in class; communicates confidence in students' ability to learn; promotes their interest in the material and motivation to come to the class and learn. In contrast, a poor teacher contributes little to their learning; induces mistrust and a tense atmosphere, which severely curtails students' ability to learn; lowers their self-confidence; and makes their learning more difficult. Consequently, students dislike the poor teacher's class, avoid attending it (voting with their feet), and in extreme cases even drop the course.

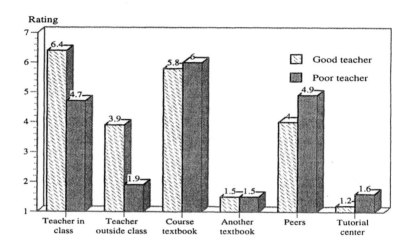

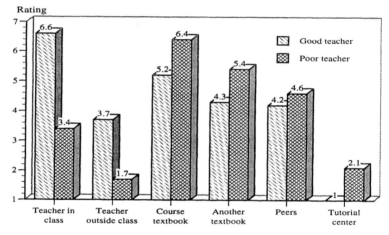

Figure 2-2: Sources for Students' Learning When the Teacher is Good Versus Poor (Upper Figure for Undergraduates, Lower for Graduate Students)

These students' responses were corroborated by the results of a survey that I administered to 240 undergraduate students, mostly freshmen and sophomores, who were neither mathematics or science majors, regarding their math teachers. I presented the same survey to 21 TAs who were doctoral students in the same mathematics department (Hativa, 1984).

The first question was: "Think about a very good/effective mathematics teacher whom you recently had. What sources for learning did you use to master the material for his/her course?" I repeated the same question but referring to a poor/ineffective teacher. Six sources for learning were offered as possible answers, formulated on the basis of a previously implemented pilot questionnaire. The rating scale went from 1 (never used) to 7 (extensively used). The means of students' ratings for each of the sources is presented in Figure 2-2.

Results suggested that the effective or good teacher serves as the primary contributor to students' learning of the course material, both inside the class and outside it (e.g., in office hours). The next-in-order contributors were the course textbook and peers, probably in the context of study groups.

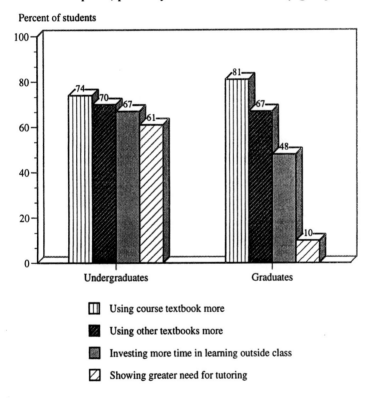

Figure 2-3: How Undergraduate and Graduate Students Compensate for Poor Teaching
(Percentage of Those Who Selected the Particular Method)

When the teacher is ineffective, we see a significant shift to textbook reading, which then becomes the primary source for student learning, and to greater reliance on peers.

We would expect graduate students to be better able than undergraduates to study independently; therefore, they should rely less on the teacher as a source for learning than do undergraduates, while using textbooks more. However, the results showed that contrary to expectations, when the teacher was good, the graduate students relied on him/her as the major source for learning, no less than did undergraduates. However, when the teacher was poor, their shift to textbooks was substantially more extreme than for the undergraduate students.

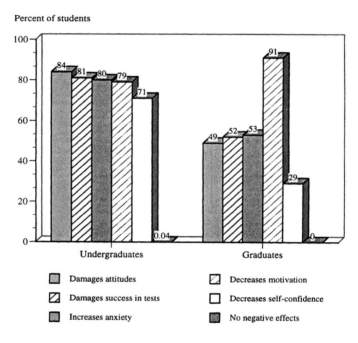

Figure 2-4: Negative Effects of Poor Teaching on Undergraduate and Graduate Students (Percentage of Students Who Reported Effects)

I furthermore asked these two groups of students how they compensated for ineffective teaching. The results are presented in Figure 2-3. That figure indicates that undergraduates compensated for poor teaching by using more textbooks, investing more time in learning, and getting more individualized help (in the tutorial center of that department). The graduates also compensated by using textbooks more, but they sought out individualized help substantially less than did undergraduates, probably because graduates study more independently than undergraduates.

To conclude, the ineffective teacher causes students to invest much more time in learning in order to gain the same level of knowledge and achievement, as compared with the effective teacher. Time is a limited resource, and students do not like "wasting" it on unnecessary learning activities.

The class discussion presented previously suggests that the quality of teaching affect not only students' cognitive learning but also affective factors, such as enjoyment versus tension. The last item in the survey (ibid.) looked at this affective aspect by asking: "How are you affected by poor teaching?" Figures 2-4 and 2-5 present the mean ratings of negative and positive effects, respectively.

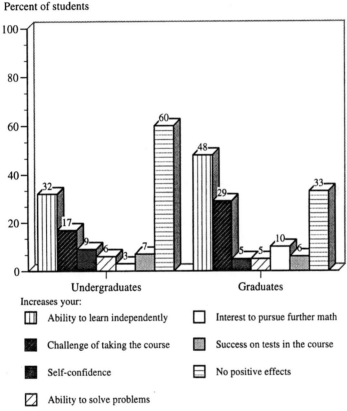

Figure 2-5: Positive Effects of Poor Teaching on Undergraduate and Graduate Students (Percentage of Students Who Reported Effects

Poor teaching seemed to produce negative attitudinal effects in undergraduate students, particularly for those in their first years of postsecondary study. It decreased their positive attitude toward, self-confidence in, and motivation for learning the material, and it lowered their performance on course tests while increasing their anxiety during studying.

For the graduate students, the main affective impact of the poor teacher was a decrease in motivation to learn the course material. However, all the other negative effects were also reported in high proportion, even if to a lesser degree than for the undergraduates.

Regarding positive effects, 60% of the undergraduates did not attribute any positive effects to poor teaching, and most of the reminder felt that poor teaching forced them to learn the material on their own. The graduate students were somewhat less critical of poor teaching, probably because they were better at self-learning; yet, one third of them did not attribute any positive effects to poor teaching.

To summarize, students' benefits from good teaching are composed of increased success on course exams and improved self-confidence and self-esteem as learners.

TEACHER BENEFITS FROM GOOD TEACHING

Successful teaching serves as a major source of satisfaction for university faculty, who gain pleasure in contributing to the lives and future professional careers of young people. As we have seen, faculty's main motivating factor in teaching is internal satisfaction from a job well done. In fact, over one third of 54 award-winning teachers surveyed by Quinn (1994) at five research universities perceived their effectiveness as teachers as a vital source of satisfaction in their academic work. Three quarters of these teachers also perceived the problems they faced in teaching, for example, dealing with student misconduct and dishonesty, managing large classes, and stimulating interest in apathetic students, as their main source of dissatisfaction in teaching.

Teachers' personal satisfaction is often promoted by students' explicit expressions of appreciation of good teaching performance. The following are illustrations taken from teacher rating forms. These comments are certainly ego boosting for a teacher.

- She is always well prepared and enthusiastic about the subject. After all, she makes the class laugh at 8 AM!!!
- She is a super teacher. She is so clear and easy to understand that she makes getting up to be in class at 8:00 worth the effort.
- He is a "ten"— a refreshing change from the majority of teachers I had so far in this department.
- This instructor is clever, sensible, and not pompous— just perfect.
- I love this woman. She is a real person professor and not condescending academia.

On the other hand, ineffective teachers receive very negative comments from students, expressing disappointment and desperation from teaching that does not contribute to their learning. How would a teacher who gets these comments feel about them and about himself/herself?

- The teacher has no idea how to present the material. Classtime is basically useless, and more can be gained from reading the text for half an hour than studying in class for a week.
- During her lectures I get lost every day. I have to learn the material completely on my own. The lectures do not help at all.
- He is really concerned for your learning and is a really nice guy. I'd be dead without the book, though.
- He doesn't know what he is doing. He is impossible to follow and has absolutely no rapport with students. Worst class I've had on campus.
- Sometimes it's difficult to do problems before they have been taught. If I could teach myself, I would buy an encyclopedia instead of paying this outrageous tuition.
- He's the most OK that we have had in the department and this is not exactly a complement.
- The only single thing that makes me happy about his lectures is that always, but always, each lesson comes to an end.
- His talents as a scientist are undoubted but his pedagogical talents are nonexistent.

Additional benefits for the instructor who teaches well are: the increase over recent years in the consideration of teaching performance during hiring and promotion processes; larger attendance in class lessons and lower proportion of course dropouts; high registration for elective courses taught by that instructor; pleasant atmosphere in class and in communications with students; and positive responses from the department head and leading faculty.

DEPARTMENTAL BENEFITS FROM GOOD TEACHING

Some departments (for example, mathematics, statistics) regularly provide "service" courses to other departments at the same university. Providing instructional services to other departments is in the interest of any department because it justifies expanding faculty size while producing additional income. The success of this service depends directly on the quality of teaching provided by the department. In the case of unsatisfactory teaching, the departments on the receiving end may decide to use their own faculty to teach these topics.

Good teaching may also attract students to take additional courses or degrees that the department offers and thus increase enrollment. There is some research support for this notion. Students in a multisection introductory course to computer programming, who attended sections where the teacher was rated high, were more likely to pursue further coursework in computer-related areas and to join the local computer club than were students in sections where the teacher was rated low (Marsh & Overall, 1980). Similarly, students in introductory courses that were taught by highly rated teachers were more likely to enroll in advanced courses in that department than were students taught by poorly rated teachers (Bolton, Bonge, & Marr, 1979).

SUMMARY

To further understand why effective teachers behave as they do, this chapter discusses teacher motivations to invest in teaching. It also presents incentives for teachers to invest time and effort in providing good teaching.

Many professors appear to be interested in the craft of teaching and to be committed to improving their competence as teachers, particularly when their institutions also have a strong commitment to teaching. Even faculty in research universities show a high motivation to teach well, and to invest in preparing their lessons. Intrinsic motivation, that is, internal satisfaction from a job well done and from students' personal feedback, is the strongest factor motivating teachers. Tangible rewards such as the use of teaching evaluation in tenure, promotion, and salary considerations only take second place, although they still demonstrate high motivating power. The department's encouragement of quality teaching also has strong motivating power.

The following are the main incentives for boosting university professors' intrinsic motivation to teach well. They are related to the students, the teacher, and the department.

Effects of teaching quality on the students. The good/effective teacher induces a relaxed and enjoyable atmosphere in class; communicates confidence in students' ability to learn; boosts their self-esteem as learners; promotes their interest in the material and motivation to come to the class and learn; and eventually promotes their learning. In contrast, poor teaching induces a negative learning climate that severely curtails students' ability to learn. It adversely affects students' success in the course as well as their attitudes, motivation, and self-confidence in learning the course material. The teacher is perceived as not contributing to students' learning and as wasting their time, and consequently students avoid attending his/her classes. They compensate for poor teaching by investing additional time and effort in learning from textbooks as well as from peers and other sources.

Effects of teaching quality on the instructor. The first and utmost benefit from good teaching is self-satisfaction, based on feelings of a job well done and on students' explicit expressions of high appreciation. Additional benefits are: the current increase in weight of teaching during hiring and promotion processes; larger attendance in class lessons and a lower proportion of course dropout; high registration for elective courses taught by that teacher; pleasant atmosphere in class and in communication with students; and positive responses from the department head and leading faculty. The disadvantage of poor teaching is students' communication of negative feelings, avoidance of attending class (voting with their feet), and in extreme cases even dropping the course.

Effects of teaching quality on the department. Good teaching may attract students to take additional courses or degrees that the department offers and thus increase enrollment. For some departments, this may increase requests from other departments to provide instructional services.

The first three chapters suggest answers to the question: "Why do teachers behave as they do?" This chapter contributes to answering that question by discussing sources for faculty motivation to teach well and to invest time and effort to achieve this aim. Chapter 1 elaborated on two categories of teachers' background characteristics that were found to affect classroom teaching behavior: The faculty's teaching aptitudes and their knowledge base for teaching. The next chapter presents a third important category: teachers' perceptions of and thinking about teaching, learning, and students.

Chapter 3

Teacher Thinking, Beliefs, and Approaches to Teaching

Part of the rationale underlying teaching practice is tacit and only implicitly known to the teachers. This rationale is based on teachers' "practical knowledge" (knowledge that exists only in use) that cannot be formulated in propositions, rules, techniques, and principles (Hirst, 1983). This feature fits the general pattern of professionals' behavior. When asked to describe principles that guide action, most people describe their "espoused theory," which often contrasts sharply with their "theory in action," which may be inferred from their observed actual behavior (Argyris & Schon, 1974). Teachers' practical knowledge is deeply embedded in their beliefs, values, understandings and attitudes. Thus, teaching should be described not only on the basis of teachers' aptitudes and knowledge base (as described in Chapter 1) but also on the basis of their beliefs, perceptions, and assumptions regarding teaching and learning (Hativa, 1998; Ramsden, 1992; Shulman, 1987). This chapter examines several issues related to implicit thinking and beliefs of university professors: (a) the goals that underlie their teaching; (b) theories and beliefs that damage teaching effectiveness; (c) orientations and approaches to teaching; (d) perception of and compliance with the contextual factors that affect teaching; and (e) the tension between the thinking and beliefs of university teachers and those of their students.

GOALS IN TEACHING

Educational Goals in University Teaching

McKeachie (1994, p. 315) defined effective teaching as "the degree to which one has facilitated student achievement of educational goals." That is, *teaching is effective when it achieves its intended educational goals.* So what are the goals of university teaching?

The overall goal, it is widely agreed, is to prepare students for their adult life, particularly for their professional life. For current university students, the 21st century workplace is expected to be characterized by rapidly changing conditions and work assignments. Hence, professional success will require original, imaginative, and non-routine thinking, the ability for self-study, and flexibility in adjusting to changing conditions. To prepare students for life in the 21st century, beyond a particular body of knowledge, *universities should offer students well-developed thinking skills and a well-founded basis for self-directed, independent learning.* From this perspective, which dominates today's thinking about teaching, knowledge is no longer considered an essence that is transferable from one person to another. Students are not empty vessels that are to be filled by teachers pouring knowledge into them, as the common maxim has it. They are not passive receptors of teachers' perceptions, beliefs, and knowledge but rather active learners who construct their own knowledge (Perkins & Swartz, 1992). This perception of the teaching/learning process is entitled the *constructivist learning theory.*[12]

In view of this theory, the weight in teaching should move from transmission of knowledge and the shallow coverage of many topics, to the in-depth teaching of fewer topics, only the most important ideas or concepts. Teaching should promote students' understanding, that is, their capacity to apply new knowledge to a variety of tasks and situations. And it should promote students' thinking by explicitly teaching them to use organizers of thoughts, decision-making approaches, and reflection, and by promoting their tendencies for thinking (ibid). In fact, these ideas are not new. Many years ago, Polya (1965, p. 100) the famous mathematician and mathematics educator, expressed the same idea:

> I have an old fashioned idea about the aim of teaching. I believe the aim, first and foremost, is to teach young people to *think... Teaching to think* means that the... teacher should not merely impart information, but should try to develop the ability of the students to use the information.

---

[12] See Chapters 4: The Constuctivist Learning Theory.

These goals of university teaching have been formulated by educational theorists and leaders. The important question is—are their perceptions shared by practitioners? How do college and university faculty perceive their goals as teachers? The question of faculty perceptions of their goals in teaching is part of a wider question on faculty thinking about teaching, learning, and students, which is discussed below.

Faculty Members' Goals in Teaching

In light of the current perceptions of the goals of education, it is important to learn about how faculty actually perceive these goals. Cross (1991) asked 2,700 teachers from 33 two- and four-year colleges (excluding research universities) which of six teaching roles they considered as primary. Results showed that the main two roles were developing students' higher-order thinking skills and teaching facts and principles. The most significant differences in choice of teaching roles emerged across disciplines. The role of promoting higher-order thinking skills was chosen by social science teachers more than by others, with math teachers in second place and science teachers last. In contrast, presenting facts and principles was selected most frequently by science and math teachers but less so by humanities and social sciences teachers. Humanities and social sciences teachers seemed to appreciate the role of student development much more than did the science and math teachers.

Franklin and Theall (1992) surveyed 466 teachers in a large private urban university. Regarding goals, engineering, math, and science teachers placed a significantly higher emphasis on facts, principles, concepts, and problem solving than did their colleagues in other departments. Humanities teachers, in contrast, emphasized creativity, attitude toward subject matter, writing, group work, oral communication skills, social skills, and self-knowledge.

In the 1989 Carnegie Foundation survey of college and university faculty, Smart and Ethington (1995) analyzed 4,000 faculty members' opinions concerning desired outcomes of undergraduate education. They found that faculty in applied disciplines (e.g., engineering) put more stress on knowledge application than did faculty in pure disciplines (e.g., mathematics). On the other hand, faculty in pure disciplines placed greater importance on knowledge acquisition (the acquisition of multidisciplinary knowledge that most often makes up the general education component of undergraduate programs) than did faculty in applied fields.

Lastly, when surveying faculty members at an Ivy League university, Hativa (1997) listed 21 teaching goals that had been identified in previous studies, although under two categories that differ somewhat from those above: (a) promoting the knowledge needed for functioning in the academic domain and in daily life, and (b) promoting students' motivation, aptitudes, and skills in the subject domain and for self-learning. Results demonstrated very high agreement among the respondents on 13 of the 21 goals: The goals perceived as important or very important by at least two thirds (67%) of the faculty belonged to the first category: helping students gain the basic body of knowledge, structure/organization, and tools of the domain; and promoting students' ability to apply methods and principles and to gain other work and thinking habits typical of the domain. For the second category, the most highly agreed-upon goals were promoting students' independent, objective, critical, original, and creative thinking; advancing their interest and motivation to continue studying in the domain; enhancing skills for oral and written expression; fostering openness to different points of view; and facilitating the ability for self-study. Thus, the main goals in teaching include the cognitive aspects of gaining knowledge and understanding, the affective aspects of promoting motivation, and the skills for learning and functioning in the workplace and in social life.

Disciplinary differences were identified in the perception of the specific goals' importance (ibid). Humanities faculty particularly appreciated the goals of "conveying the contribution of their discipline to humanity," "developing students' oral and written expression skills," and "openness to a variety of ideas and points of view," whereas faculty in engineering—a professional school—assigned the greatest importance to the goal of "promoting knowledge needed for professional work" and the least importance to the "promotion of learning of research methods in the domain." Faculty in mathematics and natural sciences appreciated "originality and creativity in thinking" significantly more than did engineering faculty, and they valued "aesthetic appreciation of the material and of the human endeavor in the domain" significantly more than did engineering and social sciences faculty.

Having defined the notion of effective teaching as well as having identified faculty perceptions of their goals in teaching as reported by several studies, we may now turn to examine faculty thinking and beliefs regarding teaching, learning, and students.

PERSONAL THEORIES AND BELIEFS THAT DAMAGE TEACHING EFFECTIVENESS

Several personal theories and beliefs regarding teaching that may be detrimental to effective teaching and difficult to change have been identified among university instructors. These theories usually develop on the basis of "intuitive assumptions, guiding principles, and stored perceptions or models that comprise a teacher's understanding of the teaching-learning process" (Carrier, 1981, p. 32). The sources of these theories are former teachers, personal experiences in the classroom, personal values, philosophical orientations, or personality attributes (ibid.). Following are the main theories and beliefs held by university teachers that are considered as detrimental to effective teaching or to the willingness to invest effort in improving teaching. These theories have been identified by a variety of sources in the literature and are supported by my own experience working with faculty on their teaching.

(a) There's nothing to be learned about teaching. College faculty members have been shown to have a very limited view of the nature of teaching (Smith & Geis, 1996). They do not associate teaching with a systematic, organized body of knowledge that is research or theory based; instead, they perceive it on the basis of their personal beliefs and own teaching experience. Many university professors believe that anyone of sound intelligence and in the possession of some experience-based knowledge can be a good teacher (Freedman et al., 1979). These professors, therefore, feel no need to learn more about teaching. This belief contrasts with the vast research connecting particular teaching behaviors and strategies to the effectiveness of student learning (e.g., Marsh, 1987b); it also contrasts with the conception of teaching as scholarly work (Shulman & Hutchings, 1997).

(b) I do the teaching, but it's not my responsibility whether or not students understand and learn. The underlying perception here is that the students are responsible for learning regardless of the way the instructor teaches, as if to say: "Send me students who can learn from the way I know how to teach," rather than "I need to learn how to teach the students I am sent" (Smith, 1995, pp. 17-18). A detrimental outcome of this view is that professors feel there is no need for them to worry about their teaching, let alone to improve it. They teach at the pace and level that seem appropriate to them, use some general notion of teaching in their field, and almost entirely disregard the particular students who make up their classes. Placing the full responsibility for learning solely on the students is typical for teachers whose orientation to teaching is teacher centered (Kember, 1997), as discussed below.

(c) I maintain my integrity and would not lower/sell myself by decreasing the level of teaching, as some of my colleagues do, to gain popularity or high students' ratings. University teachers have been found to mistakenly regard any adjustment of their teaching to suit students as lowering the level of teaching. These same teachers also tend to blame their own low ratings on their high demands from students (Hativa, Forthcoming). However, there is substantial evidence (e.g., Marsh, 1987a) that students are not "bribed" into

giving higher ratings by the teacher's "lowering" of the level of teaching or responding to student demands, and that high requirements from students ("course difficulty level") are not related to the evaluation of the teacher's overall performance.

(d) Students do not have the tools to fully appreciate my teaching at present. However, in future years, when they become professionals and look back, they will realize how much knowledge and understanding they gained from my course. This myth (Hativa, Forthcoming) is based on anecdotal evidence where these professors remembered some of their own teachers, who were regarded as either poor or good at the time of study, but now are considered by these professors as the opposite. However, established research evidence (e.g., Blackburn, Boberg, O'Connell, & Pellino, 1980; Feldman, 1989b; Marsh, 1987a) indicates that, on average, when looking back, graduates rate their former teachers very much like they rated them when they were students.

(e) My teaching is good enough; there's no need for me to improve. Most of those faculty members perceived by their students as less than excellent teachers are unaware of their problems in teaching and actually consider themselves good teachers (Berman & Skeff, 1988; Blackburn et al., 1980; Cross, 1977; Feldman, 1989b). For example, Blackburn et al., surveying about 2,000 faculty at 24 institutions, reported that about 90% of the faculty judged themselves as above average or superior teachers. These results contradict what would be expected from a statistically normal distribution of ratings, which would find only about 50% of the population rated above the statistical average. Berman and Skeff (1988), in a survey of faculty at a research university, found that about 75% of the respondents rated their lecturing ability as either very high or high, whereas students' ratings indicated a much lower proportion of very good teachers. These repeated findings suggest that faculty have a high sense of self-competence for teaching, believe they are already doing a good job as teachers, and therefore do not feel a need to improve.

(f) Teaching cannot be improved—good teachers are born, not made. This very common fatalistic belief that good teaching is an inborn ability, that "you either have it or you don't," diminishes teacher willingness to develop their teaching through the acquisition of skills and knowledge (Cross, 1977; Gaff, 1976; Smith & Geis, 1996). This belief contradicts all research evidence on success in improving the teaching of university professors (Hativa, 1995; Marsh & Roche, 1993; Weimer & Lenze, 1991).

(g) To teach well, all that is needed is good knowledge of the material (Berman & Skeff, 1988; Smith, 1995). Most professors regard knowledge of the material as a necessary and sufficient condition for good teaching. They tend to describe teaching in terms of content. They "define excellence in

teaching in terms of scholarship and knowing the subject matter. Thus, they direct their teaching improvement efforts toward keeping abreast of new developments and carrying out research or other scholarly activities" (Smith & Geis, 1996, p. 134). This belief runs counter to research findings that suggest that there is no relationship between excellence in research (which does necessitate good knowledge of the subject matter) and excellence in teaching (Cohen, 1990; Smith & Geis, 1996).

(h) I need to cover most of the course curriculum in class. Content coverage is a major component in the perception that identifies teaching with information transmission. This perception is widespread among college professors (Hativa, Forthcoming) who often define their central problem in teaching as "too much content, too little time" (Smith, 1995, p. 15).

(i) I use strict lecturing and do not need to change it. Many professors believe that strict lecturing is the most appropriate way to teach university classes, and the only possible way to teach medium and large classes. They believe that the best way to develop learners is by structuring the subject matter for them (Kember, 1997; Smith & Geis, 1996). These professors would not consider other teaching methods that are more student-centered, because these clash with their perceptions of the essence of good teaching. This perception of teaching opposes the current constructivist learning approach that maintains that teaching should accommodate students' needs to construct their knowledge independently and to be active during classroom instruction.[13]

PROFESSORS' ORIENTATIONS AND APPROACHES TO TEACHING

Kember (1997) integrated recent findings regarding professors' approaches to teaching and organized them in terms of relationships among teachers, students, and content. He identified five teaching approaches along a continuum ranging from teacher-centered/content-oriented on one pole and student-centered/learning-oriented on the other, with the middle approach, that of student-teacher interaction, as a transitional approach:

1. Imparting information. In this approach, teaching is purely a transfer of information. The instructor uses the lecturing method, relying on notes prepared in advance. The student is mostly ignored in this vision of teaching and is perceived, metaphorically, as a vessel into which knowledge is poured. This approach involves the beliefs (b), (g), (h), and (i) discussed above.

---

[13] See APA Psychological Principles for learning, in Chapter 4.

2. Transmitting structured knowledge. The transmission metaphor is still used in this approach, but the quality of presentation is emphasized. The teacher structures and arranges the presented knowledge in a clear, logical, and simplified manner so that it can be understood by the students, and thus interest and motivate them. The student is more likely to receive the information concisely than in the previous approach, but he/she is still a passive receiver.
3. Student-teacher interaction. Focusing on the interaction between teacher and students, this approach emphasizes students' understanding and discovery. Lecturing is modified by greater stress on learning activities such as experiments or problem solving in class.
4. Facilitating understanding. The main role of the teacher here shifts toward that of helping the student to learn. Students are recognized as individuals with differing needs rather than as a homogeneous audience.
5. Conceptual change/intellectual development. This approach views the main role of the teacher as that of changing students' conceptions within a sympathetic and supportive environment.

According to Kember's (1997) continuum, the teacher-centered orientation focuses upon the communication of defined bodies of content or knowledge, whereas the student-centered orientation "takes a developmental approach toward students and their conceptions of knowledge. It focuses upon students' knowledge rather than the lecturers'" (ibid., p. 264). To illustrate how instructors' approaches to teaching affect students' learning, Hativa (1998) presented a case study of a university professor whose approach to teaching was strictly that of imparting information. This approach led to teaching that was ill adjusted to the students' level of understanding; and as a result, it negatively affected their home-study strategies and, in consequence, their learning outcomes.

Gow and Kember (1993) and Kember and Gow (1994) showed that university departments whose predominant orientation to teaching is teacher-centered are more likely to promote a surface approach to studying. Departments that approach teaching as facilitating students' understanding or as changing their conceptions are more likely to use interactive and student-centered teaching methods and to establish a learning environment that encourages meaningful learning.

TEACHERS' PERCEPTIONS OF AND COMPLIANCE WITH CONTEXTUAL VARIABLES

The context of teaching—the multiple and embedded situations and settings within which teachers work—affects a teacher's thinking and perception of variables such as disciplinary norms, organizational patterns, and institutional variables (Ramsden, 1992). Contextual variables—mainly the institution, the department or discipline, the particular students in class, and the academic peer organizations in the same domain[14] have been shown to make a considerable, even crucial impact on teaching and student learning in higher education (Hativa & Marincovich, 1995; Ramsden, 1992). Therefore, teachers should achieve a good grasp of this multifaceted context (Shulman, 1987), to contend with those context-related factors that may hurt teaching effectiveness, as follows.

Unawareness of or Noncompliance with the Institution's Educational Goals

Each educational institution has its own educational mission or vision, which it expects all faculty members to comply with, support, and promote. For example, Ford (1980) suggested that the modern universities' new mission is generally pluralistic, international in scope, with a focus on preservation and enhancement of quality and diversity, advancement of social justice and constructive change, more effective governance, and more effective use of resources. Teachers who are unaware of the specific goals and norms of their institution, or who do not comply with them, may come into conflict with administrators and students. To illustrate, the movie "The Dead Poets' Society" describes a new teacher (played by Robin Williams) in an elite preparatory high school that has taken on the mission of maintaining tradition and excellence in learning. Teaching in that school is strictly teacher-centered with rote learning, whereas the new teacher uses mostly student-centered methods and encourages students to think and learn meaningfully. His teaching goals and methods collide with the school's "mission," which leads to a bitter conflict with the principal and his eventual dismissal.

Unawareness of or Noncompliance with the Teaching-Related Norms of the School/Department, and the Related Student Expectations

The teaching-related culture of particular academic disciplines and departments plays a crucial role in effective teaching (Hativa & Marincovich, 1995). Different clusters of disciplines sometimes have divergent course objectives (Hativa, 1997; Stark & Lattuca, 1994), and

---

[14] For example, APA: American Psychological Association; MAA: Mathematical Association of America.

teachers in various disciplines plan their courses differently (Stark & Lowther, 1990). The separate academic disciplines have been associated with different frequencies of teacher classroom behaviors (Murray & Renaud, 1995) and with selective considerations in student ratings of instructors (Cashin, 1990; Feldman, 1978). These findings imply the need for specialized teaching methods and effective teaching patterns for each academic department (Cashin & Downey, 1995).

Students adapt themselves to the departmental culture and norms, developing expectations concerning the way courses are structured and grades are assigned; the nature and style of teaching, tests, and assignments; the responsibilities they are required to take on; and the relationships between themselves and the teacher. Teachers who do not conform to these expectations may develop conflicting relations with their students. Students may perceive them as ineffective or outdated, or as posing unacceptable demands on them. Thus, teachers should be well aware of the teaching-related culture of their department. The following four cases of instructors teaching undergraduate courses (three in physics and one in chemistry, respectively) illustrate the conflict caused by noncompliance with the department's culture or with the students' expectations, a situation that brought about their low ratings by students:

> *[The first physics instructor]* made requirements and/or used teaching methods that were very different from those of most other departmental physics teachers, and with which students felt they were unable to conform. For example, he would not discuss in class problems that students experienced in doing the assigned homework, demanding that they come to his office for personal explanations. He proved to have a firmly principled approach toward teaching and students' learning duties and would not change his approach in spite of the instructional consultant's suggestions. He continued to be rated low by his students (Hativa, 1995, p. 401).

> *[The second physics instructor]* also had a fundamental problem that prevented improvement in his global ratings. The structure and approach of the course he taught were very different from those of almost all other physics courses in the department, and students perceived them as chaotic. Although the teacher often explained the point of teaching this specific topic through this particular approach, the students continued to dislike this type of presentation, particularly the weaker ones who rated him very low. Thus, because of his inability or unwillingness to change the structure of the course, his mean ratings did not rise in spite of the tremendous improvement in his classroom presentation following two semesters of intensive consultation support (Hativa, 1995, pp. 401-402).

> *[Regarding the third physics instructor who taught a course for physics majors.]* Students' main complaints were that his presentation was very boring; its level was too low, and he covered the textbook exactly so that class attendance almost seemed a waste of time... He felt insulted and angered by the students' perceptions of his teaching and

vehemently denied the allegation that he was teaching exactly what was written in the textbook.... Although he was assigned to the same course for the following year, he refused and insisted on teaching only non-physics majors. In the next year, his ratings in the two new (required) courses for non-physics majors soared.... although he taught basically the same material and used the same teaching methods as before.... The students, being of a lower level and with lesser aspirations than physics majors, highly appreciated his faithful adherence to the textbook and his systematic, organized, and clear presentation. In these classes, he created a very pleasant atmosphere. He continued to teach the same two courses during the follow-up year and to be rated very high (ibid, p. 394).

[Regarding the chemistry instructor]. Interviewing several students of a low-rated teacher identified their bitter feelings toward him because he used to ask them to self-learn parts of the course curriculum by reading a textbook in English. [Most science courses in Israeli universities do not have textbooks in Hebrew.] The teacher's own undergraduate and graduate studies all took place in physics departments in Israel where the students were required to study by themselves from English textbooks, and he adopted the same method in his current teaching. He was unaware, after teaching 25 years in the chemistry department, that other teachers in his department almost never assigned students to self-learn new material from English textbooks, a fact that was validated by several sources. [Taken from own experience of working with this teacher.]

Unawareness or Lack of Knowledge as to How to Adjust Teaching to Diverse Student Populations

Students with different approaches to or needs in learning are likely to define good teaching in ways that reflect those approaches and needs (Hativa & Birenbaum, 2000). Therefore, teachers need to adjust their teaching to a heterogeneous student body in the classroom—to students' diverse aptitudes, background, learning and experience, interests, and approaches to learning.[15] However, research evidence (e.g., Marsh, 1987b) has shown that teachers are rated, on average, higher in graduate courses (that is, among better and more motivated students) than in undergraduate courses; in elective (that is, among higher-motivated students) than in required courses; and in small than in large classes. This evidence suggests that on average, teachers are less proficient at adjusting their teaching to less advanced or less motivated students, and lack the knowledge necessary to optimally adjust teaching to the diverse population found in large classes.

---

[15] Chapter 12 discusses teaching for a diverse student population.

TENSION BETWEEN THE THINKING AND BELIEFS OF UNIVERSITY PROFESSORS AND THEIR STUDENTS

A survey questionnaire answered by almost all faculty and a representative sample of undergraduate students in a law school at a research university (Hativa, 2000) revealed major discrepancies between the law faculty's and the students' perceptions of issues related to teaching and students. These discrepancies pinpoint the serious tension between student and faculty expectations and goals regarding the teaching/learning process. The two parties—faculty and students also exhibited opposing views on the responsibility for students' failure in learning, each placing the blame on the other. Another disparity relates to teaching effectiveness. Faculty perceived themselves as satisfactory and even good teachers who have sufficient pedagogical knowledge and who apply it well in practice, whereas students rejected these perceptions and strongly denounced the level of instruction. Students perceived the teaching provided to them as very poor—mainly of material coverage at the surface level of "knowledge" rather than of "understanding," as monotonous and boring lecturing with almost no intellectual challenge, as lacking student participation or any other form of student activation, and with teachers showing very little concern for them and their learning.

Comparing faculty perceptions of goal importance with their perceptions of success in actually achieving these goals indicates that they perceived themselves as failing to a large extent to actually achieve all the teaching goals that they considered important. In their view, they particularly failed to promote student abilities to think in a creative, original, and innovative way, and to encourage self-study. Altogether, faculty would have preferred their teaching to be more student-centered, aiming at developing their students and caring for their learning, but felt that they were not able to achieve these aims in their teaching. Students, on their part, felt that their teachers failed to achieve the large majority of goals that these teachers regarded as being important for them, or that they thought they achieved in their instruction.

The extreme gap between students' and faculty's perceptions regarding teaching and students in the law school examined was shown to arouse student dissatisfaction with their studies, and to the resulting problematic behaviors—voting with their feet (avoiding classes) or coming unprepared to class. We therefore suggest that this kind of a gap may exist in other higher education institutions.

SUMMARY

Teachers' practical knowledge is deeply embedded in their beliefs, values, understanding, and attitudes. Thus, teaching should be described on the basis not only of teachers' aptitudes and knowledge, but also of their beliefs, values, perceptions, and assumptions regarding teaching and learning. Teachers' thinking and beliefs, including their approaches to teaching, were found to affect student learning. This chapter examines several issues related to implicit thinking and beliefs of university professors, as follows.

(a) *Goals that underlie teaching.* Faculty of all departments share similar perceptions regarding the goals of teaching: promoting the knowledge needed for functioning in the academic domain and in daily life; and boosting students' motivation, aptitudes, and skills in the domain and their ability to think and self-learn.

(b) *Theories and beliefs that damage teaching effectiveness.* The sources for these damaging beliefs, misconceptions and maladaptive theories, as revealed by research, are: former teachers, personal experiences in the classroom, personal values, philosophical orientations, or personality attributes.

(c) *Professors' orientations and approaches to teaching.* Two types of teachers' orientations and approaches to teaching have been identified: The *teacher-centered orientation* includes the approaches of imparting information and of transmitting structured knowledge, whereas the *student-centered orientation* includes the approaches of facilitating understanding and conceptual change/intellectual development.

(d) *Professors' perceptions of and compliance with contextual factors that affect their teaching.* The context—mainly the institution, the department or discipline, the particular students in class, and the academic peer organizations —has been shown to render a considerable, even crucial effect on teaching and student learning in higher education. Context-related factors that may damage teaching effectiveness are: unawareness of or noncompliance with the institution's mission and educational goals, the teaching-related norms of the school/department, and the related student expectations; and unawareness or lack of knowledge as to how to adjust teaching to diverse student populations.

(e) *Tension between the thinking and beliefs of university professors and their students.* A particular study reveals major discrepancies between faculty's and students' perceptions of the issues related to teaching, learning, and students. These pinpoint the serious tension between students' and faculty's expectations and goals regarding the teaching/learning process. The extreme gap between students' and faculty's perceptions lead to students' dissatisfaction with their learning, and to voting with their feet (avoiding classes) or coming unprepared to class.

This chapter has presented university teachers' thinking and beliefs regarding teaching, learning, and students, and their approaches to teaching. The next chapter presents the parallel issues with respect to students, that is, students' thinking and beliefs regarding teaching and their approaches to studying. It also presents the current thinking of how students learn and should be taught, and examines students' diverse learning needs as well as their preferences for teacher characteristics and teaching methods and styles.

Chapter 4

Students' Learning and Their Teaching Preferences

Any efficient teaching device must be correlated somehow with the nature of the learning process (Polya, 1965, p. 102).

Learning depends primarily on the behavior of students (Cross, 1993). Therefore, teaching for effective learning requires understanding of how people learn, where and why learners have difficulty, what are their preferences in teaching, and what practices are most effective for helping them progress toward more complex and sophisticated understanding. Only when this understanding is achieved can we promote students' meaningful learning (Kreber, 2000). The following are two summaries of principles of learning (at all school levels) prepared by relevant educational associations.

THE APA PSYCHOLOGICAL PRINCIPLES FOR SUCCESSFUL LEARNING

The American Psychological Association (APA) has made a comprehensive attempt to define the current perceptions on psychological principles that pertain to the successful learner and learning process. A large task force of experts prepared a document in this regard on the basis of multidisciplinary research (APA, 1997). The principles listed there focus on psychological factors that are primarily internal to and under the control of the learner, but also acknowledge environmental or contextual factors that interact with learner factors. Altogether, the APA document lists 14 principles organized into four categories, including a short explanation and instructional implications for each principle. The principles should be understood as an organized set so that no principle is viewed in isolation. Because of their significance for understanding effectiveness of student

51

learning, and their important implications for teaching, I hereby cite them almost intact from the APA source.

Cognitive and Metacognitive Factors

1. Nature of the Learning Process

The learning of complex subject matter is most effective when it is an intentional process of constructing meaning from information and experience.

Successful learners are active, goal-oriented, self-regulating, and assume personal responsibility for contributing to their own learning.

2. Goals of the Learning Process

The successful learner, over time and with support and instructional guidance, can create meaningful, coherent representations of knowledge.

The strategic nature of learning requires students to be goal directed. To construct useful representations of knowledge and to acquire the thinking and learning strategies for continued learning success across the life span, students must generate and pursue personally relevant goals. Initially, students' short-term goals and learning may be sketchy in an area, but, over time, their understanding can be refined by filling in gaps, resolving inconsistencies, and deepening their understanding of the subject matter so that they can reach longer-term goals. Educators can assist learners in creating meaningful learning goals that are consistent with both personal and educational aspirations and interests.

3. Construction of Knowledge

The successful learner can link new information with existing knowledge in meaningful ways.

Knowledge widens and deepens as students continue to build links between new information and experiences and their existing knowledge base. The nature of these links can take a variety of forms, such as adding to, modifying or reorganizing existing knowledge of skills.... Unless new knowledge becomes integrated with the learner's prior knowledge and understanding, this new knowledge remains isolated, cannot be used most effectively in new tasks, and does not transfer readily to new situations. Educators can assist learners in acquiring and integrating knowledge by a number of strategies that have been shown to be effective with learners of varying abilities, such as... thematic organization or categorizing.

4. Strategic Thinking

The successful learner can create and use a repertoire of thinking and reasoning strategies to achieve complex learning goals.

Successful learners use strategic thinking in their approach to learning, reasoning, problem solving, and concept learning... to help them reach learning and performance goals and to apply their knowledge in novel situations. They also continue to expand their repertoire of strategies by reflecting on the methods they use to see which ones work well for them, by receiving guided teaching and feedback and by observing or interacting with appropriate models. Learning outcomes can be enhanced if educators assist learners in developing, applying, and assessing their strategic learning skills.

5. Thinking about Thinking

Higher order (metacognitive) strategies for selecting and monitoring mental operations facilitate creative and critical thinking.

Successful learners can reflect on how they think and learn, set reasonable learning or performance goals, select potentially appropriate learning strategies or methods, and monitor their progress toward these goals.... They also can generate alternative methods to reach their goals.... Instructional methods that focus on helping learners develop these higher order (metacognitive) strategies can enhance student learning and personal responsibility for learning.

6. Context of Learning

Learning does not occur in a vacuum but is influenced by environmental factors, including culture, technology, and instructional practices.

Teachers play a major interactive role with both the learner and the learning environment. Cultural or group influences on students can affect many educationally relevant variables, such as motivation, orientation toward learning, and ways of thinking.... The classroom environment, particularly the degree to which it is nurturing or not, can have a significant impact on student learning.

Motivational and Affective Factors

7. Motivational and Emotional Influences on Learning

What and how much is learned is influenced by the learner's motivation. Motivation to learn, in turn, is influenced by the individual's emotional states, beliefs, interests and goals, and habits of thinking.

Students' beliefs about themselves as learners and the nature of learning have a marked influence on motivation. Motivational and emotional factors also influence both the quality of thinking and information processing and an individual's motivation to learn. Positive emotions, such as curiosity, generally enhance motivation and facilitate learning and performance.... However, intense negative emotions (e.g., anxiety, panic, rage, insecurity) and related thoughts (e.g., worrying about competence; ruminating about failure; fearing ridicule, or stigmatizing labels) generally distract from motivation, interfere with learning, and contribute to low performance.

8. Intrinsic Motivation to Learn

The learner's creativity, higher order thinking, and natural curiosity all contribute to motivation to learn. Intrinsic motivation is stimulated by tasks of optimal novelty and difficulty, relevant to personal interests, and providing for personal choice and control. Intrinsic motivation is facilitated on tasks that learners perceive as interesting and personally relevant and meaningful, appropriate in complexity and difficulty to the learners' abilities, on which they believe they can succeed.... Educators can encourage and support learners' natural curiosity and motivation to learn by attending to individual differences in learners' perception of optimal novelty and difficulty, relevance and personal choice and control.

9. Effects of Motivation on Effort

Acquisition of complex knowledge and skills requires extended learner effort and guided practice. Without learners' motivation to learn, the willingness to exert this effort is unlikely without coercion.

Effort is another major indicator of motivation to learn... Educators need to be concerned with facilitating motivation by strategies that enhance learner effort and commitment to learning and to achieving high standards of comprehension and understanding. Effective strategies... enhance positive emotions and intrinsic motivation to learn and methods that increase learners' perceptions that a task is interesting and personally relevant.

Developmental and Social Factors

10. Developmental Influence on Learning

As individuals develop, they encounter different opportunities and experience different constraints for learning. Learning is most effective when differential development within and across physical, intellectual, emotional, and social domains is taken into account. Individuals learn best when material is appropriate to their developmental level and is presented in an enjoyable and interesting way. Because individual development varies across intellectual, social, emotional, and physical domains, achievement in different instructional domains may also vary.... Awareness and understanding of developmental differences among learners... can facilitate the creation of optimal learning contexts.

11. Social Influences on Learning

Learning can be enhanced by social interactions, interpersonal relations, and communication with others,

Learning can be enhanced when the learner has an opportunity to interact and to collaborate with others on instructional tasks. Learning settings that allow for social interactions and respect diversity encourage flexible thinking and social competence. In interactive and collaborative instructional contexts, individuals have an opportunity for taking perspective and for reflective thinking that may lead to higher levels of cognitive, social, and moral development, as well as self-esteem. Quality personal relationships that provide stability, trust, and caring can increase learners' sense of belonging, self-respect, and self-acceptance and provide a positive climate for learning.... Positive learning climates... can help learners feel safe to share ideas, actively participate in the learning process, and create a learning community.

Individual Differences Factors

12. Individual Differences in Learning
Learners have different strategies, approaches, and capabilities for learning that are a function of prior experience and heredity.

Individuals are born with and develop their own capabilities and talents. In addition, through learning and social acculturation, they have acquired their own preferences for how they like to learn and the pace at which they learn. However, these preferences are not always useful in helping students reach their learning goals.... The interaction between learner differences and curricular and environmental conditions is another key factor affecting learning outcomes.... Educators need to be sensitive to individual differences... and attend... to these differences by varying instructional methods and materials.

13. Learning and Diversity
Learning is most effective when differences in learners' linguistic, cultural, and social background are taken into account.

The same basic principles of learning, motivation, and effective teaching apply to all learners. However, language, ethnicity, race, beliefs, and socioeconomic status all can influence learning. Careful attention to these factors in the instructional setting enhances the possibilities for designing and implementing appropriate learning environments. When learners perceive that their individual differences are valued, respected, and accommodated in learning tasks and contexts, their levels of motivation and achievement are enhanced.

14. Standards and Assessment
Setting appropriately high and challenging standards and assessing the learner and learning progress—including diagnostic, process, and outcome assessment—are integral parts of the learning process.

Assessment provides important information to both the learner and teacher at all stages of the learning process. Effective learning takes place when learners feel challenged to work toward appropriately high goals. Therefore, appraisal of the learner's cognitive strengths and weaknesses and knowledge and skills is important for the selection of instructional material of an optimal degree of difficulty. Ongoing assessment of the learner's understanding of the curricular material can provide valuable feedback to both learners and teachers about progress toward the learning goals. Standardized assessment of learner progress and outcomes provides one type of information about achievement levels both within and across individuals that can inform various types of programmatic decisions. Performance assessment can provide other sources of information about the attainment of learning outcomes. Self-assessment of learning progress can also improve students' self-appraisal skills and enhance motivation and self-directed learning.

THE CONSTRUCTIVIST LEARNING THEORY

Principles 1 through 3 present the currently most widely prevailing theory of learning—the *constructivist learning theory*. This theory holds that meaningful learning is possible only on the basis of previously acquired knowledge. There is substantial research evidence that meaningful learning, as compared with rote or "technical" learning, increases the comprehension and retention of the material studied. Meaningful learning takes place when the learner relates new material in a substantive fashion to an already existing cognitive structure. What we learn in school and in daily life is retained in our cognitive structure as a framework of interconnections between ideas, skills, procedures, facts, and other types of information. When new learning occurs, this existing framework influences what we pay attention to, how we perceive and interpret new information, and the degree to which it is processed. The more prior relevant knowledge and interconnections learners possess, the better are they able to analyze, understand, and interpret what is received, the less time they spend on acquiring information, and the more time they spend on organizing and interpreting the new information. Students learn and remember information well or "meaningfully" when they can make cognitive associations and interconnections with this information. Learning of isolated information is more difficult and less permanent because the information is not connected to a network of other material. For meaningful learning to occur, then, new knowledge should be embedded within one's existing cognitive structure—one's conceptual framework.

This theory implies that most students cannot learn effectively by being passive listeners, and they do not simply record and store what they are taught. Rather, they learn well only when they are active in the learning process, when they construct their own understanding, and when they use what they are taught to modify their prior knowledge. In this process, they develop their own interpretation of the material presented to create a theory that makes sense to them. They then connect the new knowledge with the personal knowledge structure that they construct.

THE COGNITIVE MEDIATION MODEL OF COLLEGE STUDENT LEARNING

The APA motivational and affective factors encompassing Principles 7 through 9 Serve as a basis of the cognitive mediation model that serves as a conceptual framework for the ongoing advancement of theory and research on how college students learn (Paulsen, Forthcoming).

The basic assumption of this model is that college students possess characteristics that may include attitudes, feelings, beliefs, thoughts, shcemas, and behaviors, that interact with and mediate the effects of task, instruction, and other ecological features of learning environments in ways that influence the quality of learning outcomes. (ibid.).

This model assumes that the student's emotional states, beliefs about themselves as learners and the nature of learning, interests, and goals affect their learning. Thus, to promote learning teachers should enhance students' positive emotions and intrinsic motivation to learn.

The 12th and 13th APA principles assume that students have different strategies, approaches, and aptitudes for learning, and that they develop their own preferences for how they like to learn and for their favored pace in learning. The rest of this chapter elaborates on these points.

DIVERSITY IN STUDENTS' APTITUDES FOR LEARNING

Increasing faculty awareness about the diversity in students' aptitudes for learning may lead teachers to use a variety of instructional methods, activities, and materials that are more responsive to the entire range of learning styles and students' characteristics. In this way, more students may be provided with the opportunity to acquire skills and knowledge and to better prepare themselves for the workplace. The following is a research-based presentation of some of the individual differences that may affect students' learning.

Diversity in Intelligence—Multiple Intelligences

According to Gardner (1993), people have learning abilities that may be termed "intelligences," such as the capacity to solve problems or to fashion products, which can facilitate learning in one context and inhibit learning in others. Gardner has identified seven intelligences: linguistic, logical-mathematical, spatial, musical, bodily/ kinesthetic, interpersonal, and intrapersonal. The two intelligences traditionally emphasized and valued in developed countries belonging to the western culture are logical-mathematical and linguistic. However, people low on these two intelligences may be high on several of the others.

The implications for teaching are that by implementing techniques to enrich all the intelligences in their teaching, faculty can help students improve their learning skills. This can be done in two ways: (a) teaching content that applies to each of the intelligences, that is, in teaching a topic, the teacher tries to present it in several different ways, catering to the different intelligences; and (b) using the intelligences as a guide for teaching styles or methods—planning to use teaching methods in the lesson that target the dominant intelligences of the students. The teacher may assign reading materials or projects so that each student or groups of students may choose their own sources for reading or their own forms of presentation (e.g., dances or music of a relevant culture, maps, written and artistic artifacts) that tap into their areas of strength.

Diversity in Students' Learning Styles and Approaches to Learning

Students' Learning Styles

There is a vast research literature on students' learning styles. Here, I present briefly only a small portion of this literature, which pertains to learners mostly at the post-secondary level. Pask (1988) identified two learning strategies: (a) the *holist strategy*; and (b) the *serialist strategy*. Students using *holist strategies* prefer, from the beginning, to look at the learning task in its wider context. They also make extensive use of illustrations, examples, analogies, and anecdotes in building up an idiosyncratic form of understanding deeply rooted in personal experience and beliefs. Students using *serialist strategies* prefer starting with a narrow focus, concentrating on details and logical connections in a cautious manner, and looking at the broader context only toward the end of learning the topic. Although the majority of students were found to show a bias toward one or the other style, some students were found to have a versatile style, comprising a readiness to use both strategies in conjunction, with the particular balance between them determined by the nature of the task.

Kolb (1981, in Stage, Muller, Kinzie, & Simmons, 1998) identified four preferred learning styles: (a) *convergers,* who are most comfortable with abstract concepts and active experimentation, prefer practical applications of ideas, and usually have specific interests; (b) *divergers,* who are most comfortable with concrete experience and reflective observation, and are able to view concrete situations from a variety of perspectives; (c) *assimilarots,* who learn most effectively through abstract conceptualization and reflective observation, and excel in working with theoretical models and inductive reasoning; and (d) *accommodators* who learn best in a setting that allows for concrete experience and active experimentation, prefer doing to thinking, rely heavily on information from other people rather than on theories, are very adaptable, and solve problems intuitively.

Claxton and Murrell (1987) grouped students' different learning styles, as identified in the research literature, into four categories: (a) *personality models,* referring to basic personality characteristics such as extroversion versus introversion; (b) *information-processing* models, referring to the way people take in and process information; (c) *social interaction* models, referring to the way students interact and behave during the lesson, and (d) *instructional preference models,* concentrating on the media in which learning occurs (watching, reading, listening).

Students' Approaches to Learning

Another point of view of students' learning styles, referred to as students' approaches to learning/studying, sorts students' strategies for learning into two categories—motivational and cognitive. However, researchers have differed in terms of either coupling each motivational strategy with a specific cognitive strategy to form a particular study approach, or perceiving these two strategy categories as independent.

One group of researchers (Biggs, 1979; Entwistle & Ramsden, 1982; 1990; Marton & Säljö, 1976; Ramsden & Entwistle, 1981) distinguished three main student approaches to the study process, each of which includes an affective (motivational) component and a cognitive component, with the cognitive component envisaging the behavioral realization of the motive. These three approaches are:

(a) The *surface approach,* consisting of external motivation and surface learning strategies.

(b) The *deep approach,* consisting of internal motivation and deep learning strategies.

(c) The *organized/strategic approach,* consisting of an achievement-oriented/competitive motivation and strategic-learning strategies.

To elaborate on these approaches: *A deep approach* stems from an intention to establish personal understanding of the material presented. To do this, the student must learn meaningfully by interacting critically with the content, relating it to previous knowledge and experience, as well as examining evidence and evaluating the logical steps by which conclusions have been reached. In contrast, *a surface approach* involves the sole intention of satisfying the perceived requirements of the lecturer, which are seen as external impositions, remote from personal interests. The surface approach can still be active, but it relies on identifying the elements within the task most likely to be assessed in an exam, and then memorizing that information through rote learning strategies. *A strategic approach* stems from the intention to compete with peers in order to attain better grades. It involves orienting the study methods to succeed in the particular type of exams that the particular teacher assigns and to use study time efficiently.

A second group of researchers (Pintrich, Smith, Garcia, & McKeachie, 1991; Schmeck, Geisler-Brenstein, & Cercy, 1991; Weinstein, Zimmermann, & Palmer, 1985) separated the motivational from the cognitive components of academic performance, a separation which is reflected in the models of student approaches to learning that they developed. To illustrate, the following is Pintrich et al.'s model, including a motivation category and separate learning strategies category.

The Motivation Category

This category is based on a broad social-cognitive model of motivation that proposes three general components:

The Value component refers to what causes students to engage in an academic task. Its three sub-components are an intrinsic goal orientation (a focus on learning and mastery); an extrinsic goal orientation (a focus on grades and approval from others); and task value beliefs (a sense of interest, usefulness, and importance of course content).

The Expectancy component refers to students' beliefs that they can accomplish an academic task. Its two sub-components are: control of learning beliefs (the belief that outcomes are contingent upon own one's effort, rather than external factors such as the teacher or luck), and self-efficacy (a sense of confidence in their ability to accomplish a task).

The Affective component includes a single sub-component—test anxiety—that taps students' worries and concerns about taking exams.

The Learning Strategies Category

This category is based on a general cognitive model of learning and information processing. It consists of two components:

Cognitive and metacognitive strategies. Cognitive strategies include rehearsal (repeating words over and over to oneself to help in the recall of information), elaboration (e.g., paraphrasing, summarizing), organization (e.g., outlining, creating tables), and critical thinking (applying previous knowledge to a new situation and critically evaluating ideas). Metacognitive strategies help students control and regulate their own cognition by planning, monitoring (own comprehension), and regulating (e.g., adjusting reading speed to the task).

Resource management strategies. These strategies are divided into four sub-categories: time and study environment (using one's time well for study), effort regulation (persisting in the face of difficult or boring tasks), peer learning (using a study group or friends to help learn), and help seeking (seeking help from peers or teacher when necessary).

STUDENTS' PREFERRED TEACHER CHARACTERISTICS, BEHAVIORS, AND APPROACHES TO TEACHING

Knowledge of students' preferences for teaching methods, characteristics, and behaviors is important as their perceptions and interpretations of the academic environment, rather than the environment in any objective sense, affect their approaches to studying most directly; this, in turn, affects their learning outcomes (Entwistle, 1987). Entwistle and Tait (1990) suggested that ascertaining students' perceptions of and preferences for their academic environment and teacher characteristics can serve faculty in selecting appropriate teaching strategies and in structuring the academic environment to better serve the students' learning needs.

Students' preferred teacher characteristics and behaviors can be inferred by analyzing their ratings of their own teachers at the end of a course. Studies of this type found that students prefer teachers who are clear, interesting, organized, and well prepared, and perceive these characteristics as contributing most to good teaching and to their success in learning[16].

Hativa and Birenbaum (2000) identified university students' preferences for teacher characteristics in a general way that was unrelated to a particular teacher. They asked undergraduate students to rate their preferences for more than 80 listed teacher classroom behaviors. Factor analysis clustered the preferred behaviors into four teacher type categories: the provider, the self-

---

[16] See Chapter 1: Main Dimensions of Effective Teaching.

regulation promoter, the good communicator, and the information transmitter.

The information-transmitting instructor describes a lecturer whose main objective is the coverage of material, demonstrating no concern or awareness of the student population attending the particular class.

The well-communicating instructor describes a teacher, primarily a lecturer, who presents the material in a clear, well-organized, and engaging manner.

The providing instructor describes a teacher who promotes students' collaboration during learning, through small groups or even pairs, encourages students to seek help when they need it, provides a supportive learning environment, helps them concentrate, and guides students in resource management and effective study methods.

The self-regulation promoting instructor describes a teacher who requires and advances critical thinking and material integration, promotes active learning, assigns tasks that require self-regulated learning, and demands effort from students.

Because Kember (1997) has also categorized university faculty's approaches to teaching,[17] Table 4-1 compares the categories of approaches to teaching identified by both Kember and (Hativa & Birenbaum, 2000).

Kember	Hativa and Birenbaum
University instructors' approaches to teaching	Students' preferred teacher approaches to teaching
Teacher-centered orientation	
1. Imparting information	The information transmitter
2.Transmitting structured knowledge	
	The good communicator
3. Student-teacher interaction	
Student-centered orientation	
4. Facilitating understanding	The provider
5. Conceptual change	The self-regulation promoter

Table 4-1: Approaches to Teaching: Perceptions by University Teachers and Those Preferred by Students

It is very plausible that students' preferences for the four approaches to teaching, identified from factor analysis of undergraduate students' answers to a questionnaire (Hativa & Birenbaum), correspond to four out of the five

---

[17] See Chapter 3: Professors' Orientations and Approaches to Teaching.

approaches to teaching identified through interviews with, and questionnaires filled by university teachers (Kember).

One very interesting finding from Hativa and Birenbaum's study is that of the four teacher types identified, students showed the greatest preference for the well-communicating teacher who uses mainly the lecture method but in a clear, interesting, and well-organized manner. Students also preferred, although to a much lesser degree, the providing teacher who encourages help seeking, promotes a supportive learning climate, provides guidance in resource management and effective studying, and helps students concentrate. Students preferred least the self-regulation promoter who advances critical thinking, promotes active learning, assigns tasks that require self-regulated learning, and demands effort from students.

The finding that the clear, organized, and interesting lecturer is most highly preferred by students substantiates the vast body of research on teaching effectiveness that is based on student-related sources, such as student ratings of their teachers.[18] On the other hand, the low preference for the self-regulation promoter is surprising, because this teaching approach is highly recommended by educational researchers and educators, as presented at the beginning of this chapter. This low preference suggests that a large proportion of undergraduate students dislike investing too much thinking effort and independent work while learning. Rather, they seem to prefer their teachers to communicate material to them in a clear and engaging manner, and to support their learning.

Students' Preferred Teacher Characteristics as Related to Their Own Characteristics

As presented in this chapter, students differ in their approaches to studying and in their learning styles and strategies. Similarly, research studies have identified differences in university teachers' approaches to teaching as well as methods and styles in teaching.[19] Thus, if we want to find out how to teach in a way that helps students learn effectively, we need to identify the relationships between, on one hand, students' approaches to studying, or their learning styles and characteristics; and, on the other hand, their preferences for teacher characteristics. Are different professors' approaches to teaching perceived by different students as equally addressing their learning needs? Or do particular student characteristics relate to their differential preferences for teaching methods and styles?

---

[18] See Chapter 1: Main Dimensions of Effective Teaching.

[19] See Chapter 3: Professors' Orientations and Approaches to Teaching.

Indeed, preferences for a particular teaching style or other teacher characteristics were found to interact with a variety of student characteristics and learning styles, such as cognitive style, personality, and hemispheric dominance (Entwistle, 1990). Teachers' attitudes toward education were found to match students' preferred teaching styles (Kerlinger, 1966; 1968). Tetenbaum (1975) found that students' specific social-psychological needs in learning were related to their ratings of teachers whose style was consistent with their needs. Emanuel and Potter (1992) identified relationships between students' approaches to learning and their preferences for teacher communication styles.

Several ATI (aptitude-treatment interaction) studies showed that congruence between students' preferred teaching characteristics and their learning-related characteristics increased student achievement and satisfaction from instruction. To illustrate, Domino (1968; 1971) showed that students' achievement orientation interacted with the teaching style to which they were exposed. Students who scored high on a particular achievement orientation performed better academically and reported greater satisfaction from their studies when taught in a manner consonant with their achievement orientations than when taught in a manner dissonant with these orientations. Pask (1988) showed that when a teaching style was closely similar to students' learning style, students learned more easily and effectively than peers whose learning style mismatched the teaching style.

The next section presents the same notion but concentrates specifically on the congruence between teaching style and students' personal approaches to learning.

Students' Preferred Teacher Characteristics as Related to Their Approaches to Learning

Several studies suggest that students' approaches to learning per se are related to their preferences for certain teaching characteristics and behaviors. For example:

> Students who adopt deep approaches to learning   show a clear preference for an environment which is likely to promote understanding, while those with a surface approach prefer situations which are thought to facilitate rote learning (Entwistle, 1987, p. 187).

Similarly, students' main goals or motivation for learning correspond to their preferences for different kinds of teaching:

> Students whose main concerns are narrowly vocational want the lecturer to provide only the minimum required to pass the examination, and to present that in the most straightforward way. In contrast, students whose concerns are more academic want to be

challenged intellectually, and to be encouraged to read widely to supplement lectures (Entwistle, 1990, p. 9).

Hativa and Birenbaum (2000) found that undergraduate students preferred teaching approaches that best suited their own learning approaches and that students with particular needs in learning preferred teachers who accommodated for these needs. Hence, the *information-transmitting instructor* was not preferred by any type of student, probably because this approach in teaching overlooks the learning needs of all students. However, students with high extrinsic motivation (who learned for the sake of the grade) and with low critical thinking, preferred the *well-communicating instructor,* whose clarity and organization helped them achieve their goal of obtaining good grades, without too much thinking effort. In contrast, students having a high level of test anxiety, who needed much encouragement and help in their learning, and who probably did not feel safe in employing their own critical thinking, preferred the *providing instructor* who nurtured and encouraged them and supported their learning. Finally, students with high intrinsic goal motivation and low extrinsic goal motivation preferred the *self-regulation-promoting instructor,* who put high demands on their learning, promoted critical thinking and material integration, and required self-regulated learning and effort investment.

Disciplinary Differences in Students' Preferred Teaching Characteristics as Related to Their Approaches to Learning

There is ample evidence that students' preferred teaching characteristics are influenced by contextual factors such as the discipline they study (Feldman, 1989a; Hativa & Marincovich, 1995). These discipline-related differences in teaching and learning have been identified in research. Students tend to study in academic disciplines that suit their approach to learning and personal characteristics, and in the course of their studies they adapt themselves to the discipline's specific needs or modes of thinking and learning (Entwistle & Tait, 1990). Good teaching is also differentially evaluated in different disciplines (Feldman, 1978; 1989a; Hativa & Marincovich, 1995; Jones, 1981). Therefore, teachers should be aware of the diversity in their students' learning approaches with respect to the different academic disciplines, and of the need to accommodate these differences in adopting a teaching style.

ASSUMING RESPONSIBILITY FOR STUDENTS' LEARNING

APA principles 1 and 5 refer to the issue of students' responsibility for their learning. These principles suggest that successful learners assume personal responsibility for contributing to their own learning and that instructional methods should enhance students' personal responsibility for learning.

Kember's (1997) study identifies differences in teachers' perceptions of who should assume the main responsibility for student learning. The two extreme approaches to teaching, those of imparting information and conceptual change, delegate this responsibility mainly to the students whereas the other approaches, those of transmitting structured knowledge, student-teacher interaction, and facilitating understanding place the responsibility mainly on the teacher. Hativa and Birenbaum's (2000) and Birenbaum study suggests that students prefer good communicators and the providing teachers who assume a major role in the responsibility for student learning, to the other teacher types who delegate this responsibility mainly to the students.

Hativa (2000) found that when the question of responsibility referred to students' *success* in learning in courses of a particular law school, both faculty and students put the main responsibility on the teacher and perceived students' responsibility to be of lower extent. However, when the question of responsibility referred to students' *failure* in learning the course material or on course tests, faculty gave high ratings to four reasons related to the students' behaviors and low ratings to two reasons related to themselves as teachers. In contrast, students gave low ratings to all four reasons related to themselves, whereas they rated high the two reasons related to teachers. The differences between faculty and students' ratings on each of the six reasons were significant. Thus, we may conclude that in general, faculty assume responsibility for students' success in learning in the course but they deny their role in students' poor success or failure, and blame those results on students' problematic behaviors. In contrast, students feel just the opposite.

SUMMARY

The chapter opens with 14 psychological principles for successful learning that have been supported by multidisciplinary research. They are arranged under four categories, as published by the American Psychological Association (1997). The principles focus on psychological factors that are primarily internal to and under the control of the learner, but also acknowledge environmental or contextual factors that interact with learner factors. They assume that students differ in their learning characteristics and styles and in their preferences for various teaching styles, methods, and characteristics.

The remainder of the chapter reviews the diversity in students' learning characteristics and aptitudes, and in their individual preferences for how they like to be taught. This diversity affects students' approaches to studying and, eventually, their learning outcomes. Therefore, knowledge of this diversity can serve teachers in selecting the appropriate teaching strategies to better serve their students' learning needs and styles.

Various taxonomies of students' approaches to learning were suggested. One group of researchers distinguished between three main approaches to the learning process: surface, deep, and organized/strategic. Each of these includes an affective (motivational) component and a cognitive (strategy) component, with the strategy envisaging the behavioral realization of the motive. A second group of researchers isolated the motivational from the cognitive components of academic performance.

Yet another taxonomy distinguishes students' preferences for four different teaching approaches: the providing instructor, the self-regulation-promoting instructor, the well-communicating instructor, and the information-transmitting instructor. The teacher most strongly preferred by students is the well-communicating instructor who is clear, interesting, and well organized. In second place is the providing instructor, who encourages help seeking, promotes a supportive learning climate, guides in resource management and effective studying, and helps students concentrate. Students preferred least the self-regulation promoter who advances critical thinking promotes active learning, assigns tasks that require self-regulated learning, and demands effort from students.

Students' preferences for particular teaching styles were found to interact with a variety of characteristics, personality, and learning styles. Several ATI (aptitude-treatment interaction) studies have shown that congruence between students' preferred teaching characteristics and their learning-related characteristics increases learning achievement and satisfaction from instruction. It was shown that students seemed to prefer those teaching approaches that best suited their own individual learning approaches. Students' preferred teaching characteristics are also influenced by contextual factors such as their academic disciplines. Students tend to study in academic disciplines that suit their approach to learning and personal characteristics, and in the course of their studies, they adapt to the discipline's specific needs or modes of thinking and learning.

Faculty seem to assume responsibility for students' success in learning in the course but they deny their role in students' low success or failure and blame it on students' problematic behaviors whereas students put on the teacher the main responsibility for both—their success as well as their failure in learning in the course.

The next part of the book (Part II, Chapters 5-7) presents research and practice related to the main teaching methods that are used or may be applied in colleges and universities. The widely used lecturing method belongs to the teacher-centered orientation, whereas methods of active learning belong for the most part to the student-centered orientation.

PART II

TEACHING METHODS AND STYLES

Chapter 5

Lecturing and Explaining

A wide range of teaching methods can be found in institutions of higher learning. This chapter focuses on the one most prevalent teaching method, used in over 90% of college and university classrooms: the lecture (Thielens, 1987). The chapter also discusses teacher explanations—a recurrent component in lecturing.

THE LECTURE METHOD

All are sleeping

Just one is preaching

Such performance is called here "teaching"

(A German jingle)

What is a lecture? It is a "comparatively uninterrupted talk by a teacher on an academic subject, usually in a classroom setting" (Thielens, 1987, p. 1), or, similarly, "a teaching period occupied wholly or mainly with continuous exposition by the lecturer" (Cockburn & Ross, 1980, p. 1). Another description is:

As a teaching device, it is undoubtedly the most economical method by which a single individual can present in the context of a personalised and continuous argument a general framework for understanding the fundamentals of a particular subject, emphasizing the key concepts and involving the audience in reflective thought which moves in time with the on-going performance. A certain air of studied improvisation retains the basic character of the lecture as an extended conversation which has been allowed to develop into a monologue because of the intensity of student interest in the thoughtful contribution of the master. (McLeish, 1968, p. 1).

The main purposes of the lecture in higher education are:
To provide a survey of a whole field of knowledge through the medium of a living personality; to relate this body of knowledge to the primary aims of human life; to arouse an active interest, leading to an independent comprehension of the subject on the part of the listener (Paulsen, 1906, in McLeish, 1968, p. 2).

Lecturing may take many different forms. Strict lecturing refers to teacher exposition with almost no student participation. Less strict lecture structures allow students to ask questions when they do not understand, integrate periods of teacher-led questions and discussion with students, use the Socratic method of developing topics through questioning, and incorporate additional types of interaction with students, as described in Chapter 6.

Lecturing is not perceived to be a stand-alone teaching method but rather should be complemented by use of other sources. The main additional sources are: textbooks and other relevant texts, homework assignments, personal or group projects, lab tasks, and quizzes and tests.

Historical Roots of Lecturing

The lecture has been established for many centuries as the teaching method of choice in higher education. We can trace its origins to the fifth century pre-Christian Academy, the public pleasure-gardens in Athens where Plato and his students foregathered. In mediaeval times, when manuscripts were scarce and expensive, it became established as the prime method in university teaching.

As practised in the universities of mediaeval Europe, not to speak of the universities of the Muslim East, the lecture developed into a *system* wherein the lively conversation was changed to the reading of, and commentary on, a book—as it happened, the lecturer had the only available copy. The dogmatic and *a priori* tone of the aged Plato set the pattern for the formal university system of instruction, which had become closely tied to the professional training of the theologian, the physician and the lawyer.... There was of course no question of adapting instruction to the needs of the individual student in those far-off days. It was the function of the auditor to sit at the feet of the master and to reproduce the artificial pearls of his wisdom when called upon to do so. With the invention of printing, the fact that the lecture system was uneconomic and inefficient was not apparent, since the system of professional training had developed its own inertia and its own set of vested interests (McLeish, 1968, pp. 1-2).

Although books and other types of printed material are widely available at present, and computer communication enables the convenient transfer of large amounts of information in a very short time, lectures still dominate teaching in higher education, as next shown.

The Lecture as the Dominant Teaching Method at the College/University

The predominance of the lecture as a teaching method in colleges and universities has been often noted. National and regional surveys in England, Scotland, the US and other countries, uniformly show lecturing to be by far the most prevalent teaching mode at the undergraduate level (Thielens, 1987). To illustrate, one survey showed that 80% of faculty in a random sample of universities in the US essentially lectured through the entire class period (ibid.). However, of these 80%, only 7% used strict lecturing with absolutely no interruptions from students, whereas the remaining 73% paused now and then for student questions and comments. An additional 9% of the faculty lectured for 15-25 minutes and then used other teaching methods, and only 11% used alternative teaching methods for most of the class period. Larger classes received more lecturing than smaller classes, and men lectured substantially more than women. However, this gender gap may be explained partially in that women were better represented in the humanities and particularly in literature, which use lecturing least intensely and strictly, as we shall see.

Disciplinary differences were apparent in the extent of lecturing. Teachers in both the physical and biological sciences lectured in about 90% of their undergraduate classes, whereas in the social sciences the level of lecturing was 81%, and in the humanities a sharply lower 61%. However, disciplines within the humanities again differed greatly between one another. Literature professors lectured only 50% of the time, whereas both historians and philosophers lectured as much as scientists. Thus, literature stands apart by giving equal weight to other modes of teaching. These findings were supported by a more recent survey conducted among faculty members of an Ivy League research university (Hativa, 1997).

College teachers tend to underestimate the extent of their lecturing, particularly when they are expected to lead discussion. Most often, discussion forms only a small part of the lesson, and the lecture still dominates (Thielens, 1987). Or, it may turn out that what was meant to be discussion was in fact a lecture, as described by Barzun (1945, p. 37):

> Lecturing comes so natural to mankind that it is hard to stop it by edict. It simply turns into bootleg form. Many teachers think that because they sit around a table with only a dozen students they are running a discussion group, but they are lecturing just the same if the stream of discourse flows only in one direction.

There are many reasons for the dominance of the lecture in the college classroom. One of these is the nature of college courses, which are often attended by many students—dozens or even hundreds; sometimes the contents of these courses build on one another; there is a large amount of material "to cover"; and so forth. All these impose multiple constraints on teachers, and the lecture appears to be the most economical way to achieve the course goals under the circumstances. However, the lecture method may have several drawbacks.

Lecturing: Drawbacks and Criticism

The jingle that opens this chapter reflects a common belief that a lecture is always boring because only the teacher is active while students are passive. The following students' comments confirm this belief; they describe lectures that are boring or unclear to them and which make no contribution to their learning beyond what they could have obtained independently by reading the textbook or the lecture notes.

- Teacher simply reads lecture notes and this makes class boring. I wonder why I spend the time sitting in the lectures when I could just glance at the notes on my own.
- Lectures merely repeat and summarize the material in the textbook and contain nothing new or insightful. If you read the book you don't need to come to class.
- The entire course consists of reading transparencies that we have Xeroxed copies of.

The lecture has not prevailed so stubbornly because it is beloved. Over the centuries, the lecture method was frequently denounced, as illustrated by the following incidents. As a young adult (in the Old Ages), Socrates told the distinguished Protagoras that he could not learn anything from lectures (Thielens, 1987). There is evidence that Sorbonne students in the Middle Ages voted with their feet against dreary and turgid commentators (McLeish, 1968). In the 18th century, Samuel Johnson claimed that he knew nothing that would be best taught by lecture, and that lectures were unnecessary when all can read the book from which the lectures are taken. There is evidence dating from 1794 that criticizes the "reading off" of lectures and the anachronism of the lecture system, which had survived the invention of printing. At the beginning of the 19th century, university rectors already sought to persuade professors to devise a technique for communicating the fruits of their scholarship that would be more modern and efficient than lecturing (ibid.). This line of criticism became even more outspoken in the last several decades, as in "The mass lecture is the ultimate denigration of the human personality" (Goodman, Wade, & Zegar, 1974, p. 197) or Kraft's (1990) complaint about the *'pencil-pushing'* passivity encouraged by the lecture, which disengages students from genuine involvement and brings them to believe that learning is tantamount to note taking. The common metaphor critics use to describe a lecture is that of a teacher pouring information into the students' brains.

Altogether, the lecture is criticized because it keeps students passive rather than allowing them to actively construct their own knowledge; it is boring; it is impersonal and lacking in human warmth; it does not add anything beyond what can be learned from other sources of learning such as the textbook; it "spoonfeeds" students; and it consists almost solely of one-way communication.

Problems with Lecturing from the Teachers' Point of View

The most common reasons faculty gave for disliking lecturing were (Brown & Atkins, 1988): unresponsive audiences, large groups, effort and time involved in preparation, feelings of failure after a "bad" lecture, and lecturing on topics disliked. Teachers criticize their own lectures as unsatisfactory when they say too much too quickly, assume too much student prerequisite knowledge, forget to provide summaries, do not indicate when making an aside (rather than a main point), and have difficulty in timing the length of a lecture.

So what are the advantages of lecturing?

Lecturing: The Benefits

In sharp contrast to the criticism of lecturing as expressed in the last section, the following students' comments attest that a lecture, if presented well, can in fact be a stimulating, pleasant, and effective method of teaching.

- She is able to transmit her confidence with the material to the class. Her lectures are also interesting. She often throws in some witty remarks and she gives a touch of humanness to mathematics.
- She is sympathetic and really gifted in her lectures: in her knowledge, the high level of presentation, the thoroughness.
- He provides a wide, comprehensive view of the material, exhibits amazing knowledge, goes out of his way to see that students absorb the material, brings out many details to illustrate the theoretical material—a superb lecturer.
- An outstanding lecturer—makes a moderately interesting course a course that is a pleasure and fun to attend.

We may conclude that the view of the lecture as an unsuccessful, ineffective, and boring teaching method is an improper generalization and that all the above criticisms can be averted by giving good and engaging lectures. The success and effectiveness of the lecture depends upon its quality—there are good lectures and bad lectures. Good lectures activate students to construct their knowledge, include a personal approach and human warmth, present content that cannot be learned from other sources, at least not directly, and contribute greatly, overall, to student learning. Bad lectures, in contrast, are a waste of their time.

The lecture has prevailed because of its manifest merits: it is an effective communication tool, answers some basic needs of teachers, and serves as a useful tool for achieving the objectives of teaching a course.[20]

Advantages of the Lecture as a Communication Tool

The cardinal importance of lecturing derives from its qualities as a means for oral and visual communication. The lecture is the most comfortable and inexpensive way to transmit a large amount of knowledge to a large number of students. But effective lecturing is much more than just communicating knowledge. It arouses interest and motivation; promotes concentration and attention; identifies and marks the most important information; and enables effective cognitive processing, storing, and information retrieval, as described below. A good lecture presents ideas, analyzes and criticizes them, demonstrates how things work, follows steps of invention or discovery, and so on.

Advantages of the Lecture in Promoting Information Processing

The currently accepted model of information processing (e.g., Gage & Berliner, 1991) suggests that information enters our cognitive structure through at least one of our five senses (see Figure 5-1). As it enters these sensory registers, it passes through screening filters, particularly those of attention and concentration. Then it moves to short-term memory, which is conscious memory—all that we are aware of at one time. This storage capacity is limited to about seven "chunks" of information. The information passes through a control mechanism, sometimes regarded as the working memory, which is part of short-term memory. At this stage, the information undergoes several processes, such as rehearsal, encoding, screening, and searching. The parts of the information that are filtered out are forgotten, and the rest is connected and integrated with "old" knowledge while being stored

---

[20] Additional advantages of the lecture are listed below under Lecturing Versus Other Teaching Methods.

in long-term memory. Long-term memory probably has an unlimited capacity. The information stored is almost never forgotten, although we may be unable to retrieve it because of a failure in how we search for it.

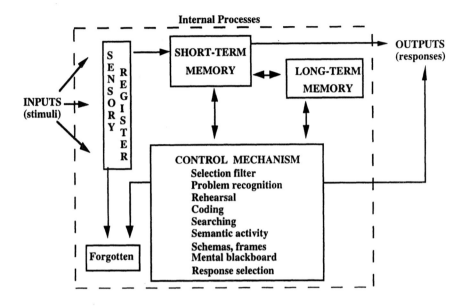

Figure 5-1: An Information-Processing Model

The information-processing model suggests that for learning from a lecture to be effective, a teacher should take care that all the processes of acquiring and processing knowledge work smoothly and effectively, without interruption. Good lecturers reduce all kinds of "noise"[21] to the very minimum. They break down the material into small "chunks" or segments, and teach the segments one by one, with pauses in between to enable deep processing by the control mechanism. They present the material in an organized and clear way that enables fast and easy screening to separate what is important from what is peripheral. This screening facilitates processing and storage of the new knowledge in long-term memory while creating the connections with old knowledge that enable effective search and retrieval.

Advantages of the Lecture for Teachers

The most common reasons teachers themselves give for liking lectures are intellectual challenge in structuring a lecture, personal satisfaction in

---

[21] See Chapter 11.

giving a good lecture, student responsiveness during a lecture, and stimulating students' interest in one's subject (Brown & Atkins, 1988).

Teachers view the lecture as the form of teaching most directly under their control. They are in charge, in command of the teaching process, and can make it a most fruitful learning experience for students. They also see the lecture as best utilizing their teaching skills, aptitudes, and knowledge in attaining the course goals, as enabling them to disseminate unpublished or not readily available knowledge, and as complementing and clarifying text material (Thielens, 1987)

In regard to attaining faculty teaching goals,[22] the lecture appears to be the most suitable method, particularly when teaching a large number of students at the same time. Indeed, teachers appreciate the power of the lecture to communicate information, and find it a comfortable and pleasant experience. They believe that it is very cost effective for transmitting knowledge of the domain, its structure and organization, and its methods. In addition, the lecture is perceived by faculty as the best response, and sometimes the only possible response, to three key needs in designing material for a course or lesson: selecting, structuring, and simplifying.[23] Faculty find lecturing the best available way to transmit to students their *selection* of the material, the *structure* of the material selected, and the most suitable method to *simplify* the material, adjusting it to students' capacities and interests (ibid.).

The following presents results of studies that compared the lecture to other teaching methods. Unfortunately, few studies of this kind are available, and of those that are, none compare the lecture to all the important teaching methods.

Lecturing Versus Other Teaching Methods

Since the turn of the century, educators have periodically mounted determined campaigns to replace the lecture with what they perceived as better forms of teaching. The new formats included discussion, independent study, television, programmed instruction, computerized instruction, student-paced instruction, and other less widely known innovations. However, none of these has produced any notable improvement, at least in overall outcome, nor have they attained to any widespread use (Thielens, 1987). Among all alternative methods of teaching, only the discussion has been found to be somewhat prevalent, in about 10% of classes, while Socratic techniques and

---

[22] See Chapter 3: Faculty Members' Goals in Teaching.
[23] See Chapter 19: Planning the Course.

other teaching methods are infrequently used (ibid.). Nunn (1996) also found discussion to be little used in college teaching.

Several studies have compared the effectiveness of lectures with other teaching methods. When measures of knowledge were used, the lecture proved to be at least as efficient as other methods for student learning (Cockburn & Ross, 1980; Costin, 1972; McKeachie, Pintrich, Lin, & Smith, 1987), whereas other methods work well usually with small-to-medium classes. However, lectures seem to be less effective in stimulating thought than are methods that give students a more active role in their learning, such as small group discussion or working on projects (Cockburn & Ross, 1980).

Lecture Versus Discussion

Findings of different studies that compared the lecture with discussion are inconclusive—some of them show the lecture to have a greater effect whereas others show the opposite. An old review of these studies (Costin, 1972) concluded that: (a) lecture is more efficient for facilitating student acquisition of information; (b) discussion is more effective for teaching cognitive skills, such as interpreting knowledge and solving problems; (c) the two methods do not differ consistently from one another in their effect on students' overall evaluation of the course.[24]

Lecture Versus Textbook and Independent Reading

Comparisons of the lecture and independent reading found no consistent differences between the effects of either method on students' acquisition of information (Costin, 1972). McLeish (1968) and Thielens (1987) argued that textbooks and other readings cannot replace the lecture, but rather complement it, and this is only when appropriate reading materials are available. In support of this notion, the following lecture characteristics may be viewed as giving it an advantage over using textbooks:

Pertinence of the teaching material to the teacher's vision. Professors usually have a clear personal view of the best possible contents to select for the course they teach, as well as the right depth and difficulty level. They also have their own perception of the most appropriate structure to give to this content. It often happens that they cannot find a textbook that shares their view. Even when they do find an appropriate textbook, it only rarely fully agrees with their choice of material and personal philosophy as described above. As one professor put it: "Textbooks bring up peripheral matters one doesn't want to cover, and class discussion sometimes gets off the subject" (Thielens, 1987, p. 13). Consequently, they may choose to either teach a course without a textbook or to use only parts

---

[24] I have not found any more recent research-based comparison of lecture and discussion.

of a textbook. By lecturing, teachers construct their presentations to fit their own visions and adjust them to the students in the particular class.

Up-to-datedness of the material. In a rapidly developing field where timely topics are relevant, these can easily be included in a lecture. In contrast, textbooks quickly become outdated.

Promptness of help available to students. Undergraduate students are often too immature to learn effectively by reading. They may face difficulties in understanding texts that are too technical or abstract for them, or in sorting the important from the peripheral. Nor can readings provide immediate answers to their questions or help them in their difficulties. In a lecture, in contrast, the teacher can identify when students face problems in learning and help them on the spot, by promptly clarifying students' misunderstandings (ibid.).

Adaptability to students. The lecture can be adjusted to the particular students in class—to their aptitudes, interests, and background knowledge—whereas books are written for a general audience and are not adjusted to a particular population. When students do not understand, the lecturer can go back to the material in different words, whereas books are usually restricted to one form of explanation.

Use of visual aids. The lecture can integrate visual aids and employ physical demonstrations and illustrations, even in motion, such as through computer animation or other computer presentations, films and videotapes. All these can add clarity and interest to the material in a way the textbook cannot.

Maintaining a human touch. The lecture can provide a human touch and aesthetic pleasure, communicate and kindle enthusiasm for a subject, and stimulate original thinking in a way that a book cannot.

Practical Applications of Lecturing

Chapters 8-16 present theory and practice related to making a lesson—particularly a lecture—organized, clear, interesting and engaging, within the framework of a pleasant classroom climate. For practical applications of the lecture, see these chapters.

EXPLAINING IN TEACHING

Those who can, do; those who can explain, teach[25]…Good teaching is good explaining (Calfee, 1986, pp. 1, 12).

This citation reflects the belief that the capacity to explain is of critical importance in teaching. Explanations are integrated into all methods of instruction—discussion, seminar, practice lesson, tutorial, and laboratory class. However, explanations seem to be of particular importance in lecturing: "The art of explaining, that is, the ability to provide understanding to others, is the central activity of lecturing" (Behr, 1988, p. 189).

What is "Explanation?"

The terms *explanation* and *explain* appear in many kinds of educational contexts, but not always with the same meaning. Generally, *to explain* involves relating an object, event, action, or state of affairs to some other object, event, action, or state of affairs; or showing the relation between an event or state of affairs and a principle or generalization; or stating the relations between principles and a generalization. *To explain* is to set forth an antecedent condition of which the particular event or process to be explained is taken as the effect, or else, to give the rules, definitions, or facts which are used to justify decisions, judgments, actions, and so forth (Behr, 1988). *Explaining* is a group of statements or a story from which the thing to be explained can logically be inferred (Miltz, 1972). At the lowest level, explaining entails the communication of a definition or a set of facts or a set of instructions on how to do something. At a higher level of abstraction, it involves the use of generalizations, cause and effect relationships, as well as reasoning leading to conclusions (Behr, 1988).

Fairhurst (1981) operationally defined an explanation as requiring (a) something to be explained; (b) an explainer or other communication source such as printed material, and (c) an explainee who is the recipient of the explanation. The role of an explanation is to make some concept, procedure, or rule plain and comprehensible (Metcalf & Cruickshank, 1991). *Explanation* in the teaching context must involve understanding. If a teacher explains in a way that students do not understand, this cannot be regarded as an explanation (Behr, 1988).

We should note, though, that students may also be required to explain in class, usually when called upon to present their observations, learning, answers to assignments, solutions of problems, outcomes of a discussion, or

---

[25] A twist of George Bernard Shaw's aphorism: "Those who can, do; those who cannot, teach."

values. Considerable insight can be gained into students' thinking, values, or their grasp of a problem or of the material taught in class through the explanations they give.

Types of Explanation

One may explain *how to do something*; *why an event occurred or a law was obtained*; or *for what reason persons or groups acted as they did* (Miltz, 1972). A teacher might explain a *concept* (e.g., global warming), a *procedure* (how to subtract), or a *rule* (we raise our hands in class to be recognized). Explanation is also used *to account for the occurrence of things,* that is, *to give reasons.* For example: why the global warming occurs; why subtraction is performed in a specific manner, and why students must prepare their homework (ibid.).

MacDonald (1991) divided explanations into three types: *descriptive* (specifies a procedure to be followed), *interpretative* (provides the meaning of concepts or terms), and *reason giving* (clarifies why something is done the way it is or why some event has occurred or is occurring). Descriptive explanations tell the listener how processes, structures and procedures operate, for example: How does a child acquire language? How does one make an overseas call from a public telephone? Interpretative explanations clarify the central meaning of a word or statement, for example: What do "epenthesis" and "apocope" mean? Answers to reason-giving explanations may be tentative or speculative, for instance, what is the cause of the nuclear power-plant disaster at Chernobyl in the Soviet Union in April 1986? A particular explanation may embrace all three of the types concurrently.

Additional types of explanations mentioned in the literature (Metcalf & Cruickshank, 1991) are:

Structural explanations (pointing out the structure of something).

Classificatory explanations (pointing out the class to which something belongs in accordance with some classificatory system).

Teleological explanations (pointing to a purpose or goal).

Sequential explanations (relating a sequence of events).

Analytic explanations (procedures and propositions that inform and clarify concepts and rules—e.g., explaining how to solve mathematical equation).

Prescriptive explanations (prescriptions for actions). These include:
- Social explanations (e.g., pointing out social rules).
- Ethical explanations (e.g., pointing out a principle of conduct),
- Procedural explanations (i.e., how to do something to achieve some goal).

- Aesthetic explanations, including value-giving explanations (e.g., the criteria for grading), and interpretive explanations (e.g., explicating a poem).

Leinhardt (1990, pp. 3-4) differentiated between two types of teaching-related explanations: *instructional* and *disciplinary*.

Instructional explanations are designed to explain concepts, procedures, events, ideas, and classes of problems in order to help students understand, learn, and use information in flexible ways. They communicate a particular aspect of the subject matter knowledge they are designed to teach. They teach in two distinct ways: (a) they convey, convince, and demonstrate; and (b) they model explaining in the discipline and self-inquiry. Instructional explanations occur in response to an actual query, an anticipated or probable query, or perceived puzzlement.

Disciplinary explanations are built around a core of conventions within each particular discipline and include features such as what are the important questions, what constitutes evidence, what may be assumed, and what is the agenda for the discipline. These explanations have rules that help the community of thinkers in that field focus on the task of constructing new knowledge and reformulating extant knowledge. They provide the legitimacy of new knowledge, they reinterpret old knowledge, and they challenge and address existing knowledge.

Disciplinary explanations differ from one particular discipline to another. To illustrate the differences in explanations between the sciences and the humanities, let us compare mathematics and history. The formalism of mathematics tightly constrains explanations. Mathematics has a "closed structure"—it is easy to define and limit the area of investigation or the variables; therefore, the components of a mathematical explanation are well defined and limited. History, in contrast, has an "open structure," with no shared or uniform view of the domain. Thus, it is not easy to delimit an area for investigation or to define the relevant variables and their functions in the explanations. Hence, disciplinary explanations differ in their functions and types, and in the procedures for their evaluation and validation. For the interested reader, the following articles involve discussions for the explanations for the several particular subject areas: Horwood (1988, science), Eley and Cameron (1993, mathematics), and Vayda, McCay, and Eghenter (1991, social science).

Properties of Good Explanations

Students and professors alike attach very high importance to good explanations. When asked to rank 75 statements concerning the ideal teacher-pupil relationship, one of the statements rated highest by students was: "The teacher's explanations fit in correctly with the student's ability and knowledge" (Hyman, 1968). The following studies show that the strategies for achieving good explanations are, in fact, the same as those for achieving effective teaching.[26]

In a survey of 93 university lecturers regarding explanations (Brown & Daines, 1981), the respondents rated the value and importance of each of 40 listed properties of an explanation. The ten most valuable properties were found to be, in decreasing order of importance: *clarity, interest, logical organization, selection of appropriate content, eliciting responses from students, focusing attention upon important points, relevance to students, use of examples and illustrations, use of diagrams, and enthusiasm.* In support, a review of the research literature indicated that good explanations have *clarity of structure* and *an interesting presentation* (Metcalf & Cruickshank, 1991).

Fairhurst (1981) suggested that an explanation be considered as satisfactory according to three points of view. From the *explainer's* point of view, it must meet the conditions of clarity, orderly presentation, and intention to explain. From the *explainee's* view, the explanation must be a gap-filler, that is, it must satisfy their curiosity or remove puzzlement, and be expressed in terms that are intelligible and related to previous experience. From the *detached observer's* point of view, the explanation must be a distinct attempt to clarify a point or situation, and it must be true, testable, appropriate, adequate, and not circular (circularity means defining a term by using a synonym that is equally ill understood).

MacDonald (1991) prescribed the following requirements of good explanation. The explanation should be *appropriate to the situation*, and it should be *thorough, accurate, and understandable— logically sound and psychologically appropriate.* This can be accomplished by adapting explanations to the learner's frame of reference (e.g., to help students rearrange and extend what they already know), providing only as much information as can be assimilated, and using techniques to enhance clarity and emphasis. The following are MacDonald's guidelines for evaluating explanations as logically sound. The explainer:

- Has a clear conception of the purpose of the explanation—either interpretive, descriptive, reason giving, or some combination of the three.
- Identifies the purpose of the required explanation from the student's request.
- States an interpretive explanation operationally.
- Avoids circularity.
- Breaks up the procedure of a descriptive explanation into parts or small steps and presents the parts step-by-step in some carefully chosen order.

---

[26] As listed in Chapters 9-16.

– Takes care that reason-giving explanations are complete.

Learning to Explain Well

Can one learn how to explain well? A survey of university lecturers (Brown & Daines, 1981) revealed that they believe that the properties of good explanations can be learned and integrated into teaching. Miltz (1972) developed and evaluated a manual for improving teacher effectiveness in explaining. His method consisted of two steps: (a) helping teachers understand the major components of good explanations, and (b) giving them guided practice in improving those components. Miltz showed that middle school teachers who were trained to improve their explanations using his method substantially improved the quality and effectiveness of their explanations, as compared with untrained teachers.

SUMMARY

The Lecture Method

Lecturing dominates the college classroom and may take many different forms. Strict lecturing refers to teacher's exposition with hardly any student participation, whereas less strict lecture structures provide for a variety of types of interaction with students.

The lecture has been established for many centuries as the teaching method of choice in universities, and it still dominates teaching in higher education. University and college teachers underestimate the extent to which they lecture. Larger classes receive more lecturing than smaller ones. Research indicates that teachers in both the physical and biological sciences lecture in most of their undergraduate classes, whereas in the social sciences the amount of lecturing is somewhat smaller, and it is sharply smaller in the humanities—particularly in literature.

Lecturing has been blamed for making students passive rather than stimulating the active construction of knowledge. It has been said to be boring and impersonal, one-way communication, "spoonfeeding," and not contributing anything to the learner beyond other sources for learning such as textbooks. However, to describe the lecture as an unsuccessful, ineffective, and boring teaching method is an improper generalization. Rather, the success and effectiveness of a lecture depends upon its quality—there are good lectures and bad lectures. Good lectures contribute greatly to student learning beyond the textbook or class notes, whereas bad lectures are perceived by students as a waste of their time.

The lecture has prevailed throughout the centuries because of its manifest merits: It is an effective communication tool; it enables teachers to select, structure, and simplify the material for the course and lesson and to control its presentation; and it serves as a good tool for achieving the goals of teaching the course. Its advantages over other teaching methods are that it enables teachers to adjust the material to their own vision; present material that is up-to-date; provide prompt help for students when they face difficulties in understanding and adapt teaching to students in other ways; use visual aids— static as well as dynamic; and provide a human touch. Research shows that the lecture is not less effective than all other teaching methods, particularly discussions and learning from textbooks. Because a lecture can be given to a large number of students at one time, it seems to be the most cost-effective method of teaching in the college classroom, at least for the goal of knowledge acquisition. However, it is most effective when complemented by other learning activities, for example, reading and problem solving.

Explaining in Teaching

The capacity to explain is of critical importance in teaching. Research shows that the properties of good explanations can be learned and integrated into teaching. "Explanation" has a variety of definitions and meanings but in the teaching context it must involve understanding and learning. Explanations should make some concept, procedure, or rule plain and comprehensible, and should account for the occurrence of things, that is, give reasons. Explanations may differ for different academic disciplines in a variety of aspects—in their functions and types, and in the procedures used for their evaluation and validation. Several criteria for good explanations are presented in this chapter. The properties of an explanation most valued by teachers were found to be, in decreasing order: clarity, interest, logical organization, selection of appropriate content, eliciting responses from students, focusing attention upon important points, relevance to students, use of examples and illustrations, use of diagrams, and enthusiasm.

The next chapter presents methods to actively engage students during the lecture. These methods enliven the presentation and promote the effectiveness of student learning.

Chapter 6

Active Learning During Lectures

In the 5th century BC, Confucius wrote:

I hear and I forget

I see and I remember

I do and I understand

It is through involvement and doing that learners genuinely participate in the learning process. They learn meaningfully only when they are doing something either mentally or physically with the information and learning materials. The following is additional evidence that aware educators believed in the notion of active learning a long time ago:

> It has been said by many people in many ways that learning should be active, not merely passive or receptive; merely be reading books or listening to lectures or looking at moving pictures without adding some action of your own mind, you can hardly learn anything and certainly you can not learn much (Polya, 1965, p. 102).

Polya also cites in this matter Kant's dictum:

> Learning begins with action and perception, proceeds from thence to words and concepts, and should end in desirable mental habits. (p. 103).

In accordance with the constructivist learning theory, meaningful learning takes place only when students actively process the new information, interpret it, and link it to their existing knowledge.[27] The implications of this theory for classroom teaching are that teachers should promote students' active involvement in the learning process, for example,

---

[27] See Chapter 4: Constructivist Learning Theory.

87

by performing some tasks that give them personal insight into the concepts being taught. Becoming active seekers rather than passive recipients of knowledge promotes students' attention, generates interest, provides opportunities for them to think, and delegates more responsibility for their learning to them.

Bonwell and Eison defined *active learning* as a process that involves students in doing things and thinking about the things they are doing. When students are active learners in the classroom they are engaged in higher-order thinking (analysis, synthesis, evaluation), and in a variety of activities such as reading, discussing, writing, and problem solving. Less emphasis is placed on transmitting information and more on developing students' understanding and skills and on exploration of their own attitudes and values. Care should be taken to ensure that, first, the students' activity is "mindful," that is, that the students understand what they are doing as well as how this activity relates to the overall course goals. Second, evaluation and feedback to students must be in accordance with the objectives of active learning—they should relate to students' understanding of processes rather than of specific contents, and credit should be given for the students' formulating the problem correctly or for their making a strong case, even if the main point made differs from the teacher's.

However, active learning can be promoted not only in teaching methods that directly involve student activity, such as discussions, but even in lecturing, in which the teacher's role is that of the presenter and authority. Active learning in lecturing comprises the ongoing involvement of students in thinking, in reflection on the material presented, and in those activities that promote cognitive construction of the material.

BARRIERS TO ACTIVE LEARNING IN THE CLASSROOM

In contrast to the importance of making students active in classroom learning, the majority of students play a relatively passive role in the classroom and see themselves as recorders of the information transmitted by the teacher (Becker, Geer, & Hughes, 1994). A major reason for this situation is the resistance found among university teachers to using active learning methods. Three of the main barriers I have identified are presented next, together with a response to each:

Waste of time. Some lecturers claim that they need to cover the curriculum material and do not have time to waste on student activities in class.

The answer to this claim may be that what matters in lectures is what and how well the students learn, what attitudes they develop toward the material taught, and what encourages them to continue learning. Rather than assuming that they themselves must cover all of the content, teachers can delegate some of it to students for independent study. Teachers should consider what they really want students to remember five years after taking the course. Active learning may provide more effective and exciting learning, which will be remembered in the long run.

Loss of control. Other teachers are concerned about the risk of uncertainty, losing control, and chaos in the classroom if they use active learning methods extensively during the lesson, particularly in large classes.

However, if these activities are well planned and organized, students appreciate being involved and challenged, and problems are unlikely to arise. To avoid losing control, the teacher may choose to incorporate into his/her lectures active learning methods that are of "low-risk,"—such as those illustrated below. These methods can still achieve high student participation and engagement even in large classes, without changing the professor's central controlling role in the classroom.

Unprepared students. Some teachers justify their avoidance of active learning methods that are based on assigned reading or other homework by arguing that students come unprepared.

The way to overcome this obstacle is to motivate students to do the reading.[28] This can be done, for example, by providing guiding questions in advance, giving brief quizzes at the start of class, or requiring short, out-of-class writing tasks based on the assigned reading, or conducting short, in-class readings that remind them of and complement the out-of-class reading.

The following sections present strategies for active learning that can be incorporated into the "safe" methods of lecturing or teacher-led discussion in the class. Teachers can decide which of these strategies are sufficiently *"low-risk"* for them within the particular teaching context— the students, course material, and culture of teaching prevailing in the institution or school. Strategies may be characterized as "low-risk" if they do not cause too much loss of control or of class time and do not induce too much chaos or uncertain learning outcomes.

So what are the basic elements of active learning in the classroom? Meyers and Jones (1993) described active learning as consisting of basic elements (talking, listening, writing, reading, and reflecting); learning strategies (small groups, cooperative work, case studies, simulations,

---

[28] See Chapter 20: Maintaining Student Motivation to Read the Assigned Reading.

discussion, problem solving, journal writing); and teaching resources (readings, homework assignments, guest speakers, teaching technology, ready-made educational materials, commercial and educational television). The basic elements for promoting active learning that can be integrated into teacher-centered instructional methods, primarily into lecturing, consist of getting students to: (a) talk and listen; (b) read or write; (c) think, pause, reflect; and (d) question (ibid.). Additional active learning strategies for use in alternative teaching methods that are more student-centered than those mentioned here are presented in the next chapter.

TALKING AND LISTENING IN CLASS

Talking, within the active learning process, is aimed to clarify thinking and promote students' public speaking and active listening skills. The teacher provides opportunities for students to present their ideas to the whole class, and to meaningfully talk with each other. Active listening is necessary for a meaningful talking-listening process; as such, it requires attention and concentration.

Note: a shadowed background in this book marks sections with practical advice, as follows.

How to promote meaningful talking and listening in class

Paraphrasing. Just asking students to talk and listen attentively to each other does not guarantee learning. Ask listeners to paraphrase what they have just heard, before they start talking. In this way they must practice active listening skills.

Special oral presentations. Assign students in class, individually or in small groups, to:

- Prepare and teach parts of the new material.
- Present their homework assignments.
- Present projects they have done.
- Present a relevant topic, for example, an interesting scientific article they have read.
- Describe personal experiences related to the topics at hand.

Amongst-student discussion/"think-pair-share." Incorporate into your lecture periods of discussion among adjacent students. For example, when building part of the lesson on students' pre-class readings, you may divide the allocated time into 10-15 minute segments, each devoted to one of the main points of the reading. You may begin each segment with a brief lecture on, or a demonstration of, a point that you wish to get across, and then present a conceptual question which tests the students' understanding of the idea or point presented. In other cases just pose a question to the students that requires reflection on the material presented. In all cases, give students 1-2 minutes to think or write an appropriate answer/response and ask them to then turn to a partner or to a group of other students—usually their immediate neighbors, share their responses, and then present them to class. You may then conduct a short follow-up class discussion, or alternatively, ask students to raise their hands in support of the answer they find most appropriate. For each answer, call on one of the students who supported it to explain his/her answer and then let the other students in class develop a discussion with that student. When working with small groups, you may ask the representatives of each small group to report their findings to the class. Require that students take turns acting as group representatives. This strategy stimulates the discussion and promotes students' reflection and verbalization.

Short debate with selected students. Assign particular students to participate in short debates during a lecture—to present opposing sides. Ask the other students in class to criticize the debates and to vote on the debated issue before and after the debate. Debates can help students recognize and overcome the biases they bring to certain topics.

Short debates with half the class. In order to maintain control in leading the debate, you may divide the class into two groups (e.g., right and left of the classroom, or front and back rows). Then ask one group to submit an agreed number of statements representing the "pro" side of the debate and the other group to submit the same number of statements representing the "con" side. You may repeat the process, including rebuttals. Before concluding, ask for two or three volunteers to summarize each side's arguments. When some students refuse to choose one side or the other, invite their additional points of view.

Panel. Assign two or more students or groups of students to study a certain issue prior to the lesson, to prepare to present their points of view on the debated issue, and to bring reasons to justify their positions. During the lesson, each member of this selected student panel will present their views and justifications, with you acting as the coordinator. Then, have the class present questions and comments to the panel. Next, ask for volunteers to make summary arguments for each side, and eventually ask all students to vote, by taking one of the two opposing sides. Ask several students to explain why they chose one side or the other, or why they abstained from voting.

"Hot seats." This is a variation of the panel method, in which the members of the panel do not present different points of view on the issue but rather they present the topic that they have prepared in advance (a solution to a problem or an issue) and lead the ensuing class discussion. All students in class may present questions to these students, come up with suggestions, and work together until a solution is arrived at. The lecture then follows from their ideas. The students leading the discussion are assigned in advance for this role, and during the discussion they sit in front of the class—in the "hot seats."

READING AND WRITING IN CLASS

Reading and writing can clarify thinking and develop students' written expression skills. Focused reading can serve as a meaningful exercise when the teacher requires students to respond either to questions that he/she provides regarding the text, or to problems and issues suggested in the text.

Writing during class challenges students to use higher-order thinking skills such as analysis, synthesis, decision-making, and evaluation. Angelo and Cross (1993) suggested a number of short yet effective writing exercises that help students learn and assess their own learning as well as provide teachers with feedback on how well they are teaching and what students are learning. The advantage of brief writing assignments is that the method works well in any class size and academic discipline.

How to promote reading and writing in class

Short reading assignments. Assign students to read, during the lesson, a short passage from a book, handout, or transparency. Then have them discuss the content in small groups, or conduct a class-wide discussion. Alternatively, assign students to critically read short assignments and respond to them orally or in writing.

Guiding questions to the assigned reading. To make in-class reading a meaningful exercise that requires students to think, provide guiding questions for the text to be read. Ask students to respond to these questions in writing, while reading.

Short writing assignments. During the lesson, ask students to perform the following tasks in writing, either individually or in small groups. The students can then submit their answers to you, to be read aloud in class for further student comment or discussion, or to be graded later. Alternatively, students themselves may read their answers aloud to promote discussion, or else ask them to pass their answers to a neighbor to be read aloud. Such tasks may include asking students:

- To **paraphrase** a key paragraph in today's reading.
- To **express their thoughts** about a discussion, a particular issue, or a topic development.

- To **answer a question** you have posed, for example: What are some of the major concepts associated with today's topic? Describe the concept of... in your own words.
- To **list the main ideas**/points of a discussion.
- To **solve a short problem** or to plan the approach for solving a problem.
- To **analyze, compare, contrast, define**, describe, evaluate, justify, prove, or integrate/synthesize.

Ask students during the last few minutes of the lesson to:

- Write down the three most important ideas they remember from today's lecture.
- Pose the **content-related questions** still uppermost in their minds.
- **Write a short summary of the lesson.** Then call on several students to read their summaries to the class. Follow this by class discussion, or copy the summary outline onto the board.
- **Reconstruct in writing as much of the lecture** as possible while their notebooks are closed—either in outline form or in tables or diagrams. This exercise in immediate recall forces students to review and consolidate key points, and helps them discover areas for review.
- **Give students a printed outline of the topic** or a table with only headings, on completion of teaching a topic. Assign them to complement the missing information in the outline or table.

Actually, students write regularly, not in the framework of special assignments, but while taking notes of the material presented. This activity can be taken advantage of to promote active learning.

Note Taking

Teachers prescribe, students transcribe...

This well-known saying reflects the common perception among both students and faculty that the students' role in lectures is to passively absorb knowledge "broadcast" by the lecturer, and to take notes mechanically. Indeed, students often do take notes automatically— writing almost each word the teacher says or writes on the board—without too much investment of thinking effort. However, many students actually do much more while taking notes. Rather than just copying down the teacher's words, they mentally process the discourse to structure contents so that it will be meaningful for them. Through this meaningful note taking, students analyze the content of the lesson, seek organizational cues, look for key concepts, and attempt to follow the teacher's mode of thinking. This mindful note taking enables students' personal construction of understanding and knowledge of the lesson content. It maintains their concentration, attention, alertness, and active thinking. A review of studies on student note taking (Hartley & Davies, 1976; 1978) supports the conclusion that annotating helps students learn, provided it is accomplished in an effective/meaningful way.

The question is how to make students activate their thinking while taking notes. Some instructors feel that they save students' time when they give them detailed lecture notes that present most of the lesson content prior to the lesson. Such notes may verily reduce or eliminate the need for students' note taking and free them to concentrate solely on the presentation. However, many students find it difficult to listen passively and concentrate on a lecture, as illustrated in the following comments:

- Taking notes makes me more involved, less likely to fall asleep.
- Writing things down helps one stay awake.
- Chalkboard makes the teacher go slower. Viewgraphs are fine and save time during lecture, but I don't pay attention as easily when I don't have to take notes.
- Although getting lecture notes in advance allows us to go at a faster pace, it makes it easy to fall asleep.
- If we have lecture notes, why go to class?

Thus, teachers should not aim to help students entirely avoid note taking during lectures; instead, they should facilitate meaningful and effective note taking. Note taking in class is ineffective when the notes are incomplete, inaccurate, and disorganized, or when note taking overloads students' cognitive capacity and consequently causes them to miss large chunks of the lecture. This may happen when students attempt to take notes on complex or difficult material that the teacher does not clarify sufficiently, or when the teacher talks too fast when presenting dense information, a process that requires simultaneous listening and writing.

How to help students take meaningful notes
Adapt to the students' rate of note taking

Speak at a rate that the students can follow while taking meaningful notes. Develop explanations gradually and be sure to give students enough time to process and understand the oral and written information.

Allow students to compare their notes with each other, provide several pauses throughout the lecture. During the lesson, encourage students to compare notes in order to clarify points they have not understood. You may even dedicate special pauses for this aim. Research has demonstrated that if a lecturer allows students to consolidate their notes by pausing three times for two minutes each during a lecture, students will learn significantly more information (Ruhl, Hughes, & Schloss, 1987).

How to design your notes so as to activate students' thinking

Avoid giving notes that substitute for lectures. Do not provide students prior to class with lecture notes that present most of the lesson content because they bring to students' passivity, as discussed above.

Design lecture notes to be user friendly. Handouts should be brief and well structured in order to be adjuncts to lectures.

Provide a priori lecture notes with only skeletal information. Include in these notes only a portion of the explanation to be presented in class, only the main points, only headings and subheadings, or only a picture or a graph, *leaving a lot of space for your students to write around your text or drawings.* Then, while explaining, allow students to add the complementing information from similar texts, graphs, and diagrams on the board.

THINKING, PAUSING, AND REFLECTING IN CLASS

Listening to lectures, or reading books, you can hardly learn anything and certainly you cannot learn much without adding some action of your own mind... the pleasure of success in intensive mental activity is the best reward (Polya, 1957, p. 38).

Polya's words remind us that what is important in teaching is activating students' thinking, and that this can be accomplished through a variety of instructional methods. Even a traditional lecture can be executed with the excellence that makes students actively think. Lectures can model the solving of a problem or can challenge thinking, inspire reverence for learning, and motivate enthusiasm for further study. A teacher can stimulate active thinking in the course of a lecture by using several basic elements of active learning: pausing, reflecting, questioning, and challenging students intellectually (Meyer, 1975).

The following students' comments express satisfaction with and appreciation for teachers who challenge them intellectually during the lesson:

- Each one of his lessons provides mental challenges and this makes for a very interesting course.

- He kept us active, stimulated and interested in the subject matter during the two hours, which can be very long.

- High level of sophistication really pushes the class.

- The course was very interesting, very advanced, very challenging.
- Very high level. You must go to every lecture to keep up. Very much worth it, though.
- Very clear lecturing style, extremely interesting and thought provoking.

These comments suggest that students perceive intellectual challenges as an important factor in making the lesson interesting, and that they prefer thinking to mere rote learning.

Challenging tasks require the investment of substantial mental effort, for example, in applying difficult concepts to problem solving. The experience of success following a difficult task is one of great satisfaction. Overcoming challenges engenders students' pride in their work, boosts their self-confidence in their learning abilities, increases their feelings of competence in understanding and mastering something new and difficult, and eventually brings pleasure. Perceptions of greater personal control have been found to be associated with greater task interest and enjoyment (Dweck, 1989).

How to promote students' thinking, pausing, reflecting, and to challenge them intellectually during the lesson

Present the material slightly beyond students' level. Students should invest at least a modest thinking effort in trying to understand the material and to apply it to solve a problem. Beware, though, of presenting the material at too high a level because this may confuse and frustrate students, making them lose confidence in their abilities.

Avoid low challenge. Avoid as much as possible "telling" your students things that you can arrive at through other teaching methods based on student thinking (e.g., presenting guiding/Socratic questions). Do not elaborate on rules and formulas that are self-evident

In all the following cases, write students' evaluations, guesses, estimations, solutions, decisions, and so forth on the board for summary or emphasis, or as a basis for comparison when you teach the topic in full.

Present controversies, paradoxes, unsolved problems, conflicting evidence, and claims based on misconceptions. Ask students to take sides in a controversy and make their case; to explain the difficulties in an unsolved problem; to suggest ways for handling conflicting evidence, and to show how misconceptions lead to absurd solutions or claims. Assign them to suggest explanations of a paradox. To illustrate, present a demonstration whose outcome is counter-intuitive or one that clashes with what is suggested in the textbook, and ask them to explain the paradox.

Pose riddles, puzzles, and intriguing and provocative questions, and discuss challenging issues or homework assignments. Responding to these challenges involves the student in taking some risks. Most people enjoy taking moderate risks when they feel confident. In taking a risk, personal involvement naturally occurs and this brings about active learning.

Involve students in problem solving. Even during straight lecturing, you can make students think about problems before you solve them.

- Present a problem and pause for several minutes to allow students to consider and deliberate the solution method or even to start solving it on paper before you take over. You may then ask the students to suggest their plan for a solution, and build the full solution from there, or assign them to complete it at home.
- Guide students in the solution process by posing questions that direct their thinking on the problem solution.
- Evaluate and discuss a solution for a problem just solved.

Assign students to guess, or to provide intuitive estimates and evaluations. Before discussing a process, procedure, or case that actually occurred, you may ask students to make an educated guess regarding the result or outcome. Assign them to make reasonable estimations or approximate the answer of a problem you present, or ask them to make an intuitive evaluation of the result of a computation or development.

Polya (1965, p. 105), the mathematician famous for his didactic approach to problem solving, strongly advocated that teachers should lead students to guess before solving a problem:

Before the students do a problem, let them *guess the result*, or a part of the result. The student who expresses an opinion commits himself; his prestige and self-esteem depends a little on the outcome, he is impatient to know whether his guess will turn out right or not, and so he will be actively interested in his task and in the work of the class.... In fact, in the work of a scientist, the guess almost always precedes the proof. Thus, in letting your students guess the result, you not only motivate them to work harder, but you also teach them a desirable attitude of mind.

Arrange for students to discover or develop new material by themselves, with your support, for example, leading them through Socratic questioning (see below).

The best way to learn anything is to discover it by yourself. This is the *principle of active learning (Arbeitsprinzip).* It is a very old principle: it underlies the idea of "Socratic method." Lichtenberg (an eighteenth century German physicist...) adds an interesting point: *What you have been obliged to discover by yourself leaves a path in your mind which you can use again when the need arises.* Less colorful but perhaps more widely applicable, is the following statement: *For efficient learning, the learner should discover by himself as large a fraction of the material to be learned as feasible under the given circumstances.* (ibid., p. 103).

Assign students to make decisions, give explanations, and provide illustrations and applications regarding the material you present.

Make students pause and reflect. Reflecting while lecturing or discussing refers to students' thinking about the topics just presented or about their learning in general. Incorporating periods for students' reflection into teaching provides them with thinking opportunities and thus promotes their active learning.

- **Pause regularly for a couple minutes,** two or three times during the lecture, to allow students to consolidate notes and develop questions about the material presented (see "wait time" below).
- **Pause to give time for students to answer your questions or to present their own questions.** Insert sufficiently long pauses for reflection after you pose a question or after you ask students if they have any questions on the material taught so far (see "wait time" below).
- **Pause for pair work.** Pause and assign students to work in pairs to organize their notes and discuss the key points of the lecture, and develop questions based on what they feel is still unclear.
- **Pause and explicitly assign the task of thinking and reflecting.** Pause and ask students to think about the content, or discuss it in pairs. Assign students to write down their reflections in journals during each class or at home after each lesson. Urge them to record some of their thoughts about what they are studying and learning and their comments on what they think and feel about issues, concepts, and events in that day's class. Collect, read, and comment on the journals at regular intervals during the term (usually three or four times).
- **Pause for summarizing.** Pause and assign one or two students to summarize orally the last topic to the whole class.

QUESTIONING IN CLASS

- The instructor asked interesting questions that offered a unique perspective in class discussions.

"Classroom questioning" here refers to questions from both the teacher and the students, and to the responses of each to questions of the other. During lectures and class discussions, questions allow the teacher to interact with the students.

Educators and researchers perceive classroom questions as an essential aspect of good teaching. There is professional consensus that questions posed by teachers have a major impact on student achievement (Gall, 1970). Teachers' questions fulfill a variety of functions, they verify student understanding, emphasize important points in the material, identify for the students points they do not understand, attract student attention, and force students to mentally scan all the material the lecturer has presented up to the point at which a question is asked (Berliner, 1969). In this way, questioning helps the teacher adjust instruction to the students in class, and promotes students' active participation, intellectual investment in the material, and lesson interest[29].

Students, too, perceive classroom questioning as an essential tool for effective teaching. The following four teacher behaviors were found to strongly discriminate between students' perceptions of clear and unclear university teachers, in the order of decreasing importance (Hines, 1982):

- Answers students' questions.
- Asks questions to find out if students understand.
- Explains and then stops for questions.
- Allows students time to ask questions.

When students were asked what makes a teacher clear, they included answers such as: "He encouraged our questions" and "She was willing to answer our questions" (Benz & Blatt, 1994).

Teacher questions can be *closed* or *open*. A closed question has a limited number of acceptable answers, most of which are anticipated by the teacher. An open question has many acceptable answers, most of which will not be anticipated by the teacher. Closed questions direct students toward an answer preplanned by the teacher whereas open questions promote students' independent thinking and verbal expression.

Teacher questions can require students to employ different levels of cognitive effort. Bloom (1956) developed a hierarchical system of thinking skills that can be arranged in the following levels:

Low: Knowledge (including memorization of facts).

Moderate: Comprehension and simple-level application.

High: high-level application, analysis, synthesis, evaluation, and judgment.

Redfield and Rousseau (1981), in their meta-analytic review of the level of teacher questions, found that the use of questions requiring high cognitive investment during instruction had a positive effect on student achievement.

Conflicting findings have been reported in the research literature regarding the extent to which questioning is employed during class time higher education. One study found college and university professors to ask about 25 questions on average per class (Duell, Lynch, Ellsworth, & Moore, 1992), whereas another study of 40 public and private colleges and universities reported that very little use is made of questions in the classroom (between 2.5% and 5.8% of class time), with no significant differences across institution type, size, course level, or academic field (Barnes, 1983).

Questions may be initiated by either the teacher or the students, and they are usually followed by responses from the other party. We next discuss the

---

[29] See Chapters 12 and 15

role of the teacher in presenting questions to students, and in encouraging and reacting to students' questions and responses.

The Teacher's Role in Presenting Questions to Students

Questions initiated by the teacher can be sorted into three categories: (a) questions for instructional applications, (b) questions for diagnostic purposes, and (c) rhetorical questions. To elaborate:

(a) Questions for instructional applications aim at soliciting students' answers regarding the material presented. For example, "OK, so what should we do here?" Or "And why should that be true?" These questions are designed to stimulate students' curiosity and motivate them to learn; to arouse and maintain their attention; to make them active and involved in the learning process; and to promote their thinking. The following is one student's expression of appreciation for this kind of questions:

• Thanks for raising questions that directed our understanding of the material.

(b) Questions for diagnostic purposes aim at getting students' feedback as to the state of the presentation, for example, "Are you with me? Am I going too fast?" or "Can you hear me in the back row?" Students' answers to these questions provide the teacher with continuous feedback concerning students' follow up of the presentation.

(c) Rhetorical questions are not aimed at obtaining feedback, but only to stimulate students' thinking and thus make them active in the learning process. For example, "And why has this happened? It happened because...."

Questions for instructional applications that particularly promote student thinking and involvement in the learning process are named after the ancient Greek philosopher Socrates (470-399 BC), one of the greatest teachers of all times.

Socratic Questioning

Socrates believed that a person (teacher) should not transmit his/her knowledge to "friends" (students) but should, rather, attempt to identify the untapped knowledge that lies deep within everyone. To achieve this end, he used the dialogue method, consisting of a sequence of questions that guides the other person in discovering "the truth" (knowledge).

In the college classroom, "Socratic questioning" refers to a systematic series of questions that channels the students' thought processes toward developing understanding of the new material along predetermined paths, leading to processes of self-discovery. The teacher poses a question that guides students to an insight, receives their answers, explains them to the whole class, then poses an additional question, and so on. Socratic dialogue helps teachers express their opinions, critically evaluate students' opinions, and promote students' imagination, creativity, and analytic thinking. The Socratic dialogue, building on the students' input, is very beneficial in promoting active learning because it stimulates the students' cognitive participation in the development of explanations.

Another type of instructional questioning is recitation.

Recitation

Recitation is a method of rapid interchange of questions during a lecture or discussion. With this method, teachers have almost total control of the classroom: They pose the questions; select the students who will answer these questions; and react to their answers. The students' role is restricted to answering questions and to listening to other teacher-student exchanges (Gall & Artero-Boname, 1995). Research at the pre-college level shows that recitation promotes better student learning than do alternative instructional methods that avoid teacher questioning, and that the more questions asked during recitation, the more effective student learning becomes (ibid.).

How to present questions to students

Use questions of a high cognitive level. Ask questions requiring students to explain or to integrate relationships among the units of information taught, to form general concepts, or to apply concepts and principles they have developed to new data and different situations, or to their own lives.

Pose questions that stimulate students' curiosity, that motivate them to learn, that arouse and maintain their attention, and that promote their thinking.

State your questions clearly, at an appropriate cognitive level for the students in class.

Make sure that your question is understood. After posing a question, ask: "Is this question clear?"

Use Socratic questioning. Build the new content using question-and-answer dialogue with the class.

Pose direct and indirect questions (related to the material you are teaching) to find out if students understand what you present.

> **Ask explicitly how many students understand** your explanation, and count the hands raised (vote count), for diagnostic purposes.
>
> **Switch teacher-students role:** Announce that you will switch roles with the students. They will collectively play the role of the teacher while you are the student. Then ask them questions about the material that you have just taught, from the point of view of a student. Challenge them, push them for answers, and challenge their answers in order to stir them more deeply.

The Teacher's Role in Encouraging Students' Questions and Responses, and in Reacting to Them

- Excellent teacher! Stops often for student questions.

The opportunity for students to initiate questions during the lesson and to respond to the teacher's questions contributes greatly to learning from classroom instruction. This situation allows students to express themselves, clarify points they do not understand, and be active in the classroom learning process. Teacher responsiveness is a very important component of successful students' questions, as shows in the following comments on teacher evaluation forms.

- Very nice person. Responsive to student questions and interests.
- She answers questions always in a good spirit and explains with a lot of patience.
- She'll cover for you if you ask dumb questions.
- Students are unhappy when teachers respond in an unhelpful manner:
- She shouldn't get flustered when students ask difficult conceptual questions.
- He didn't allow for many questions and didn't answer well the ones he did take.
- Sometimes when we ask questions he doesn't really go back far enough to clarify our understanding; as a result, we become less eager to ask questions.
- I feel stupid to ask questions for if I did even ask a specific one, the teacher would spit back the answer without showing the development of the answer. I feel very insignificant in this situation.
- At times when a student asks a question because he doesn't understand, the teacher thinks that this is because the student hasn't listened or that he wants to distract the teacher so then the teacher makes fun of the student.
- The course involves very difficult material and he responds to students' questions by saying: "This is trivial." For a professor this might be trivial but for undergraduates it is certainly not!

- He should understand that there are no stupid questions and he shouldn't answer impatiently!

As can be deduced from these comments, students expect their teachers to answer questions willingly, patiently, and in good spirits; verify if students understand the answers; never make fun of or patronize a student who asks a poor question; cover for students who ask poor questions; and explain the reasons for their answers. Thus, the teacher plays a crucial role in creating a supportive environment in the classroom, one in which students feel free, safe, and comfortable enough to ask relevant questions, or to answer teacher questions. Students should not feel threatened by the possibility that they might be wrong or exposed as not particularly clever. The teacher needs to ensure that all students, rather than only the better students or those who usually dominate in class, get the opportunity to respond, as expressed in the following student's comment:

- The students who ask or answer questions in the lesson are those who understand and the others don't dare (although I think they are the majority).

However, reality indicates that not many teachers do provide such a supportive, safe, classroom climate. In a summary of studies, students were found to pose only few questions in the classroom (Karabenick & Sharma, 1994). The reason for this reticence was teachers' poor support, indifference, or even negative reaction to students' questions. Considerable variation was found among teachers in the support they provided for student questioning and among students with respect to the threat they felt in class. Students who perceived greater teacher support reported being more motivated and active in the learning process, and used more self-regulating learning strategies. Students who perceived their teachers as less supportive achieved lower academic success. They reported being confused, and not daring to ask the very questions that could assist in alleviating that confusion.

How to encourage and support students' questions and answers to your questions

Arrange for opportunities to ask questions. After the completion of each unit of instruction, stop, look around, and ask the class if everything is clear and if there are any questions.

Solicit questions and answers from your students. Strongly encourage them to ask questions or to answer your questions.

Show your interest in their questions/answers by positive verbal and nonverbal behaviors.

Praise students for a good question/answer.

Cover up unclever questions/answers, and do not put students down whenever they provide inappropriate questions or answers. Avoid criticizing their questions or answers.

How to get all students to answer

Direct your questions to, and encourage questions of, the whole class.

Pause for sufficient time after asking a question, before getting or providing an answer. Pausing enables students to think, and shows that you are concerned with their learning.

Assign your students to write down their answers before raising their hands. This policy may encourage the less strong students to participate.

If no one answers, repeat the question, rephrase it, or provide additional information that leads to the answer.

Avoid calling on the first person to raise a hand. Such behavior may prevent other students from evaluating the response for themselves and may interrupt their own thinking process. Rather, wait until many students raise their hands. Then, distribute the opportunity to answer equally among the students.

How to demonstrate listening to students' questions and answers

Listen carefully to the student. Do not interrupt even if you think he/she is heading the wrong way, unless the answer is too long or diverts too much from the lesson topics. Students may learn as much from an incorrect response as from a correct one.

Show clearly that you are listening to the student: use nonverbal gestures to indicate your understanding, confusion, or support; head nods, facial expressions, or hand gestures to signal the student to continue; or general body language to indicate that you are thinking about the student's answer.

Avoid nonverbal responses that communicate a negative reaction such as boredom or disagreement with the answer. While a student is making a point, avoid looking at your notes or at the board, or ruffling papers.

How to respond to students' questions and answers

Rephrase the student's answer and check with him/her to ascertain that you have understood it.

Repeat or rephrase the student's answer so that it can be heard by students in the back of the classroom, particularly if the student who answers the question sits in one of the front rows.

Follow up the student's answer and analyze it promptly. If you identify areas of misunderstanding, respond by clarifying these areas. Ask the student for more information or explanation.

Use student responses to **lead to the next question** or **to make a point.**

Provide positive reinforcement to create a safe environment for students to speak out and try new ideas. Encourage students by praising good answers and using positive nonverbal communication such as smiling, nodding, or encouraging facial expressions. However, the effect of praise depends on what students attribute it to—what they see as the cause of the praise. "Overpraise" or praise given too often loses its value[30].

Propose a plan for obtaining information or evidence that will facilitate answering the question.

Suggest resources where the student can find information to answer the question.

Avoid conducing a questioning dialogue with a single student while all others feel excluded and stop listening

Briefly acknowledge a response that is off target or incorrect, but do not spend much time on it, and then move onto the correct response.

Avoid responding negatively to a student's response. Do not disapprove or criticize, but rather approve and encourage. Here are some responses to avoid (Gage & Berliner, 1991, p. 549):

That's not right! Wrong! Stop that! You didn't do that very well! Your answer indicates that you haven't read the assignment! Both your facts and your logic are wrong!

Clarify the misunderstanding when a student's question indicates a lack of understanding.

Provide full, clear, and appropriate answers to students' questions during the lesson. For particular types of questions, as next explained, defer your answer.

Defer your answer to a student's question when it is too complicated or tangential to the course material; or when you judge it as lacking general interest, or as being below or above the class level; or when the student is the only one who does not understand, and a simple answer will not clarify the point; or when you don't know how to answer; or when the answer will be discussed in a future lesson. Your answer should be deferred to either after class, right before the next class, or during office hours. When deferring a student's question, always

---

[30] See also "praising" in Chapter 16

acknowledge the question and the student who posed it, and briefly explain why you will not be answering it at this time and when the student can receive an answer. If the reason for deferment is that you don't know how to reply to a student's question, admit this and promise to look for the answer and report back to the class in the next lesson. Make sure you actually do return with the answer.

Use probing. Help a student answer his/her own question by repeating the question using different words, asking additional—simpler or lower level— questions, pursuing the implications of the student's first response to the question, providing cues, and thus leading the student to the correct response.

Redirect the question to the class, that is, ask other students in the class if they can answer the question. This strategy forces the class to continue thinking about the question and encourages interaction among students.

Deferral, probing, redirection, and wait-time (see the next section) were found to increase students' involvement in the lesson and, consequently, their achievement (Gage & Berliner, 1998).

Answer the question yourself if you do not have enough time for probing or redirecting.

Leave sufficient wait-time after a student's question before answering it as elaborated next

Pausing—"Wait-Time"

"Wait-time" is the time a teacher allots to a pause, either after posing a question to the class or after receiving a student's question. Wait-time is introduced before taking any action such as answering it him/herself, repeating it, rephrasing it, adding further information, making a comment, or posing another question. A large body of research in fields other than education, such as psycholinguistics or speech communication, demonstrates that uninterrupted pauses during speech are positively related to the level of cognitive activity (Rochester, 1973). Similarly, providing sufficient wait-time in teaching is beneficial because it gives students time to organize their thoughts for better answers or for posing their own questions. When wait-time is too short, students do not have the opportunity to elaborate their answers, particularly when questions are complex or intellectually demanding; the quality of their reflection is diminished, and they are deprived of the opportunity to respond.

Wait-time is an important ingredient in teacher-student interactions. Rowe (1974) found that the quality of the verbal interaction that occurred in pre-college classrooms was related to the duration of pauses separating speakers. When the average length of pauses was greater than approximately three seconds, desirable characteristics of student behavior were evident in the number of appropriate responses, their length, the number of less able students answering, the number of student-to-student interactions, and the number of student questions. In addition, longer wait-time led to significant improvement on three teacher variables: greater response flexibility; increased expectations of the performance of students regarded as slow learners; and increased number and improved type of questions asked by the teacher (Rowe, 1974; 1986; Tobin, 1987).

However, in the classroom reality, long pauses are a neglected technique. Wait-time research suggests that the typical rate of exchange between university teachers and students is far too rapid. For example, Duell et al. (1992) found the average wait-time to be about 2.25 seconds after teacher questions and 0.45 seconds after student responses. The lack of silent time in the college classroom may be explained by the fact that teachers feel responsible for maintaining the flow of discussion and tend to speak as soon as the student pauses or falters. Similarly, students are accustomed to having the teacher speak as soon as they pause.

Using longer wait-time can substantially improve student classroom learning in the college and university. The length of the optimal wait-time depends upon the level of questions posed and on student characteristics, such as familiarity with lesson content. More time is required for students to respond to questions at a higher cognitive level than at a lower level (e.g., for integrating material versus recalling factual information). The mean wait-time threshold should be higher at the college/university level than the optimal three seconds identified for pre-college classes, reflecting the greater complexity and abstractness of the questions. However, too long a wait-time (more than 20-30 seconds) can be detrimental to student participation. When no one seems to be able to answer a question, more wait-time will not solve the problem.

ADDITIONAL CLASS ACTIVITIES DURING A LECTURE

"Attention-getters"—activities for the start of a lesson. Begin class by first having students brainstorm problems that remained unresolved from the previous lecture, or raise questions from the previous lecture or questions relating to their reading assignment. Then address these issues while proceeding with the day's topic, responding to student input while covering new material.

Class vote: Give each of your students a set of differently colored index cards to hold up for their answers, each color representing another option. Pose a question to the class and suggest several options for answers. Ask your students to raise the colored card that reflects their answer. You may call on a student who chose the correct answer or an incorrect answer and have him or her explain the response. The colored cards can be replaced by a show of hands, or with forms for an optical scanner in a computerized voting system.

Interactions like these actively involve the students in thinking about the material and enable you to poll students' ideas or understanding. This enables you to get feedback about what was learned, and how well they have been learning. In this way, all students can be stimulated to participate in thinking and answering, even in very large classes.

Student contests. Organize contests related to the lesson material among students or among groups of students. Organize competitions on specific issues. For example, assign five minutes for students to list as many components of an issue/process/phenomenon as possible, related to the lesson topic or to the reading material for today. Offer a reward (either a tangible one, or only writing the winner's name on the board) to the student(s) who succeeds in listing the largest number of components.

Stretching/exercising. Pause for a minute in the middle of each long lesson and ask students to get up from their seats and stretch.

SUMMARY

Most students cannot learn effectively by only listening, and the majority do not simply record and store what they are taught. It is through involvement and activity that learners participate genuinely and meaningfully in the learning process. This engagement enables them to modify their prior knowledge and construct their own understanding.

The implications for classroom teaching are that students' active learning should be promoted in all methods of teaching, even in lecturing, where the teacher's role is that of the sole presenter and the authority. Active learning in lecturing relates to the ongoing involvement of students in doing things and thinking about what they are doing. Students should not only be engaged in listening, but should also be intellectually challenged and participate in higher-order thinking (analysis, synthesis, and evaluation), and in the cognitive construction of the material. The basic elements for promoting active learning that can be integrated into teacher-centered instructional methods, primarily into lecturing, consist of getting students to: (a) talk and listen; (b) read or write; (c) think, pause, reflect; and (d) ask questions and answer the teacher's questions. The main barriers to active learning are teachers' concerns about wasting class time, loss of control, and unprepared students.

Talking and Listening in Class. Talking, within the active learning process, is aimed to clarify thinking and promote students' public speaking skills and active listening skills. The teacher provides opportunities for students to present their ideas to the whole class, and to meaningfully talk with each other.

Reading and Writing in Class. Reading and writing can also clarify thinking; challenge students to use higher-order thinking skills such as analysis, synthesis, decision-making, and evaluation; and develop students' written expression skills. The teacher can promote students' meaningful note taking. In this process, students analyze the content of the lesson, seek organizational cues, look for key concepts, and attempt to follow and make sense of the teacher's mode of thinking. This mindful note taking enables students' personal construction of understanding and knowledge of the lesson content, and maintains their concentration, alertness, and active thinking.

Thinking, Pausing, and Reflecting in class. Activating students' thinking is one of the most important aspects of teaching. It can be accomplished through a variety of instructional methods. Even a traditional lecture can be executed with the kind of excellence that makes students actively think by using several basic elements of active learning: pausing, reflecting, questioning, and challenging students intellectually.

Questioning in Class. Students, educators, and researchers perceive classroom questions-and-answers as an essential tool for lesson clarity and student engagement, that is, for effective teaching. The functions of questioning are to emphasize important points in the material; practice the new knowledge; make students aware of issues they do not understand; attract student attention; and introduce diversion into the presentation by inserting "pausing breaks" in the fluency of presentation. Questioning also helps the teacher adjust instruction to the students in class as it promotes students' active participation and intellectual investment in the material.

The Socratic method is a systematic series of teacher questions that channels the student's thought processes toward developing the new material along predetermined paths, leading to self-discovery. *Recitation* is a frequently used method of rapid interchange of questions during lectures or discussions, in which teachers have almost total control of the classroom: they pose the questions; select the students who will answer these questions; and react to these answers.

Teacher questions may be closed or open and may require a variety of levels of cognitive effort. Questions that require a high cognitive level of thinking posed during instruction were found to have a positive effect on student achievement. There is no agreement among studies on the average level of questions actually used in the college classroom nor regarding the frequency of use of classroom questioning.

Wait-time is the time a teacher allots to a pause, either after posing a question to the class or after receiving a student's question. Wait-time precedes any response such as answering it him/herself, repeating it, rephrasing it, adding further information, making a comment, or posing another question. Wait-time is an important ingredient in effective classroom interactions. Students need time to organize their thoughts for better answers to teacher questions, or for posing their own questions. Wait-time research suggests that the typical rate of exchange between teachers and students is far too rapid, and that increasing the wait-time can substantially improve students' classroom learning. However, too long a wait-time can be detrimental to student interaction.

Chapter 7

Teaching Methods for Active Learning

The previous chapter presented several active learning methods—that can be incorporated into the lecture to avert student passivity and facilitate students' meaningful learning. However, there are student-centered instructional methods available in which active student involvement is the norm. The main ones are discussion, group work, "community of learners" strategy, role-playing, simulation, case-method teaching, problem-based learning, and experiential learning. Because these methods may introduce some chaos into the classroom and may lead to some uncertain learning outcomes, they are regarded as more "high risk". None of these methods should be used solely during a whole lesson period. Rather, they should be integrated with one another and with the lecture method, to enliven it.

The teacher's role in these methods is that of a *facilitator, director, consultant,* or *moderator.* Active learning in the classroom requires that the teacher spend less time as a *presenter* and more time as a *designer, choreographer, orchestrator,* and *manager* of the learning environment and teaching process. In other words, the teacher acts as chairperson, guide, listener, observer, monitor, initiator, summarizer, and referee.

When employing these methods, students talk and listen, interact, communicate, and collaborate with the other students in class. Social interaction, interpersonal relations, communication, and collaboration on instructional tasks can enhance learning. Furthermore, interactive and collaborative instructional contexts provide individuals with an opportunity for perspective-taking and for reflective thinking, activities that may lead to higher levels of cognitive, social, and moral development, as well as greater self-esteem. (APA, 1997).[31]

The main teaching methods for active learning, as listed above, are presented next.

THE DISCUSSION METHOD

Discussion is a teaching method in which students are encouraged to actively participate in the learning process by talking to the teacher and to one another during the lesson. The discussion method may take several forms, ranging from student-centered to teacher-centered structures. The most extreme student-centered discussions are conducted in the form of *discussion groups,* in which all the students in the class are divided into small groups, each discussing some issue that may be either the same for all groups or different for each group. In contrast, in teacher-centered discussions the teacher leads the discussion with the whole class by posing questions and guiding students' answers (Thielens, 1987). The latter form is the most prevalent in the college classroom and is the one referred to most frequently in this chapter.

Discussions are valued by educational leaders because they encourage students to actively participate in the lessons—to think about the material and about its connections with other things, and to talk about the material—to explain, summarize and question. A summary of research on student participation in the college class indicates a positive relationship between students' participation in classroom discussion and their learning, motivation, and problem-solving ability (Nunn, 1996).

Students, too, value discussion, as expressed by the following comments:

- The discussions were really helpful in making me realize how many different perspectives on these issues there are out there.
- The discussions made us so aware of sooo much!

Students appreciate discussion that is carefully directed by the teacher because of the opportunities it creates for them to be active, to generate and be exposed to new representations of knowledge and ideas, and to provide possible confirmation or denial of their own ideas. According to students, the most successful class discussions are those that provide opportunities for autonomous thought, for personal expression, and for representing information in ways that are personally meaningful to them. This type of

---

[31] See first section in Chapter 4

discussion widens the pool of available ideas and enables them to advance their thinking in ways that they cannot achieve alone (ibid.).

However, although discussion is the second most frequently used method of teaching in the college and university classroom, it is used in only about ten percent of these classrooms (Thielens, 1987). The following are several obstacles that may be responsible for the meager use of discussions as compared with lectures, along with practical suggestions of how to overcome them.

Problems in Conducting Discussions

The main problems that reduce the use of discussion in class are: low student participation, habitual participants and discussion monopolizers, students' impression that they do not learn much from discussion, negative emotional reactions to discussion, and perceived low expertise of discussion participants.

Low Student Participation

Research shows that teachers devote little time to interaction with students during class and that few students actually participate in classroom discussions (Nunn, 1996). Reasons for students' lack of participation can be boredom, lack of knowledge, lack of sufficient preparation (e.g., not having done the assigned readings), general passivity, insecurity about talking in public, and fear of being exposed as not clever. In support, Becker, Geer, and Hughes (1994) found that more than two-thirds of the students who were asked to explain their nonparticipation in classroom discussions presented the following five reasons, arranged in decreasing order of frequency, with only small gender differences in the rank order:

1. I didn't do the assigned reading.
2. I feel I don't know enough about the subject matter.
3. The class is too large for me to speak.
4. I feel that my ideas are not formulated well enough.
5. The course simply isn't meaningful to me.

Thus, insufficient knowledge resulting from insufficient preparation is a major obstacle to conducting those discussions that build on the assumption that students have acquired some of the background knowledge necessary for making contributions. Faculty are very dissatisfied and frustrated by insufficient preparation. In a survey of faculty in a research university on problems faced in teaching (Hativa, 1997), out of 20 possible problems listed, those that ranked second and third in frequency (noted by about one third of the respondents) were: "Many students show insufficient background preparation/ reading of the assignments" and "Many students fail to review material taught in previous lessons, which then serves as background for the new lesson."

The following are practical suggestions for overcoming low levels of student participation in discussions.

How to encourage student participation

Encourage all students to participate. Do this explicitly and frequently.

Explain the values and advantages of participation, or conduct a short discussion of this topic and let students offer a list of advantages.

Demonstrate a supportive approach through praise, approval, and interest.

Encourage elaboration of students' contributions. Respond and build the next part of discussion on students' questions and answers. Encourage other students to respond to their peer's question or answer.

Get students acquainted with one another at the beginning of the term to promote a friendly class atmosphere that encourages participation.

Arrange the seats in the classroom in a circle for small or even medium size classes. This creates a friendly classroom climate.

Encourage/assign students to write down their initial responses or arguments before presenting them in class. This enables them to effectively formulate their ideas and may boost their self-confidence in their answers.

Enable/assign students to first discuss their answer or arguments in pairs or small groups before expressing them in the general discussion. This has the same effects as the previous point.

Start a discussion by posing "non-risky" questions that do not call on specific knowledge, such as: "What is your opinion about...?" or "How do you feel about...?"

Assign students to lead a discussion. Assign a few students to lead a discussion on a particular topic. Repeat this procedure for each new topic, assigning other discussion leaders for each.

Assign silent/nonparticipating students to present a particular topic in class. Identify those students who never raise their hands or participate in other ways in class. Assign them to prepare and present some topic of their interest to the class and to conduct a discussion on this topic.

Habitual Participants and Discussion Monopolizers

In many college classrooms, a "consolidation of responsibility" emerges (Becker et al., 1994). Almost inevitably, a small group of students forms, who can be counted on to respond to questions asked by the professor, or to generally have comments on virtually any issue raised in class. When asked, more than 90% of the students agreed or strongly agreed with the observation that usually only a very small number of them are responsible for all talk that occurs in class. Once the group of "talkers" becomes established and identified as such, the remaining students develop a strong expectation that these "talkers" can be relied upon to answer questions and make comments, and thus they free the others of the responsibility to participate. A phenomenon to be particularly avoided is the emergence of a discussion monopolizer—a student who talks so much that the teacher and other students become irritated.

How to handle discussion monopolizers

When you have one or more students in class who monopolize the discussion, you may use the following ideas:

Raise the question of participation in discussion: Lead a discussion on the question, "Would the class be more effective if participation were more evenly distributed?"

Assign the monopolizer to serve as an observer of the discussion for one or more class periods. Assign him/her to report his/her observations back to the class.

Videotape a portion of class discussion. Play it back in class, and ask the students to suggest what might be done to improve the discussion (McKeachie et al., 1987).

Students' Impression That They Do Not Learn from Discussion

One of the main risks of discussion is that students develop the feeling that they do not learn much in the process and so their time is wasted. They feel this way when other students talk at too great a length, or apparently not to the point; when other students say things they deem irrelevant; or when the discussion goes on and on, ostensibly leading nowhere.

How to make the students aware of their learning from discussion

Supervise and guide the discussion so that it does not go off on tangents and so students do not talk at too much length. In this way, students feel that the discussion is focused and beneficial for them.

Clarify how the goals of the discussion were achieved. During the process of discussion write on the board or on an overhead transparency the main points of view and questions that were suggested by the participants, and what issues are left to explore.

Summarize all conclusions of the discussion—the variety of points and issues raised. Generalize the results and conclusions. Lead students to understand and formulate the underlying ideas, points, rules, or principles of the discussion.

Negative Emotional Reactions to Discussion

During discussion, students may respond to others' opinions by feeling frustration, rejection, dependence, or other discouraging or negative feelings.

How to handle students' emotional reactions

Develop a positive learning environment in class[32] to avoid arousing students' negative feelings about other students during discussion. Avoid forcing either your own opinion or a single solution to a problem. Build a sense of community, which enables students in class to confront one another openly and helpfully (McKeachie et al., 1987).

Perceived Low Expertise of Discussion Participants

Some students reject discussions by saying that they came to college/university to learn from experts (faculty), and not from peers who are at their own level. They complain that they did not pay such high fees to listen to students "who are just as ignorant as I am", or that they would "rather hear a poor lecture by an expert, than a discussion—even lively—by fellow novices." Another problem related to low expertise is that some teachers avoid discussion because they, like their students, perceive themselves as significantly less expert and effective at leading discussion than at lecturing (Nunn, 1996).

Additional Ideas for Conducting Effective Discussions

How to increase student appreciation for the discussion method

You should increase students' appreciation for discussion in order to promote their motivation and willingness to participate.

Frequently explain to your students what are the advantages of the discussion method. During a successful discussion, emphasize the benefits of that particular discussion to the students.

---

[32] See Chapter 16

How to start a discussion

Pose an opening question: Raise a question about the main topic planned for the discussion, the reading for today's lesson, or controversy in the field.

Build on students' oral input: Ask students to pose questions for discussion that are relevant to the general topic, to describe their related experiences, or to suggest headings and key points for the discussion.

Build on students' written input: Allot several minutes in class for students to write opinions regarding the topic, questions about the topic, or experiences related to the topic. Then, use these writings for discussion.

How to integrate lecture and discussion

Probably the best way to overcome the deficiencies of either the lecture or the discussion is to combine both methods in a lesson. You can make the lecture somewhat informal and more loosely organized by integrating periods of discussion within the lecture frame. This gives the students the opportunity and responsibility to raise and answer questions, which makes them more intellectually involved.

GROUP-WORK, COOPERATIVE LEARNING

Cooperative learning refers to students working together in small groups to accomplish a common goal under three main conditions: "positive interdependence," where all members must cooperate to complete a task; "group accountability," where all group members are accountable for the final outcome; and "personal responsibility," where students take on responsibility for their peers, and are held accountable by them. When they engage in cooperative activities, individuals seek outcomes that are beneficial to themselves and to all other group members.

A summary of research studies on cooperative learning in higher education accentuated the beneficial effect of this method (Johnson, Johnson, & Smith, 1991). This summary showed that the more students worked in cooperative learning groups, the more they learned, the better they understood and remembered what they had learned, and the better they felt about themselves, the class, and their classmates.

Incorporating pair- or small-group work or discussions into the lesson can be beneficial even if does not take the form of cooperative learning and is limited to working together on a common problem or assignment. Most contemporary real-life jobs require employees to work together to complete tasks; hence, the skills in communication and group dynamics that students acquire during group learning activities are transferable to real-life situations.

How to conduct group work

Assign your students to work in pairs, threesomes, **or other types of small groups.** Students can be divided into groups early in the term, and encouraged to exchange phone numbers and addresses. Then assign specific projects that the group works on during the lesson, or even those that require groups to meet outside of class.

Assign group tasks. The groups can discuss a particular topic or idea, make inquiries, answer questions in a handout you distribute, or solve problems; work out a case study representing a real-life event; generate ideas in preparation for a lecture or videotape presentation; predict the results of a demonstration; summarize the main points in a lecture, lesson segment, text, reading, process, film, and so on; complement missing information in a given skeletal structure; review exams, quizzes, and homework assignments; compare and contrast issues and interpretations; or apply the material taught to some particular area, or to daily life. Groups might be responsible for starting discussion, presenting important concepts, or reporting on research. The following are a few more elaborate illustrations of group tasks:

–   When the objective is solving a problem, the task for each group can be to discuss and solve a different aspect of the problem, or suggest a different method for its solution.
–   When the objective is to make some decision, the task for each group can be to discuss a different argument for the decision, or another aspect of the relevant background.
–   When teaching material where the identification of pros and cons may be relevant, assign the group teams to develop either a pro or a con argument on the topic; then pair teams of opposite orientations and ask each team to present their arguments to the other team. Subsequently, each team formulates counter arguments to rebut opponents' arguments and presents these to opponents. Finally, engage the class in a general discussion where all teams voice their views and arguments.

Give both oral and written directions on the assigned learning task, and reiterate the directions frequently.

Check on your students' progress as often as possible.

Take care that each student in the group performs a clearly specified role that is essential for completing the entire project. You either may allow students to elect group leaders, recorders, researchers, and so forth, or you may determine their roles for them.

Monitor the groups carefully to ensure that they are working on their tasks. Walk around the room and periodically ask each group questions about their progress.

Have each group present to their classmates the projects/assignments, when completed. In doing so, students will realize the value of pooling individual talents for the benefit of the entire group.

Plan the group work in stages so that at first each student works alone on the task for some time. In the second stage students work in groups, and in the third, the different groups compare their input or a representative of each group reports the results to the whole class. Next, you may conduct a full-class discussion, summarize the findings of all the groups, write the summary on the board, and build the continuation of the lesson on that summary. Feedback on group assignments will be given to the group rather than to individuals.

Initiate competition between groups: Divide the whole class into two or three groups (which may be fairly large) and organize a competition to solve a problem or on some other issue.

Arrange for numbered heads. Members of learning teams are each given a number—1,2,3,... Pose a question to be discussed in the team setting. Following some discussion, call a specific number (which students do not know in advance), and the person with that number in each group responds as the group spokesperson. In this way, all students are motivated to become actively involved with the material.

Community of Learners

This title belongs to a particular method of group work. It is based on the recognition that we cannot teach everything but that we still need to create a curriculum that is intellectually honest. The most accepted solutions to this dilemma are (a) coverage of most of the curriculum material, and (b) teaching only the structures of the subject matter, the essential questions of the disciplines and their applications. Both methods have fatal flaws (Shulman, 1997, pp. 24-26)[33]. The *community of learners model* suggests a third approach. This approach argues that "we must be prepared to live in a world where different people have come to know different things in depth, and where they develop the capacity to collaborate with one another when there are problems to solve, problems that transcend what any individual can do alone." (ibid., p. 26). This is the way the world of work and play is evolving; therefore, this is the way that learning should go.

---

[33] The description here is an adjustment to the college level of a method described by Shulman for the precollege level.

So how is the community of learners method implemented? Instruction in the course begins with a series of "benchmark lessons." The purpose of these lessons is twofold. The first is to create a foundation, a base of knowledge shared by all the students, so that after this sequence of lessons, everyone starts the course topics at more or less a similar place. The second purpose is to present the course's goal, where all of this is going, where the students will be at its end. The second phase involves working in research groups, where each group investigates and becomes knowledgeable in a different topic or different aspect of a topic. All students conduct active investigation, reading, writing, interviewing, and communicating by computers with experts and databases. Thus, through its own research, the group becomes expert on its assigned topic. Periodically, the members of the different groups talk to one another to see what the other groups are doing. The teacher coaches and monitors the work of the groups and periodically brings all the students together for additional benchmark lessons. In the third phase, the specialists from each group engage in a "jigsaw." One or more members of each of the specialist groups comes together in a new group, whose responsibility it is to solve a problem that can be solved only by synthesizing the knowledge that was previously possessed only by the separate groups. In this phase, students take turns teaching their ideas to one another.

Peer Teaching

The community of learners model is largely based on students who become expert on a particular topic and teach what they know to their peers. Peer teaching in pairs or in small groups uses the same principle, thus providing an additional solution to the problem of curriculum coverage, but without going through the three separate phases of the community of learners model. Another advantage of peer teaching is that it provides more individual instruction for students who are struggling with the material. This is particularly beneficial when teaching difficult concepts.

How to use peer teaching

Version 1: Assign some students who already know some parts of the new material to teach it to those who do not know it and supervise the process during class time.

Version 2: Divide your class into groups and assign the students in each group to study a particular portion of the course curriculum by themselves (e.g., to read different parts of the same article) or research a particular topic. Then regroup the students so that each new group contains one member of each of the previous groups. Assign each member of the new groups to teach the other members the material he/she has learned in the former group.

Version 3: (a variation on Version 2): After each group becomes knowledgeable or expert on the topic it has studied or researched, each group in turn teaches that topic to the whole class. In its presentation, the group should integrate a variety of teaching methods: lecture, discussion, role-play, simulations, and more.

Version 4 (a variation on Version 2): Divide an assignment or topic into several parts and create learning teams with a like number of members (e.g., four). Within each group, the assignment parts are distributed, so that each student volunteers to become an "expert" on one of the parts. The experts on each topic then form separate groups to work together to master their fourth of the material, and also to discover the best way to help others learn it. All experts then reassemble into the original learning teams, whose members they then teach.

ROLE-PLAYING AND SIMULATIONS

Role-playing and *simulation* require students to place themselves in a particular situation or take a committed position on a key issue in the course. Here the attempt is to model some real-life problem situation in order to achieve an educational goal. The teacher presents a hypothetical but realistic situation and a cast of characters. The students then improvise dialogue and actions to fit their views of the situation and the character they are playing in it. For example, students might become actors in an historical event, requiring that they research positions and argue for certain actions or decisions. In scientific fields, students can become actual representatives of a physical process, acting it out to make it more concrete.

The incorporation of short simulations, games, and acting may provide important learning experiences, keep students involved in new and enjoyable ways of learning, motivate them, promote interaction among them, and present relevant aspects of real-life situations (Gage & Berliner, 1998). Lepper (1985) and Lepper and Chabay (1985) showed that games lead to high attention and deep processing, and thus contain a large potential for promoting learning.

How to administer role-playing and simulations

You may use a variety of role-playing and simulations for teaching, including computer-based and other activities. Computerized simulations are available in abundance in the market. Examples of non-computerized simulations are:

- If you teach some literary or historical topic (e.g., Othello), each of several students can be assigned the role of a key person in a simulation of a particular historical event. You may have students play out their roles with costumes, make-up, scenes, and so forth.
- In an anthropology class, role-play can simulate the life of a tribe in a particular context.
- If you teach the steps of selling a product, have students act out the sales situation in class.
- In a computer science class, when you teach the functions of different components of the computer, you can assign each of several students to represent a different component of a computer; for example, one student serves as an input device, another as an output device, and so on. Then, describe a computer task and let each participant play his/her role in the process of task performance.
- In any class, ask two students to volunteer to act out two people with opposing views who are trying to arrive at a difficult decision, or two scientists thinking aloud about the significance of an experiment, or two social workers handling a family crisis. Issues involving value conflicts, moral choices, and timeless human dilemmas related to the students' world usually work best.

Use the following stages of a simulation or of role-playing:

- **Start by establishing the context and setting** for the simulation/role-playing through a short lecture.
- Divide the class into a number of small groups.
- **Give each group a specific concrete task.** Assign each group a topic, issue, or idea to work on; or to propose a position and course of action. The role of each group should be clearly delineated. Each group receives a different assignment and keeps it confidential from the other groups.
- Provide clear instructions, debriefing to the groups.
- **Give students time in class** (or have them prepare this as homework) to plan and rehearse acting out a scene which presents their assignment.
- **Assign each group to make a presentation to the whole class,** who should then be able to identify the issue or idea from the act.
- **Discuss in class the presentations made by different groups.** Show assertive leadership—hear the presentations of different groups and promptly summarize them and incorporate them into your lecture.

THE CASE-METHOD TEACHING

The *case method* employs stories (case studies) builds on real-life examples or situations and places students in the role of a decision-maker or problem-solver. The case studies offer background data; the students need to make sense of the information provided to them and come to appropriate conclusions regarding the next action to take, or the kind of data they will need in order to appropriately resolve the problem. Cases typically involve consideration of several possible alternative approaches for action or solution, and require the evaluation of each approach under different criteria, mainly cost-effectiveness. Case-based teaching requires students to apply the theories and models they are currently studying in the course, as well as those they have learned in other courses. This method helps students see the connection between theory and practice, and realize that theories and models may be more problematic when applied to real-life situations than they appear in textbook illustrations and examples. They also learn that there is no one "correct" solution to a problem. The ambiguities inherent in many cases spark discussion, forcing students to weigh the credibility and validity of different arguments and the reasoning behind them.

The case-method teaching thus provides contextualized learning that aims to increase student interest and motivation in learning. This method promotes students' active learning and use of higher-order thinking skills, for example, analytic and problem-solving skills. Students also become more responsible for their learning because they must read and think about the case ahead of time in order to be prepared to discuss it in class. The case method provides problem-solving heuristics that can be applied in a variety of teaching situations. Legal, medical, and business training are largely dependent on the case method, but this method is easily adapted to many other disciplines.

The teacher's role in case-method teaching is to select cases that embody particular rules and principles, to guide the discussion of all aspects of the case, and most importantly, to summarize at the end of discussion and lead students to understand and formulate the underlying rules or principles. Teachers who do not summarize or generalize, leave students wondering what they have learned from the exercise.

How to use the case method in teaching

Present the case to students. Prepare the case in printed form. Present a detailed description with supporting documentation. If the description is long (e.g., printed on several pages), distribute it to students in advance.

Use a variety of sources for cases. The most timesaving way to find case studies is to base them on actual events or experiences. You may draw cases from your own and your peers' research and practice experiences and also from existing publications such as newspapers, magazines, journal reports, and special books with case descriptions (e.g., Zeaks, 1989). You may also ask students to present cases resting on their own experiences.

Select stimulating cases. Use cases that are thought provoking, present a conflict, have real elements, lack an obvious right answer, and demand that students take a position and make a decision.

Sequence the cases. If you present several successive cases to teach a principle, arrange them in some logical sequence, for example, in increasing level of difficulty.

Prepare students to use a case study. Provide clear instruction on what their responsibilities are in preparing to discuss a case in class. Give them a list of questions to guide them through the case. Ask them to prepare a short outline of the central problem and their plans for resolving it. You may organize them into groups to prepare comments before class discussion of the case.

Conduct the case study. Pose questions to the student-presenters and guide discussion in class. Avoid lecturing or telling the "right" answer.

Write students' input on the board. Start by writing the main details of the case, and add points students make while discussing the case.

Role-play the case. You may use role-playing by students to make the case more vivid.

Summarize and generalize. When the discussion of the case is done, summarize and generalize the case, or lead students to state the generalization. Ask them: What have you learned from the case? What principles and rules does the case support or offer?

PROBLEM-BASED TEACHING

Problem-based learning is an instructional method that is based on working in groups to achieve understanding or resolution of complex real-world problems. This method aims to promote students' problem-solving skills, to help them think critically, to learn how to learn, and to acquire communication skills.

Formats for Problem-Based Teaching

Problems can be incorporated into a variety of teaching formats: small-group cooperative activities, large-group case method discussion, laboratory experimentation, and even in interactive lecturing. The following are the main formats for problem-based learning:

Small-group discussion with a faculty tutor. This is the original format, as used in medical education. Students meet as a group with a faculty member who serves as a facilitator and occasional expert resource in their discussion of problems.

Collaborative learning groups. Students meet as a group in the classroom, to solve problems, with a teacher who is available to all groups as a consultant, as needed.

Case-method problem-based teaching. This method, frequently used in business and law schools, engages a large group of students in the discussion of a problem that has been carefully analyzed by the students prior to the class session, often through study in informal peer groups. Class discussion is orchestrated by the teacher to promote critical analysis, exploration of multiple perspectives, application of newly learned ideas, and the making of well-supported decisions.

Problem-based lectures. The teacher begins a lecture by presenting a problem for class discussion. The problematic case is used to raise interest in the topic of the lecture. The teacher incorporates students' comments into the following lecture.

Community of learners. As described above, the third phase of this teaching model is assigning students to solve problems in the framework of group work, by synthesizing and bringing together the knowledge that was previously possessed only by the separate groups.

How to promote problem-based learning through teaching

- Use the following critical components for problem-based learning:
- Use problems that are central to learning rather than those serving as mere supplements to the lecture.
- Introduce problems that raise compelling issues for new learning.
- Actively involve students in the discussion of these issues.
- Provide appropriate feedback and corrective assistance.
- Build the process of learning expecting students to draw on previous learning and experience, pose questions, set personal learning goals, take responsibility for their own learning through independent reading and study, and teach one another (Wilkerson & Feletti, 1989).

Ensure that students involved in problem-based learning work through the following process:
- Guide students so that they confront the problem, identify its nature and dimensions, suggest procedures to resolve it, generate hypotheses to explain it, request additional data to support or challenge the proposed hypotheses, identify questions for additional independent study, and determine how to proceed.

- Allow opportunities for students to engage in independent study by selecting and locating resources; manage information overload and time; and develop active study strategies including peer discussion, note taking, charting, and more.
- Enable students to return to the problem by sharing new learning with other students, examining and prioritizing original hypotheses in light of new learning, selecting and criticizing potential solutions, raising new questions for additional study, and summarizing, organizing, and synthesizing what is now known.

EXPERIENTIAL LEARNING

Experiential learning builds on the notion that learning must be rooted in the student's own experience—that knowing and doing are connected. Originally, the term experiential learning referred to special educational experiences such as fieldwork, internship, and on-site education in the workplace, whether in business or industry. However, experiential learning can be practiced also during regular lessons in the classroom. This means either building the learning sequence on previous student experiences, or building an experience into the learning sequence. In order to transform students' involvement in the experience into learning, students need to reflect on that experience—to step back and ponder the events, and to extract some meaning or knowledge relevant to other experiences (Cantor, 1995; Hutchings & Wutzdorff, 1988).

Professional and technical disciplines such as education, health services, and social work, use experiential learning to provide students with the competencies necessary to pursue successful careers upon graduation. These experiences promote students' professional skills and give them job experience. Some disciplines of a more theoretical nature also have a history of making learning experiential and concrete, for example, the integration of laboratory work into the sciences. In the other domains, experiential learning should be specifically planned if it is to be used at all.

How to promote experiential learning in teaching

Introduce experiential learning methods such as the following examples (Hutchings & Wutzdorff, 1988):

- In learning how to write (composition), ask students to think about a time they felt satisfied with something they wrote, and to describe how they wrote it. Through this process, students will uncover many of the essential points.
- In the first lesson of a social science class, assign students to groups, choose a social issue to investigate, and begin to work—all with only minimal instruction or intervention. In the frustration and confusion that inevitably follow, students

experience the issue central to the course—how groups select leaders, how social systems make decisions, and how they handle conflicts.
- In a literature class, assign students to enact a poem, giving form to the concepts of tension, climax, and resolution.
- In a nursing course, a student might spend a day in a wheelchair to understand the reality of being handicapped.

SUMMARY

There are instructional methods in which active student involvement is the norm. The main ones are: discussion, group work, simulation, role-play, case-method teaching, problem-based learning, and experiential learning. These methods may be regarded as "high-risk" active learning strategies because they may introduce some chaos in the classroom and some uncertain learning outcomes. None of these strategies should be used solely during an entire lesson period. Rather, they should be integrated with one another and with the lecture method, to enliven it. Active learning in the classroom requires that the teacher serve less as presenter and more as a designer, choreographer, orchestrator, facilitator, director of student learning, consultant, moderator, and manager of the learning environment and teaching process.

Discussion in class may take several forms, ranging from teacher-centered to student-centered ones. The teacher-centered form is the most prevalent in the college classroom. Discussions are valued by educational leaders because they encourage students to actively participate in the lesson; to think about the material and about its connections with other issues; to talk about the material; and to explain, summarize, and question. Students, too, value discussions because of the opportunities created for them to be active, to generate and be exposed to new representations of knowledge and ideas, and to provide possible confirmation or denial of their own ideas. In students' view, the most successful class discussions are those which provide opportunities for autonomous thought, for personal expression, and for representing information in ways that are personally meaningful to them. However, in spite of its potential advantage, the discussion is used relatively little in colleges and universities, probably due to the following factors: (a) low student participation, caused by boredom, lack of knowledge, insufficient preparation for lessons, general passivity, lack of confidence to talk in public, and fear of being exposed as not clever; (b) the emergence of a small group of students that are "frequent participants" or, in the most extreme case, discussion monopolizers who talk so much that the teacher and other students become irritated; (c) students' impression that they do not learn much from discussion; (d) negative emotional reactions from discussion, and (e) perceived low expertise of the discussion participants.

Incorporating *pair- or small-group work* into the lesson has proved to be very beneficial to students' learning. It promotes the communication and group dynamics skills that students will need in their future work situation.

Community of learners is a teaching method that provides a solution to the dilemma of the teacher's inability to cover the entire course curriculum within the time frame of the class sessions. The community of learners model prepares students to live in a world where different people have come to know different things in depth, and to develop the capacity to collaborate when problems arise, problems that transcend what any individual can do alone. Instruction in this method begins with a series of "benchmark lessons." These lessons are designed to create a shared knowledge base, so that following this sequence of lessons, everyone starts the course topics from a more or less similar position. A second purpose is to present the goal of the course. The second phase involves working in research groups, where each group investigates and becomes knowledgeable about a different topic or different aspect of a topic through active investigation, reading, writing, interviewing, and communicating by computers with experts and databases. Thus, through its own research, the group becomes expert on its assigned topic. Periodically, the members of the different groups see what the other groups are doing. The teacher coaches and monitors the work of the groups and regularly brings all the students together for additional benchmark lessons. In the third phase, specialists from each group engage in a "jigsaw." One or more members of each of the specialized groups form a new group, whose responsibility it is to solve a problem that can be solved only by synthesizing the knowledge that was previously possessed exclusively by the separate groups.

Peer teaching is part of the community of learners model, but it can be used in other ways, too, whenever students who become expert on some topic teach it to the other students taking the course.

Role-playing and simulation require students to place themselves in a particular situation or take a committed position on a key issue in the course. The incorporation of short simulations and student acting into teaching may provide important learning experiences, keep students involved in new and enjoyable ways of learning, motivate them, promote interaction among them, and present relevant real-life situations.

Case studies are stories, often based on real-life examples or situations, which place students in the role of a decision-maker or problem-solver. Case-method teaching requires that students apply the theories and models they are currently studying; this helps them see the connection between theory and practice. It promotes their active learning and their use of higher-order thinking skills. Students also become more responsible for their learning because they must read and think about the case ahead of time in order to be prepared to discuss it in class.

Problem-based learning is based on working in groups to achieve understanding or resolution of complex real-world problems. This method aims to promote students' problem-solving skills, to help them think critically, to learn how to learn, and to acquire communication skills.

Experiential learning builds on the idea that learning must be rooted in the student's own experience and that knowing and doing are connected. This means either building the learning sequence on the experience the student brings to the learning situation, or introducing experience into the learning sequence.

Chapter 7 concludes the second part of the book. Part III (Chapters 8-16) presents a structured model for effective teaching, consisting of teaching dimensions and strategies that were identified as most crucial in effective teaching.

Communication research perceives teaching as a process of oral communication where a commonness of understanding is created between a sender (the teacher) and a receiver (the student). That process consists of a sequence of events whose desired effects on the receiver can be arranged in the following order (DeLozier, 1979):

1. Getting and maintaining attention/awareness.
2. Gaining understanding.
3. Developing or changing attitudes (e.g., toward the topic being taught to create an atmosphere for learning).
4. Learning.
5. Action (application of the material learned).

Teachers can achieve all these five components by making the presentation organized, clear and interesting/engaging, and maintaining a pleasant classroom climate. These are the main dimensions of effective teaching.

PART III

A MODEL OF DIMENSIONS AND STRATEGIES FOR EFFECTIVE TEACHING

Chapter 8

Course and Lesson Organization

The term "organization" in the context of teaching is defined as a systematic arrangement or design; as arranging in a coherent form, forming a strategy for a plan, introducing a deliberate order, arranging, and outlining. Organizational procedures enable students to follow the presentation during each lesson, identify the location and relation of each topic to the general framework of the course and lesson, structure the new material, and absorb and embed it into their existing cognitive structure in a way that makes it easily retrieved.

A teacher who organizes the course and lesson well can be likened to a tour guide who, at the beginning of the tour, presents the road map illustrating the whole plan of the tour, and explains the rationale for visiting each site and for the particular order. Then, on each day of the tour, he/she again shows the full tour map, indicating where they have been until now, and pointing out the current day's plan. The guide then zooms in and shows an enlarged map of the sites planned for that day, and explains in advance where the stops will be and why. Then, at the end of the day, he/she summarizes the visits made throughout the day, and again shows the general tour map, indicating the next day's plan. The well-organized teacher, likewise, starts the course by presenting a structured syllabus—mapping out the plan for the course and its rationale. Then, the teacher starts each lesson by showing the full course plan, indicating which parts of the plan were accomplished until now, and pointing out the current lesson's plan. Then, at the end of each lesson, he/she summarizes the topics covered during the lesson, and indicates the next lesson's plan.

STUDIES OF COURSE AND LESSON ORGANIZATION

Organization has traditionally been considered by educators, psychologists, and communication specialists as essential for effective oral communication. Surveys in the domain of oral communication, all conducted in the 1970s, revealed that most basic speech courses and all popular college-level speech-communication textbooks had units/chapters on message organization (Gibson, 1974; Kelley, 1970). Several experimental studies in this domain showed that message organization made a significant difference in listeners' comprehension—the better organized the message, the better it was understood (e.g., Spicer & Basset, 1976; Thompson, 1960). Similarly, psychological research found that the more organized the material, the easier it was learned, the better it was retained, and the faster it was retrieved (Baddeley, 1976; Loftus & Loftus, 1976). The fact that organization improves retention is widely accepted. The psychological rationale for this is that we know much more than we can recall, and that organization of information aids effective location/storage and fast retrieval from memory (Baddeley). Organization is important not only for the lecture method, but also for more student-centered methods such as discussion, group work, and problem solving. Students need to know where the discussion or group work is going, what are their aims, and what are the aims of the problems presented.

Few studies in the domain of education have investigated the role of organization in student learning. These took place mostly in the 1960s and 1970s. The Stanford Program on Teaching Effectiveness (1976) found that high structuring of recitation lessons was positively related to student achievement. Miltz (1972) found that the organization and clarity of explanations highly correlated with the quality of the explanations: Explanations presented in a clear and organized fashion were better understood than were less clear and disorganized explanations. A review of studies on teaching effectiveness in higher education (Feldman, 1989a)[34] found "teacher's preparation and organization" to be one of the two (out of 22) teaching dimensions most important for all four main indicators of effective teaching: correlation with student achievement, correlation with overall evaluation of the teacher, and statement of importance by faculty and by students. That is, course and lesson organization are highly related to student learning and satisfaction from instruction and are highly appreciated by teachers and students alike.

Several studies found that the use of teaching strategies that represent components of organization also increased comprehension and retention of the material presented. Some of the organizational strategies examined were:

---

[34] See Chapter 1: Main Dimensions of Effective Teaching.

making the structure of a message explicit (Eylon & Reif, 1979; Thorndyke, 1978), presenting behavioral objectives (Begle, 1979), and proper use of transitions (Thompson, 1967).

The organization of each lesson is embedded within the general organization of the course. Thus, this chapter will first discuss course organization and then lesson organization. Figure 8-1 presents a flowchart of course and lesson organization and their components.

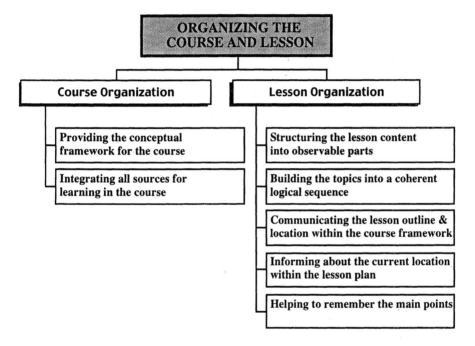

Figure 8-1: Dimensions of Course and Lesson Organization

COURSE ORGANIZATION

Effective course organization requires that teachers: (a) organize and link the different course topics within a structure—a conceptual framework—and communicate this structure to students, and (b) integrate the different sources for learning into the course.

Providing a Conceptual Framework for the Course

Students' comments often refer to the importance of transmitting the course's conceptual framework to the class:

- He emphasizes the general frame of the theory and the philosophy underlying it.
- He always integrates in his teaching references to topics we learn in other courses in that department.
- She showed the bigger picture and the major trends.

However, students' comments also frequently reflect the negative impact rendered by the absence of a clear conceptual framework:

- This is the seventh lecture and the topic of the course is still unclear. I haven't got a clue about what he intends to teach during the semester or even during the present lesson.
- I am terrified of the final because although I have done all the work, I still don't have a clear understanding of the course's concept.
- I'm not sure exactly of what I learned in this class. I certainly know more about the history of Paris or Rome but I haven't been able to correlate knowledge with historical circumstances—how events were placed in historical context.
- Course material didn't seem relevant or oriented to a particular theme.
- This is the last week and I'm still not sure what the point of the class was.
- Need a more coherent, defined overall framework. Otherwise it seems like a lot of hot air.
- I would have liked a stronger historical context for the works we read.
- He presents a variety of results of experiments that either support or refute the classical physics, but there isn't any guiding idea or unifying theory.

These comments point to the need to present to students a general framework of the course topics, a guiding idea, a unifying theory, a context, a theme, or a sense of the bigger picture or of the major trend to be explored. The course framework serves as an infrastructure for laying out the concepts, notions, ideas, and knowledge developed throughout the course.

In addition to providing the general framework, the teacher should ensure that the themes or topics of the course are well integrated and clearly related to one another. Here is one student's positive comment:

- Last lecture was brilliant—it integrated the overall themes of the course.

However, most student comments in my accumulated database reflect negative experiences regarding the integration and interconnection of course topics. For example:

- It isn't clear to us what the main topics of the course are, what are the connections between the different topics, and where the course is going.
- Lectures weren't connected very well, and I didn't really understand how some course topics tied together. I felt I only gained bits and pieces of knowledge.

• I had a difficult time putting all the materials together.

In sum, the teacher should organize and link the different course topics into a conceptual framework, and frequently communicate this framework to the students.

How to provide a conceptual framework for the course

Provide the general framework for the course, and explain how the course topics are organized in order to achieve these objectives:

- **Describe a unifying theory**—the whole picture, the main theme, the leading line of thought.
- **Situate the course content within a wider context**—within the general structure of courses in the department or within the curriculum for a particular academic degree. Connect the course to related courses that students might have taken in other departments; to up-to-date topics in the domain; to students' future professional work; and to their daily-life experiences.
- **Provide a rationale for the framework.** Explain your considerations in selecting and organizing and connecting the specific course topics within the conceptual framework of the course. Explain how and why you have selected the particular topics from the overall content of the domain and why you have organized them as you did—to be parallel to the chapters in the course textbook, chronologically, or on another basis that should be made known to the students. Explain also what topics you have excluded and why.

Communicate the course organization to students clearly and continuously: Introduce and explain the course framework and organizational structure in the first lesson and repeat it throughout the course. Clarify the structure of the framework—the interconnections among the different topics and their relations to other topics students have already learned:

- **Give a printed syllabus** in the first lesson that lists all main topics in the order to be taught, all central notions, themes, and theses of the course.
- **Prepare a "roadmap"**—a graphical representation of the course topics and the links among them. Prepare a graph in a coordinate system, a chart, a tree-diagram, or a summary table.[35]
- **Give the printed "roadmap" to the students** as a handout or prepare it on a transparency.
- **Use the graphical representation to inform students where you are in each lesson.** At the beginning of each lesson or whenever you start a new main topic, show the graph of the general framework (either on the transparency or in students' handout) and where you are within this framework—what came before

---

[35] Illustrations of graphic representations of chapter frameworks are presented by tree diagrams in several of the chapters in this book. See Figures 8-1, 9-1, 10-1, 11-1, 12-1, 13-1, 14-1, 15-1,16-1.

> and what will follow. Only after the students understand the organizational
> structure should you go into detail.
> – **Use the "skeleton" method to build the framework transparency** so that only
> the main topics are first presented. As you advance in the material, add sub-
> topics onto the transparency (during the lesson).

Integrating All Sources for Learning into the Course

Students may need to accommodate a variety of sources for learning the
course material, primarily the lectures, the practice lessons, the textbook,
other readings, the assignments, and the lab. The teacher should establish
connections among all these sources to help students integrate and use them
in a way that promotes their learning. Of all the sources mentioned above, I
elaborate only on the integration of the readings into class lessons.

The integration of the textbook and the assigned readings into the course and lesson framework.

The following two comments illustrate a lack of good integration of the
assigned readings into the lesson:

• I feel like I read a lot of cool stuff, but I'm not sure I see how they fit together to build
  some kind of coherent story, to provide a full picture of the course topics.

• I didn't have a good sense of how to integrate the lectures and readings together.

These students' comments suggest that reading assignments should be an
integral part of the course content, and need to be smoothly and coherently
integrated into the lessons.

Unfortunately, only rarely does a teacher find a textbook that fully shares
his/her view of the course material.[36] In addition, many students face
difficulties in understanding texts that are too technical or abstract for them.
Teachers thus need to make their own modifications during the lesson,
adjusting the topics in the textbook to their students' needs.

How to integrate readings into the course framework

> **Adapt the textbook to your students** using the following steps:
>
> – **Complement the textbook content during class**: Present oral or visual aspects
>   that the text does not provide; use demonstrations; present the material in
>   alternative ways than those in the text so that students have an additional
>   approach; provide additional points or views and different types of explanations
>   than those in the book; add up-to-date topics not included in the book; develop

---

[36] See chapter 5: Lecture Versus Independent Reading.

some topics more deeply; give your own point of view or interpretation on the topic; and add anecdotes, analogies, and metaphors.

- **Give students directions** on how to use the textbook to benefit their learning.
- Identify the textbook's most important points/sections.
- **Clarify and simplify text passages** and issues that students may find difficult.
- Make frequent summaries of the book's readings.
- Complement deficiencies in students' background necessary to understand the text.

Integrate the assigned readings into the lesson content:

- **Motivate students to read the assigned readings** by ensuring that it is a prerequisite for understanding the lesson content and to participating in the discussions.
- **Plan the reading** and the lesson so that the main issues in the readings are discussed in the lesson.
- Explicitly clarity the connections between the lesson and the reading for the students.
- **When you assign the reading, provide several questions** that will connect it to the lesson content and direct student thinking. Assign students to submit written responses to these questions.

LESSON ORGANIZATION

Lesson organization makes it easy to follow the lesson development and its content. Effective organization of a lesson consists of (a) structuring the lesson content into observable parts under headings and sub-headings; (b) arranging the lesson topics in a coherent logical sequence; (c) communicating to students the objectives and structure of the lesson content and its place in the general framework of the course; (d) frequently updating students on their current location within the lesson plan; and (e) helping students identify and remember the main points of the lesson.

Structuring the Lesson Content into Observable Parts

- He starts with a general presentation of the topic, then provides the details, and concludes with a summary and a fast review tying up all ends.

A well-known adage says: *Tell students what you're going to tell them, tell them, and then tell them what you've told them.* This three-part lesson structure—introduction, body, and conclusion—provides students with a frame of reference throughout the lesson. The introduction provides motivation for learning and a framework on which subsequent learning can be based. The body covers the content and should be divided into observable topics and subtopics, with headings and subheadings. The teacher should mark the move from one heading to the other. The conclusion summarizes and reviews the principal points.

Building the Lesson Topics in a Coherent Logical Sequence

Lack of logical order of the lesson topics reduces students' ability to follow the presentation. Here are positive and negative students' comments related to this issue:

- She stays with the subject at hand and progresses logically to new subjects instead of jumping back and forth between concepts as other teachers do.
- He presents the topic in chronological order, according to its historical development by scientists.
- He presents the topics in an extremely disorganized way. It is impossible to understand from the presentation what causes what, what results from what.

The lesson topics should be given some logical structure, that is, be connected in a coherent way, be arranged under a leading line of thought, which should be adhered to without too many digressions from the objectives of the lesson. The topics in a lesson may be arranged on various bases: classificatory, historical, hierarchical, topical, spatial, inductive, deductive, or climatic, among others. The teacher should make the basis for the arrangement of topics explicit; once this basis is understood, the sequence is simpler to follow and retain. The teacher should also tie the different topics together in a coherent way, so that the material flows smoothly (see also "Coherence and smoothness of explanations" in Chapter 10).

However, it is possible to present well the different topics or ideas in a nonlinear organization. The organization can be circular—ideas can be presented in several circles, each converging onto the main theme. Ideas can also be presented in what may seem as random order. Students may not initially understand where the lecturer is heading, and only become aware of this gradually, as everything eventually "falls into place."

Communicating the Lesson Framework and its Place in the General Framework of the Course

- He does a good job of letting us know what topics he is going to be covering in class on a given day.

- She provides a wide, comprehensive view of the topic before going into detail.

Research at the pre-college level shows that effective teachers begin a lesson with a short statement of goals (Rosenshine, 1986). By this statement, they communicate the framework of the lesson to their students. Making the structure of a message explicit was found to increase comprehension and retention (Eylon & Reif, 1979; Johnson, 1970; Meyer, 1975; Thompson, 1967; Thorndyke, 1978). A teacher should communicate the general lesson structure, the basis for arrangement of the topics, and the place of the material presented within the conceptual framework of the course. Providing the lesson outline, main objectives, and conceptual framework before teaching begins is called "advance organizing," and has been shown to facilitate understanding of the material (Ausubel, 1978; Luiten, Ames, & Ackerson, 1980).

In presenting the material, the teacher should stick to the main line of thought and avoid too many diversions so that students do not lose track of the general framework of the lesson, as indicated in the following student comments:

- She doesn't focus on important points and gives too much detail.
- She does not give us any direction in class. The lectures proceed in an orderly manner but toward no anticipated conclusion.
- I'm not sure exactly of what I learned in this class. The lessons lacked focus.

How to communicate the lesson's framework

Outline the lesson topics, list objectives, provide a general overview. You may state the lesson outline or objectives orally, but it is better to write them on the board before the lesson starts, in the extreme left or right column, and leave them there throughout the lesson. You may also list them in a handout to students.

Use a "micro-outline" or "micro-objectives." Tell students what you are going to do in the next segment of the lesson or what the objectives of the coming segment are. For example: [37]

Next we'll define a sequence of complex numbers.

First of all, we should make a couple of definitions.

This was a geometrical explanation. Now, let's look at the analytic proof.

---

[37] The illustrations in all the following sections are taken from transcriptions of university math and science lessons that I have studied. Unfortunately, sources for citations from other subject areas that illustrate these particular points were not available to me.

Updating Students on Their Location Within the Lesson Framework

- Sometimes it was hard to know where we were and where she was going.

Students should be frequently updated throughout the lesson of where the teacher is within the lesson plan—where he/she is coming from and going to. For students who miss parts of the presentation due to note taking or lapses of concentration, this procedure provides the knowledge needed to reintegrate themselves into the lesson.

How to update students on your current location within the lesson plan

Refer to your outline/objectives. Refer to each outline item or objective, in turn, during the lesson. If the lesson outline is written on the board, point to each item when moving to teach it. Referring to the outline helps students identify where you are within the general framework of the lesson. For example:

As I've told you at the beginning of the lesson, we're now going to start several applications of...

Refer to your "micro-outline" or "micro-objectives." State the next few points to be discussed and refer to each in turn. For example, your micro-outline may be:

There are three ways for ... and we'll look into them one by one.

Then, refer to the micro-outline by going over these three ways and marking the shift from each to the other:

The first way is.... the second, ... and the last one is ...

Mark shifts/transitions during the lesson. Communicate to students that you are moving from one topic to the next.

Mark/signal verbally the start and completion of any part of the lesson, and any component of the content such as a case, a topic, a definition, a proof, an algorithm, a procedure, or any of their components or steps. This technique informs the students where you are at a given moment and what is to come next. For example:

So these are our assumptions; now, let's move on to the description of the study.... So that's the argument—what should the decision be?.... These were the given conditions, and now the proof is.... Now I'm going to state the conditions and the conclusions: The first condition is,..., the second,...., the third condition is.... These are the conditions, so the conclusion should be....

Here are examples of markers indicating completion of a topic:

Thus, the theorem is satisfied.... This is precisely what the theorem tells us.... That was the definition.... From all the above you know that they are similar triangles.... OK, that's the amount of light expressed in terms of the variables.... This is the expression we've got for dv/dt.... This is what it means to converge.... By this, the proof has been completed....

Mark/signal moves between points. Use special words or phrases to alert students to the fact that you have completed a point and are moving to the next one. Commonly used words for this purpose are:

"Now," "well," "O.K.," "all right," "allright?" "so," "but," "let's."

Commonly used phrases are:

"O.K. But," "But now," "Let's see what happens....," "Well, let's take for example ....,""Now then, ..." "First of all....," "Shall we move on?" "The next thing we want to know....," "On the other hand,....," "Of course we can now look at...."

Helping Students Identify and Remember the Main Points of the Lesson

Good lesson organization helps students by providing devices for facilitating retention, such as summaries or mnemonics. Some teachers object to "teaching students to remember things." However, the teacher behavior of "showing how to remember things" was identified by Hines (1982)[38] as behavior that highly discriminated between clear and unclear teachers. In other words, students feel that it is important for their learning that the teacher provide them with tools for organizing the newly learned material. Such tools impose a structure that facilitates the material's efficient storage in memory and subsequent retrieval.

How to help students remember the main points

Summarize the most important points you have presented during the lesson.

Use tables of comparisons and contrasts. Compare and contrast the main issue discussed in the lesson and arrange the pro and con arguments in parallel columns in a table.

Provide mnemonics to aid students in remembering certain concepts, formulas, theorems, and procedures. Examples are:

RST for the three properties of equivalency—Reflective, Symmetric, Transitive;

FOIL for the order of product of two binomials—First, Outer, Inner, Last;

---

[38] See Chapter 9: Research on Components of Clarity in Teaching.

"My Dear Aunt Sally" for the order of operations—Multiplication and Division come first and then Addition and Subtraction.

Use algorithms. Break down a procedure into components that should be followed in the given order to attain the objectives of that procedure. Organizing a procedure in the form of an algorithm helps students to store and retrieve it as one unit. The following is an example of an algorithm for solving a system of two linear equations with two variables:

To solve linear equations: First step, use the distributive law to get rid of parentheses, then combine like terms in each side of the equation. Now use the addition-subtraction rule so as to place all terms containing the variable on the same side of the equation, and the numbers on the other side. And lastly, use the division rule to get your variable.

Divide into categories. When you consider different instances of the same topic (e.g., when providing several applications to some theory), explain in what way each instance/application differs from the others, and in what instances one should use each as a model for solving the problem. This helps students identify what algorithm to retrieve in each case. For example:

If you have a variable in the numerator, use the quotient rule, but if you have a constant at the top, just take the negative power and take the derivative. Don't use the quotient rule for this one. You can use it, but it'll take longer.

Assign labels or titles. Assign names to procedures and algorithms to serve as direct access for the procedure's storage, location, and retrieval from memory. Examples of this are:

Using the quadratic formula, combining like terms, solving motion problems, and proving congruence of triangles.

SUMMARY

Organization of the course and lesson refers to the teaching procedures that enable students to follow the presentation during the lesson, identify the location and relation of each topic to the general framework of the course and lesson, structure the new material, and absorb and embed it into their existing cognitive structure in a way that makes it easily retrieved. Research shows that the quality of course and lesson organization relates to student learning and satisfaction from instruction.

Effective course organization requires that teachers: (a) organize and link the different course topics within a conceptual framework and communicate this framework to students, and (b) integrate the different sources for learning, such as the textbook and the readings, into the course.

Lesson organization consists of (a) structuring the lesson content into observable parts under headings and sub-headings; (b) arranging the lesson topics in a coherent logical sequence; (c) communicating the objectives and structure of the lesson content and its place in the general framework of the course; (d) frequently updating students on their current location within the lesson plan; and (e) helping students identify and remember the main points of the lesson.

Chapters 9-13 discuss "Making the lesson clear"—a main dimension of effective teaching.

Chapter 9

Clarity in Teaching: Importance and Components

As an introduction to the next four chapters on strategies for promoting clarity in teaching, this chapter presents, in brief, a number of studies that have identified these strategies, as well as studies that established the essential role of clarity for teaching effectiveness.

IMPORTANCE OF CLARITY IN TEACHING

Clarity is one of the main effective teaching dimension (Feldman, 1997). A review summarizing almost two decades of research on teacher clarity concluded that:

> Although there is evidence to suggest that a number of teacher behaviors facilitate learning (e.g., enthusiasm, variability, task orientation), there also is growing evidence that clarity of explanation may be the requisite of effective teaching, at least effective expository teaching (Cruickshank & Kennedy, 1986, p. 43).

The following comments, made by students, emphasize the importance of teaching clarity for understanding the material presented and for learning:

- I don't know a professor who could have made the difficult ideas of this course clearer.
- She has an excellent grasp of the material; makes the material very clear and accessible, easy to understand.
- The lessons are clear and understandable. The instructor has a gift for communicating in a clear and concise manner.
- Presentations are well organized, thorough, interesting and very easy to understand.

- She makes a difficult course clear and understandable.

On the other hand, unclear teachers confuse students and force them to invest extra time and effort in learning from sources other than the teacher, particularly the textbook.

- She didn't make connections between different concepts very clear. I relied heavily on the book because I rarely understood lectures.
- Confusing lectures, I got lost in lectures at some point every week. I wasn't sure how things fit together.
- Some lectures were obtuse, sometimes hard to understand. Explanations were unclear, some concepts were explained vaguely, very confusing at times.

Clarity in teaching also increases students' satisfaction from instruction. Hines (1982), and Hines, Cruickshank, and Kennedy (1985) showed that students who perceived their teacher to be clear tended to feel more satisfied with their learning experience than did students who perceived their teacher to be less clear. But what is the meaning of clarity in teaching?

The Notion of "Clarity in Teaching"

Studies of teaching clarity rarely define this notion, which is apparently taken to be self-explanatory. The few studies that have defined it (e.g., Hines, 1982) have related clarity to student understanding of the material taught, as illustrated by the cited comments. Hines identified those components of clarity in university teaching which differentiate between clear and unclear teachers. The teacher behavior component with the highest discriminating power was "Gives explanations students understand." Its complement, low clarity, was found to be associated with a lack of understanding. In a case study of a successful physicist whose clarity in teaching was very low, students showed to have acquired only little understanding of the material presented in his lessons, and to be strongly dissatisfied with his instruction (Hativa, 1998). We may thus conclude that clarity in teaching means teaching in a way that students understand. Yet, what does it mean to "understand?" Hence, we adopt the following definition:

> Understanding refers to an individual's ability to use knowledge in novel situations, for example, to solve problems, fashion products, or create stories... Understanding is the ability to think with knowledge, according to the standards of good practice within a specific domain, such as math, history, ceramics, or dance (Boix, 1997, p. 382).

The following are research-based findings regarding the validity and reliability of clarity in teaching, and students' perceptions of the importance of clear teaching.

"Clarity in Teaching" as a Valid Component of Teaching Effectiveness

Land and Smith (1981), Smith and Land (1980a), Evans and Guymon (1978), and Snyder et al. (1991), all found that college students successfully distinguished between clear and unclear lessons. Bush, Kennedy, and Cruickshank (1977) examined relationships between teacher clarity and several status and demographic variables, such as teacher age and gender and student gender. Of all the variables examined, almost none showed a relationship to clarity. Only teacher age showed a low relationship, with younger teachers perceived as clearer. Hines (1982), and Hines et al. (1985) similarly found that students' judgments of teacher clarity were not affected by extraneous student and teacher variables. The latter two studies also reported that students of clear teachers displayed higher achievements than students of less clear teachers, suggesting that students actually learn more from clear teachers. Thus, "teacher clarity" is a valid component of effective teaching.

Reliability and Consistency of "Clarity in Teaching"

A sequence of studies conducted at Stanford University about three decades ago (Belgard, Rosenshine, & Gage, 1971; Fortune, Gage, & Shutes, 1966; Gage et al., 1971) indicated that pre-college teachers differ in their ability to explain material clearly and that this ability is consistent over lessons and across groups of students (even in different grade levels). Teacher characteristics that inhibit their clarity of presentation, particularly those related to vagueness (as explained below)—were also found to be consistent for across lessons (Hiller, Fisher, & Kaess, 1969).

Students have proven to be consistent in evaluating teacher clarity (Bush et al., 1977; Kennedy, Cruickshank, Bush, & Myers, 1978) and in their perceptions of the components of clarity in teaching across age groups (junior high school, high school, and college); geographic regions and countries; and socioeconomic status. Williams (1984; 1985) demonstrated that the same teacher receive consistent ratings on clarity and its components from both students and observers over a period of one week. Marsh and Overall (1979) found that performances by the same teacher teaching the same course in different terms or years produced highly correlated ratings on "organization and clarity." For performances by the same teacher teaching different courses, the correlation was lower but still substantial and significant (r=.54). In comparison, the correlation coefficients between ratings of different instructors teaching either the same course or different courses were almost zero. Similarly, Hativa and Raviv (1996) showed that teachers' ratings by students on clarity were stable in the same course given in different years and also within the same course at mid- and end-of-semester. All in all, the findings of these studies suggest that student ratings of teachers on clarity and its components are fairly stable across time and courses.

Students' Perceptions of the Importance of Clarity in Teaching

Disciplinary Differences

As described above, clarity in teaching relates to student understanding whereas "understanding" refers to thinking with knowledge within specific domains or disciplines. Gardner and Boix (1994) advocated that teaching should promote understanding that builds upon disciplinary content, notions, approaches, and culture. Thus, we would expect disciplinary differences in students' perceptions of what makes lessons clear. Indeed, clarity is perceived by students as important particularly in mathematics, natural sciences, and engineering courses (Hativa, 1984; 1993; Hativa & Raviv, 1993), more so than in the humanities and social sciences (Feldman, 1976; Holland, 1979; Jones, 1981). Jones (1981), for example, asked university freshmen from six disciplines (arts, science, law, engineering, commerce, and medicine), to rate 40 items describing teacher behaviors in terms of their importance to learning. Results showed that the science and engineering groups regarded clear explanations, thorough lesson preparation, and ease of taking notes as the primary characteristic of good lectures. Other teacher behaviors that they considered as highly important included two components of teaching clarity: good blackboard work and clear speech. In comparison, students of other disciplines did not assign great importance to these behaviors. To test these perceptions, Pohlmann (1976) assigned students of different disciplines to rate their teachers on a list of classroom behaviors. Of all the teacher behaviors listed in the rating form, science and mathematics teachers were rated lowest on two components of clarity—"spoke understandably" and "knew if students understood him". In comparison, faculty in education, social science, humanities, and business rated high on at least one of these components and did not rate low on either of them. Holland (1979) attributed the special importance of clarity in mathematics and science courses to these sequential/hierarchical topic structure.

Course-Level Differences in Perceptions

On average, undergraduate students rate their teachers consistently lower than of graduate students on overall performance as well as on clarity (Feldman, 1976; Jones, 1981), suggesting that clarity in teaching is especially important for undergraduate students.

Discrepancies between Faculty and Students' Perceptions

Benz and Blatt (1994) identified discrepancies between faculty and students' perceptions of clarity. From the students' perspective, clarity indicated that they understood the content presented; it was manifested through teaching methods such as repetition, orderliness, examples, and relevance to their lives. From the faculty's perspective, clarity indicated being logical and organized, presenting questions to students, and encouraging students' questions in class.

In order to help teachers improve their clarity, we need to identify what makes teaching clear, that is, to identify components of clarity—that is, teaching behaviors and strategies that promote clear teaching.

RESEARCH ON COMPONENTS OF CLARITY IN TEACHING

> Everybody understands that there is a phenomenon called teacher clarity, but no one can, with any confidence, denote its peculiar parameters (Metcalf & Cruickshank, 1991, p. 107).

This section presents evidence for teacher behaviors that contribute to, or represent components of, teacher clarity. As shown above, students relate *clarity* to their *understanding* of the material presented. Similarly, they relate *lack of clarity* to *low understanding*. What do teachers do to make their lessons incomprehensible to students? Brown (1979; 1980) found that students were dissatisfied with lecturers whose presentations were incoherent, who failed to present the subject matter at a level appropriate for the students or to emphasize main points, who were inaudible, whose speed of delivery was too fast to allow for proper note taking, and who showed poor chalkboard work. All these behaviors may be regarded as components of clarity, as discussed below. Poor performance on these behaviors results in unclear teaching and in students' dissatisfaction.

Following are several studies that more systematically identify the components of clarity. One sequence of studies explored the components of teacher clarity through the identification of behaviors that discriminate between clear and unclear teachers. A preliminary study (Cruickshank, Myers, & Moenjak, 1975) asked over 1,000 junior high school students to provide open-ended descriptions of the behaviors of teachers they considered to be clear. The list of behaviors thus compiled was subsequently used to ask students in different schools and grade levels to rate *the frequency* with which their *most clear teachers* performed these behaviors, and to do the same for their *least clear teachers*. Discriminant analyses performed on their answers identified specific teacher behaviors that significantly differentiated between clear and unclear teachers. Table 9-1 presents the first 28 "prime discriminators", arranged in decreasing magnitude of discriminating power:[39]

1. Gives explanations that students understand.	15. Tells students what they are expected
2. Uses examples when explaining.	to do/know.
3. Encourages students to ask questions.	16. Explains things simply.
4. Presents content in a logical manner.	17. Gives enough time for practice.
5. Repeats things when students do not understand.	18. Repeats things that are important.
6. Answers students' questions.	19. Stays with the topic until students
7. Summarizes the material presented in class.	understand.
8. Teaches step-by-step.	20. Asks students if they know what to do
9. Emphasizes important points.	and how to do it
10. Explains the assignments and the materials	21. Distributes time adequately over topics.
students need to use.	22. Explains and then stops for questions.
11. Asks questions to find out if students	23. Stresses difficult points.
understand.	24. Describes the assignments and
12. Compares new material with what students	how to do them.
know.	25. Shows how to remember things.
13. Teaches at an appropriate pace.	26. Shows similarities and
14. Explains and stops for students to think	differences between things.
about it.	27. Goes over difficult problems in class.
	28. Explains meaning of unfamiliar words.

Table 9-1: Prime Discriminators Between Clear and Unclear Pre-College Teachers

Most strikingly, all the other studies in this sequence identified similar behaviors as prime discriminators, although these studies were conducted in diverse locations in the US and in Australia, and for two school levels: middle school and high school (Bush et al., 1977; Kennedy et al., 1978). Hines (1982) replicated the same procedure at the college level. Her set of teacher clarity behaviors consisted of 42 behaviors drawn from previous

---

[39] In educational research, these behaviors are termed "low-inference teacher behaviors"—see Low Level Dimensions in Figure 1-2.

studies for the pre-college level and an additional 11 behaviors modified or introduced especially to fit the university level. Discriminant analysis revealed that both the 42 items and the combined set of 53 items each had even higher discriminatory power in differentiating between clear and unclear teachers at the college level when compared with the pre-college level. Table 9-2 presents the 28 prime discriminators she identified from among the 53 items, arranged in decreasing magnitude of discriminatory power. Several items are congruent with the previous list for the pre-college level:

1. Gives explanations students understand.	15. Explains and then stops for questions.
0. Presents content in a logical manner.	16. Tells students what they are expected to do/know.
1. Explains things simply.	17. Stresses difficult points.
2. Teaches at an appropriate pace.	18. Describes the assignments and how to do them.
3. Answers students' questions.	19. Teaches step-by-step.
4. Asks questions to find out if students understand.	20. Allows students time to ask questions.
5. Repeats things that are important.	21. Writes important things on board or in handouts.
6. Repeats things when students do not understand.	22. Shows how to remember things.
7. Points out what is important to learn.	23. Uses examples when explaining.
8. Stays with the topic until students understand.	24. Shows similarities and differences between things.
9. Summarizes the material presented in class.	25. Compares new material with what students know.
10. Asks students if they know what to do and how.	26. Goes over difficult problems in class.
11. Distributes time adequately over topics.	27. Explains meaning of unfamiliar words.
12. Explains the assignments and the materials students need to use.	28. Explains and stops for students to think about it.

Table 9-2: Prime Discriminators Between Clear and Unclear College Teachers

The following are several other studies on components of teaching clarity that do not belong to the above sequence and that use other research methods. Smith (1978) used trained raters to rate the videotaped classroom teaching of 99 community college teachers. The ten behaviors that Smith found to be most highly related to overall teacher clarity are presented in Table 9-3:

1. Uses examples with explicit referents.	6. Shares overall structure of lecture with students.
2. Lets students ask questions.	7. Teaches step-by-step.
3. Answers student questions.	8. Prepares students for what is upcoming.
4. Asks questions related to material being taught.	9. Uses verbal markers of importance.
5.. Encourages students to ask questions.	10. Summarizes material at appropriate points in the resentation.

Table 9-3: Community College Teachers' Behaviors Most Related to Clarity

A more recent study (Benz & Blatt, 1994) used qualitative methods to identify components of teaching effectiveness. University students were asked to explain in writing why they rated their teachers as they did on the standard rating questionnaire. The most frequent explanations for ratings of teacher clarity were: The teacher explained the subject matter well, understood it, repeated key concepts, presented in an orderly manner, used personalized examples, and used frequent questioning.

The substantial similarity of the behaviors identified as components of clarity in the different studies, conducted in different types of institutions, locations, and using different research methods, validate these clarity components.

An additional group of studies (e.g., Hiller et al., 1969; Land & Smith, 1981; Smith & Land, 1981) identified teaching behaviors that inhibit clarity. The main inhibitors were: "frequent use of vagueness terms," "mazes in speaking," "low verbal fluency," and "providing irrelevant examples."[40]

On the basis of the results of all of the above studies and of my analysis of about 40 hours of videotaped lessons of award-winning university teachers, I have sorted behaviors that contribute to teaching clarity into four major categories—intermediate level dimensions[41]—as presented in Figure 9-1.

---

[40] These studies and their findings are discussed in more detail in Chapter 11 on "noise" in teaching.

[41] See also Figure 1-2.

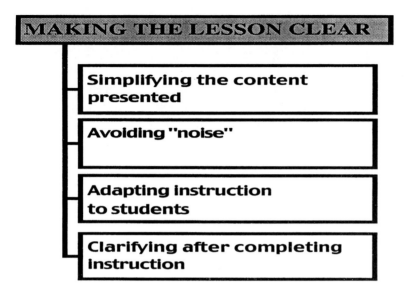

Figure 9-1: Intermediate Level Dimensions of Teaching Clarity

The following four chapters discuss and elaborate on these categories.

SUMMARY

University faculty and students perceive clarity as of utmost importance to student learning. They judge teaching to be effective, to a large degree, on the basis of its clarity. Indeed, students appear to learn more from and are more satisfied with clear teachers.

Clarity in teaching means teaching in a way that enables students to understand. Research shows clarity to be a valid, distinct, and stable construct, unaffected by extraneous student or teacher variables. Students are able to distinguish between clear and unclear teachers and to identify the behaviors that contribute to or distract from clarity of presentation. Their ratings of teachers on clarity and its components are fairly reliable and consistent across time and courses.

Disciplinary differences were identified in students' perceptions of the importance of clarity. Students in math, natural sciences and engineering courses consider teacher clarity to be more important to learning than do students in humanities, arts, education, and social sciences.

Several dozen teacher behaviors were identified as components of clear teaching at the college level. Some of the main behaviors were: using examples and illustrations; presenting the material in a simple and logical manner; teaching in a way that students understand; adjusting the pace and level of teaching to students; using questioning in class to gauge student understanding; repeating, stressing, and summarizing important points; Breaking down the material into small steps and teaching step-by-step; and guiding students in their learning.

Chapter 10

Clarity in Teaching:
Simplifying the Material Presented

It is elementary, my dear Watson!

By saying this, Sherlock Holmes meant that he had explained the solution to a complicated problem in terms so simple that even Watson, whose intellectual abilities he did not to overly appreciate, could comprehend.

In learning new contents, students need to understand a variety of types of topics: concepts, laws, rules, formulas, cases, theorems, criteria, processes, models, and theories. Teachers can alleviate students' difficulties in understanding and applying the new material by "simplification" or "elementarization"—reducing the complexity of the topics presented. "The teacher sees his job as one of processing very tough material into more easily digestible nutrients for rather simple minds" (Fox, 1983, p. 153). Thus, simplification is a major clarity technique for promoting student understanding, as illustrated by the following comments about teachers skilled in this technique:

- He simplifies the material to understandable explanations.
- She simplifies the material so that students with no background in the topic can still follow it.
- Her explanations make even difficult material seem trivial. Other explanations (especially in the text) pale by comparison.

Supporting the importance of the *simplification* strategy, Polya (1965, p. 102) states:

Abstractions are important; use all means to make them more tangible. Nothing is too good or too bad, too poetical or too trivial to clarity your abstractions. As Montaigne put it: The truth is such a great thing that we should not disdain any means that could lead to it.

There is also research support for simplification: Kennedy, Cruickshank, Bush, and Myers (1978), and Hines (1982) found that the behavior "explains things simply" was rated as the top behavior for junior high school teachers, and in fifth place for college teachers, within a list of about 30 behaviors that are "prime discriminators" between teachers considered very high and very low in clarity.[42]

The term simplification may evoke strong objections among faculty members who interpret it as "pruning," "dumbing down," "watering down," or lowering the level of the material; that is, achieving understanding by reducing the extent and difficulty level of the targeted meaning. Faculty suspect "pruning" when a teacher looks to accommodate students who have low aptitudes or who lack sufficient background for learning the course material. When used in this book, simplification refers to reducing the complexity of the material without lowering the intended requirements for student comprehension and application.

Figure 10-1 presents four strategies to achieve simplification, based primarily on research literature and on my analysis of videotaped lessons of outstanding lecturers. These strategies will be elaborated in this chapter.

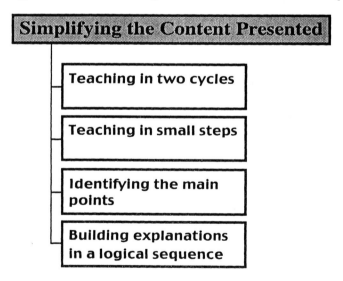

Figure 10-1: Dimensions of Simplifying the Content Presented

---

[42] See Chapter 9: Research on Components of Clarity in Teaching.

TEACHING IN TWO (OR MORE) CYCLES: FIRST OR CONCURRENTLY PRESENTING A SIMPLIFIED VERSION

- He illustrates first solving simple examples and then goes on to complex ones.

This teaching strategy refers to starting out by presenting the easier-to-comprehend aspects of the material or a simplified version of the material, and teaching the more complex aspects only after the first stage is sufficiently understood. Once students grasp the general idea, their minds are free to cope with all the complexities presented in additional cycles. The cycles are arranged in increasing level of complexity, abstractness, and difficulty, and may not be mutually exclusive. They are not necessary ordered sequentially but may be presented concurrently, in parallel, yet integrated with one another.

The pedagogical principle of simplification through teaching in two or more cycles agrees with the view of the American Psychological Association (APA, 1997, Principle 3)[43] about the optimal ways for teaching. In this view, based on the way people process new information (see Figure 5-1), "Effective and meaningful student learning may be achieved through a continuous process of students' linking the new knowledge to their experiences and existing knowledge base. This process brings about to widening and deepening the new knowledge and to integrating it with students' prior knowledge and understanding" (ibid.). The more cycles of elaboration that take place, the greater the number of links are formed, and the deeper is the understanding of material.

This pedagogical principle has been known and used for a long time. The well-known method called the "spiral principle" (Bruner, 1960) rests on the same idea: Teach a topic in a few cycles—start with the simplest and proceed to the following ones so that each is progressively somewhat more complicated and difficult. Polya (1957, p. 114) applied this principle to problem solving. He suggested a useful procedure for heuristic solutions, as follows:

> If you cannot solve the proposed problem do not let this failure afflict you too much but try to find consolation with some easier success, *try to solve first some related problem*; then you may find courage to attack your original problem again. Do not forget that human superiority consists in going around an obstacle that cannot be overcome directly.

Polya advocates that when one is not able to see how to proceed with a problem, he/she should try to think of a familiar simpler problem that resembles the given problem; then use the method for solving the simpler problem as a plan for solving the more complicated one.

---

[43] See Chapter 4: What Makes Effective Learning? Psychological Principles.

The notion of what constitutes a simplified version of the material is highly context dependent. It depends on the discipline involved, the students in the course, and the professional expertise of the target audience, as explained below. To elaborate:

The disciplinary context: What may be regarded as simple in one discipline may be complicated in another. For example, in engineering, an applied discipline, a simpler version of a mathematics-based process would be its end result or its practical application, whereas the more complex underlying mathematical procedures would be explained only in the following cycle. On the other hand, in mathematics and physics, which are pure/theoretical domains, the simpler version may be the mathematics of some process, leaving the applied interpretations for the second cycle.

The students' context: What may be simple to understand for students of high aptitude or those having knowledge in topics similar or related to the material presented may prove to be very difficult for lower-aptitude students or for those lacking the necessary background.

The expertise context: What may be perceived as simple by experts in the subject's domain (i.e., professors), may be much more complex and difficult to understand for students. For example:

> A mathematician talks of "simplifying" a proof if he can eliminate extraneous concepts and machinery, which often means that the arguments become more refined and less obvious, and thus more difficult for the student. Or else, the didactician tries to make questions "easier" to understand by explaining the concepts, terms, variable, expression— which the classroom teacher may see as complicating the matter (Kirsch, 1976, p. 98).

Thus, a teacher who uses simplification should be well aware of what makes explanations simple in the respective discipline and should take into account the students' background knowledge and aptitudes.

Types of Simplified Versions

The simplified version of a new concept or procedure, presented in the first cycle, can be of different forms: (a) a reduced version; (b) the core notion; (c) a comparable familiar case; or (d) a visual or intuitive interpretation. These forms are not mutually exclusive, that is, some teaching strategies may belong to more than a single form.

(a) Presenting a Reduced Version

When producing a reduced version, the teacher strips the topic of its most complex aspects or of its qualifications and conditions, and presents only its simplest elements.

How to present a reduced version

In presenting a concept whose description or definition needs to be learned accurately but is hard to understand, you can start with an **inaccurate (rough) but easier-to-understand notion**, avoiding the subtleties. Only when this notion is understood, should the more accurate but complex version be presented.

In explaining a visually complex drawing, chart, diagram, picture, design, or pattern, you can first present a **simplified sketch** that includes only the layout or the main features of the drawing.

In teaching a complex verbal plot, scheme, plan, or program, you can first present the **outline or main points**.

In teaching a complex theory, you can first present a **less complex model** of the theory, either verbally or pictorially, which includes only the **main features**. Only when these features and their operations are understood, should all the other parts of the theory be added.

On presenting new material, at first use **terms and concepts familiar to students**, those that students understand with no need for translation. Only after this version is comprehended, you may repeat it using the specialized terms and concepts.

Before teaching a complicated topic, you can **lay out the teaching plan** regarding what the main steps or procedures will be, what is the aim of each, which method you will use, and what are the guiding questions. The full presentation refers to the plan each time you start a new step, to show where you are within the framework of the plan.

(b) Depicting the Core Notion

In this simplification method, the teacher starts by presenting the main idea of what is being taught.

How to depict the core notion

First, present the core notion of what is being taught: the main idea, the heart of the matter, the culmination of the topic, or the "bottom line." Or, you can start with presenting the end results: the summary, the outcomes of a process or procedure, or a targeted conclusion.

Restate and rephrase the core notion or end results several times, at different stages of the explanation. Emphasize them through variation in intonation or in speech rate, or by writing them on the board and underlining or circling them. Only after they are understood, or even applied, should the full explanation be presented. To illustrate:

- In teaching a complex theory, rule, law, or process that can be summarized in a simple short statement, you may start with this simple summary statement, explain its meaning, illustrate it with several examples, and show a few applications. Only after this heart of the matter is understood should you explain how it was arrived at, and what the full theory or rule is.

- In teaching a complex mathematical derivation that culminates in some equations, you may first present the target equations, explain their importance, the role of each term in the equation, and how to apply the equations in solving problems. You may demonstrate using them to solve several problems and assign students to solve problems on their own. Only then would you go through the full process of deriving the equations mathematically.

(c) Introducing a Comparable Familiar Case: Examples and Illustrations, Analogies and Metaphors

In this method, new knowledge is built on the students' existing knowledge by first or concurrently presenting a similar/comparable case that is familiar to them. The case can come from their life experiences, conceptions and intuitions, or prior learning. These comparable cases can be presented through examples and illustrations, analogies and metaphors, and discrepant and conflicting events (Kinnear, 1994).

Examples and Illustrations

Examples and illustrations describe some particular features of the case in an attempt to make ideas, concepts, and principles concrete to the learner. *Non-examples* are instances of cases where the theory or rule does not work. They should be raised after presenting a few examples to prevent students from developing misconceptions regarding the generalization of the theory or rule.

Research has consistently supported the notion that the use of examples is a major tool for achieving clarity in teaching. Piaget (1955) suggested that the individual becomes aware of the symbolic nature of language only gradually and that concrete understanding precedes a more abstract grasp. Indeed, most students understand an abstract concept better if they are first offered a concrete example because examples and illustrations stimulate knowledge that is already available to the students. This process lays the foundation for understanding the more abstract, unfamiliar concepts to be learned. Smith (1978), after rating videotaped classroom teaching of college professors on overall clarity and on a list of clarity behaviors, found that the behavior most highly related to overall teaching clarity was: "Uses examples with explicit referents." Similarly, Hines (1982) found "Uses examples when explaining" as one of the behaviors most discriminating between clear and unclear university teachers. Observers of university lessons, who rated the frequency of use of 60 components of classroom teaching behaviors, identified "Giving multiple examples" as one of the most powerful discriminators of overall teacher effectiveness (Murray, 1983). Highly effective teachers gave examples significantly more frequently than less effective teachers. Benz and Blatt (1994) asked university students to explain in writing why they rated their teachers on the standard rating questionnaire as they did. One of the most frequent explanations for rating teachers high on teaching clarity was that "the instructor used examples." These students' comments present the importance of examples for achieving teaching clarity and effectiveness:

- She makes a difficult course understandable through carefully chosen examples.
- Excellent lecturer. Brings along many illustrations from daily life and from the natural world.
- Her examples strike students as being real, they provide a rich picture, and look valid.
- Boring! Should bring more concrete examples.
- We didn't do enough examples in class so we were lost on homework.

Analogies and Metaphors

- She makes the material juicy by presenting illustrations and analogies.
- His examples and the analogies he draws to other fields of study are helpful in visualization.

The use of analogies and metaphors is little valued by higher-education teachers as beneficial for student learning. In a survey of 93 university lecturers regarding 40 properties of explaining (Brown & Daines, 1981), analogies and metaphors were chosen as two of the ten least valuable for student learning. Science and medicine faculty rated analogies higher than art and social science lecturers, and vice versa regarding the rating of metaphors. Let us begin with analogies.

Analogies
Sara: Jacob, you've got to come over! I've taught my dog to sing the national anthem...
Jacob: Well, let's hear it!
Sara: Come on, Fido! Sing the anthem...
Fido: Howw, howw!
Jacob: Where's the anthem?
Sara: I said I taught him; I didn't say he learned it!

This anecdote assumes that teaching can occur even if learning does not. Opponents of this assumption liken the teaching-learning interaction to that of selling-buying. We would not say that somebody sells unless another person buys, that is, if there is no buying, there is no selling. Similarly, these opponents reject the above definition saying that if there is no learning, there is no teaching. This comparison is essentially an analogy: The teacher corresponds to the seller, and the student to the buyer. An additional example is that of cataloging a book for storage in a library as an analogy to the process of cognitively storing information in long-term memory.

Analogy is defined in Webster's Dictionary[44] as, "A comparison between things essentially or generically different but strikingly alike in one or more pertinent aspects" or "Resemblance in some particulars between things otherwise unlike; similarity, correspondence, parallelism." In the example above, cataloging a book resembles storage in one's memory in that both are characterized by finding a relevant place for stockpiling and creating connections to other related topics. Otherwise, both are very dissimilar. The "thing" that functions as the basis for the analogy, as the familiar element in the comparison, is called the *source,* whereas the "thing" that is being explained or learned through drawing the analogy is called the *target.* In the library analogy, the library is the source whereas long-term memory is the target. An analogical relation is symmetrical, so that the source and target may switch roles. Therefore, using an analogy is essentially a two-way process that involves interchanges between sources and targets.

In using analogy in teaching, the teacher first identifies the source and target and then establishes the correspondence between them through an *analogy elaboration* process. This process is presented as a map-and-analyze cycle, in which the source and target are situated, followed by comparison, problem solving, and inference production. Analogy elaboration is an iterative process of hypothesis formation, testing, and revision. In the said library example, analogy elaboration involves explaining how cataloging a book in a library is actually performed so as to facilitate its retrieval by linking it to its various identifiers (keywords); The source is then compared to storing information in long-term memory.

A large body of research has been conducted on the use of analogies in science teaching. An entire issue of the *Journal of Research in Science Teaching* (Vol. 30, No. 10, 1993) was dedicated to this topic. The main results of these studies suggested that analogical reasoning facilitates comprehension and problem solving when learning science in the pre-college level.

However, the use of analogies in teaching is not automatically beneficial. Analogies were found to fail when the students: (a) were not familiar with the source domain or had erroneous ideas about it; (b) did not properly understand the relations between the source and the target; and (c) were not

---

[44] Different editions and versions of this dictionary give the same or similar definitions.

able to draw conclusions from the analogy regarding the target domain (ibid.).

How to select the analogy type

When planning to use analogies in teaching, you can consider three types of analogies:

Analogy with the source and target in the same domain. Such an analogy compares two phenomena in the same field. To illustrate, in mathematics and any mathematics-based field, a source for an analogy of a two- or three-dimensional equation or graph is a one-dimensional equation or graph of the same type, one that students already know. The binary (base 2) number system can be taught as the target of an analogy whose source is the very familiar decimal (base 10) system.

Analogy with the source and target in different domains. This analogy compares the new notion or procedure to some notion or procedure taken from a different domain. To illustrate, an analogy compares electrical induction (the target, taught in an electricity course), to the harmonic oscillator (the source) which students have already learned in a mechanics course.

Analogy based on students' life experiences. This type of analogy compares the new material to features and phenomena that are familiar to students from life experiences. For example, in the analogy of storing books in the library to information storage in long-term memory, the source—books in the library—is familiar to students from life experience. Other examples are the analogy of water flowing from a higher to a lower place (a source familiar from daily life) when teaching the concept of the flow of electrons from a high to a low potential (the target—from physics), or the analogy of a child's swing (source) to an electric oscillator (target).

What steps to use in presenting an analogy

When presenting an analogy, all of the following six steps should be included: (a) introduce the target concept; (b) recall a source concept and ascertain students' existing knowledge before using it; (c) identify similar features of the two concepts; (d) map similar features; (e) draw conclusions about the concepts; and (f) indicate where the analogy breaks down, that is, identify for your students the differences between the two domains to avoid misconceptions. Differences always exist because an analogy is never based on an exact fit between the source and the target.

When selecting the source concept, beware of too big a "jump" from the source to the target, as this runs the risk that students may not be able to perceive the analogy.

To illustrate the steps in presenting an analogy, a physics professor who teaches the concept of electrical induction in an electricity course may (Step a) start by reviewing definitions and formulas related to the harmonic oscillator; (b) show the analogy between components of the formulas for the harmonic oscillator and those of electrical induction; (c) explain the similarities between the respective equations; (d) draw conclusions regarding electrical induction; and (e) indicate the differences between these two phenomena and the equations involved.

Metaphors
- The atom is a miniature solar system.
- Fractions are pieces of a pie.
- The universe, as finite but unbounded, is a sphere that expands like a balloon.
- The heart is a water pump.
- The immune system is a defense barrier, with the white blood cells soldiers fending off microscopic enemies.

All these are metaphors, but how can we characterize them? Metaphor is an implicit comparison between two concepts. Some attributes of one concept are carried over to the other, and this projection may change one's view of the second concept (Howard, 1989).

Metaphor is closely related to analogy: While analogy makes its comparison explicitly, for example, by using words such as "like," "similar to," and so forth, metaphor does so implicitly. To illustrate, each of the two metaphors "education is shepherding" and "a teacher is the captain of a ship" implicitly compares two notions: education to the role of a shepherd, and a teacher to a ship's captain. In both, the grounds for the comparison are not mentioned, and are left for the user (reader or listener) to construe or identify. The metaphor usually highlights features or relations that would usually be absurd if taken literally. They always contain some elements of surprise or provocation, and by highlighting some major dissimilarities, they incite the mind to search for similarities. This again contrasts with the analogy, which clearly indicates and stresses the identity of parts of structures. However, analogy and metaphor can transform into one another. Adding aspects of surprise and provocation to an analogy can make it a metaphor; and elaborating the comparisons may make metaphors function as analogies.

The following are some common metaphors used in teaching:

For the mathematical concept of recursive processes:

- A box of Quaker oats has a picture of a boy holding a Quaker oats box with a picture of a boy holding a Quaker oats box....
- A fisherman caught a goldfish that promised to grant him three wishes. The fisherman's third wish was that the goldfish grant him three more wishes....

For internal inconsistency:
- Bertrand Russell's barber story: In a certain village, a barber has set a rule that he only cuts the hair of those villagers who do not cut their own hair. Question: What does this barber do about cutting his own hair?

The use of metaphors in teaching is not always recommended because not all aspects of one concept may readily transfer to another and obviously because a student's existing metaphors may interfere with new learning.

(d) Presenting Visual or Intuitive Interpretations

The benefits for learning of presenting visual or intuitive interpretations of the topics are well known:

A picture is worth a thousand words.

This adage reflects the usefulness of promoting visual or intuitive understanding of the concepts at hand either before or concurrently with the formal teaching of a difficult topic. Visual representations present the concept's most salient features. In the pedagogical literature (e.g., Bruner, 1960), intuition is often related to perceptual knowledge, that is, to concrete objects, pictures, and diagrams. Only after perceptual understanding is achieved is the abstract concept presented. However, intuition can be evoked other than by visual objects. The intuitive verbal description of the topic to be studied may appeal to the students' common sense or to their direct or immediate understanding, and renders the abstract material meaningful. Experts from a wide variety of academic domains—for example, science, the arts, and economics— perceive intuitive thinking as a very important component in their respective areas, as students themselves remark:

- The instructor extrapolates to nature and our life experiences by providing physical or intuitive meaning.
- No time is spent on an intuitive understanding of what is happening.

Webster defines intuition as "quick and ready insight"; "immediate apprehension or cognition"; "the act or process of coming to direct knowledge or certainty without reasoning or inferring"; "immediate

cognizance or conviction without evident rational thought and inference";
"revelation by insight or innate knowledge"; and "immediate apprehension
or cognition." Similarly, Bruner (1960) wrote: "Intuition implies the act of
grasping the meaning, significance, or structure of a problem or situation
without explicit reliance on the analytic apparatus of one's craft." Fischbein
(1987) presented the following meanings of intuition as conceived by several
philosophers, psychologists, and educators:
- The source of true knowledge.
- A mental strategy which allows reaching the essence of phenomena.
- Cognitions that are directly grasped without, or prior to, any need for
  explicit justification or interpretation.
- An elementary, commonsense, popular, primitive form of knowledge; or,
  in contrast,
- The highest form of knowledge through which the very essence of things
  may be revealed.

Intuitive thinking differs from analytic thinking in that it does not
advance by well defined, sequential steps. Rather, the person who thinks
intuitively makes logical and cognitive leaps, skipping steps and making
shortcuts on the basis of an implicit perception of the problem to be solved.
That person arrives at a solution, either right or wrong, with little if any
awareness of the process by which it was reached. Educational literature
advocates the frequent use of intuitive devices in teaching and in the
promotion of students' intuitive understanding. Bruner (1960, p. 59)
recommended that in designing curricula, in mathematics and the sciences
particularly, it is "of the first importance to establish an intuitive
understanding of materials before we expose our students to more traditional
and formal methods of deduction and proof." Artists, mathematicians,
natural and social scientists all stress the value of intuitive thinking in their
respective areas, and teachers in these areas are encouraged to develop their
students' ability to think intuitively.

> Rolle's Theorem is in fact the Mean Value Theorem *tilted on its side...* [from a math
> lesson].

Nevertheless, intuition should be promoted with caution. Numerous
studies in science education (many of which appeared in the *Journal of
Research in Science Teaching 30*(10), 1993) have indicated that some
intuitions are based on misconceptions, and that it is very difficult at times to
replace them with the correct conceptions. A teacher should be aware of the
existence of these misconceptions and take care that students abandon them
before starting to teach the correct conceptions.

How to present visual or intuitive interpretation for promoting intuitive understanding

You may use:

Two-dimensional static representation of the topic: graphs, diagrams, drawings, or pictures.

Three-dimensional static representation of the topic: presentation or manipulation of a three-dimensional model, changing its spatial orientation (e.g., a reflection, enlargement, rotation).

Technology based static presentation: use of an overhead or slide projector to present static pictures, charts, or diagrams.

Technology based dynamic presentation: use of films, video clips, demonstrations, computer graphic presentations, or computer programs of simulations, virtual reality, and models of abstract concepts that can be visually manipulated (e.g., rotated, translated, or reflected). An abundance of computer programs of this type is now available.

Verbal intuitive description of the topic may appeal to the students' common sense or to their direct or immediate understanding and renders the abstract material meaningful.

Following the model of effective teaching dimensions presented in Figure 1-3, Figure 10-2 illustrates the breakdown of "Clarity" into four strategies.[45] These strategies may be thought of as belonging to Layer 1of the intermediate level dimensions.

As suggested in this chapter, one of these strategies—"Simplifying the material presented"—can be broken down into four strategies that form a second layer of the intermediate level dimensions. One of these sub-strategies—"Teaching in two cycles"—is further broken down in the figure into several classroom techniques that guide the teacher in what to present in the first of the two cycles.

---

[45] See Chapter 9: Figure 9-1.

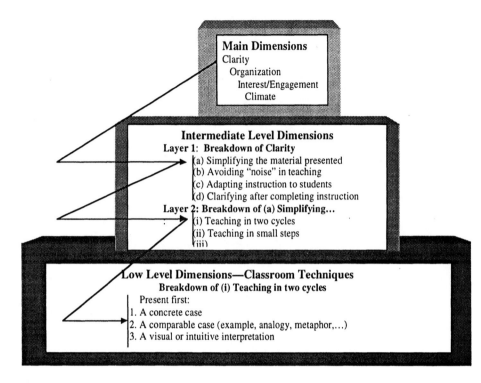

Figure 10-2: Classroom Strategies for Teaching in Two Cycles in Order to Simplify the Material Presented to Achieve Clarity in Teaching

TEACHING IN SMALL STEPS

Research at the pre-college level has established the notion that teaching step-by-step is beneficial for student learning. Effective teachers in well-structured subjects were found to present new material in small steps, with students' practicing after each step until they understand the material, before going to the next step. Well-structured subjects are those in which the objective is to master a body of knowledge or to learn a skill, such as certain aspects of mathematics, vocabulary, grammar, and science. Teaching step-by-step is particularly important when learning sequential or hierarchical material because subsequent learning builds upon well-formed prior learning. This is doubly true when the material is difficult for the learners (Rosenshine, 1986).

Current information-processing theory[46] pinpoints the limits of our working memory and the importance of elaboration and practice. This theory

---

[46] See Chapter 5: Figure 5-1

suggests that learners have a limited capacity of information that they can attend to and process effectively. When too much information is presented at once, their working memory is swamped; they then become confused and unable to complete the processing correctly (ibid.).

The limits of working memory necessitate that when teaching new or difficult material, the teacher proceeds in small steps and guarantees understanding before going on to the next step. In this way, the learner can concentrate his/her somewhat limited attention to processing manageably sized pieces of information or skills.

Breaking down a topic into small parts and teaching these parts one-by-one have also been identified to be important components of clear teaching in higher education. One of the teaching strategies discriminating between clear and unclear college teachers, as perceived by students, is "teaches step-by-step" (Hines, 1982). This strategy simplifies the explanation and helps students understand complex concepts, processes, and procedures.

How to simplify explanations

Break down a complex or long explanation/development **into several smaller steps.** Arrange the steps in a logical sequence: from familiar to unfamiliar, from easy to more difficult, or from concrete to abstract. Teach each step separately until a good level of understanding is achieved. When finished, combine all steps to show students the whole picture. The combination can be done by summarizing, overviewing, and more.

IDENTIFYING THE MAIN POINTS OF THE MATERIAL

In each lesson, the amount of information presented is very large, sometimes complex, and cannot be fully absorbed by the students. To simplify the selection of parts of this information that should be taken in and stored in the student's long-term memory, the teacher should indicate during the lesson what are the most important things to understand and retain. Research has shown that marking the importance of particular points within the material significantly discriminated between teachers of high-achieving students and teachers of low-achieving students (Pinney, 1970). The following are typical students' comments on teachers who do not provide such indications:

- It is difficult to distinguish in class which information is especially relevant or important from that which is only supplementary. Therefore, I spend most of my time writing and little time understanding what he is teaching.
- We cannot see the forest for the trees.

Teachers inform students about the main points of the material by emphasizing, repeating, and summarizing. These strategies/techniques have been shown in research to contribute to lesson clarity. For example, of the 28 behaviors that discriminate between clear and unclear university teachers identified by Hines (1982), five relate to these strategies:
- Emphasizes important points.
- Repeats things that are important.
- Tells students what they are expected to do/know.
- Stresses difficult points.
- Summarizes the material presented in class.

Emphasizing or Stressing Main Points

- All the material is presented in the same monotonous tone, and only when we read our class notes and the textbook at home do we succeed in deciphering the more important points of the lesson.

Placing emphasis on the main points alerts students to pay special attention to what is being said, thus helping them identify and remember the most important points of the message. This helps students keep the essential aspect in focus while it reduces the intrusion of non-essential details.

How to emphasize main points:

Vary your intonation. Changes in voice level and varying intonation are cues for students on the relative importance of the material presented.

Write on the board. Write definitions, theorems, or a list of main topics or major ideas. Put those of special importance in frames or encircle them.

Stress points verbally—use marking and signaling. Identify and verbally stress the main points, the most significant information in each topic. Use special phrases to emphasize topics for special qualification. Special phrases can serve as "verbal markers" of importance, difficulty, interest, usefulness, elegance, and so on. To illustrate:

Now, the important thing to remember is that...; These are two critical assumptions: ... ; Write this down! This is a very *important* application...; Pay attention to this *critical* fact...; It's *easy* to do it this way; This is the *beauty* of the theorem; The next thing we're going to see is quite *difficult*; This is a very *simple* method to solve it; Here's a very *interesting* example; It would be *beneficial* for you to understand; *Surprisingly*, both lines will get us into the same parabola; And you'll find that geometrically, this theorem is *very useful*; "Certainly...;" "We are sure that...;" "Of course we know...;" "The problem is that...;" "We're interested in...;" "Notice that...;" We must show...;" "I would stress that...;" "You should remember...;" "I claim that...;" "I do want to state ... ;" "You should write this down ...."

Repeating Important Points

Repeating the same explanation or content in the same or different words alerts students to the importance of the topic. Repetition also helps students identify the key issues within the material presented. The repetition and emphasis of main points in a conclusion, delivered at the end of lesson, have been shown to strongly relate to student achievement (Kennedy et al., 1978; Pinney, 1970; Shutes, 1970).

Summarizing the Main Points

Summarizing aids students in identifying the main points, and in organizing and clarifying the material already presented. A general summary of the main topics of the lesson usually takes place at the end of the lesson. *Micro-summaries* take place at the end of an explanation, a proof, a procedure, and so forth, when the teacher restates the rule, the theorem, or the result/conclusion of what has been presented up to that point. For example:

So let's review what we have talked about so far. We have talked about functions, and that every function has a domain, and a range... Now we need to add a third thing ...

Up to now, the three cases that we have counted ...

BUILDING THE CONTENT PRESENTED IN A COHERENT, LOGICAL SEQUENCE

A good way to simplify students' perception of the topic and thus to promote their understanding, is to arrange the ideas presented in some ordered sequence that gradually builds toward a conclusion, without skipping steps or digressing to unrelated topics. Material that is presented with logical internal connections can be stored and retrieved as a single chunk, which simplifies its understanding and retrieval. On the other hand, presenting ideas in a way which lacks logical development makes it difficult for the students to follow the line of thought (Jones, 1979). Hines (1982) found that of 28 teacher behaviors that discriminated between clear and unclear university teachers, "Presents content in a logical manner" was second in discriminating power. The behavior "Sequencing topics and subtopics in a hierarchy" was found to increase comprehension and retention of the material presented (Eylon & Reif, 1979). Cruickshank (1985, p. 44) described logical progression as one of the four behaviors most central to achieving clarity:

> Clear teachers, as opposed to unclear teachers, are consistently concerned that their students understand. They try to ensure understanding by providing students with appropriate opportunities to learn, utilizing abundant illustrations and examples, logically organizing and reviewing the material to be learned, and assessing student learning.

Evans and Guymon (Evans & Guymon, 1978) presented to each of two groups of university psychology students a different videotaped version of the same teacher teaching the same content. The versions differed on two clarity behaviors: (a) appropriate/inappropriate use of examples, and (b) good/poor logical sequencing of instruction. The version combining the appropriate use of examples and good logical sequencing significantly correlated with student achievement on a test and with their satisfaction from instruction, whereas the other version did not show such correlations. Students become very disconcerted when lecturers skip steps in a sequence, in proofs, developments, or explanations; or when they leave out pieces of information for students to fill in themselves without clear guidance on how to do this. Teachers who make frequent errors or "jump around" in their presentations, confuse students and diminish their capacity to learn (Jones, 1979). Therefore, teachers should refrain from skipping material unless the gaps are clearly marked and explained, and they should also coherently tie together the different ideas in the presentation. A coherent presentation concentrates on the main line of thought, and flows smoothly from one idea or step to the logically next one (ibid.).

Students tend to bitterly complain about teachers who present material without a logical, coherent progression:

- The teacher was hard to understand, moved very fast and skipped steps that were not obvious.
- Occasionally in his lectures he skips several steps in the interest of time, but then the class is lost as to how to solve the problems on their own.
- Too many jumps from idea to idea which makes it difficult to understand.
- This particular teacher seems to pride himself on announcing he didn't prepare the lecture and he launches a random attack on the material, jumping around from idea to idea and from board to board, which makes the lecture impossible to follow.
- She didn't make the connections between the different concepts very clear and I rarely understood the lectures.

In contrast, teachers who do maintain logic, coherence, and smoothness of explanation receive positive comments:

- He ties everything in together in a coherent way, thus making comprehension easier.
- Doesn't get bogged down in unnecessary detail. Gets to the heart of the problem and the principles to be understood.
- Very good in showing all steps.

Proper use of transitions (transitional phrases) is necessary to achieve continuity from one topic to another, that is, to increase coherence and smoothness. A transition is a word, phrase, sentence, or paragraph that indicates the relationship between what has been said, what is being said, and what will be said. Examples of transitions are linking words like: and, but, also. Examples for transitional phrases are: in addition, consequently, however, therefore, nevertheless, despite the fact that, finally, and so forth. Thompson (1967) found that adding transitions to oral messages increased comprehension and retention.

SUMMARY

Simplification or "elementarization" is a major strategy for achieving clarity in teaching. It facilitates the understanding of new material by reducing the complexity of the explanation while avoiding the lowering of cognitive requirements, that is, without decreasing the level or extent of understanding to be achieved by the learner. The following are four strategies for achieving simplification:

1. Teaching in two (or more) cycles: First or concurrently presenting a simplified version. In this method, the explanation goes through at least two cycles. The first cycle presents a simplified version of the new concept or procedure, a reduced form of the notion to be explained that has been stripped of qualifications and conditions. Once students have the general idea, their minds are able to cope with all the details and qualifiers presented in the next cycle more effectively. The cycles are not necessarily sequential and may also be presented concurrently, in parallel, or integrated with one another. The notion of what makes a simplified version depends on the context, such as the discipline involved or the students in the course. The simplified version may be: a rough notion; a verbally simplified description; the core notion or end result; a plan for action; a comparable case that is already familiar to students either from their life experiences, their conceptions and intuitions, or their prior learning (i.e., an example, an illustration, an analogy, a metaphor, or discrepant and conflicting events); or a visual or intuitive interpretation such as presenting a graph, chart, diagram, drawing, video clip, animation, picture, or physical model of the concept or procedure to be explained.

Analogies and metaphors, examples, illustrations, and tools for promoting intuition support constructivist learning[47] by connecting new knowledge to what is already available or easily perceived by students. These devices help teachers simplify the material presented by serving as the first, simpler step in the teaching of a new complex concept; they adapt the material to the students by making it relevant to their prior background knowledge and life experiences; and they make the presentation more interesting by maintaining students' attention.

In spite of all their expected benefits, research showed only little value for the use of analogies and metaphors for student learning.

Analogy is a comparison between the structures of two domains: the "source" and the "target." An analogical relation is symmetrical, so that source and target may switch roles. After identifying the source and target, the correspondence between these two should be presented through an *analogy elaboration* process. For analogies to facilitate student understanding, it is crucial to ascertain students' existing knowledge of the source domain, to avoid too big a "jump" from the source to the target, and to help students draw conclusions from the analogy in the target domain.

Metaphor is an implicit comparison between two concepts. Some attributes of one concept are carried over to the other, and this projection may change one's view of the second concept. Metaphors are closely related to analogies, but the grounds for the comparison are not explicitly mentioned and are left for the user to construe or identify. The metaphor always contains some elements of absurdity, surprise, or provocation.

Promoting intuition. Educational literature advocates the promotion of students' intuitive understanding. Intuitive thinking differs from analytic thinking in that it does not advance by well-defined and sequential steps. One should be aware that some intuitions that students bring from their daily experience are based on misconceptions, and it is very difficult at times to replace them with correct conceptions. A teacher should be aware of the existence of these misconceptions and know how to handle them before starting to teach the correct conceptions.

2. Teaching in small steps. Breaking down a topic into small parts and teaching them one-by-one has been identified in research as an important component of clarity in teaching. The teacher may teach each of these steps

---

[47] See Chapter 4: Constructivist Learning Theory

separately until a good level of understanding is achieved. Only then are all steps combined and students shown the larger/full picture.

3. Informing students about the main points of the material. The teacher indicates the most important things to understand and retain throughout the lesson. Toward this aim, teachers use the techniques of emphasizing, repeating, and summarizing.

4. Building explanations in a coherent, logical sequence. Coherence is important for making smooth connections between the topics being taught. The coherent lecture flows smoothly and logically from one topic to the next, neither skipping intermediate steps nor getting sidetracked to irrelevant material. The topics in a lesson or the ideas within one topic should be arranged to gradually build to a final conclusion. The teacher should make explicit on what basis the ideas have been arranged. Maintaining continuity between one statement and the next requires proper use of transitions. Transitions contribute also to clarification of the relationships among, and to marking relative importance of these statements.

Chapter 11

Avoiding "Noise" in Teaching

Professor Smith introduces many clarity-promoting behaviors in his classroom teaching. He always presents examples, either before or after explaining a new concept; encourages students to ask questions and willingly answers these questions; summarizes the material; repeats important or difficult points; and emphasizes main concepts and topics. He presents the material step-by-step in a logical progression and adjusts the pace to the students' assimilation rate. Every so often, he asks questions to gauge student understanding, and he pauses for the students to digest difficult points. He uses analogies and metaphors, explains things simply, and gives many examples and illustrations. Does using all these clarity-promoting behaviors necessarily make Professor Smith's a clear teacher?

Let us consider Professor Smith's other classroom behaviors. His sentences are long and complex, and he mumbles and stammers slightly. He writes on the chalkboard with one hand and promptly erases it with the other, not leaving students much of an opportunity to read the written text. His handwriting on the board is small and hard to read, and he often talks with his back to the class, which makes it difficult to hear what he says. He frequently digresses from the central topic, or makes errors in computations or in formulas. He does not deal with students who chat loudly in class, distracting others. Considering these behaviors, should Professor Smith still be perceived as a clear teacher?

The first set of behaviors described above are a necessary but insufficient condition for clear teaching. For clarity, it is essential that the teacher reduce to minimum behaviors of the kind described in the second set, entitled "noise-inducing behaviors." These behaviors disrupt students' attention; distract them from the core aspects of explanations; increase their doubt, conflict, or confusion; and eventually reduce their capacity to follow the presentation and learn the material. It is probably impossible for a teacher to totally refrain from producing any noise-related behaviors. In effect, the presence of these behaviors in small doses and low frequencies does not substantially reduce clarity. Noise behaviors impede learning only when their frequency crosses a certain threshold, that is, when the noise is "turned up too loud."

STUDIES OF NOISE IN TEACHING

Studies of the relationship between noise in teaching and student learning have used mostly experimental methods (Hiller et al., 1969; Kennedy et al., 1978; Land & Smith, 1979; Land & Smith, 1981; Smith & Land, 1980a). In one type of study, the same teacher presented the same learning content to several groups of students, while varying types and degrees of noise. The different versions were videotaped and students' performance on the same posttest for the different noise versions was compared. In another type of study, different teachers taught the same content to different groups of students. Their lessons were videotaped, transcribed, and analyzed for noise behaviors. Again, students' learning was examined by a posttest. The findings across the studies consistently produced a negative relationship between the frequency of noise-related behaviors and student achievement and satisfaction from instruction. That is, the higher the noise, the lower the students' achievement and satisfaction. We may conclude that noise behaviors reduce student understanding and learning.

DIMENSIONS OF NOISE BEHAVIOR IN TEACHING

How does teachers' noise behavior interfere with student understanding and learning? On the basis of the theory of information processing,[48] we may sort the negative effects of noise behaviors into four main categories:
1. Noise disrupting hearing and listening comprehension.
2. Noise disrupting seeing and visual comprehension.
3. Noise disrupting making sense of the information already absorbed (noise in the logic of presentation).
4. Noise reducing internal motivation to take in and process information (internal noise).
The first two categories interrupt the information's entry through the senses, whereas the two latter categories disrupt the stage of initial

---

[48] See Chapter 5: Advantage of the Lecture in Promoting Information Processing

processing of the information. Figure 11-1 presents these categories, which are elaborated in the following sections.

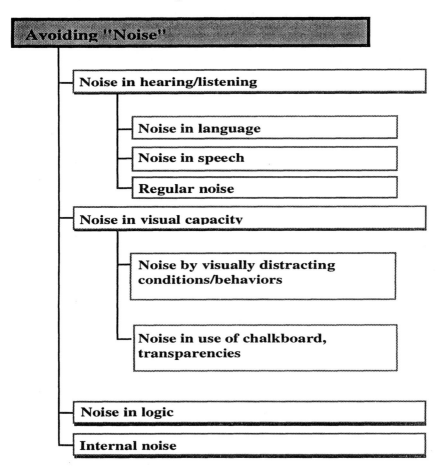

Figure 11-1: Dimensions of "Noise" in Teaching

Noise Disrupting Hearing and Listening

Noise that reduces hearing capacity and listening comprehension consists of anything that interferes with students' ability to hear the teacher, listen to his/her speech, and interpret it. It also relates to anything that students hear which distracts them from concentrating on the material presented, such as noise in language, speech, and in daily life.

Noise in Language

Noise in language is caused mainly by two factors:

Speaking in written language. Generally, speech communication experts argue that spoken language differs from written language. Sentences in spoken language are shorter and more succinct, and they use simpler vocabulary, more familiar words, more personal references (e.g., "I"), and more repetitions and redundancy than do written sentences. Therefore, using written language while speaking, as in reading lectures aloud from notes, gets in the way of listening comprehension.

Presenting vague content. Vague content may hinder the listener's ability to follow the presentation and may make it difficult to understand the content. Vagueness here is defined as incomplete verbal information resulting from approximation, lack of assurance, and ambiguity in the intended meaning. Approximation and lack of assurance convey to the listener that the teacher is not well prepared for the lesson and cannot remember or does not thoroughly know or understand the material he/she teaches (Smith & Land, 1980a).

How to avoid noise in language

Use spoken rather than written language. Use simple vocabulary, familiar words, personal references, and redundancy. Do not read from written material.

Use succinct, short, and simple sentences. Reduce the number of clauses and commas in a sentence, and avoid excessive verbosity—the use of unnecessary words.

Use language that is conversational rather than formal.

Use language that is meaningful for the students.

Avoid vague content. Vagueness-related words and phrases to be particularly avoided are:

- Ambiguous designations (e.g., all of this, things, somewhere, somehow, other people).
- Negated intensifiers (e.g., not all, not many, not very).
- Approximation (e.g., about as, almost, pretty much, somewhat, sort of, mostly).
- Error admission (excuse me, not sure, maybe I made an error).
- Intermediate quantification (a bunch, a couple, few, some, several, various).
- "Bluffing" (e.g., to make a long story short, anyway, as you all know, of course).
- Possibility (e.g., may, might, chances are, could be, perhaps).
- Probability (e.g., probably, sometimes, ordinarily, often, frequently, in general, usually).

Noise in Speech

Clear speech is essential for listening comprehension:

- His language is easy to understand and he has a loud, clear, modulated voice.

By the same token, unclear speech diminishes understanding:

- It is hard to follow and understand what he says. He mumbles most of the time.
- Her resonant, semi-monotone voice makes listening difficult and puts people to sleep even if the material presented is interesting.
- He has this horrible way of saying "umm" or "OK, uhh" all the time which affects the clarity of his lectures.
- We need an amplifier to hear her. She also swallows words and speaks to the blackboard.
- The biggest problem in his class is to be able to reserve a good place in the lecture room so that we can hear him.
- He talks to himself with his back to the class.

These students' comments identify problems of mumbling, unintelligible speech, a resonant and monotone voice, a difficult-to-hear voice, and unpleasant utterances or vocalizations.

How to avoid noise in speech

Speak clearly. Clear speech consists of the following factors:

Articulation: clear pronunciation, neither mumbling nor speaking in a husky or hoarse manner.

Smoothness: smooth, fluent, easy-going speech, without staccato bursts.

Breathing: silent or barely audible inhalations occurring at the ends of major phrases rather than noisy inhalations in the middle of sentences.

Distinct utterance of words fully facing the class. It is much easier for students to listen and to hear teacher's speech in these conditions.

Speak pleasantly. Speak in a listener-friendly mode, in the optimal conditions for listening. Pleasant speech fluctuates and maintains attention, thus preventing boredom. It consists of the following factors:

Pitch: ranging melodically between high and low tones rather than using merely one or two notes monotonously, neither being too low and deeply resonant, nor too high and shrill.

Inflection: emphasizing some words or sentences more than others.

Variation: occasional changes in the volume, rate, and pitch of voice.

Relaxation: tone of voice that imposes a sense of comfort.

Speak at a proper rate—neither so rapidly as to make it difficult to follow, nor so slowly as to make it boring to listen and cause drowsiness.

Speak at a proper volume—loud enough to be heard from the back of the classroom but not so loud as to make listening uncomfortable.

Speak fluently. Verbal non-fluency is caused by verbal disruptions that distract listeners from the content of the lecture, thus decreasing their understanding. As these disruptions do not provide any additional meaning, they cause noise that hinders fast and clear processing of the meaning of a statement. Avoid the following most frequent verbal disruptions:

Avoid large proportion of clauses: The larger their number, the greater the frequency of disruptive structures.

Avoid vagueness in speech caused by using an excessive proportion of words that indicate haziness and ambiguity such as:

- Hesitation in speech: Hesitation consists of verbal mazes—words or groups of words that either show hesitation (e.g., oh, eh, uh, umm, ahh, ur); a tangle of words; a false start; or redundantly repeated words.
- Redundant, repeated words, a kind of stammering, for example, "If we look at, at, at the theorem ...," or "And the, and the, the derivative is...."
- Vague expressions, not belonging to the explanation, such as: "You know," "Let's say" (as in the sentence, "We haven't had it, let's say, in the book.")
- False starts of sentences, halts in speech, and any unit of discourse that does not make semantic sense (mazes), for example, "It equals to, it's got to be...," or "There might be, it might look like..."

Avoid errors in word pronunciation, sentence structure, or grammar. All these communicate to students that the teacher is not confident in his/her knowledge and understanding of the material, probably because he/she is not well prepared for the lesson or has a low command of the material for some other reason.

Avoid making distracting sounds: frequent clearing of the throat, other annoying vocalizations, squeaky shoes as you pace about, squeaky chalks when you write on the board, and so forth.

Use pauses. Pause after each difficult step to allow students some breathing space in which to think, digest, complete their notes, and ask questions.

Take care that each student who speaks up in the lesson is heard by the other students. When the student who speaks is not heard by the other students, repeat clearly aloud and in your own words what the student said. Otherwise, you may be perceived as communicating with that particular student whereas all others, feeling excluded, may attend to other issues meanwhile.

Regular Noise

* The class is very noisy, students are chattering but he doesn't care and continues to teach in spite of the impossible conditions.

Regular noise during a lesson decreases students' ability to hear what the teacher says and may distract their attention from the lesson content. Disruptions can come from either outside or inside class.

How to avoid regular noise

Check the classroom conditions in advance. Are there creaking chairs, knocking windows and doors? Take care of those noise problems that you can control. During the lesson, try to reduce noise caused by students' chatting by making the lesson interesting and engaging.

Try to take care of noise from sources outside class such as typewriters, telephones, and chats in the corridors, among others.

Stop talking when students' chatter is too noisy and find out what is the reason for noise. Pose questions to identify student understanding, encourage students to ask if they do not understand, and pause to enable students clarify their notes with their neighbors.

Visual "Noise"

* The handout notes were hard to follow.
* Her transparencies were unintelligible.

The visual presentation should be clear to the audience. Noise affecting students' visual capacity and comprehension comprises any visual stimulus that diminishes their ability to concentrate on the lesson content; to watch the teacher and whatever he/she does, shows, or writes; and to interpret it. This type of noise may be caused by improper use of the chalkboard or other audiovisual devices, repeated nervous movements, or a garment whose irregular design or unusual colors averts students' attention from the content presented.

How to avoid visual noise

Four sources for visual noise may be identified: (a) general noise; (b) noise in use of the chalkboard; (c) noise in use of transparencies and other visual devices, and (d) noise in class demonstrations.

(a) Avoiding general visual noise

Attend to visually distracting classroom conditions in advance. Take care of an overly shiny chalkboard, insufficient lighting of the chalkboard, or too dark a room.

Avoid visually distracting behaviors. Do not stride rapidly back and forth in front of the class for a long time, do not clean the board with your bare hands, and do not fiddle continuously with your glasses.

Maintain a pleasant and correct appearance. Dress in a way that will not distract student attention—not too shabby or provocative, not in eccentric colors or styles, and so forth.

(b) Avoiding noise in use of the chalkboard

Here are several students' remarks on improper chalkboard techniques:

- His blackboard organization is a disaster—he jumps from corner to corner when doing a problem that makes it impossible to follow the solution.
- She writes too fast on the chalkboard and skips steps so that all the time I lose connection with what she writes.
- She writes with one hand and after one second erases with the other hand. We can't follow or take notes.
- Her lectures are presented to the blackboard. She stands in front of what she is writing and won't step aside until she has completely finished a problem, and in this process the students get completely lost.

These comments suggest that improper blackboard techniques interfere with students' ability to follow and understand the material during the lesson and to take notes in class. On the other hand, a teacher with a good chalkboard technique is highly appreciated by students:

- She writes figures extremely neatly and easily understandable. Super diagrams.

How to use the chalkboard effectively, while avoiding visual noise

Write and draw legibly and large enough to be seen from the back of the classroom.

Draw aesthetically appealing graphs, drawings, and charts, and mark all legends clearly and meaningfully.

Explain the components of graphs and drawings—what each axis of a coordinate system stands for, what each element in a graph means.

Keep illustrations, diagrams, and summaries simple, brief and readable from the back of the class. Give the audience enough time to view them and, if necessary, to copy them. If the illustrations are available in a book, give the full reference. While the class is looking at the illustration, tell them what to look for.

Use colors functionally—use the same color to emphasize similar figures and different colors to show differences.

Use good organization and placement of the writing so that the materials have continuity:

- Divide the board by vertical lines into wide columns.
- Start to write from the upper left corner of the left column going down the column until it is full, move to the next column to the right, and so on. When you arrive at the right-most column, erase the left-most column and continue from there.
- Use the column on the extreme right for summarizing important points, rules, and formulas that need to stay on the blackboard throughout the whole lesson.

Prepare your organization of the board in advance. If you face difficulties in keeping well organized during the lesson, you may plan chalkboard organization in advance by writing everything on paper beforehand.

Mark important points by putting them in rectangular frames, by use of color, or by use of a different letter size or type.

Do not erase the board too soon after writing on it.

Erase the board well, leaving it clean.

Avoid blocking the students' view of what you write on the board or of what you demonstrate.

(c) Avoiding noise in visual presentations when using transparencies, when printed handouts, and visual devices

Use these visual presentations particularly in the following cases:

- When you do not have a legible handwriting.
- When you do not draw adequately.
- When the drawings you use are too complex and too time consuming to perform on the board in class.
- When you want to exhibit texts, pictures, or graphs taken from sources unavailable to students in class.
- When you do not have an appropriate board in your classroom.

Use visual aids effectively:

Do not use them **excessively.**

Clearly indicate which features of the material to look for while using visual aids.

Pose questions to students while they are watching the visual aid to ascertain that they understand its content, encourage a brief discussion afterwards, and then summarize the main points and link them to the relevant parts of the lecture.

Using transparencies

The use of transparencies on an overhead projector is a distinct communicational medium. Therefore, you should not design transparencies using principles of book design but concentrate instead on making them "eye-friendly." Most of the above effective chalkboard techniques are relevant to transparencies. The following are additional ideas.

How to effectively design transparencies

Use clear, readable text. Printed text is preferable to handwriting.

Present information in a systematic and organized way, with headings, sub-headings, numbering, and so forth.

Include uncommon, unexpected, or humorous elements: a humorous drawing or saying, or a striking visual illustration of the topic, among others.

Introduce variety in the elements presented: integrate text and drawings, pictures, fonts of different sizes and types, and several forms of emphasis (e.g., underline, frame, use color). But do not distract with exaggerated variety.

Write and draw in an aesthetic, properly spaced, and optimally sized form so that the writing or drawing can be seen from the very back of the classroom.

Provide only skeletal information on the transparencies. Write only a portion of the explanation, only the main points, or only headings and subheadings, leaving a lot of space to write comments or add drawings.

How to effectively use transparencies

Do not overuse transparencies, for example, for presenting all the lesson material, or throughout the whole lesson.

Use the transparencies dynamically, as if they were a chalkboard. Write and draw on them, adding complementing information as you speak and the topic develops. Mark on them important points while you talk—by writing, drawing, underlining, enclosing in frames, and using color.

Reveal the information in stages rather than presenting all of it at once (if needed). You may do this by covering parts of the transparency and uncovering them when you talk, by writing on the transparency, or by using special presentation software in which the information appears step by step.

Don't stick to the overhead projector but rather step aside and walk around when you talk about the transparencies' content. Point to them directly at times and at other times point at their projection on the screen.

How to effectively design handouts

All the ideas listed for effective transparencies, except the last two, are relevant also for the design of handouts.

(d) Avoiding noise in class demonstrations

Practice the presentation in advance.

Explain, when you start, the aim of the demonstration and the steps of performance you are going to take, or draw a rough illustration on the board.

Give a simple explanation for each step as you proceed throughout the demonstration.

Observe students throughout to make sure your pace is not too fast or too slow.

Summarize the demonstration at its end or assign students to do this.

After completing the demonstration, explain again the underlying concepts and how the demonstration illustrates them. Draw a picture/scheme of the demonstration on the board, and review the key points with the class.

Noise in the Logic of the Content Presented

• She should exclude all unnecessary information. The necessary info is hard enough to deal with, without separating it from things that don't matter.

Noise in the logic of the content presented interferes with students' capacity to process and make sense of the information already taken in. This kind of noise is created when the teacher presents the material using a logically faulty structure. Numerous factors that may damage the logic of the presentation were identified in studies by Huh (1986) and Needels (1984), as next listed.

How to avoid noise in the logic of the content presented

Avoid the following:

Irrelevance. Avoid presenting irrelevant or nonessential content.

Errors. Come very well prepared to class, with a thorough knowledge and understanding of the material you plan to teach. This will help you to avoid making errors. If you err, promptly acknowledge your error and correct it.

Apologetic expressions like: excuse me, not sure, maybe I made an error.

Gaps in explanations, definitions, and descriptions.

Incomplete explanations. When explaining a new, complicated concept, present all its properties, and be careful not to omit any necessary information.

Logically incorrect causal relationships. Present cause-and-effect relations accurately and correctly: present all necessary assumptions; avoid attributing a cause to the wrong factor, reversing the order of the relationships, omitting essential premises, or mentioning the result—the effect—while giving only partial causes or none at all.

In addition:

Explain unfamiliar words, terms, or technical notations. Explain the meaning of each term in a development; each element in a graph, a table, a pictorial illustration, a demonstration, and where it comes from.

Show how the examples or illustrations that you present support the concept taught.

The following is especially relevant student's comment:

○ He presents the material in an extremely disorganized way. It is impossible to understand from his presentation what causes what, what results from what.

Avoid negative/unclear transitions:

Using thrusts —interrupting the flow of the lesson with an irrelevant announcement.

Using dangles—starting one activity, only to leave it in suspended animation for completion after other relevant stimuli are attended to.

Incoherence. Avoid discourse in which the meaning expressed in a sentence or a paragraph is not connected well with the meaning of what follows or precedes it, so that the statement, as a whole, creates confusion. Avoid improper use of linking words—*and, or, but, so*—and of transitions.

Inconsistency. Avoid statements that inadvertently contradict a previous argument or statement; avoid accidental shifts in the meaning of terms in mid-argument; avoid accepting student responses that are inconsistent with, or non-responsive to, your original question.

Contradiction. Avoid making self-contradicting or semantically anomalous statements.

Vague intentions—rationalize (as next explained).

Let students to decide. You may present the pros and cons for each of several options and ask your students to vote on each to make them feel that they are partners in decision making regarding instruction.

Internal "Noise"

Internal noise refers to all factors associated with the students themselves that diminish their motivation to study or decrease in some other way their capacity to concentrate on the lesson content. These factors may relate to students' physical or mental condition, such as fatigue, personal problems, or low motivation. A student who comes to class tired or in a bad mood due to some personal problems may face difficulties in concentrating. The teacher should create a positive classroom climate for listening to help students overcome their internal noise, stay open to input, and develop and maintain intrinsic motivation to listen and learn.[49]

Rationalizing/Explaining Decisions and Intentions in Teaching

Taking actions and decisions in teaching (e.g., why topics are taught in a certain way or order), without explaining them to the students may create confusion and frustration. Such actions can promote "internal noise." Rationalizing intentions and decisions in teaching helps students comprehend the progression of the topics and conclude what to study at home in order to compensate for the material that was skipped in the lecture. The following comments illustrate how important rationalizing teaching intentions is for the student:

- It is important for us that he clarifies why we need this material for our learning.

---

[49] See Chapter 16

- He always explains the background, like why are we doing this, and what is it used for. These explanations help me understand the material.

- Although some of the examples and explanations are clear, the context in which they were introduced is unclear.

The following are several illustrations of how teachers have rationalized their teaching decisions:[50]

We make these assumptions for historical reasons.

We'll introduce the theorem here even though it won't be used completely until sometime later in the course. It is an important theorem and it has several practical applications.

I'm not going to give an analytic proof because you can find it in your textbook, and it's more important to understand the theorem in terms of the geometry, the graphical meaning.

I'm going to discuss this topic because it will be helpful to you in your homework assignments.

Let's solve some problems in order to be sure that you did get the material.

The theorem is stated in this form and not in the other form because of the usefulness of this form in applications.

How to overcome internal "noise"

Demonstrate interest in and caring for students by personalizing the classroom environment—call students by name, ask for frequent feedback from students, use personal e-mail, and so forth.

Make classroom material "listenable" through a variety of techniques designed to maintain students' engagement and interest level. Make the most of your communication strengths: dynamism, interactive abilities, personableness/ rapport, humor, drama, storytelling, analogies, enthusiasm for the subject, organization, clarity, and ability to pinpoint areas of confusion. Some of these techniques are:

Relate the material you present to students' life experiences.

Use stories, examples, and anecdotes for illustration.

Interact with your students and **activate** them in other ways.

Move around the room and particularly in the students' sitting area to increase teacher-student contact.

---

[50] Taken from transcriptions of mathematics lessons (Hativa, 1983).

Avoid the common pitfalls that cause students to stop listening and tune out:

— **Avoid lowering your credibility** by transmitting the feeling that the way you present the information might not be optimal or that what you're saying might not really be important to all of the students, that is, that you expect some of the students, at least, not to listen.

— **Prevent "emotional deafness."** Avoid emotionally charged words or phrases, as this can cause students to switch off; do not insult students; show respect to everybody; avoid racist, sexist, or religiously slanted comments.

Explain your intentions, actions and decisions in teaching: explain your selection of topics, problems, and techniques for solution before or while you take the specific instructional steps. It is always a good practice to rationalize your decisions and explain them to students whenever you select to emphasize in class and teach in depth particular topics and skip others in the textbook, when you change the order of material from that in the book, when you assign particular readings or other types of homework, and so forth.

SUMMARY

Behaviors that promote clarity in teaching are a necessary but insufficient condition for clear teaching. To be perceived as a clear teacher, it is essential that the teacher reduces to a minimum noise-inducing behaviors—those which disrupt students' attention; distract them from the core elements of explanations; diminish their concentration; lead to their doubt, conflict, or confusion; and eventually reduce their capacity to follow the presentation and to understand and learn the material.

Noise-inducing behaviors are sorted here into four main categories that negatively affect students:

1. Capacity for hearing and listening comprehension—noise in language, in speech, and regular noise;

2. Capacity for seeing and visual comprehension—general visual noise, noise in use of the chalkboard, noise in use of transparencies, printed handouts, and other visual devices, and noise in class demonstrations;

3. Capacity to process and make sense of the information already taken in, caused by noise in the logic of the content presented.

4. Internal motivation to take in and process information

A teacher should reduce to a minimum all types of noise-inducing behaviors.

Chapter 12

Adapting Teaching to Students

What can one conclude from the following authentic comments of university students about their teachers?

- The professor tried to go too much in depth, too difficult and abstract material. This is an introductory course, not an advanced one.
- He doesn't understand our needs nor is he sensitive to our problems.
- She dwells on easy topics and speeds up on difficult ones.
- He gives examples that are too easy and does not explain difficult problems.
- She does not relate the material to our lives.
- Could really push us more, toward more complex and critical thinking.
- He is immersed in theory while we are struggling to learn practical applications because that is what we are graded on.
- Too easy course, material too simple.

These comments describe university professors who do not adjust their teaching to their students. They base their teaching on knowledge that students do not have and present the material at a pace and level that are either too slow and easy, or too fast and difficult for the students to understand. Indeed, a survey (File, 1984) found that lecturers' improper speed of presentation, inability to communicate, and wrong assumptions about students' prior knowledge were among the major reasons cited by first year university students for their difficulties in understanding material during lessons. For students who do not understand, teachers showing these behaviors are perceived as displaying a low level of clarity. This chapter presents strategies for adjusting teaching to students' needs and abilities so as to increase clarity.

STUDENT DIVERSITY

Students have different strategies, approaches, and capabilities for learning that are a function of prior experience and heredity. Through learning and social acculturation, individuals acquire their own preferences for how they like to learn and the pace at which they prefer to learn. The interaction between learner differences and curricular and environmental conditions is a key factor affecting learning outcomes (APA, 1997).

Problems in Teaching Due to Student Diversity

Clarity in teaching is not an absolute notion but is, rather, contingent on the audience of learners. The student audience in a course is always heterogeneous in terms of background knowledge, motivation, study orientation, needs, expectations, areas of interest, and styles of and aptitudes for learning. The same lesson may be perceived as very clear by students with the proper background knowledge and tools to understand it, and may be totally unclear for others who lack that background and those tools. This diversity evidences itself in the differences in teacher ratings on clarity provided by different students in a class. The following is an illustration of the gap, taken from written comments by two students *attending the same course, and regarding the same teacher:*

- The professor assumed too much of an anthropology background from us, which left me guessing and not understanding several of the topics presented.
- I sometimes felt the course was too introductory and basic to fulfill the anthropology major requirements. I wouldn't have minded a more advanced approach.

Thus, for the first student, a non-anthropology major who does not have the relevant knowledge, the lessons were unclear, whereas for the second student, an anthropology major with the proper background, the presentation was of too low a level and lacked challenge.

In a survey among professors in five major schools (humanities, social sciences, education, math/natural sciences, and engineering) at an Ivy League research university (Hativa, 1997), the respondents selected the main difficulties they faced in teaching undergraduate courses from a 20-item list. Four of the six difficulties found to be most disturbing related to student diversity, in decreasing frequency of responses, were:

- Many students display an insufficient background (experienced in the highest frequency by humanities and social science respondents).
- Many students do not review material taught in previous lessons before the new lesson (experienced in the highest frequency by social science and math/natural sciences faculty).

- The student population is too diverse.
- Many students do not read the required texts for the lesson.

These answers reveal that student diversity and insufficient preparation (e.g., lack of reading or doing the assignments for the lesson) cause difficulties in teaching for substantial numbers of teachers. If this is the situation for a university that is very selective in admitting students, what happens in less-selective universities and colleges?

Problems When Teaching Does Not Fit Student Diversity

Learning is most effective when differences in learners' linguistic, cultural, and social backgrounds are taken into account (APA, 1997). Other factors in student diversity should also be accommodated in teaching. For example, when students and professors were asked what contributes to the ideal teacher-pupil relationship, they chose: "The teacher's explanations fit in correctly with the student's ability and knowledge" as a major contribution (Hyman, 1968).

Teaching that is ill-suited to many students in a course, that does not adapt the material to students' needs, life experiences, or prior learning, may bear negative consequences. For example, when a teacher presents the material at a level above the students' ability to understand, the students may become frustrated, even angry, and may disengage from listening:

- He assumes that we know too much or that things are obvious when they aren't.
- She just goes right over our heads.

Teaching below the students' level also endangers negative results—students may become bored, unchallenged, inattentive, and feel that their time is being wasted:

- You could demand more of us, ask tougher questions, make us clarify our ideas. You give us too many hints, too much help.

Adapting pace to students is likewise essential for maintaining their concentration. Too slow a pace results in boredom and mental wandering, whereas too fast a pace prevents students from following the lesson, discourages them, and makes them quit listening. Indeed, "Teaches at an appropriate pace" was found by Hines (1982), to be fourth (out of over 50 teacher behaviors) in discriminating power between clear and unclear university teachers. Here is a description of the effect of improper pace, transcribed from an interview with a student:

I attend a lecture on a topic which is difficult to understand, the content is abstract, full of entirely new ideas, and I feel that I'm missing out on something—the lecturer goes on and on at a steady pace but my mind does not. Sometimes he states an idea that I do not quite grasp. I stop for a minute to struggle with it and what happens? I miss what he's saying in the meantime and then understanding becomes more difficult. Or something that he says sets off a chain of related thoughts in my mind—again I'm lost. If this situation continues on and on, I'm totally lost and teaching becomes very unclear.

And a few written comments by students on too fast a pace:

* She runs with proofs on the board and there isn't enough time to copy them and also to think and understand.

* Too much was covered in a short time so that not enough time was given to understanding a concept.

* Transparencies on an overhead projector should be replaced at a slower pace to enable us to follow.

Adapting instruction to student diversity requires the teacher to address three issues:
- Gaining knowledge of the learners prior to teaching, that is, identifying students' background knowledge and aptitudes and their problems in learning the particular material.
- Keeping track of the ongoing adjustment of teaching to students throughout the lesson and the term (formative evaluation).
- Designing and implementing the adjustment of teaching to the wide diversity among students on the basis of the students' identified background characteristics and ongoing formative evaluation.

The following sections break down each of these issues into their dimensions and presents classroom strategies for adapting instruction to students, as illustrated in Figure 12-1.

GAINING KNOWLEDGE OF THE LEARNERS, BEFORE TEACHING

To adjust teaching to students, teachers first need to increase their *knowledge of learners*, that is, "knowledge of student characteristics and cognitions as well as knowledge of motivational and developmental aspects of how students learn" (Wilson, Shulman, & Richert, 1987, p. 114).

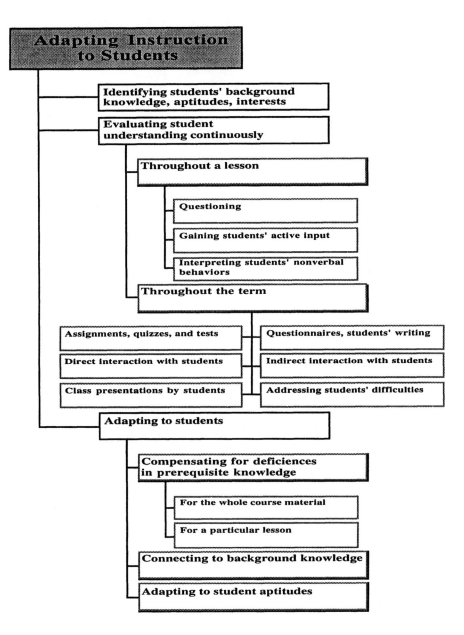

Figure 12-1: Dimensions and Strategies for Adapting Teaching to Students

Knowledge of learners is one of several types of knowledge essential for a teacher (ibid.); it plays an important role in teachers' thinking about classroom teaching, about managing classroom events, and about the content presented (Calderhead, 1983). Teachers should obtain information about their students' interests, life experiences, aptitudes, problems in learning the particular material, and course expectations, before beginning to teach the course.

How to obtain information about students before teaching

All of the procedures suggested next should be administered either at the beginning of a course, at the start of a new unit, or prior to introducing a new topic.

Identify and list the needed prerequisite knowledge. When planning a course or a lesson, think out and analyze each new topic in detail, and then identify and record everything that is required for understanding the new material.

Ask directly in class. Ask the students in class directly whether they have learned the specific topics you plan to rely on.

Find out outside class. Assign groups of students during the first one or two weeks of the term to meet with you (possibly at lunchtime). In each meeting, informally discuss their backgrounds, relevant experiences, and expectations from the course.

Use a self-made questionnaire. Give students a questionnaire with closed and open questions that provide relevant information on their backgrounds, interests, and experiences. For example, ask them what magazines/journals do they regularly read, what do they expect to gain in this course, what are their concerns, what helps them learn, what are their areas of interest, and what makes them excited in class. You may add specific questions tapping their knowledge of prerequisite material, previous courses, and relevant experiences.

Use a test/quiz. Give your students a diagnostic test, either anonymous or not, probing their knowledge which is prerequisite to the material of the particular course/unit/topic. Notify students that the aim of this test is to help you better adjust your teaching to their aptitudes and needs and that they will not be graded on this test.

Use group discussion. Divide your class into small groups, where each group discusses and agrees on answers to the same kind of questions that are posed in the former two procedures.

Identify the content of prerequisite courses. Examine what previous courses most students took and whether the curriculum of these courses covers all prerequisite knowledge for your course.

Administer a standard questionnaire on students' aptitudes. Administer a questionnaire that identifies students' learning styles or motivation orientations. There are several standard questionnaires for these aims.

Obtain information on students from the registrar office. Information available on students from their registration records may serve as a source of knowledge about students. If students' personal information is kept confidential, you may ask that the registrar's office provide you with a summary (means, frequencies) of relevant information such as the results of psychometric tests, GPAs, or high school grades for particular subject matter.

Identifying Students' Problems in Learning the Particular Material Through Reflection

One way to identify students' problems in learning the course material is to reflect on past experiences in teaching the same or similar courses.

To be able to use this experience fully, you should make special preparations. To reflect on your past experiences in teaching the same or similar courses, record after each lesson that you teach the problems that you encountered. Use your notes to analyze and identify the causes for the problematic themes/issues. Document students' difficulties throughout the course and use these records and documents when you prepare lessons the next time that you teach the same course or similar courses.

Utilizing the information on students that has been obtained, teachers can formulate course or topic unit plans that are adapted to students' backgrounds and aptitudes.[51] However, teachers will need to receive continual feedback during the course in order to maintain the match between their teaching and student learning.

EVALUATING STUDENT UNDERSTANDING CONTINUOUSLY THROUGHOUT THE LESSON AND THE TERM—THE "CLASS BAROMETER"

Often, professors are unaware of how well they are doing while teaching—do students actually understand their explanations? Are they attentive? In a survey of faculty on difficulties they face in teaching undergraduate courses (Hativa, 1997), one quarter of the respondents selected the item "You aren't aware of when students don't understand" as a problem in their teaching, and 14% agreed with the item "You aren't aware of when students are bored."

---

[51] See Part 3 of this chapter.

Adjusting teaching to students may be likened to steering a ship. From moment to moment, the helmsman must make small corrections to stay on course. Periodically, though, measurements are made to decide if the course itself needs correction. Location, direction, wind flow, and water current are checked, and the helmsman uses this information to adjust course. Similarly, if teachers want to adjust their teaching to students, they need to obtain ongoing feedback on students' understanding and interest throughout the lesson and the course. Evaluation conducted in the course of action, for the purpose of improving performance, is called *formative evaluation*. It takes place in addition to *summative evaluation*—tests and other graded evaluations given regularly at the end of the term. Obtaining continuous feedback from students serves as a *class barometer*, it helps teachers to frequently "measure the temperature" of students' understanding and learning.

To conduct ongoing *formative evaluation*, teachers can:

(a) Evaluate students' understanding *throughout the lesson* by questioning, assigning students a variety of writing tasks and interpreting their nonverbal behaviors.

(b) Evaluate students' understanding *throughout the term* by means of assignments, quizzes, and tests; questionnaires and students' writing; direct and indirect interactions with students; and class presentations by students.

Evaluating Students' Understanding Throughout the Lesson

When preparing a lesson, the teacher should plan checkpoints for evaluating student understanding. The appraisal can be done through (i) questioning, (ii) students' active input, and (iii) interpreting students' nonverbal behavior. These methods prod students to think while providing you with feedback about their understanding of the material you present.

Evaluating Student Understanding Through Questioning

Questioning in class may have a variety of purposes. The following are ideas for questions designed to evaluate students' understanding throughout a lesson.[52]

How to pose questions to reveal students' understanding
  Pose direct questions regarding particular aspects of the material you have just presented.

---

[52] See Chapter 6: Questioning.

Pose indirect questions. Ask students to repeat, rephrase, or explain what you have just taught; to guess and evaluate what the next step in the development of the topic will be; or to suggest the next step in a solution to a problem that you develop on the board. Present a demonstration or an example and ask students to explain it and connect it to the topic taught. Give students enough time after you pose a question, so that all students can reflect and answer.[53]

How to solicit questions from students when they do not understand

Solicit questions from students. Stop after each unit you teach and ask if there are any questions. Look around throughout the lesson and encourage students to ask questions whenever they do not understand.

Answer students' questions willingly and clearly.

Make sure your answer is understood. When you complete your answer to a student's question, ask that student if he/she understood the answer, and then ask all students in class if they have any further questions in this regard.

Evaluating Students' Understanding Through Their Active Input

Use speaking/verbal discussion. Begin the lesson by inviting students to call out everything they know about a topic, or to explore the multiple meanings of key words, or as many definitions as they can for a certain term. From students' answers you may find out quickly what students already know and do not know or even their misconceptions.

Utilize problem-solving. Assign students to solve problems based on the material presented, and go over their solutions to identify problems in understanding.

Assign writings. For each of the following suggestions, collect the papers at the end of the lesson, read them, respond in writing, record for yourself points where many students show problems in understanding, and return them at the next class session. You may then read to the class a selection of the responses, respond to them orally, ask if there are any additional comments or questions, and re-teach the topics that were shown to be unclear. You may also explain the rationale for these assignments clearly, emphasizing that they are not to be graded, but rather will provide you with feedback on students' level of comprehension.

Interactive papers. At different points during the lesson, ask your students to respond in writing to questions that you pose. For example: What is the point in my presentation so far? What is the conclusion? What are your difficulties

---

[53] See Chapter 6: Pausing—"Wait-Time."

understanding this explanation? What do you think of this topic? What questions do you have on your mind now? You may also assign students to describe any frustrating situation of their choice that occurred that day during class time. Alternatively, at the beginning of a lesson give students a handout with questions related to topics to be presented in the lesson, and stop appropriately during the lesson for students to write their responses on the handout.

"Minute Papers" (Wilson, 1986). This procedure serves to examine if students have understood the main topics of the lesson and to identify what questions they still have. At the beginning of the lesson write on the board two questions that you will ask students to answer in the last minutes of the lesson:

- What was the most significant idea of today's class?

- What questions are still outstanding for you?

Leave the questions on the board during the lesson and during the last minutes of the lesson. Ask students to answer these questions either providing their names (for taking class attendance) or anonymously.

Ask for student-originated key ideas. This technique is a modification of the "minute papers" in which you replace the two questions with asking students to identify the three key ideas taught in the lesson and to explain each.

However, Experience shows that most students, when asked to write and explain the key ideas of a lesson, select to write on whatever topics they remember from the lesson, not necessarily key ideas. At times they select as key ideas even very minor and unimportant points, as illustrated with a statistics instructor who asked his students to list key ideas (Angelo & Cross, 1993).

> He found that, as a group, his 35 students came up with as many as 20 different important points from the same lecture. Many of the points they listed were ones he considered details; others were distortions of things he had said; still others were points he was sure he had never mentioned at all!

Therefore, a further modification of the "minute paper" procedure is that, rather than asking students to identify the key ideas by themselves, this task is delegated to the teacher.

Provide teacher-generated key ideas. Prepare in advance, on a transparency (or on paper and copy it on the board), a list of the three ideas that you consider the major ones in that lesson. Present this list a few minutes before the end of the lesson and ask students to give you their written answers.

Evaluating Students' Understanding Through Their Nonverbal Behavior

Maintain eye contact with all students throughout the lesson. Look into their eyes and watch their body language and facial expressions to identify if they are not understanding or when they get bored.

Ask students if everything is clear when you suspect misunderstandings. When you identify boredom, use methods to engage students, as suggested in Chapters 6, 7, and 15.

Evaluating Students' Understanding Throughout the Term

Teachers are often unaware of what is going on in their classes throughout the term, and how well their overall teaching is understood and received by their students. It is important that teachers gain a general conception of their teaching by getting frequent feedback. They should take care to obtain this feedback continuously throughout the term and not only from the end-of-term student evaluations. Teachers can obtain this type of feedback through: (i) assignments, quizzes, and tests; (ii) questionnaires and students' written feedback; (iii) interactions with the students outside the lessons; (iv) indirect interaction with students using mediators; and (v) class presentations by students.

Assignments, Quizzes, and Tests

Give frequent homework/assignments. Assign homework every week. Check them or a sample if the class is large. Summarize or ask your assistants to summarize for you the main difficulties students face, and the main types of errors that they make.

Administer frequent quizzes and tests. Students usually do not like these techniques, but they help teachers keep track of their teaching, of students' doing the assigned reading for each class, and of students' learning. You may use different ways to administer quizzes. For example, you may start each lesson with a short quiz on the topics covered in the last lesson, or on the assigned reading for today; you may administer a weekly quiz on the material studied that week; or you may administer 3-4 mid-term tests. To ease the burden of frequently grading quizzes, you may either grade only a sample of the whole class (for each quiz grade another group of students), or have your assistants grade them all. Summarize all types of errors and difficulties in understanding.

Questionnaires and Students' Written Feedback

Here are several suggestions of how you can obtain this type of feedback. Additional techniques can be found in Angelo and Cross (1993). You may comment on some of the students' pieces of writing and give them back. Also respond orally in class to issues that arise from students' writing and that may concern the whole class.

How to administer in-class written responses

Arrange for weekly evaluations. These can be done on evaluation forms individually completed or by discussion groups, in the last lesson each week. The evaluation forms may include rating items on several main teaching-behavior dimensions (e.g., clarity, interest, organization) and/or open-ended comments. In a medium-to-large class, analyzing weekly evaluation forms may be too much of a burden on the teacher. To alleviate this burden, you may assign a different group of students each week to individually answer the forms. Another option is to divide the students in class into several discussion groups. All members of a group discuss and decide together how to score each item on the evaluation form and what open-ended comments to write. After class, summarize the numerical ratings (means, standard deviations) and the open answers.

Assign open-answer evaluations. Three or four times a term, assign your students to answer an in-class anonymous form with open-ended questions such as: What has happened so far in class? How do you feel about it? What do you like in class? What would you like to see changed? Then compile the responses, cluster them, and write this on an overhead to share with the class. You can then respond to their concerns, explain what may be changed, invite their suggestions, and explain anything in the course structure that is unclear. It is important that students' feedback be acknowledged and addressed.

How to administer out-of-class written responses

Assign learning diaries. Assign your students to put on your desk, at the beginning of each class or once a week, a short written communication related to the last lesson or last week's classes, or to the homework assignment for today. For example: comments, thoughts, summaries, critiques, questions, doubts, insights, and experiences.

Assign "Dear Professor" letters. Once in several weeks, assign students to answer in their homes a list of questions that you pose. The questions will deal with whatever you are interested in learning about your teaching in the course—what do students find interesting? Difficult? What are their problems?

What do they think of the textbook? Of the homework assignments? Of the discussion/recitation/problem-solving groups? Of the lab work?

Request E-mail feedback. Arrange a computer account for the class so that any student can log on to this account without identifying him/herself. Assign your students the task of reporting a weekly message to your e-mail account to tell you what was unclear in the last week's lessons, to comment on these lessons, and to make suggestions. Alternatively, rather than giving students your e-mail account, arrange that when they log on to the class account, they are invited by the software to tell you whatever they want to say about the class. When they close the file, its content is automatically sent to you so that no other student can read it.

Run a class newspaper. In large classes, set up a class newspaper to answer students' questions, and pose questions to students. Assign one student as the editor.

Direct Interaction with Students Outside the Class

Encourage office-hour feedback. Encourage students to use your office hours. Frequently mention throughout your lessons that you expect them to come to consult with you. When they come to your office, inquire about your teaching, how well they think it is going, what do their classmates think of it, what are their suggestions for modifications.

Enable before- and after-class feedback. Come ten minutes early to each of your classes and remain several minutes after the class ends. Talk to your students and ask them how the class is going, and other related questions.

Indirect Interaction with Students, Using Mediators

Set up a "Hot line." Encourage your students to call your office after working hours and leave you a message on the voice mail. They may ask questions or comment about the last lessons and keep their anonymity. In the next class meeting you may answer these questions and concerns in front of the whole class.

Use Mediation. To keep students' anonymity and still get their sincere feedback on your teaching, you can use mediators to communicate with the students. Mediators can be either a single student from the class, a class committee ("advisory group"), or an outsider (e.g., an expert on faculty development, a representative of the teaching center in the university). The following are suggestions regarding mediator selection, ways the mediators can obtain class feedback, the desired content of the class feedback, and your response to the feedback.

How to select the mediator(s)

Volunteering students: At the beginning of the course, ask for one or more volunteers to represent the class. The volunteers can be assigned for the whole term or may switch roles every fixed period.

Class selection: The class elects a feedback committee of students— an "advisory group" which consists of a small group of students (e.g., one from each practice section of a large class).

Teacher-selected students: You appoint either a single student or an advisory committee.

Mediators other than students: Use the course teaching assistants (TAs), or faculty developers—probably representatives of the teaching center in your institution.

How can the mediator(s) obtain class feedback

Student-initiated feedback: Encourage your students to communicate to the mediators their suggestions, requests, and complaints, throughout the term.

Mediator-initiated feedback: For feedback, the mediators can survey the students (orally or in writing) weekly in class.

"Class monitors:" The mediator selects a few students in a class through the department's secretariat, to serve as the feedback source. The selected students are anonymous to you and represent all levels of success in learning on the basis of their cumulative GPA (e.g., very good, good, and moderate GPA). The mediator contacts each of them in person or by phone at the end of each week, interviews them about what was good and what went wrong in that week's lessons, and asks for their comments and suggestions for improvement (Hativa, 1995).

TA feedback: Ask your TAs to inquire about your teaching from students in their practice classes and to provide you with a weekly report on this student input, on student performance on homework assignments, or on students' problems in understanding the topics that you have taught in class, including a summary of typical students' errors or difficulties.

How can the mediator(s) interact with you

Have the mediators contact you as soon as they obtain students' feedback to communicate it to you frankly, and discuss with you possible reactions. The feedback the mediators communicate to you may deal with how the course is progressing, aspects of the course that students like and dislike, topics that students did not understand, other difficulties experienced by them, and additional students' suggestions for improvement. If the mediator is a teaching expert (e.g., a faculty developer), you may consult with him/her on strategies for improvement.

Communicate with the mediators through a variety of channels: written reports (the mediators transcribe students' comments and deliver them to you on paper or through e-mail); telephone calls; and in-person meetings.

Reacting to the information provided to you by the mediators. Respond to students' comments and concerns and ask the mediators to deliver your responses back to the particular students who initiated the comments. If the comments are of general interest, discuss them in the next class session or modify your teaching if necessary.

Class Presentations by Students

Assign students to present a start-of-lesson or end-of-lesson summary. In each lesson, assign one student or a pair of students to summarize the lesson content, five minutes before the end of the class or, alternatively, to present a five-minute summary of the previous lesson content at the beginning of the next class. The start-of-lesson presenters may prepare handouts summarizing the lecture or even bring additional information. These summaries enable you to pinpoint areas that were unclear in the previous lecture and to complement the students' summary. Rather than assigning students for presenters, you may ask for volunteers and give them bonus points that count in their final grade.

Have students present their homework. Assign each student (taking turns) the task of explaining their solutions to homework assignments to the class. From these explanations, and from students' responses to these explanations, you may learn to what extent students have grasped the material.

ADAPTING TEACHING TO STUDENTS

Here is what some teachers do to adapt instruction to students, as described by their students:

- When he discovers that we do not know certain material that he thought that we were supposed to know, he explains to us in detail.
- She doesn't assume prior knowledge.
- The professor always asks questions to be sure that we've understood the material, and encourages our questions. He doesn't leave "holes" in our knowledge and answers any question.

- If she finds out that we do not follow her or that we do not have the tools to answer her question, she provides the necessary background and she helps us understand.

- This TA contacts students in his section whom he thinks are not learning the material and he makes them tell him how they feel about the class. He then advises them how to learn the material.

These teachers are described as continuously examining students' current understanding and as filling any gaps in knowledge they identify by adjusting explanations to students' level of understanding. However, there are professors who do not adapt their teaching to their diverse student populations:

- There was too wide a discrepancy in the technical backgrounds of education students and the teacher spent half the course on issues which I already knew [Course on educational uses of computers].

- He relies on knowledge that we don't have and doesn't provide definitions of basic concepts that he uses.

How can teachers use the information they obtain on their students to adapt teaching to them? They can use three main methods:
1. Compensating for students' deficiencies in prerequisite knowledge;
2. Embedding in cognitive structure—connecting teaching to students' background knowledge, and
3. Adjusting teaching to students' aptitudes.

Compensating for Students' Deficiencies in Prerequisite Knowledge

Teachers should help students compensate for deficiencies in prerequisite knowledge.

How to compensate for deficits related to the course material as a whole

Give students sufficient time and guidance to fill in the gaps in their background knowledge necessary for the course. You may use the following methods:

Provide information regarding the course's prerequisite knowledge, and direct students toward appropriate readings. Provide students in advance, before the course starts, with information regarding knowledge that the course will rely on, along with a list of sources (books, reports, and so on) and means for gaining this knowledge independently.

Arrange special help outside class. Assign the course TAs to tutor students with deficient background knowledge, give special complementary lessons, or refer students to appropriate literature and guide them in their reading.

Provide a written summary of prerequisite knowledge. Before the beginning of the course or in the first lesson, provide your students with a handout which summarizes the main prerequisite background knowledge for the course: concepts, definitions, models, theories, theorems, formulas, along with their meaning and definition, main issues, and more.

Administer a test. Test students in advance on prerequisite knowledge for the course. You may consider screening out students who fail this test.

How to compensate for deficits related to a particular lesson

Help students complement material that is prerequisite for a specific lesson, as follows.

Inform students of required knowledge. Inform them at least one week in advance as to the prerequisite material for the next week's lessons, and direct them in self-learning of that material. Guide them in sources and means for learning this material.

Provide a written summary of prerequisite knowledge. Rather than having students look for the missing material by themselves, give them a handout with a short summary.

Provide assignments that promote self-learning of the required knowledge. Assign students, as part of their homework, to read, write, or solve problems that rely on and apply knowledge that is prerequisite to the next lesson. These homework assignments should be performed or even submitted by students before the particular lesson.

Administer a test. Test students in advance on prerequisite knowledge for particular lessons. This will motivate them to complement this material on their own.

"Embedding"—Connecting to Students' Background Knowledge

The following are student descriptions of professors who successfully connect new knowledge to the students' prior knowledge and interests:

- The professor incorporates comments that connect the material to other courses we've taken.

- I especially appreciated her effort to bring together our disparate backgrounds and interests.

Two of the main behaviors discriminating between clear and unclear university teachers (Hines, 1982) were: "Compares new material with what students know," and "Explains meaning of unfamiliar words." These behaviors describe methods that very clear teachers use to help their students to integrate new knowledge with their prior knowledge.

The constructivist learning theory holds that meaningful learning is possible only when the learner relates new material in a substantive fashion to an already existing cognitive structure. Students will learn and remember information better when they can make more cognitive associations with this information and more interconnections between the new and the already known.[54]

It follows that teachers need to ascertain the existence of students' prior knowledge and to activate it at the start of any instructional sequence. One way to do this is by reviewing prerequisite knowledge. Research at the pre-college level shows that effective teachers begin a lesson with a short review of previous learning (Rosenshine, 1986). During that review, teachers make explicit links between old and new learning. *Linking* of this kind is particularly important in courses of a hierarchical/sequential nature. When topics are arranged sequentially, students will need to master one topic before learning the next in the sequence. Linking is likewise very important in courses that rely on the knowledge of a large number of technical terms, concepts, laws, rules, theories, processes, models, and so forth. When students complain about teachers' use of jargon in basic courses, it is because these students lack prior knowledge of the terms used in class. Once they become acquainted with the context, they are able to decipher the meanings of the new terms (Svinicki, Hagen, & Meyer, 1996). This applies especially to such fields as mathematics, sciences, and engineering.

How to "embed—to connect the new material to students' background knowledge

Check for the existence of relevant prior knowledge. There are several methods for identifying relevant prior knowledge, as suggested in the previous section. The most practical and simple one is asking students in class whether they have learned the specific topics you plan to rely on. You may use a *class vote* for this aim, that is, name a specific topic that is prerequisite for the material you intend to teach and ask students to raise their hands if they have learned or are familiar with that topic. Other methods mentioned above are asking students outside class, or using a quiz or a questionnaire.

---

[54] See Chapter 4: Constructivist Learning Theory.

Activate relevant prior knowledge. If you identify a sound number of students who do not have some prerequisite knowledge, review the required material, or ask students in class to share what they know about this particular topic. Make sure that most students in class understand this related material before presenting the new material.

Make explicit links between old and new learning. For embedding the new knowledge into prior knowledge, it is crucial that students have a clear and organized framework of the relevant prior knowledge. For this reason, during the first lesson you should provide the framework for the course, and in each lesson you should connect the lesson topics to that framework, and present the framework for that particular lesson[55]. Then explicitly link each topic you present to the frameworks of the course and lesson, and to the prerequisite knowledge that you have already identified and reviewed. The linking can be done by showing the location of the new topic within the existing frameworks, reminding students of relevant available knowledge, comparing and contrasting new with old knowledge, showing interrelations between new and old concepts, and using examples and applications from areas with which students are familiar.

Adapting Teaching to Student Aptitudes

Among the main discriminators between clear and unclear teachers (Hines, 1982), four relate to teachers adapting their teaching to student aptitudes:
- Teaches at an appropriate pace.
- Repeats things when students do not understand.
- Stays with the topic until students understand.
- Teaches step-by-step.

Because students' aptitudes are so diverse, they differ largely in the pace and ways they perceive, digest, and comprehend new material. Thus, a teacher should pave a "golden path," teaching at a pace and level that fit most students in class, while taking care that the better students are not bored and that the lowest-level students are not too frustrated. However, each teacher has his/her own thinking as to which audience classroom teaching should be adapted to. Should it indeed be adjusted to *all* the students in class or only to those from a certain level of knowledge or aptitude and above? In other words—should teaching be directed to and designed for the level of the "lowest common denominator" in class, or should one "teach to the mean," that is, at the level of the average student in class? In some extreme cases, teachers may even teach at the level of the best students in class.

---

[55] See Chapter 8: Providing a Conceptual Framework for the Course, and Communicating the Lesson Framework and its Place in the General Framework of the Course.

Teaching to the lowest level of students may cause well-prepared students or those of high aptitude to get very bored and remain unchallenged, and it may impede the coverage of the full course curriculum because of the slow pace. On the other hand, teachers whose main goal is the full coverage of the course material, with no regard for the particular students in class, may teach above the level of many students in class.

Methods for adapting teaching to the range of students' aptitudes include repetitions and elaborations, multiple representations, pauses, stimulation of students' intuition and imagery, and planning for anticipated difficulties in teaching.

Repetitions and elaboration. Research at the pre-college level indicates that effective teachers use many repetitions and elaborations. The effectiveness of this method may be explained by the information processing model,[56] which assumes that the new information that remains after being screened through the senses, goes through several processes such as rehearsal, encoding, screening, and searching in a control mechanism—the working memory. The parts of the information that are filtered out are forgotten, and the rest is connected and integrated with "old" knowledge while being stored in the long-term memory. Teachers can facilitate this process by elaborating, reviewing, rehearsing, and summarizing the new material (Rosenshine, 1986). As shown in the following comments, repetitions and elaborations help students who have not understood an explanation the first time it is presented:

* He goes very fast but repeats until I understand by the second or third time.
* She realizes that some material is too difficult to be absorbed the first time so it is presented and repeated for more complex subjects.
* Each point is presented with more than an adequate number of explanations.

Multiple representations. Students differ in the ways they perceive and digest new material. Some students understand oral explanations better, while others prefer visual material. Therefore, an important method for catering to students' aptitudes is to present each explanation in several different modes. The more channels a teacher uses in presenting the same material, the better the students will understand it. For example, listening is insufficient for effective learning and sight is at least as important. In fact, the concurrent use of both senses— hearing and seeing—is most beneficial, as students can absorb the content presented via two channels simultaneously. The two senses complement one another and enhance understanding.

---

[56] See Figure 5-1.

The pausing principle. Rowe (1975) identified lapses in students' concentration and attention throughout a lesson. She found that lapses always occur; that their frequency increase as the subject matter becomes more complex; and that not everyone in the class suffers lapses at the same points in the lecture. Rowe suggested to help students catch up with their thoughts by using what she called the "pausing principle." If a lecturer pauses at least three times during a lecture for, say, two minutes, and has students in adjacent seats share notes and comments, more of the content of the lecture will be learned and retained by more students. Sharing by three students provides sufficient variety in notes and interpretations to recover what each student might have lost. In addition, the immediate rehearsal and elaboration of the ideas occasioned by the pause reinforces new concepts and reduces the probability that students will learn incorrect or partial concepts. Furthermore, the pause forces students to use each other as resources; this promotes peer teaching, which is viewed as an effective promoter of student learning.

How to adapt instruction to students' aptitudes

Repeat and elaborate. Repeat a theme, an explanation, or an idea, either in the same or in different words, until the students understand it. When elaborating, the repetition involves enrichment of the previous ideas, or highlighting them from a different viewpoint, or presenting them at a higher difficulty level.

Adjust the pace. Check students' understanding frequently throughout the lesson, using methods suggested above, to identify the appropriateness of your pace for your audience. Make adjustments, as you find appropriate.

Facilitate note taking. Develop explanations gradually, but at a rate that most students can follow while taking beneficial notes. Be sure to give students enough time to process and understand the oral and written information so that they are able to meaningfully summarize it in their notes.

Use multiple representations. Use different types of examples/illustrations/demonstrations—numerical, concrete, those that build on students' experimentation and intuition, and those that stimulate their imagery. Present the same content through as many types of representations as possible. For example, use verbal, graphical, pictorial, mathematical, two- or three-dimensional representations, or present a demonstration. When using more than one single representation, it is very important that you show the connections among the different representations.

Pause. Make it a habit in your teaching to stop two or three times during a lesson for a moment to let students catch their thoughts and complement their note taking. You may use the "pause principle"—ask students to form pairs or triads to share their notes and comments and explain to each other what they do not understand.

Stimulate students' intuition and imagery. Connect explanations to students' intuitions, conceptions, and visual perceptions. For stimulating intuition, invoke preexisting knowledge of graphing principles or of plane and solid figures to promote perception of new concepts[57].

Plan for anticipated difficulties in teaching. When you prepare a lesson, use the information on students that you have gathered (as suggested above) to identify sources of likely difficulties in the material to be presented. Think how you can handle these difficulties—which examples, illustrations, analogies, applications, or multiple representations to use. In class, dedicate extra time and effort to difficult topics, dwell on them, and elaborate them from various directions and points of view.

Adapting Teaching to Students in a "Very Heterogeneous" Class

Every class is heterogeneous. There are no two students with the same background knowledge, aptitudes, interests, and so on. However, it happens that a class consists of two or more different populations, each of which is relatively homogeneous in terms of certain topics or aptitudes. An example is a basic general-requirement course in science that requires a strong background in math and science, and which is attended by students with and without such background. In a course of this type, the teacher faces a serious problem in presenting the material to suit both the weak and the strong group.

How to adapt teaching to students in heterogeneous classes

Develop a method of teaching *"in two voices."* On the one hand, guide the weak group to make up for the lacking prerequisite material or background knowledge at the beginning of the course; teach material in a very clear and organized way without skipping steps; and use all the methods presented above for adjusting teaching to the students. At the same time, take special care to present the strong group with thinking challenges—pose to them every so often a difficult but interesting question; develop the material through the Socratic method[58]; use challenging examples, applications, and riddles; use group work; and promote their interest and intellectual challenge in other ways.[59]

---

[57] See Chapter 10: (d) Presenting Visual or Intuitive Interpretations.
[58] See Chapter 6: Socratic Questioning.
[59] See Chapter 7 for additional ideas.

Tailor the course differently to different student groups through providing different curriculum. Differentiate the treatment to students with different aptitudes or prerequisite knowledge by dividing the course material into two parts. The first involves the basic concepts and essential processes that all students need to learn and understand. The second, smaller part, involves the more difficult and complex/abstract material, which is optional. Only students who desire their excellence to be recognized, or those with special interest in the material, are tested on this.

Tailor the course differently to different student groups through adjustment of the course requirements and the grading policy. You can allow students to select one of several options for fulfilling the course requirements, which vary in the extent of demand from the students.

To illustrate, here is how an outstanding teacher at Stanford University handles this problem. The professor teaches an introductory general-distribution electrical engineering course attended by several hundred students with a wide variety of backgrounds and aptitudes. They come from many different disciplines—humanities, social science, and science—whereas only 10% are actually from engineering. They range from freshmen to graduates. Here is his description of his policy (Salsibury, 1995, pp. 1-2):

To present this material and grade the students in a way that is fair to everyone, that gives both the fuzzies and the techies equal opportunities to do well, I provide students with multiple paths:

- In the standard path, the student does the homework, midterm and the final. Homework accounts for 25% of the final grade, while the two exams count for 75%. Because the homework and the exams include problems in which calculations are required, the techies have a distinct advantage.

- To level the playing field, fuzzies can do an optional paper. If they do, then the paper counts for 35% of the grade, the homework 25% and the midterm and final are reduced to 40%. Notice that I don't make the paper extra credit. If I did, I'd get 500 lousy papers, which would be absolutely numbing to read through. This way I get a few, very good papers.

- Students with strong science and math skills who want to get more out of the course can choose to do a set of optional problems. In this case, the added problem set is worth 35% of the grade, homework accounts for 25%, while the midterm and final make up 40%. These problems are much harder than those included in homework. A number involve material that is in the textbook but not covered in the lectures, so the students must learn it on their own. To reduce the temptation to cheat, student choosing this option also must take an extra class test in which they are asked to answer three out of five of these problems correctly.

- On top of this I have set up two ways in which students can earn bonus points: reading and summarizing 50 newspaper articles that appear during the course of the class dealing with issues related to the class, and writing a critique of an article I select. I have worked out a way to grade all these options so that those who do only the homework, midterm and final are not put at a disadvantage by other students doing additional work.

- Essentially, extra effort can raise an individual's grade without reducing that of other students.

SUMMARY

Clarity in teaching is contingent on the audience of learners. Learner diversity is very problematic for many teachers, who face difficulties in adapting instruction to this diversity.

Adapting teaching to the students in class consists of: (a) identifying students' background knowledge and aptitudes; (b) keeping track of/supervising the ongoing adjustment of teaching to students throughout the lesson and the term (formative evaluation) and (c) designing and implementing the adaptation of teaching to the students on the basis of the students' background and the ongoing formative evaluation.

1. Identifying students' background knowledge, aptitudes, and interests, including their needs and expectations in learning, learning styles, life experiences, and current relevant knowledge. This information may be gleaned through directly inquiring students about these issues in and outside class; letting students fill out a questionnaire on these issues; administering diagnostic tests/quizzes on prerequisite knowledge; using group discussions; analyzing the content of prerequisite courses; using standard questionnaires that identify their learning styles, aptitudes or motivation orientations; and obtaining relevant information from the registrar's office.

2. Evaluating student understanding continuously throughout the lesson and the term (formative evaluation):

Evaluating student understanding throughout a lesson is achieved by questioning, gaining students' active input through students' verbal feedback, writing (e.g., interactive papers, "minute papers," explanations of key ideas), solving problems, explaining steps in development, and interpreting students' nonverbal behaviors.

Evaluating student understanding throughout the term is achieved by using: assignments, quizzes, and tests; questionnaires and students' written feedback (weekly evaluations, open-answered evaluations, learning diaries, "Dear professor" letters, e-mail feedback, and class newspaper); direct interactions with the students (office-hour feedback, before- and after-class feedback); indirect interaction with students using mediators (volunteer or elected students or TAs; class presentations by students (start-of-lesson or end-of-lesson summary, homework assignments); and anticipating and planning for students' difficulties. The teacher should document students' difficulties by identifying them from all of the above sources and use this document when preparing lessons the next time he/she teaches the same or similar courses.

3. Adapting teaching to students is achieved by complementing for deficiencies in prerequisite knowledge. For deficits related to the whole course, adaptation can involve: informing students of prerequisite knowledge, directing their reading, offering special help outside class, providing a handout with a written summary of prerequisite knowledge, and testing. For deficits related to a particular lesson, adaptation can include: informing students in advance of the prerequisite material for that lesson; providing a written summary of prerequisite knowledge; giving an assignment to promote self-learning of the required knowledge; embedding—linking teaching to students' background knowledge; using an outline or visual presentation; reminding students of or reviewing related known topics; making students review the material of the last lesson; explicating and linking the various elements among themselves; and integrating multi-sources for learning. Adapting teaching to student aptitudes and learning styles can be done by repeating and elaborating; adjusting pace; facilitating note taking; using multiple representations, analogies, metaphors, examples, illustrations, and applications; using the "pause principle," stimulating students' intuition and imagery; and planning for anticipated difficulties in teaching.

Chapter 13

Clarifying After Completing Instruction

Clear teaching is teaching for understanding[60]. However, gaining a full and meaningful understanding of the material taught is established only when students can apply this knowledge by demonstrating *"understanding performances"*—performing some thinking tasks that are based on the material. The tasks can be of a diverse nature such as explaining, providing illustrations and analogies, comparing and contrasting, providing evidence and justification, putting into context, generalizing, applying and transferring to new situations, and solving problems (Perkins, 1992; 1998). A full level of understanding is gained gradually during the lesson and after the lesson (e.g., through solving related problems or doing other homework assignments). Nevertheless, to deepen students' understanding within the framework of the lesson and help them retain and apply the new material, teachers should add clarification procedures after completing instruction of each subject.

As can be seen in Figure 13-1, the main clarification procedures used after teaching a subject has been completed are:

1. Looking back (i.e., laying the basis for "understanding performances").
2. Sharpening the meaning (i.e., demonstrating "understanding performances").
3. Helping apply learned material (i.e., training or guiding in "understanding performances").

[60] See Chapter 9: The Notion of "Teaching Clarity."

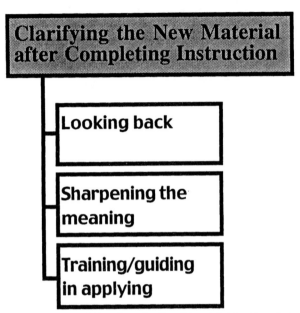

Figure 13-1: Dimensions of Clarifying the New Material After Completing Instruction

LOOKING BACK

In this teaching strategy, upon completion of the explanation of a complex concept, topic, procedure, and so forth, the teacher looks back critically on the issues and steps presented so far. The teacher thereby examines the strengths and weaknesses of the ideas and findings, and looks for ways to improve the results, to connect or apply them to different domains, and to explore their accuracy or validity. Thus, looking back lays the groundwork for demonstrating "understanding performances."

Looking back is considered to be a very important step in any problem-solving procedure. Polya (1957, p. 15) advocated that:

> A good teacher should understand and impress on his students the view that no problem whatever is completely exhausted. There remains always something to do; with sufficient study and penetration, we could improve any solution, and, in any case, we can always improve our understanding of the solution.

In effect, looking back offers an opportunity to investigate the connections of one problem with other problems and issues.

How to look back

Recapitulate the core idea. Upon completion of an explanation, clarify the meaning of the concept, notion, theory, procedure, and so forth, by recapitulating the main points, the core ideas, or the end results.

Simulate the process or review the steps. In this technique, when the explanation refers to a long procedure or to an elaborate process with many steps, you may go over all the steps one by one. If different initial conditions produce different results when going through the process, you may repeat going through the process, where each repeat starts with a different initial condition.

Follow the steps suggested by the following list of questions while looking back on a problem you have solved, as suggested by Polya (ibid, p. xvii): "Can you check the result? Can you check the argument? Can you derive the result differently? Can you see it at a glance? Can you use the result, or the method, for some other problem?"

SHARPENING THE MEANING OF NEW CONCEPTS OR PROCEDURES

An important step to be taken prior to having students show their "understanding performances" is for the teacher to demonstrate some of these performances in class. Toward this aim, the teacher can repeat the procedures for achieving clarity (e.g., give more complex and comprehensive examples and illustrations, analogies and metaphors, summaries, and reviews) described in the three previous chapters. To sharpen the meaning of concepts and processes, the teacher can provide positive instances as well as negative instances—what a concept is not. Such negative examples delineate the boundaries of a definition and so increase clarity. Another strategy for sharpening meaning is to show similarities and differences between the new content and previously known material. One of the 28 teacher behaviors that most strongly discriminated between university teachers high and low on clarity (Hines, 1982) was "Shows similarities and differences between things." Cognitive learning theories indicate that it is difficult to learn ideas that appear similar unless the differences between them are emphasized. Alternatively, it is easier to learn disparate ideas if their similarities are emphasized (Lowman, 1984). Additional sharpening strategies include the discussion of limit cases, special cases, extreme cases, unusual events, the extrapolation of the material, and so forth.

How to sharpen the meaning

Provide additional examples and illustrations, use rule-example-rule sequence. Upon completing an explanation, present examples and illustrations, additional to and more complex than those already presented during the development of the explanation. After teaching a particular rule, support it with a few examples, and then restate the rule, thus creating a *rule-example-rule* sequence. You may extend the sequence to *rule-example-rule-example,* or change the order to *example-rule-example-rule,* and use like structures of combinations of examples and rule formulation.

Provide additional analogies, metaphors, and visual or intuitive interpretations. Upon the completion of an explanation, present additional analogies, metaphors, or other visual and intuitive interpretations of the material presented. Here also you may build combinations of sequences such as *analogy-rule-metaphor;* or *example-metaphor-rule-example-analogy.*

Discriminate between similar cases, indicating where students typically err or confuse the cases.

Show similarities between different cases.

Bring positive as well as negative examples and applications to illuminate the concept from different aspects.

Present cases of use and misuse of the new concept, and cases of "non-examples"—when concepts or procedures do not work. Present counter-examples and discriminate between cases.

Stress main attributes of the concept.

Present special cases, limit/border cases.

Present applications in the same field, for other fields of study, for professional use, and in daily life.

Identify the type/category of each case.

State which cases would apply in what conditions/occasions.

HELPING STUDENTS TO APPLY THE NEW MATERIAL

The last step for deepening students' understanding, before letting them experience independent "understanding performances," consists of teachers training or guiding students in carrying out these performances. "Research studies have shown that comprehending an abstraction does not certify that the individual will be able to apply it correctly. Students apparently also need practice in restructuring and clarifying situations so that the correct abstraction applies" (Bloom, 1956, p. 122). Indeed, in Bloom's hierarchical taxonomy of educational objectives, the category of "Application" follows the two lower-level categories of "Knowledge" and "Comprehension."

The following are illustrations of applications within various disciplines, as suggested by Bloom (ibid., p. 124):

Application to the phenomena discussed by a paper, of the scientific terms and concepts used in other papers.

Application of social science generalizations and conclusions to actual social problems.

Practicing the probable effect of a change in a factor on a biological situation previously at equilibrium.

Applying science principles, postulates, theorems, or other abstractions to new situations.

Applying principles of psychology in identifying the characteristics of a new social situation.

Relating principles of civil liberties and civil rights to current events.

Applying the laws of trigonometry to practical situations.

Developing some skill in applying Mendel's laws of heredity to experimental findings on the genetics of plants.

However, the more recent perception of "understanding" (Perkins, 1998) entails demonstrating "understanding performances." Therefore, training and guiding students in applying the new material to new situations is an important component of teaching for understanding. To do so, a teacher can guide students in solving problems by demonstrating methods for solutions. Hines (1982) found the technique "Goes over difficult problems in class" to be one of 28 teacher behaviors most discriminating between clear and unclear teachers. Here are several students' complaints about teachers who do not provide this type of guidance:

- The guy doesn't explain any problem. He spends forever confusing the class with theory that we can't apply.

- Do sample problems in class and do different examples than the book does! The reason everyone does so poorly on exams is we have only been taught the formulas and their derivations, not how they are used.

- Do more problems and better prepare students for what is going to be tested so we don't end up thinking we understood the lectures and concepts but we remain utterly clueless as to how to approach and solve problems.

Another way for guiding students in solving problems is to provide them with a printed sequence of solved examples, arranged in increasing difficulty and complexity. Several studies on learning mathematics at the pre-college level have shown that when students are provided with a well-structured sequence of worked-out examples, they can learn to solve problems independently and, moreover, learn a substantial amount of the theoretical material by themselves (Sweller & Cooper, 1985; Zhu & Simon, 1987).

How to guide students in applying learned material

Provide questions to direct students' thinking while reading or writing. You can provide several questions on reading or writing assignments to direct students' thinking while doing the assignments, or even ask students to submit written answers and commentaries.

Demonstrate solutions to problems. You may solve sample problems on the board while explaining how to think about the problem and how to approach and plan the solution process.

Provide a sequence of solved out examples. You can replace guiding students in problem solution in class by distributing a printout illustrating a sequence of problems with fully explicated solutions.

Provide an algorithm for solution. An algorithm is "a procedure for solving a problem which, if followed accurately, guarantees that in a finite number of steps you will find a solution to the problem if the problem has a solution" (Bruner, 1960, p. 63). Providing an algorithm for the solution of a category of problems helps students in the first steps of solving problems of this category. Eventually, after students achieve confidence in their ability to solve the problems, their understanding is deepened and increased.

Suggest a plan for action. A plan for action is an elaborated algorithm for solution—it consists of a sequence of meta-cognitive questions that learners may ask themselves in order to proceed.

To illustrate, use Polya's (1957) four-step plan for action in heuristic problem solving: understanding the problem, devising a plan, carrying out the plan, and looking back:

First you have to *understand* the problem. Second, find the connection between the data and the unknown. You may be obliged to consider auxiliary problems if an immediate connection cannot be found. You should obtain eventually a *plan* for the solution. Third, *carry out* your plan, and fourth, *examine* the solution obtained (pp. xvi-xvii).

For each of these steps, you may add Polya's (ibid, p. xvii) sequential list of questions that the solvers should ask themselves in order to accomplish each step successfully. For example, the steps for devising a plan or algorithm are:

Have you seen the problem before? Or have you seen the same problem in a slightly different form?

Do you know a related problem? Do you know a theorem that could be useful?

Look at the unknown! And try to think of a familiar problem having the same or a similar unknown.

Here is a problem related to yours and solved before. Could you use it?

If you cannot solve the proposed problem try to solve first some related problem. Could you imagine a more accessible related problem? A more general problem? A more special problem? An analogous problem? Could you solve a part of the problem? ...

How to make your students demonstrate "understanding performances" of the new material

After guiding students in applying the new material through providing questions to direct thinking while reading or writing, demonstrating solutions, and providing algorithms and plans for actions, you may assign students to demonstrate their own "understanding performances." Ask them to:

Explain relations among the units of information you have presented, to integrate them and form general concepts.

Apply the new concepts and principles to new data and different situations, or to their own lives.

Solve problems.

Give opinions, demonstrate skills, react to feedback, and so forth.

SUMMARY

Clear teaching is teaching for understanding. However, gaining full and meaningful understanding of the material taught in a lesson is established only when students can apply this knowledge, that is, perform thinking tasks—"understanding performances"—based on that material. A full level of understanding is gained gradually during the lesson and after the lesson. To deepen students' understanding within the framework of the lesson and help them retain and apply the new material, teachers should add clarification procedures after students have supposedly gained basic comprehension of the material. The main clarification procedures teachers use are:

Looking back. In this teaching strategy, which lays the foundation for "understanding performances," upon completion of the explanation of a complex concept, topic, procedure, and so forth, the teacher looks back critically on the issues and steps presented, examines the strengths and weaknesses of the ideas and findings, and looks for ways to improve the results, to connect or apply them to different domains, and to examine their accuracy or validity.

Sharpening the meaning of new concepts or procedures. Teachers should sharpen the meanings of the material just taught. This may be done by providing additional, more complex and comprehensive examples and illustrations, analogies and metaphors, summaries, and reviews; by presenting cases of use and misuse of the new concepts; and more. These additional items strengthen and deepen students' understanding of the new material and promote their ability to apply it.

Training students in applying the new material. The last step for deepening students' understanding, before having them demonstrate independent "understanding performances," is training and guiding them in carrying out these performances. Students need supervised practice in restructuring and clarifying situations so that the correct understanding applies. Therefore, training and guiding students in applying the new material to new situations makes an important contribution to clarity. The training can be done by means of demonstrating solutions to problems and providing plans for action.

Chapters 14-15 present "Making the lesson interesting and engaging"— a main dimension of effective teaching.

Chapter 14

Promoting Student Motivation

Along with clarity and organization, presenting material in an interesting and engaging way is another main dimension of effective teaching[61]. How does an interesting/engaging presentation of the material contribute to student learning? An interesting presentation helps students concentrate on the material and keeps them alert and attentive. On the other hand, when the presentation is dull, students stop listening. They daydream, fall asleep, or become engaged in activities other than learning.

As shown in Figure 14-1, a teacher can achieve student interest and engagement throughout the lessons by using three main methods:
1. Motivating students to learn the material.
2. Gaining and maintaining students' attention.
3. Activating students and their thinking.

This chapter concentrates on the first step in making a lesson interesting and engaging—promoting students' motivation to stay open to input and to study the material presented. The second method—gaining and maintaining students' attention—is elaborated in the next chapter. The third method—activating students and their thinking—was elaborated in the previous chapters 6 and 7.

---

[61] See Chapter 1: The Main Dimensions of Effective Teaching.

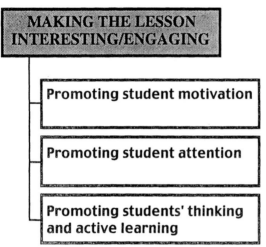

Figure 14-1: Dimensions of Making the Lesson Interesting and Engaging

MOTIVATING STUDENTS TO LEARN DURING THE LESSON

Remember, the customer is always right in principle, and sometimes right in practice. The lad who refuses to learn [your subject] may be right; he may be neither lazy nor stupid, just more interested in something else—there are so many interesting things in the world around us. It is your duty as a teacher, as a salesman of knowledge, to convince the student that [your subject] is interesting, that the point just under discussion is interesting, that the problem he is supposed to do deserves his best effort (Polya, 1965, p. 105).

People cannot learn by having information pressed into their brains. Knowledge has to be sucked into the brain, not pushed in. First, one must create a state of mind that craves knowledge, interest and wonder. You can teach only by creating an urge to know (Weisskopf, 1997, p. 194).

The following comments, taken from students' evaluation sheets of an anthropology teacher, illustrate how making the presentation interesting can motivate students to learn the material.

• She loves her subject and works very hard to make it interesting to all of us.

• Perhaps one of the most enthusiastic professors I have yet encountered in my university

 career!! She seems to live and breathe the material and does an exceptional job of drawing

 on classical and contemporary examples to further our understandings of certain themes.

 She motivates us to explore the incredible cultures around us.

- Professor "x" was a very enthusiastic lecturer who fostered interest in any topic she spoke about.

- She really built my interest in a topic I had found totally dull before. I took this course solely to fulfill the requirements and I was going to blow it off and take it with no credit. However, I ended up liking the class a lot. I went to all the lectures and did all the reading.

- She instilled interest in the students—her own love and knowledge was inspiring and infectious. Lectures were great!

According to the constructivist learning theory, meaningful learning develops through an active process of thinking and building networks of bodies of knowledge.[62] However, the mere exposure to knowledge, even if it is clearly presented by the lecturer, does not ensure meaningful learning. A prerequisite for meaningful learning is that students want to concentrate on the presentation and to open themselves up to input, that is, that students are motivated to study the material. What and how much is learned is influenced by the learner's motivation.[63] The learner's creativity, higher order thinking, and natural curiosity all contribute to motivation to learn.

To foster studying—to make students want to learn the new material—a teacher should provide motivation for the whole course, lesson, or unit of study at the beginning of the course, the lesson, and every time a new topic is presented. The teacher should inspire students to learn a whole topic, an idea, a proof, an experiment, a development, or a process.

WHAT AFFECTS STUDENT MOTIVATION FOR LEARNING IN THE COURSE?

Motivation for learning in an academic course is enhanced when (Eccles, 1983):

- The goals of a course are consistent with the immediate or long-term goals of the student (for example, majors are usually more highly motivated than non-majors).
- The students see an immediate application of the content.
- The task itself represents a challenge.
- The presentation of the task is novel or otherwise interesting.

A prerequisite for promoting student motivation to learn is an effective presentation. Poor teaching reduces students' motivation to study. When the material presented is not clear or boring, or when the classroom climate for

---

[62] See Chapter 4: Constructivist Learning theory.
[63] See Chapter 4: (APA, 1997, Princples 7-9).

learning is unpleasant and tense, students feel frustrated and unhappy. They then tend to lose interest:

- The lesson has no pace, which decreases our motivation to absorb the material.

What is the role of the nature of material for learning in promoting student motivation?

> If we wish to stimulate the student to a genuine effort, we must give him some reason to suspect that his task deserves his effort...The [learning material] should appear as meaningful and relevant from the student's standpoint; it should be related, if possible, to the everyday experience of the students, ...it should start from some very familiar knowledge; it should have, if possible, some point of general interest or eventual practical use (Polya, 1965, p. 105).

Thus, to promote motivation it is also important that the learning tasks are perceived by students as personally relevant, meaningful, appropriate in complexity and difficulty to their abilities, and in which they can succeed. Motivation is also facilitated by tasks that simulate real-world situations and meet students' needs for exercising choice and control.

THEORIES OF LEARNING MOTIVATION

Motivation is what energizes us and directs our behavior and activity (Gage & Berliner, 1998). It can thus be likened to an automobile's engine and steering wheel. *Motivation to achieve* is the degree to which individuals make an effort to achieve goals they perceive as meaningful and worthwhile (Johnson & Johnson, 1995). Following are several theories related to *achievement motivation in learning*. They are not mutually exclusive and share some ideas. A more detailed account of these theories may be found in any textbook on educational psychology (e.g., Gage & Berliner, 1998). Additional sources for reading are also presented below.

Theories of the source of motivation distinguish between external and internal motivation to study. *External motivation* is any motivation caused by environmental factors, having tangible/observable rewards such as a monetary award or a high grade. *Internal motivation* is behavior resulting from some innate drive, without apparent reinforcement from the outside, that appears to be unaffected by environmental factors. Generally, a person with low internal motivation does not feel committed to the task and reacts to circumstances rather than controlling them (ibid.). More particularly, a student with low internal motivation is not committed to learning and adjusts his/her learning to the circumstances—for example, to the teacher's requirements or to the daily events that affect him/her.

The theory of self-fulfilling teacher expectations suggests that teachers' expectations of their students' success or failure tend to materialize. Most often, students expected to succeed do succeed, whereas those expected to fail, fail. This assertion that teacher's expectations function as a self-fulfilling prophecy is named the *Pygmalion Effect*. To explain, the trust teachers express in students' ability to learn reduces anxiety when students do not understand the material immediately, and promotes their perseverance when they face difficulties. Teachers communicate their expectations in subtle ways— both verbal and nonverbal. These expectations affect students' beliefs in their ability to learn, as we explain next.

The theory of student expectancies for success in learning contends that students who believe a learning task can be accomplished and that they are able to learn difficult material have greater motivation to try, to invest effort in studying, and to persist. A history of success, and a match between the learner's skills and the task's demands, both increase expectancies for success (Svinicki et al., 1996).

The theory of attributions in learning states that the reasons to which students attribute their successes and failures in task performance affect their work on subsequent tasks. This theory is concerned with students' perceptions of the causes (a) of their own and others' behavior, and (b) of the events that occur to them (Graham & Golan, 1991). Causes can be *dispositional* (within people) or *situational* (within environment). In this theory, students perceive their behavior as either originating in themselves or as being the result of external pressures. For example, they can attribute the causes for success in learning to either their ability or the amount of effort they exerted (dispositional causes), or to the ease of task or to their luck (situational causes). If students believe that causes of events are beyond their control, for example, that causes are arbitrary or capricious, their achievement motivation declines. When students believe that they are studying because they freely choose to do so, that they operate under their own control and are personally committed to learn, then their learning motivation increases (deCharms, 1976).

The theory of attributional retraining holds that adults can be trained to increase their achievement motivation (McClelland, 1985). Perry, Hecher, Menec, and Weinberg (1993) reviewed studies that examined the effects of special training for at-risk university students whose causal attributions led to low motivation for investing effort in learning. The retraining was aimed at changing these attributions by increasing students' expectations for success in learning and their belief in their control over factors related to success[64]. Results indicated an increase in motivation for investing effort in

---

[64] See a detailed description in Chapter 16.

learning and consequently increased success in learning, among the participating students.

Teachers may affect the attributions students make about the causes of their success or failure even without special student training. This can be done through teachers' behaviors toward students, particularly through the emotions they communicate to students in response to their success or failure. For example, teacher sympathy for failure tends to be interpreted by students as indicating their low ability, while teacher anger or impatience with failure is interpreted as indicating low effort on their part.

The theory of self-esteem suggests that teachers can promote students' perceived competence. Perceived competency influences students' willingness to invest effort in their learning, particularly in task accomplishment and persistence in the face of failure (Bandura & Cervone, 1986). This perception is heavily influenced by initial encounters with novel tasks. Students who experience initial success or failure in some new undertaking tend to infer that they possess a respectively high or low aptitude or competence in that area. Once formed, these beliefs are resistant to change.

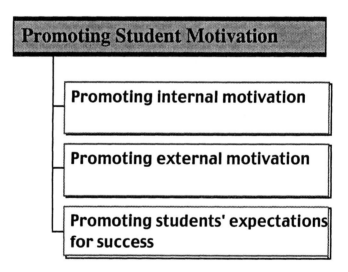

Figure 14-2: Dimensions of Promoting Student Motivation

WAYS FOR PROMOTING STUDENT MOTIVATION FOR LEARNING

A teacher can promote students' internal as well as external motivation, and their expectations for success, by changing students' attributions for causes of success or failure and their self-esteem, as suggested next.

How to Promote Internal Motivation

Appeal to the permanent interests and immediate concerns of students. Show them that the content is worth putting effort in learning because:

- **It is relevant** to their life experiences, interests, or prior learning, or it supports their attitudes, opinions, and needs. Use relevant examples and illustrations. Allow students to select topics of personal interest for discussion, projects, or papers; and build on their personal experiences.
- **It is intrinsically beautiful, challenging, intriguing, interesting.** Use *motivational cues* such as: Isn't that nice? Beautiful? Marvelous? Exciting? Greatest? Wonderful? Or by stating: this is very interesting, important, applicable, useful, and so forth.
- **It is related to contemporary issues.** You can use up-to-date examples and illustrations and present cutting-edge knowledge.

How to Promote External Motivation

Emphasize the benefits of learning the material. Make students want to learn the material because they realize that it is important for them and that it will benefit them either now or in the future. Tell students what the tasks they are doing are good for, how these tasks prepare them to do other things, and why they are important. Show or tell them that the material you teach is important or useful to them because:

- **It is beneficial for them to learn.** Learning the material will benefit their lives at present or in the future, their personal or professional needs, their present learning in this course or in other courses, and their future learning in other fields of study or contexts. Give students some notion of the rewards they will gain if they make an effort to learn.
- **It may lead to achieving their goals.** These goals can be good grades, the solution to an intellectual problem, success in a career, satisfaction of curiosity, the ability to help other people, or a chance to earn more (Gage & Berliner, 1998). Tell students that the final exam will include questions on the particular topics that you present in this lesson.

How to Promote Students' Expectations for Success

In light of the theories of learning motivation presented above, in order to increase students' motivation you need to modify their attributions for causes of success and failure:

Communicate your belief in students' ability to learn the material well and your expectations for their success in learning in your course.

Communicate expectations that students invest the time and effort needed to succeed.

Avoid communicating sympathy for students' failure.

Specify clear, explicit learning goals to help learners see and assess their progress toward achieving their goals.

Help students set their own goals to enhance their perceptions of control over the environment.

Define success for each student as improvement relative to his/her own prior performance rather than comparing to other students (if possible).

Guide students to attribute both their successes and failures to causes within themselves rather than to uncontrollable external causes. Help them see the relationship between their efforts and success in the course tests. Show and convince them that their success is related to their effort or learning strategy rather than to coincidence.

Ensure that all students experience some success early in a learning sequence. At the beginning of each new class or with every new type of task, make students experience success to help them believe in their aptitude for the subject area or task.

Invite students who failed a midterm test and try to identify their perception of the causes for their failure. Encourage them and convince them that the reason for failure is not a lack of luck but rather inefficient preparation for the test or insufficient background. Guide them in how to complement the missing background and to effectively prepare for success in the next test.

Enable students who failed in the first midterm to compensate for their failure by getting good grades in the following tests, quizzes, and homework assignments. See a vivid description in the foreword to this book by Douglas Osheroff.

SUMMARY

Motivation for learning is a prerequisite for meaningful learning to occur. *Motivation* is what energizes us and directs our behavior and activity. *Achievement motivation* is what drives individuals to commit effort to achieve goals they perceive as meaningful and worthwhile. *External motivation* is any motivation caused by environmental variables having tangible or observable rewards, whereas *intrinsic motivation* appears to be unaffected by environmental variables.

Factors that may increase students' motivation to study the course material include teaching that is effective—organized, clear, engaging, and that leads to a positive classroom climate In addition, the goals of the course should be consistent with the immediate or long-term goals of the student. Students should also see an immediate application of the content, and the learning task should represent a challenge.

Theories of learning motivation suggest that teachers' expectations for the success or failure of their students tend to come true (the Pygmalion Effect). Students who believe a task can be accomplished have greater motivation than do others to try, to invest effort in studying, and to persist. Students attribute their success in learning either to (a) causes within themselves or that are under their control, such as their ability or the amount of effort they have exerted, or to (b) environmental factors beyond their control such as luck or the ease of the task. The more students believe they operate under their own control, the greater is their learning motivation. Students can be trained to increase their achievement motivation for learning and thus increase their success in learning.

Even without special training, teachers may affect the attributions students make about the causes of their success or failure through their behaviors toward students, particularly through the emotions they communicate to students in response to their success or failure. Teachers should explicitly guide students to attribute both their successes and failures to causes within themselves, which are under their control. They should promote students' perceived competence, for instance by providing them with success experiences at the beginning of a new type of task.

Chapter 15

Making the Lesson Interesting and Engaging: Promoting Student Attention

- Class lectures were pretty boring, and it wasn't surprising to see course attendance slip so much.
- She gets it all in but does not overwhelm you, and can lull you to sleep.
- The lecturer goes on and on at a rather uniform pace but my mind does not. I frequently suffer from lapses of attention and eventually I totally lose my ability to follow the presentation and my motivation to stay alert. I even find myself falling asleep.

Anyone who has attended a dull, boring lecture has had the experience described in these students' comments, when their attention failed and they drifted off, when their motivation to attend class and concentrate faded, or when they became involved in activities other than learning. An engaging presentation, in contrast, helps listeners focus on the material and keeps them alert and attentive throughout the lesson, as reflected in the following students' comments:

- A delightful lecturer—very engaging, never boring. Gold stars!
- Excellent teaching style! Fun and entertaining even for a techie! [in a humanities general-distribution course]

From the point of view of oral communication, gaining and maintaining the receiver's attention is the first step in communicating between a "sender" and a "receiver" (DeLozier, 1979). Thus, in order for students to understand and learn the material taught in class, they must first of all be attentive to the teacher. According to models of information processing,[65] a low level of

---

[65] See Chapter 5: Figure 5-1.

attention, or the lack thereof, obstructs the first step of this process—it prevents the taking-in of information through the senses—so that this information does not penetrate active memory.

Gaining and maintaining student attention is not a simple task. Pollio (1984) found that while teachers are lecturing, students are not attending to what is being said 40% of the time. Communication experts suggest that students' level of attention is uneven throughout a lecture—as a lesson proceeds, students lose their initial interest, and attention levels continue to drop. McKeachie (1999) quantified this decrease in attention, which indicated that on average, in the first ten minutes of the lecture, students retain about 70% of the information presented, whereas in the last ten minutes, only 20%. Similarly, Wlodkowski (1985) found that most people's attention wanes after 15-25 minutes of listening.

Indeed, sitting passively for 45-50 minutes during a lecture is a difficult task. How can teachers help students concentrate and stay alert? We have already mentioned two main methods: arousing students' motivation[66] and fostering students' physical and cognitive activity—making them read, write, and talk meaningfully during the lesson, think and be intellectually challenged, stretch and even exercise during long lectures[67]. Additional strategies, suggested here, are: presenting content that promotes listeners' attention, and behaving in class in ways that attract and maintain student attention.

This chapter presents these additional behaviors and strategies arranged under two categories: (a) attention-getting content, and (b) attention-getting teacher behavior, as shown in Figure 15-1.

ATTENTION-GETTING CONTENT

Teachers can gain and maintain student attention through the content they present. They can dramatize the content and present unexpected elements; incorporate related anecdotes, analogies, humor, examples and illustrations; use self-disclosure; and present cultural aspects of the domain taken from history, philosophy, sociology, current events, and prospective developments. More specifically:

---

[66] See Chapter 14.
[67] See Chapters 6 and 7.

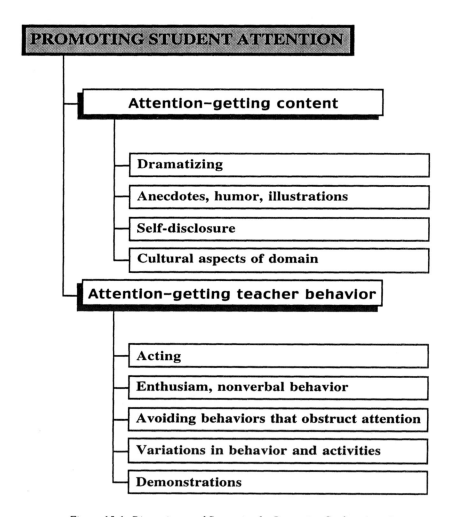

Figure 15-1: Dimensions and Strategies for Promoting Student Attention

Dramatizing the Content—Using Suspense, Surprise, and Uncertainty

"An occasional departure from what students have come to expect has the effect of attracting their attention and getting them involved" (Gage & Berliner, 1991, p. 372). Dramatizing the content takes place when teachers promote student curiosity and the desire to explore; raise doubt or conflict regarding held beliefs; stimulate the perplexity or uncertainty coming from unexpected contents, results, or fantasy; and elicit the feelings of suspense, tension, surprise, and excitement that arise when expecting something important or unusual.

To illustrate dramatized content, I refer to one of the physics lessons I observed given by a university professor who was well known for his exemplary teaching. On that day, he presented the principle of the elastic collision of two bodies. After he had demonstrated several different cases of such collisions (of bodies of either equal or different masses), he presented a graph describing the behavior of two train cars after their collision. The graph indicated the unexpected behavior of one of the cars. The teacher led the class through a step-by-step analysis of the graph, creating suspense by gradually unfolding unexpected processes. The analysis surprised students by revealing the existence of an unknown body within that car, which was responsible for its strange behavior after the collision. Then the teacher made an analogy of this process to the way elementary particles of the atom were discovered: they, too, could not be observed until a through analysis of graphs of their behavior following collisions was undertaken. In this way, the professor succeeded in explaining to first-year physics students material that was in the forefront of scientific discovery and whose formal explanation requires many years of study. The students were extremely excited by their success in understanding these contemporary physics issues.

Strategies for Dramatizing the Content

How to create a climate of suspense

Infuse the presentation with suspense, with a sense of dramatic tension. Create a sense of anticipation that leads students to expect something important or unusual. Build the material to lead toward a climax, surprise students with absurd, unexpected results or connections.

Save the conclusions or most crucial points until the end, having teased the students along the way with key questions, leading questions, and dropped clues.

Build the material as an unfolding story of discovery. Reveal the most interesting point gradually rather than exposing it outright.

Ask for students' intuitions or guesses regarding the results of some process or the solution to a problem. Then develop the process or solve the problem correctly.

Use dramatic elements in content. Use exaggeration, provide astonishing and startling facts, create controversy, show contradiction, use intriguing and surprising illustrations or demonstrations, or describe a paradox, puzzle, captivating experiment, or surprising case study.

Complement missing information. Present a table with empty cells, or a tree-diagram without its headings to be completed as the lesson proceeds.

Tell captivating stories to support points you make. Almost any teacher can learn to be a good storyteller if he or she relaxes inhibitions and is responsive to the suspense inherent in most contents.

Infuse interest in the main parts of the lesson structure. These entail the introduction, conclusion, and body of the lesson:

- **Introduction.** Start the lesson with an attention-getter such as a story, anecdote, personal incident, interesting activity, or example. Create expectations that something interesting, important, or worthwhile is going to be presented during the lesson. Toward this aim, begin by posing a key question or a problem to be answered or solved, or with describing a paradox or a controversy to be explained later. Alternatively, ask students, as they arrive to class, to call out questions about today's topic that they hope will be answered that day. List the questions on the board.
- **Conclusion.** Conclude the lesson with something that is likely to leave an impression—a summarizing graph or table, an interesting example, a surprising application, a thinking challenge to be answered in the next lesson, or some words that transmit the central thesis of the lesson.
- **Body of the lesson.** Throughout the lesson, organize the topics around one to three themes that you present at the beginning and to which you return every so often from different points of view or from different examples and applications. At the end of each unit, ask students to finish (either orally or in writing) the sentence: "A question I still have about this topic is..."

Present different/clashing approaches, points of views, or solutions, as exemplified by the following illustrations based on my class observations:

A math professor solves the same problem in at least two different ways, not only because this method demonstrates the use of different problem-solving strategies but also because it stimulates their interest in whether he will get the same answer each time.

An engineering professor presents several assumptions for a particular process that he is going to teach and polls students on which of these assumptions they think are the correct and most crucial ones. This practice adds the excitement of competition to the class.

A history professor opens up students to the possible varieties of historical explanation by posing what he calls "counterfactuals," or "what ifs," that is, what if things that happened wouldn't have happened.

Incorporating Anecdotes, Analogies, Humor, Examples and Illustrations

- She tells good stories to keep us listening during the lecture.
- He often brings interesting anecdotes that awaken the students.
- Good use of examples in class—kept it interesting.
- She always tries to show us the beauty, the elegance in the stuff she's presenting.
- Her good sense of humor makes her lessons lively.
- He can joke with us and still teach.
- I like his awkward jokes.

Incorporating relevant anecdotes, analogies, examples and illustrations into teaching promote not only clarity[68] but also makes the lesson interesting. Such strategies provide variation and breathing spaces for students and connect the lesson topics to their personal and professional interests. Some of the benefits attributed to humor include increased student attentiveness and interest accomplished by making learning exciting and effective (Bryant, Comisky, & Zillmann, 1979; Korobkin, 1988; Powell & Andersen, 1985)[69].

How to incorporate anecdotes, analogies, humor, examples and illustration

Tell related anecdotes. Describe the work of great scholars or scientists in your domain and their innovations or discoveries, or other important events that are relevant to the present lesson.

Use analogies and metaphors that shed a new light on the topic presented.

Incorporate relevant examples and illustrations from a variety of sources such as industry, economics, research, and daily life.

Highlight the positive qualities of the topics presented. Show the beauty, interest, elegance, importance, and so forth, of the course material.

Infuse your presentation with humor. Prepare jokes and humorous anecdotes that are relevant to the topic taught[70].

Build on students' experiences. Incorporate examples, illustrations, and applications into your teaching that students themselves have suggested on the basis of their life or professional experiences. Ask your students to describe any interesting or relevant experiences that they have had or things that they have read regarding the topics presented.

---

[68] See Chapter 10: Teaching in Two (or More) Cycles.
[69] These topics are discussed in more detail in Chapters 17 and 19.
[70] See Chapter 19

> Start a topic by asking students to call out everything they know or think about the topic, or to explore the multiple meanings of key words. Ask students to call out as many definitions as they can for a concept or term. Write every offering on the board. Build the ensuing presentation on students' input.

Using "Self-Disclosure"—Telling about Oneself, and Presenting Personal Knowledge and Point of View

- Great lecturer, keeps audience interested and alert with personal stories and humor.

By telling something that happened to them personally, professors provide a personal context to the topic taught. They can thereby show why the subject interests and excites them, and how they have used it in their own experience. Self-disclosure can succinctly demonstrate that the subject matter may have a practical application in one's own life; thus, the subject is worth learning about. Students like to hear about their professors' lives and professional experiences. Indeed, the use of self-disclosure was found to distinguish award-winning teachers from other teachers (Javidi, Downs, & Nussbaum, 1988). Students also like to hear their professors' perceptions and interpretations of current issues and events, and they appreciate teachers who exhibit independent thinking and who stand up for their own ideas even if these ideas are less accepted in public or in the academic world.

How to use self-disclosure

> Tell about your own life and professional experiences, or your studies in the domain.
>
> Describe your own stand or thinking regarding controversial issues in the field, even if your opinions contradict the prevailing view. Convey your personal thoughts or feelings about this and explain and justify your approach.
>
> Present your own interpretation of central issues and your expectation of future developments.

Presenting Cultural Aspects of the Domain

- He presents material that is in the forefront of scientific research and this makes the lesson exciting.
- The marvelous combination of literature and history with ample commentaries by modern writers was smashing.

Infusing the presentation with historical, philosophical, or sociological aspects of an academic domain, as well as describing current events, expected scientific developments, crucial new discoveries, and wide-scale debates and controversies in the domain can arouse considerable student interest during the lesson.

How to present cultural aspects of the domain

Introduce historical, philosophical, and sociological aspects of the particular topic that you teach. Transmit ways of thinking and of validating knowledge in the domain; general methods of the discipline; the nature of the course and learning in it; and the distinctions between the domain and related domains. Present stages in the historical development of the domain; tell about future developments that can be expected; and describe central figures and inventions. Present unusual information such as the personal correspondence of key figures in the field or little known literature that contradicts the consensus in the domain, to provoke interest and attention. Present examples and illustrations, controversies and debates, key experiments, and developments of important techniques. Tell about historical events that are related to the current topic; describe how the great discoveries in the field were made; simulate the steps of scientific discovery or of historical events.

Incorporate your knowledge of the world into the topics you present— integrate into your teaching what is happening outside of your area, or insert relevant topics from outside the strict course curriculum. Connecting course content to outside events adds validity to your area of expertise and allows students to integrate this knowledge and understanding on a variety of levels.

Present domain-related knowledge of current events and of scientific progress. Present in your lessons, whenever relevant, contemporary issues. Update your students on relevant current events such as controversial or major issues, innovative research methods, or new professional articles and books. Go beyond the curriculum to introduce topics on the forefront of your scientific domain. Students like to learn topics that are at the center of current interest.

ATTENTION-GETTING TEACHER BEHAVIOR—ENTHUSIASM AND DYNAMISM

Teaching obviously has much in common with the theatrical art... if you appear bored, the whole class will be bored. So pretend to be excited about the proof when you start it, pretend to have bright ideas when you proceed, pretend to be surprised and elated when the proof ends. You should do a little acting for the sake of your students who may learn, occasionally, more from your attitudes than from the subject matter presented. I must confess that I take pleasure in a little acting. (Polya, 1965, p. 101).

Teachers can promote and maintain student concentration and attention during the lesson not only through the content presented but also through their behavior in the classroom. They may introduce dramatic behavior including enthusiasm, dynamism, and acting; use nonverbal behaviors that attract attention; avoid "noise" promoting behaviors; and frequently vary their behavior.

Dramatic Behavior, Acting

Dramatic behaviors such as those that startle people will gain their attention (DeLozier, 1979). Student attention and interest can be generated through the use of "dramatizing devices," including the development of a dramatic personality by the teacher (Bruner, 1960). Dramatic style is one of the highest correlates of teacher effectiveness (Sallinen-Kuparinen, 1992). University teachers who received speech and drama training showed a small but significant improvement in student ratings relative to control teachers (Murray & Lawrence, 1980).

Dramatic behavior can captivate students. The use of drama in the classroom can startle, stir, stimulate, incite, and illuminate. Learners attend to provocative, creative, and inspiring teaching performances. When we use surprise, doubt, perplexity, bafflement, or contradiction, we arouse a kind of conceptual conflict in students. Their motivation tends to last until the conflict is resolved (Gage & Berliner, 1991).

In large classes, in order to communicate effectively with students and to capture their attention, the teacher must give a performance. The teacher should feel as if on stage—an actor performing—and should send and receive messages through voice, dress, body language, and even silence. Many college professors believe that they lack any dramatic ability and cannot act in class. However, interviews with professors who exhibit dramatic behavior in large classes strongly suggest that no special personality or acting talent is required (Hativa, 1998-9). Teachers may adopt techniques used by actors to communicate ideas and emotions on the stage, such as variation in loudness and pitch, movement and gesture, use of pauses, eye contact, facial expression, space utilization, animation in body language and use of props.

The extent to which dramatic behavior should be employed is dependent, of course, on the size of the class. Superior teachers who use drama when teaching large classes suggest that the smaller the class, the less drama is needed, and that in a very small class, this kind of behavior may even be totally out of place (Hativa, 1998-9). Thus, dramatic behavior is particularly appropriate in large classes with students of varied backgrounds. However, using drama even when teaching large classes is not absolutely required. Teaching a large course in a well-organized, clear, and interesting manner can avoid the addition of drama.

Nonverbal Behaviors that Attract Attention

Teachers may convey as much non-verbally as they do verbally. The main nonverbal classroom behaviors that promote student attention are: enthusiasm; dynamism; animated voice, body language, gestures, and facial expressions; eye contact; and use of the classroom space.

The physically dynamic teacher moves, exhibits a high energy level, and supports his or her explanations by an animated tone and gestures, but avoids distracting movements or mannerisms. Dynamic enthusiasm and "business-like" animated behavior are perceived to be associated with both student attention and achievement.

The following comments illustrate that teachers who deliver the lesson material enthusiastically communicate the feeling that they like the material they present, that they find it interesting and exciting, and that it is therefore worthwhile for students to put effort into its learning. Such modes of communication thus increase not only student attention but also their motivation to learn the topics.

- She is an amazing lecturer. She has a lot of energy and spunk, which is encouraging to students, and she enjoys teaching.
- He is so enthusiastic about the subject that I actually stay awake, have a good time, and learn a lot from the class.
- It is very evident that he loves the material that he teaches. He lives it, gets excited, and conveys his enthusiasm to the students.
- The professor's lectures were superb—she was animated and energetic—really expressed a passion for her area of study.
- She was always excited about what she was talking about and her enthusiasm was contagious. What a great woman!

Humor can be manifested not only in content but also in teacher behavior. Chapter 19 elaborates on this topic and presents suggestions for teachers in learning how to integrate humor into the classroom teaching.

- This teacher has comic talents, which prevent his lectures from being boring.

Actors are taught the importance of keeping their faces directed toward the audience as much as possible, and so should college teachers. It is in fact, crucial for teachers to maintain face-to-face contact with students at all times. Every time teachers turn their backs to the class, they risk "losing the house." If they stay like this for more than five seconds, they will find most of their students looking elsewhere or preoccupied with other matters.

Maintaining eye contact forces students to look at the teacher and helps keep them alert and concentrated. Eye contact also enables the teacher to identify problems in his/her presentation by observing signs of boredom or puzzlement that indicate a lack of understanding. Typical indications are chair shuffling, whispering, and, most importantly, avoiding meeting the teacher's eyes.

How to dramatize behavior, acting, nonverbal behavior that attracts attention

Be physically dynamic. Use gestures. Move, exhibit a high energy level, and support your explanations by an animated tone and gestures, but avoid distracting movements or mannerisms.

Show enthusiasm and use enthusiastic expressions. Exhibit enthusiasm in your behavior. Use enthusiastic verbal expressions regarding the material by using superlatives such as: wonderful, exciting, extraordinary, fascinating, fantastic, surprising, beautiful, elegant, and so forth.

Face the class and maintain eye contact with students throughout the lesson. Maintain eye contact by turning sideways when writing on the board, by regularly looking at the students, and by glancing around the classroom when a student is making a long comment or asking a question.

Demonstrate humorous behavior.

Avoiding Behaviors that Obstruct Student Attention

Teachers should also avoid any behavior that obstructs the maintaining of attention. This diminishes the students' capacity to take in the information being presented in class. Behaviors that reduce attention may be "noise" factors or those that cause boredom and lull students to sleep.

"Noise" reduces not only clarity[71] but also concentration and learning, as the mind fatigues more rapidly under "noisy" circumstances. "Noise" in a lesson is any teacher behavior that disrupts students' attention, distracts them from the core aspects of an explanation, or leads to doubt, conflict, or confusion. Such boredom-inducing behaviors cause the presentation to be monotonous and students to be passive. The teacher's reading from written text, as illustrated by the following students' comments, is one of those behaviors:

- The professor just read the notes and wrote them word for word on the board. Very boring.

- He's a very poor lecturer. He just photocopies pages out of the book and talks for an hour.

[71] See Chapter 11.

- His class presentation follows the textbook very closely. In fact, large parts of his lectures may be viewed as dictated from the book, almost word by word. No additional examples, illustrations, or even answers to students' questions are provided. Therefore, the classes are very boring, a waste of our time. It is enough to read the book and completely unnecessary to come to class.

How to avoid behaviors that obstruct student attention

Never dictate from a written text—whether it is a book, your notes, or transparencies. Remember—your lesson should convey far more than anything that students can read by themselves. When students merely copy from transparencies or write down every word the teacher says, they become very passive in the learning process.

Varying Teacher Behavior and Activities, Addressing Multiple Senses

Less obviously, teaching has something in common with music... the teacher should not say things just once or twice, but three or four more times. Yet repeating the same sentence several times without pause and change may be terribly boring and defeat its own purpose. Well, you can learn from the composers how to do it better. One of the principal art forms of music is the *air with variations*. Transposing this art form from music into teaching you begin by saying your sentence in its simplest form; then you repeat it with a little change; then you repeat it again with still more color, and so on. And you may wind up by returning to the original simple formulation. Another musical art form is the *rondo*. Transposing the rondo from music into teaching, you repeat the same essential sentence several times with little or no change, but you insert between repetitions some appropriately contrasting illustrative material. I hope that when you next listen the next time to a theme with variations by Beethoven or to a rondo by Mozart you will give a little thought to improving your teaching (Polya, 1965, pp. 101-102).

This flavored description by Polya presents the importance of variations during the lesson. The following are students' comments indicating their appreciation of the teacher's varying behavior and activities.

- I liked the variety of literature, film, music, poetry, discussion and lecture combination.
- Excellent lecturer—always new ideas, use of visuals, fresh approach.
- Class needs more variety, not just plain lectures every day.
- Texts and topics assigned were diverse in nature and scope, making the class more interesting and holistic.
- This is one of the most interesting compilations of texts/movies/poems/essays I have had in a class here.

- I really liked the multimedia treatment of the material.
- Wonderful variety of materials, very valuable.

Communication research suggests that people tend to pay more attention to things that are changing than to things that are stable and static (Wlodkowski, 1985). Students will tire during any lesson if it proceeds too long without a change. A teacher should enliven the class every so often to revive student interest when it appears to be flattening out. This can be done by introducing a particularly interesting example, some humor, an intriguing question, or a good mini summary. This can also be done by varying the channels of communication. Varying sensory channels has been found to help gain and maintain people's attention. "Multiple sensory messages produce greater attention than messages appealing to a single mode of perception. Sight, sound, smell, touch, and taste are the five sense modes to stimulate" (DeLozier, 1979, p. 21). The same author suggested that switching the channel of communication from the oral to the visual, even momentarily, causes changes in the response patterns and attention mechanisms of students.

Variety can also be attained by going to extremes and turning to the unusual. Communication experts suggest that the greater the strength or intensity of a stimulus (within acceptable limits), the greater its attention value (ibid.). Loud sounds and bright lights are examples, as are novel ideas and objects. Since people adapt to familiar surroundings, we reawaken their attention by introducing the unusual and exceptional (provided it is not too exceptional).

Using Class Demonstrations and Visual Aids

As suggested in the previous section, the use of visual stimuli introduces variety into the lesson and thus promotes interest and student attention. Teachers can use many types of visual aids: writing or drawing on the board, demonstrations, and transparencies. Objects in motion, or apparently in motion, attract greater attention than static objects (DeLozier, 1979). Therefore, audiovisual presentations such as clips from movies, filmstrips, videotapes, and animated microcomputer presentations are effective for maintaining student attention.

However, we should be aware that the mere use of visual devices does not in itself enhance learning. Like other techniques, visual devices must be used effectively, as suggested in the next section.

How to introduce variety into lesson

Make frequent variations in:

Teacher behavior: Change your behavior, activities, and teaching methods every 10-20 minutes. Be aware of when students start becoming bored—look at your audience for nonverbal clues of decreasing attention, watch their faces to see if they are following you. Use a lot of variation in all aspects of the lesson, but without overdoing it. Excessive use may impede attention.

Teacher oral presentation: Vary your voice inflection, tone, pitch, intonation, and level. Vocally emphasize important points.

Teacher physical behavior: Sit, stand, walk, move around the classroom space, use hand and body gestures, present dynamic behavior, write on the board, use audiovisual devices, interact with students, vary your teaching methods, and so on.

Teacher's pace of lecture: Go at a fast pace in some appropriate places, and slow down in others.

Mode of presentation: Lecture, discuss, simulate, demonstrate, present examples, show a film, play a simulation game, provide "breathing pauses," organize students into groups, pose regular or rhetorical questions, draw questions from students, seek feedback from them, try a new approach to the material, describe a process, present and solve a problem, have an introduction and a summary. Make some parts of the lectures somewhat informal and more loosely organized than others, such as in a combined lecture/discussion format.

Source of presentation: Invite guest speakers, particularly experts in topics related to the course material who come from the "real" world, to speak to your class. These outside speakers may offer real life examples of the material and ideas you have discussed in the classroom. They can clarify areas of knowledge and expertise that you lack, introduce a teaching style different from your own, provide and discuss materials, artifacts, and research that are otherwise inaccessible, offer a different viewpoint— disciplinary, cultural, gender-related, and so forth—on an issue within a discipline or topic of discussion, and serve as an expert or eyewitness for students to interview.

Other ways of varying the source of presentation are to assign a few students to present particular curricular topics in which they have a special interest, or that they have prepared for presentation as a special project; invite TAs or supervised master and doctoral students to present the topics they are involved with and on which they can contribute interesting points of view.

Communication channels: Use graphs, pictures, chalkboards, and technology-based visual media for both static and dynamic presentations: physical models, films, videotapes, slides, overhead transparencies, computer presentations, educational software, demonstrations, experiments, and props (showing an actual physical object, passing the object around the room when possible). All these introduce variety and arouse curiosity in a way that mere verbal descriptions cannot.

Students' activities: To keep students alert and active, offer them various activities, even during a lecture. Students should alternate among listening, watching, writing, drawing, thinking, or working cooperatively with other students, perhaps even making some physical changes during the lesson.[72]

SUMMARY

Making the lesson interesting and engaging is one of the most important characteristics of good teaching. To gain students' attention and to maintain it, teachers can:

Present attention-getting content. Teachers can gain and maintain student concentration and attention through the content they present. They can dramatize the content and present unexpected elements; incorporate related anecdotes, analogies, humor, and examples; use self-disclosure and present cultural aspects of the domain.

Present attention-getting classroom behavior. Teachers can promote and maintain student concentration and attention during the lesson through their own enthusiasm and dynamic behavior. They may introduce dramatic behavior like acting, and nonverbal behaviors that attract attention. They can avoid "noise" promoting behaviors and can frequently vary their behavior and students' activities.

---

[72] See Chapters 6 and 7 for suggestions for students' activity during the lesson and for introducing variety into this activity

Chapter 16

Promoting a Pleasant Classroom Climate

Professor Patron's lectures are high on the three main effective teaching dimensions that we have discussed so far: organization, clarity, and interest/engagement. His lessons are well organized and quite engaging, and he presents the material in a very clear fashion. However, he sometimes offends a student who asks a question that he thinks is insufficiently clever, and at times he patronizes or demeans students. He is very distant—never smiles, praises students' answers, or shows interest or care for them or for their difficulties in learning. Considering this entire set of classroom behaviors, is Patron an effective teacher? Does he promote students' effective learning?

The professor's insensitive behavior may produce "internal noise" and shut down many of his students. Those offended by his comments may become frustrated and angry, feelings that tend to reduce the ability to concentrate on the presentation. Most of the time, students who do not understand the material presented will avoid asking questions in fear of being ridiculed. Altogether, many students feel they benefit only little from the positive aspects in his lessons because the negative classroom environment that he creates is counterproductive to learning.

Learning is not merely a cognitive process; it is substantially affected by emotional factors. Teaching can thrive only in an environment of trust that encourages students to attend, think, and learn. Students need a supportive climate that provides generous room for trial and error, enables them to learn from mistakes, encourages them to take risks in overcoming difficulties in learning, and promotes their confidence in their ability to learn. A positive learning climate can help to establish the context for healthier levels of thinking, feeling, and behaving. Such a context helps learners feel safe to share ideas, actively participate in the learning process, and create a learning community. All in all, promoting a pleasant classroom climate that is conducive to learning is a necessary condition for effective teaching, and can be regarded as the fourth main dimension of effective teaching.

Communication research distinguishes between a supportive and a defensive communication climate. A supportive climate is characterized by efficient communication—effective listening behavior and clear message transmission. In a defensive climate, individuals tend to mistrust and misinterpret communication (Darling & Civikly, 1987).

The following comments illustrate behaviors that promote a supportive climate:

- The lectures are so good because she enjoys the subject, knows what she's teaching, is very responsive to students' questions, and aware of their difficulties.
- He has excellent responses to the students' misunderstandings of problems.
- She behaves very sympathetically toward students.
- I'm content with her great willingness to explain the stuff again and again to students who don't understand.
- Super nice, funny, approachable guy who loves to help and engage students.

And behaviors which promote a defensive climate:

- He doesn't care whether we follow him or understand what he's teaching.
- He always gives us the feeling that he intends to fail three quarters of the students in the course.
- She doesn't care about the students, behaves disrespectfully toward them, and answers questions impatiently, sometimes even sarcastically or disdainfully.

What do these comments tell us? Students highly appreciate a teacher who is pleasant, who encourages them to ask questions and responds patiently, and who demonstrates interest in and willingness to help foster their understanding and learning. Alternatively, the negative student comments presented here and in the following sections reveal that some teachers behave very negatively toward students. Evidently, these teachers are unaware of the devastating effects of their behavior on student motivation and learning.

University professors are often unaware of the effects of classroom climate on student learning. Some professors believe that they are not responsible for maintaining a pleasant environment in class and promoting students' motivation for learning but, rather, that the students themselves bear the full responsibility for their learning and that they themselves should develop the intrinsic motivation necessary to study on their own[73]. However, the need for encouragement and praise, and for a generally good feeling, are basic human needs that are not restricted by age and level of education.

How, then, can a supportive classroom climate that is conducive to learning be achieved? Figure 16-1 lists teacher behaviors that may contribute to this aim.

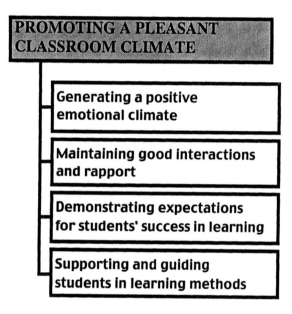

Figure 16-1: Dimensions of Promoting a Pleasant Classroom Environment That is Conducive to Learning

GENERATING A POSITIVE EMOTIONAL CLIMATE IN CLASS

In order to enhance student learning and motivation, teachers can cultivate a relaxed, warm, and pleasant climate in their classes by:
a) Generating favorable attitudes toward the teacher.
b) Exhibiting an intrinsically favorable attitude toward the students and nourishing good feelings in the students.
c) Avoiding development of internal noise.

---

[73] See Chapter 3: Personal Theories and Beliefs That Damage Teaching Effectiveness.

The last category is discussed in Chapter 11. The following is a discussion of the other two categories.

Generating Favorable Attitudes of Students Toward the Teacher

Presenting Pleasant Behavior and a Sympathetic Personality

The following comments describe a sympathetic teacher:

- Really a cool guy.
- Nice attitude, laid back, friendly, a good man.
- Nice person, dedicated and approachable, friendly and patient with all students, enjoys teaching.
- Very easygoing and flexible.
- The Prof. is very humane.

> **Communicate a pleasant demeanor** to your students, for example, by being relaxed, open, patient, friendly, good-hearted, self-confident, and so on.
>
> **Avoid showing negative feelings** in class when you are in a bad mood or suffer from anger or frustration.

Presenting Own Knowledge, Expertise, and Achievements

- He's involved in the real world of the topic. His cutting-edge experience gives a new perspective to the theory.
- Professor has complete mastery of material, a thorough understanding of the subject.
- He is brilliant and can answer any question we pose.
- Very knowledgeable, very intelligent.
- A great teacher and a very smart person, with a thorough command of the subject matter.
- Excellent knowledge of the material and of her field of study.

Students feel good about a teacher they appreciate as a person and as a scientist. They need to feel that in addition to being pleasant, their teacher is intelligent, reliable, expert, and knowledgeable in the area he or she teaches.

> **Promote students' appreciation** by positively presenting yourself through telling about your professional work and achievements.
>
> **Demonstrate a wide knowledge in areas beyond your academic domain** to show students that you are not limited to your narrow professional work.

> **Avoid excuses for gaps in your knowledge** or insufficient preparedness for the lesson. These excuses lower your credibility as an expert in the subject matter and as a lecturer.

Coming to Class Well Prepared

- Extremely well prepared and organized—wonderful lecture notes.
- The demos never worked.
- Should be better prepared to do experiments - none of them worked.
- He should come to class more prepared. If he mentally ran through an entire lecture beforehand, this might help us understand.

Students are very negative toward teachers who show a lack of command over the material they present—those who make frequent errors in formulas and developments, or who often do not know how to answer students' questions. On the other hand, students appreciate teachers who come to class well prepared. These teachers communicate that they take their teaching seriously, and that they care about their students' learning.

> **Prepare a detailed lesson plan** for each lesson in advance.
>
> **Fully solve any problem** that you plan to solve in class.
>
> **Try out any demonstration** you plan to exhibit in class.
>
> **Check all the audiovisual equipment** before the class starts.

Using Humor

Humor can greatly contribute to a positive emotional climate and to fostering a classroom climate conducive to learning.[74]

Exhibiting an Intrinsically Favorable Attitude Toward the Students and Inducing Good Feelings in Students

Highly regarded teachers express warm and accepting attitudes toward students (Ryans, 1960). Inducing good feelings in students can be done through: (i) supporting their learning; (ii) exhibiting favorable attitudes and respect toward them as persons, and (iii) creating a secure and relaxed classroom climate.

---

[74] See Chapter 17: The Benefits of Humor in Teaching.

Supporting Student Learning

The following teaching strategies are four of the behaviors found to be most discriminating between clear and unclear university teachers (Hines, 1982):
− Explains the assignments and the materials students need to use.
− Goes over difficult problems in class.
− Explains the meaning of unfamiliar words.
− Tells students what they are expected to do/know.

These behaviors describe a teacher who anticipates and takes care of problems that students may face in learning and in doing homework assignments, and who clarifies to students his/her objectives for learning. Indeed, students' comments, as illustrated next, indicate that they appreciate teachers who demonstrate that they care about students and who address their needs and problems in learning. These teachers encourage them in their learning.

- She is excited by the subject matter and wants us to learn.
- He runs after the student who asks a question with more and more answers until he's sure that that student understands him.
- She appears to care about students quite a bit, taking time to notice our needs and address them.
- He shows very good intentions to help students.
- Professor showed deep concern about how well students understood and engaged in the topics taught and succeeded in the course.
- Very devoted, spends a lot of time with the student.
- She is probably the most caring instructor I have ever had. Wonderful attitude.
- Professor showed a real concern for students that isn't found often.
- Was very understanding when I needed an extension on an assignment.

Of all the encouragement techniques available to a teacher, praise is the easiest and most natural. Learning motivation theories indicate that students increase their effort if rewarded rather than punished (Gage & Berliner, 1998). Indeed, teacher encouragement and approval were found to positively relate to student achievement, whereas teacher criticism and disapproval produced a negative effect. Reinforcement, praise, approval, encouragement, and acknowledgment of students' ideas were also found to increase students' achievement motivation (ibid.).

How to help students to learn (in additional ways to those above)

Demonstrate interest in students' learning, in meeting their study needs, and in helping them to learn. Communicate to students that it is important to you that they understand and succeed in learning. Show a willingness to repeat explanations until most students understand, and to help them overcome their problems in learning

Promote students' learning in other ways. Guide them and promote their motivation to invest effort and overcome their difficulties.

Try to meet their needs in learning. Use the information you gather at the beginning of the term on your students[75] and provide examples and applications that build on their interests and future profession.

Show readiness to modify your teaching on the basis of students' feedback, to adjust it better to their needs.

Give a second chance to students who fail at mid-term. Invite them to meet you, try to identify their problems and difficulties, and encourage them to try again.

Cater to individual students' special needs, even in a very large class. The following is an illustration of how this can be done, through a description by an exemplary engineering teacher of his "ten percent factor" principle:

In any class, there are about 10% of the students who have something weird happen to them that makes you deal with them separately. For a class of 30, that is, about three students. But for a class of 500, it is about 50. I've had students who have broken their arms on the way to exams, students who have thrown up during exams, blind students, deaf students, dyslexic students—all of whom you must treat individually. I even had one class where three students each had to take time off because a parent died.

To handle these exceptional cases, I have set up my "oddball file." When one of these special circumstances arises, I put a note in this file and then, at the end of the quarter, review it when determining individual grades. This assures that I don't forget any of these unusual circumstances (Salsibury, 1995).

Provide encouragement and praise:

- **Praise a student's question, comment, answer** to your question, or performance of some task. You may praise a single student or the class as a whole.
- **Make positive comments and accept and acknowledge students' ideas.** This behavior demonstrates that you consider students' ideas worth taking seriously.
- Give praise only when it is warranted

---

[75] See Chapter 12: 1. Identifying Students' Background Knowledge, Aptitudes, and Interests Before Teaching.

– **Use praise effectively** (Brophy, 1981): deliver praise contingently; specify the particulars of the accomplishment; provide information to students about their competence or the value of their accomplishments; show spontaneity, variety, and other signs of credibility when praising; reward attainment of specified performance criteria; use students' own prior accomplishments as the context for describing present accomplishments; recognize noteworthy effort or success on difficult tasks; and attribute success to effort and ability, implying that similar successes can be expected in the future.

– **Avoid using praise** in the following manner (ibid): do not deliver praise randomly; do not reward mere participation without consideration of performance processes or outcomes; do not encourage social comparisons of performance; do not attribute success to ability alone or to external factors such as luck or the ease of the task; avoid over-praising or praising too often.

Exhibiting Favorable Attitudes, Empathy, and Respect Toward Students as Persons

Quality personal relationships that provide stability, trust, and caring can increase learners' sense of belonging, self-respect, and self-acceptance in addition to providing a positive climate for learning (APA, 1997)[76]. Here is how some teachers achieve this climate:

- He treated students as equals, as colleagues, showed great respect for students.
- Great attitude toward students, very friendly.
- Professor makes a genuine effort to relate to all of us honestly as *people*, not just students. I appreciate this.
- She truly displayed a passion for her class and instruction and her ability to pass it on to the students was definitely appreciated.
- She relates well to students and understands what it is like to be a student.
- Taught to students and not at students.
- Very receptive to our ideas in class and outside of class.
- Very patient with students.
- Willing to meet students on their terms, over their issues.

How to exhibit favorable attitudes, empathy, and respect toward students

Show students that you respect them and care for their feelings and their problems in learning.

---

[76] See Chapter 4: What Makes Effective Learning? Psychological Principles.

Show a friendly approach toward them. You may even use a parental approach.

Treat students in a patient and non-patronizing fashion.

Personalize the classroom environment. This gives students the feelings that you care for them and are interested in them, as illustrated in the following students' comments:

- Very friendly and personable, Reached out to the students. Extremely valuable in such a large class.
- Very pleasant and supportive. She made her lectures personal.
- Seems eager to get to know individual students.

Use students' name in class:

Polaroid pictures. Take pictures in the first week of the term, write on the back of each picture the student's name and then try to remember the names (possible mainly in small classes).

Name stickers/tags. Prepare name stickers for all students in your course and ask them to wear the stickers during your lessons.

Name tags. Prepare for each student a large-print name tag, to be posted in front of them throughout the lesson so that you can read it from your position in the classroom.

Class roster. Use the roster to call on students by name to answer your questions.

Demonstrate positive nonverbal behaviors. Both students and teachers may make inferences about one another's feelings or attitudes simply by observing particular nonverbal behaviors. You may communicate to students your impressions and expectations, intimacy or liking, and so forth (Patterson, 1983). Students interpret the teacher's facial expression, physical proximity, gesture, tone of voice, or posture, and they respond to these nonverbal behaviors (Woolfolk & Galloway, 1985).

Thus, to demonstrate positive nonverbal behaviors to students: Smile often at students, address them with a positive facial expression; nod positively with your head; increase your proximity to them—walk among them, come close to their seats; express positive feelings with your tone of voice, gestures, and posture; and use body and hand language that communicate approval.

Creating a Secure and Relaxed Classroom Climate

Students need to feel secure and comfortable in class in order to dare and ask questions when they do not understand. They need to feel safe, without experiencing the emotional/internal noise that may be produced when teachers communicate negative attitudes to students, offend them for asking questions that they consider as not clever, give an improper answer, or express a controversial opinion in a discussion.

- The professor is never condescending or patronizing.

How to create a secure and relaxed classroom climate

Allay students' anxieties regarding the material.

Express your confidence in their ability to understand, to study, and to overcome their difficulties.

Avoid exposing students to failure in the presence of their peers.

Do not call on students by name in class to answer difficult questions that require a high thinking level, unless this is a part of the professional requirements. There are students who cannot think under the pressure of the classroom situation.

Cover for a student who fails to answer a question or makes an improper comment.

Avoid behaving toward students in a patronizing, demeaning, or **disdainful manner,** or **offending them** in any other way.

PROMOTING INTERACTION AND RAPPORT BETWEEN TEACHER AND STUDENTS AND AMONG STUDENTS

Promoting interaction and rapport between teacher and students contributes to students' good feelings and is crucial in optimally adapting teaching to their needs. One of the most important contributions to teacher-student relations is adjusting explanations to students' ability and knowledge (Hyman, 1968). Ongoing communication throughout the term is essential to gain awareness of how well students understand the material being taught, how they perceive teaching, and what difficulties in learning they are experiencing.[77] Teachers can then modify their teaching accordingly.

Promoting Teacher-Student Interaction

To promote interactions with students, teachers should create an environment that is favorable for such interactions by being approachable. A large part of teacher-student interaction can take place outside of class, mostly during office hours. A teacher who encourages students to approach him/her outside class can nurture beneficial interactions with them and increase opportunities to help them in their learning.

- The professor was extremely approachable and open to students' questions and suggestions, very interactive.
- He is easily the best professor I ever had. His devotion to the class is exemplary, as shown by his long office hours and preparation of lecture notes.
- Extremely approachable teacher. She always made time for me and I am very grateful for her dedication to students.
- She made extra efforts to hold additional office hours to ensure that students were learning.
- Professor is the epitome of an available professor - she is available to students and makes an excellent attempt to answer questions and get to know them—it's great!
- Extremely willing to meet with all students outside class to discuss papers and class concepts - thanks!

How to promote your interactions and rapport with the students[78]
Use questioning and discussion.

Come earlier to class—about ten minutes before the class starts. Encourage students who are in the classroom to talk with you, either individually or in a group.

Stay in class after the lesson ends to talk with students. Questions might have occurred to them during the lesson that they would like to have answered right away, while the material is still fresh.

---

[77] See Chapter 12: 2. Evaluating Student Understanding Continuously Throughout the Lesson and the Term—the "Class Barometer."

[78] Many additional ideas for promoting teacher-students' interactions can be found in Chapter 12: Evaluating Student Understanding Continuously Throughout the Term.

Arrange for an introductory meeting with you—allow each student to select a time slot.

Dedicate special times for tutorials on difficult topics, which you will announce in advance. Encourage students to come.

Ask students to leave you messages on your answering machine in your office after office hours (e.g., between 5 PM and 9 AM of the next day) regarding anything related to their learning in the course. You may also give your telephone number at home. Experience shows that even in very large classes, a teacher receives only a small number of calls from students.

Maintain an open-door policy. Encourage your students to come to talk to you if they need to, when your office door is open, or while you work in the lab or workshop.

Talk informally to your students. You may create opportunities for informal exchanges through visiting the tutorial or learning center where students get help in their studies, if there is one, or by visiting open spaces in dormitories where students work on their assignments or learn in groups.

Arrange an informal bag lunch with a few students every so often.

Promoting Interaction Among the Students Themselves

Students' interaction among themselves (e.g., through participating in class discussions) is a main contribution to a pleasant classroom climate:

* He induced a wonderful feeling of camaraderie among the class members.
* Great comments and insights from classmates.
* Should promote more interactive dialogue amongst students.

Increasing interaction among students can be accomplished by getting students acquainted with one another. When students know one another, they perceive the classroom climate as intimate, friendly, and pleasant. Satisfactory interaction is particularly important for freshmen who arrive from the more intimate climate of their local high school to an unfamiliar, often distant college.

Other interactions that teachers can promote are helping students get organized in study groups or working together on projects, on problem solving, and on other homework assignments.

How to promote interactions among students

Ask all students, in the first lesson, to introduce themselves. Or, organize students into pairs in order to get acquainted with each other. Then each student introduces his/her partner to the class.

Get students organized into groups for lunching together.

Insert a break in the lesson for informal conversation, once or twice a term.

Emphasize explicitly, during the lessons, the importance of cooperating in learning the course material, in working on homework or on problem solving, or in preparing for the course tests.

DEMONSTRATING EXPECTATIONS FOR STUDENTS' MOTIVATION AND SUCCESS IN LEARNING

• She should push students to be accountable for the kind of learning that is supposed to happen.

Chapter 14 describes studies of teachers' expectations of students' learning, showing that these expectations tend to come true (the *Pygmalion Effect*) and promote students' motivation to learn. Therefore:

Communicate your expectations for your students' success in learning, as well as your belief in their ability to study and overcome their difficulties.

Inform students that you hold them responsible for their learning, that their success depends on the efforts they invest.

Prepare students mentally before teaching difficult material, for example, by telling them that the material is going to be difficult but that it is definitely not beyond their ability, and that if they make the effort they will understand and learn.

Encourage students to be creative and independent in dealing with the material.

Encourage students to take risks, to try, and if they err, to try again.

Do not tell students that they can master the material because it is easy to learn or too simple (e.g., do not say that it is "elementary," "self-evident," or "trivial") because this demeans, frustrates, and decreases the self-confidence of those students for whom the material is not so easy to understand.

GUIDING STUDENTS IN THEIR LEARNING AND IN EFFECTIVE STUDY METHODS

Teachers can help students improve their learning by guiding them in improving their own study methods. Hines (1982) found that two of the most discriminating behaviors between clear and unclear university teachers involve this strategy:

– Asks students if they know what to do and how to do it.
– Describes the assignments and how to do them.

Teachers can also help students develop their metacognitive skills (skills in thinking about their own thinking and learning), so that they can take full responsibility for their learning and become independent learners. Research has shown that studying strategies can be taught to students (McKeachie, 1999).

The following is an illustration of the immense value that guiding students in study strategies can have (Treisman, 1985, pp. 1-3).

In the early 1980's, faculty members in the department of mathematics at the University of California at Berkeley were bothered by the fact that most of the white students from blue collar and farm families and most of African-American students were not succeeding in the calculus course for engineering and science students. After only 11 weeks of college, their very low grades in introductory calculus (the mean was close to failure) dashed the academic aspirations of many of them because this course provides a crucial basis for many other university courses, particularly science and engineering. Various remedial programs were tried (e.g., tutoring, self-paced instruction, and short courses aimed at the development of study skills) that failed.

A faculty member of the department, Prof. Uri Treisman, investigated this phenomenon and identified methods to solve the problem. First he polled the faculty, asking them about the reasons for African-American students' low grades. The faculty responses were the usual "blame the victim" type reasons: the students who flunk are stupid, lazy, do not study much, do not know high school mathematics, and so forth. Then, Treisman decided to actually move into the student dorms and observe African-American students for 18 months. He found that all the stereotyped faculty responses were wrong. These African-American students at U.C. Berkeley were smart, highly motivated, and very hard working. Many of them had even studied calculus in high school. Almost every one of them had at least one parent who encouraged their academic pursuits and urged them to go to college.

With all these characteristics predicting success, then why were they doing so poorly in calculus? What Treisman discovered, in essence, was that they had ineffective learning strategies. They were using the same strategies that brought them success in high school, and thus they were spending too much time memorizing too many formulas and prescriptions for calculations and doing lots of computations with an emphasis on getting the correct answer. However, this type of approach left these students perplexed and frustrated when confronted with a problem that was slightly different from the ones they had been trained to do. They did not try to gain understanding or to develop a facility with the important ideas and techniques of the subject. The overemphasis on testing, skill development, and fact-level content in high school seemed to have inhibited their motivation, interest in learning, ability to work with and enjoy ideas, use of creativity, and satisfaction from an educational experience. Treisman found that entering college freshmen were severely limited in their ability to read critically, synthesize information, interact effectively with peers and teachers in academic settings, and participate actively in discussions. While high school emphasizes skill acquisition, college emphasizes understanding. This mismatch of goals results in a difficult transition from high school to college for many college freshmen. Treisman also found that neither African-American nor white students had been reading their math textbooks. Only foreign students read them, with the aim to improve their English!

Treisman also intensively observed first-generation Chinese-American students (whose first language was Cantonese) as they studied in the student dorms. These students were succeeding very well in the same studies despite having received similar mean SAT scores. Most of them used a different learning strategy; they regularly spent two to three hours per day studying by themselves, and then would meet in groups to criticize each other's work and to work on difficult problems. They felt no shame in asking a teacher or older student for help after a team of four could not solve a problem.

On this basis, Treisman suggested to the African-American students that they form study groups, but they felt that "one is supposed to be self-reliant." This was also the reason why they did not make use of the available free remedial programs. As this was the American spirit of rugged individualism, many white students shared the same attitude. In addition, many college freshmen did not consider their fellow students to be a useful resource. Treisman also detected that African-American students were suspicious of remedial programs specifically aimed at helping them, because of the focus on minority students.

Over several years, Treisman developed an alternative learning environment for training college students is how to learn. The core of his program was that students spent ample time solving problems both individually and cooperatively, with timely intervention by the teachers to save the students from floundering, from much frustration, and from going on wild goose chases. Group learning took place in a non-graded, low stress, nurturing learning climate. Altogether, students were trained how to learn by participating in an efficient learning environment. The results showed that once the African-American students changed their learning strategy, in an effective learning environment, they did very well, not only in calculus, but also in subsequent courses.

This description and additional ones about this project (e.g., Treisman, 1983; 1992) have indicated that many students come to their freshman studies without appropriate learning habits and strategies, and that the study skills they need in the university context differ greatly from the kind of skills that suited their pre-college learning. Inappropriate learning strategies cause many freshmen to experience difficulties in learning and even to fail courses. It is very important that college professors, particularly those teaching freshman courses, guide students in effective learning strategies, that is, how to approach a problem to be solved, how to prepare for each lesson, or how to prepare for a test. They can do this by giving advice during the lessons, or by organizing students in learning groups.

Another means of helping students in their learning relates to their motivation to learn and their attributions of success and failure in learning. A special method for helping failure-oriented students, termed attributional retraining, was developed by Perry (e.g., Menec & Perry, 1995). The method is a therapeutic technique for individuals who are at academic risk because they experience motivational deficits. The method works through increasing their motivation. Attributional retraining is based on the premise that students' attributions for the cause of their achievement outcomes influence their subsequent motivation, and, as a result, performance on future tasks. It is designed to change students' attributions for failure. Students who believe that they cannot control the causes for their failure in learning, be it on tests, term papers, or oral presentations, and that these causes are random—a matter of luck—have low motivation to learn. For these students, academic failure, particularly if it occurs repeatedly, can have a profound negative impact on subsequent motivation and achievement. Short-term consequences range from reduced study efforts, to absenteeism, and even to dropping out. Students are trained to believe that their failures are not caused either by their lack of ability or by luck, and that success is attainable by investing sufficient effort, being persistent in their studying, and improving study strategies. This therapeutic method engenders in the students a sense of personal control, thereby increasing their motivation.

How to guide and support your students in learning and enhance their personal responsibility for learning

Create meaningful learning goals that are consistent both with students' personal and educational aspirations and interests.

Develop, apply, and assess students' strategic learning skills.

Developing their higher order (metacognitive) strategies.

Promote students' natural curiosity and motivation to learn. This may be achieved by attending to individual differences in learners' perceptions of optimal novelty and difficulty, relevance, and personal choice and control.

Enhance students' effort and commitment to learning and to achieving high standards of comprehension. This may be achieved by using purposeful learning activities, guided by practices that enhance positive emotions and intrinsic motivation to learn, and by increasing learners' perceptions that a task is interesting and personally relevant.

Provide positive interpersonal support and instruction in self-motivation strategies. These methods can offset factors that interfere with optimal learning, such as negative beliefs about competence in a particular subject, high levels of test anxiety, negative sex role expectations, or undue pressure to perform well.

Help students examine their learning preferences and expand or modify them, if necessary. You should be sensitive to individual differences in general, and attend to learner perceptions of the degree to which these differences are accepted and adapted to by varying instructional methods and materials.

Design and implement appropriate learning environments. When learners perceive that their individual differences in abilities, backgrounds, cultures, and experiences are valued, respected, and accommodated in learning tasks and contexts, their levels of motivation and achievement are enhanced.

SUMMARY

Learning is not only a cognitive process; it is substantially affected by emotional factors. Teaching can thrive only in a supportive environment that encourages students to attend, think, and learn. Teachers can make learning, besides being cognitively challenging and requiring effort, into a pleasant and enjoyable experience so that students will like coming to class. However, one should not confuse a pleasant environment with entertainment or spoon-feeding. Students should expect to work hard and persevere.

Teachers can create a supportive classroom climate that is conducive to learning by:

1. Generating a positive emotional climate in class. This is achieved by generating favorable attitudes of students toward the teacher (i.e., being pleasant and displaying a sympathetic personality; presenting one's own knowledge, expertise, and achievements; coming well prepared to class; and using humor); and by exhibiting an intrinsically favorable attitude toward the students (i.e., demonstrating interest in students' learning, in meeting their needs, and in helping them to learn; exhibiting favorable attitudes, empathy, and respect toward students; personalizing the classroom environment; creating a secure and relaxed classroom climate; providing encouragement and praise; using positive nonverbal behaviors, and reducing "emotional noise").

2. *Promoting interaction and rapport between* teacher *and students, and among students.* This is achieved by promoting: (a) teacher-student interaction by enhancing the teacher's approachability, using questions, and establishing interactions through written communication; and (b) social and academic interaction among the students themselves.

3. *Demonstrating expectations for students' motivation and success in learning, and holding students responsible for their learning.* Teachers should communicate to students a belief in their ability to overcome the difficult material and to learn. Teachers communicate their expectations of their students in subtle ways—verbal and nonverbal.

4. *Guiding students in effective learning methods.* This can be done, for example, by organizing learning in study groups, and by attributional retraining which changes students' attributions for failure.

Humor can greatly contribute to a positive emotional climate in class. The next chapter discusses the role of using humor in fostering a classroom climate conducive to learning and presents ideas of how to learn to integrate humor into teaching.

Chapter 17

Using Humor in Teaching

From a professor's diary of nightmares[79]:
A student comes to me and says—"You're such a wonderful teacher that if I wrote down everything you say in class, I should no longer have to read or think..."

I dream that I come to class totally unprepared and when I awake I find myself there...

THE BENEFITS OF HUMOR IN TEACHING

Students like humor in teaching. Surveys of learners' opinions about the qualities which they hope to find in their teachers often mention a sense of humor (Myers, 1968). Javidi, Downs, and Nussbaum (1988) found that award-winning teachers (nominated most often on the basis of students' evaluations) used humor significantly more than did less successful teachers.

Why do students appreciate humor in teaching? Mogavero (1979) found that most students perceived humor as increasing the effectiveness of the material's presentation, explained by the fact that humor eases the tension between student and teacher and helps to establish rapport. It maintains attention and it generates interest.

Indeed, the use of humor was found to foster a classroom climate conducive to learning (Kaplan & Pascoe, 1977; Mogavero, 1979; Powell & Andersen, 1985).

If students adopt a positive attitude toward a learning task and to their teacher, then they are more likely to approach the task with enthusiasm and perhaps wish to come to share the interests, attitudes, and knowledge of the teacher. This view sees humor, and enjoyment generally, as being features of a classroom environment which is more apt for

[79] Collected by the author in a conference on college and university teaching.

273

the production of learning than one from which they are absent. (Powell & Andersen, 1985, p. 80).

Humor therefore serves psychological, social, and cognitive purposes. Shared laughter is a powerful way to reinforce learning because it links the students and teacher through enjoyment, making them learn while laughing together (Korobkin, 1988). Humor can mold a collection of individuals into a group with a clear sense of togetherness; Mark Twain said, "Grief can take care of itself, but to get the full value of joy you must have somebody to divide it with." Because of the collective nature of laughter, humor increases students' active involvement in classroom work and inspires them to participate by encouraging them to take risks by softening the blow of failure. Humor relaxes and engages an audience, raising the motivation to listen and absorb. In addition, teachers often use humor as a means of managing undesirable student behavior, such as arriving late to class, chatting with neighbors, or reading newspapers or other irrelevant material during the lesson. In this case, humor indicates disapproval but without embarrassing the culprit. Properly used, humor sends the message that the teacher is confident, comfortable, and in control.

Student perception that the use of humor increases teacher effectiveness and student learning is supported by research (Carrier, 1981; Clabby, 1979; Warnock, 1989). However, Ziv (1988) found that the positive results depend on certain conditions: that humor is used in optimal doses (three to four instances per hour), and that it is relevant to the concepts, examples, and illustrations presented in class. The effect of humor on student learning has been explained by several reasons: that it contributes to students' perception that the learning material is exciting and effective (Bryant et al., 1979); that it cultivates freer interaction in the classroom by promoting group cohesiveness while reducing social anxiety, conformity, and dogmatism (Ziv, 1976); that it aids comprehension and retention of lecture material (Kaplan & Pascoe, 1977); and that it positively affects students' perceptions of the teacher's competence and likability (Tamborini & Zillmann, 1981).

Thus, although some teachers may be reluctant to use humor in their classrooms for personal reasons, its profusion of benefits to the teaching process should induce teachers to at least attempt to integrate some humor into their classrooms.

TYPES AND CATEGORIES OF HUMOR THAT CAN BE USED IN TEACHING

Humor can occur in a lesson in one of two forms: *spontaneous* or *planned*. Spontaneous humor is most common in teaching, usually in the shape of funny comments and witty remarks through which the teacher alerts the students to elements that are surprising or different from what they expected. Spontaneous humor requires that the teacher create a proper classroom environment conducive to accepting humor, but the humorous incidents are not preplanned, whereas planned humor requires the investment of time and effort in its preparation and performance. Planned humor can be derived and adapted from existing humor or it can be created from scratch. The latter necessarily requires a degree of originality and creativity.

Bryant et al. (1979) investigated the extent to which humor was used by university teachers through an analysis of the content of 70 tape-recorded lectures. Findings showed that 20% of the teachers used no humor at all, 50% had one to three humorous episodes in their lecture, and 5% introduced humorous elements on more than ten occasions. Most of the humor seemed to emerge spontaneously, and was closely related to the content of the lecture.

We may distinguish among types of humor that are expressed verbally, in writing or drawing, or non-verbally, through teacher behavior.

Verbal Humor

Jokes

Telling jokes is one of the most prevalent ways of using humor in teaching. Hill (1988, p. 69-71) described the structure of jokes as follows:

> In general, jokes are patterned constructions that set the listener up for a response, but quickly subvert what is expected with an alternate meaning in the form of a punchline. Setups are crucial to joke formats. In fact, jokes work precisely because the thought processes that follow any setup are predictable. Jokes take advantage of the expected by delivering something unexpected. This is called "switching"... Once you have a listener in a joking frame of mind, it is easier to increase the playfulness of communication.

Thus, the main components of a joke are: *setting, incongruency, surprise,* and *brevity*.

How to present a joke

Setting: A crucial component of success in telling a joke is "tuning the audience"—getting them into the right frame of mind. The listeners need to know in advance that they should not take seriously what will be said next. You can tune the audience by adopting a comic look such as wearing a hat or putting on funny glasses; through humorous facial expressions or funny body language; via a change of voice; or through a verbal statement such as "Yesterday, I just happened to hear a great joke that exactly fits this topic..."

Incongruency should be formed to create tension between what is expected and results.

Surprise of something unexpected should come after forming the incongruency, in the form of a sting, a punchline.

Brevity. All parts of a joke, but particularly the punchline, should be concise in their wording and short in duration. Jokes have the largest effect when they are worded succinctly. Ideally, do not use more than three to four bits of information, followed by a punchline.

Here is an illustration of the parts of a joke that builds on the rivalry between two groups, in this case theoretical and experimental physicists (Devine & Cohen, 1992, p. 20):

[Setting] *Theoretical physicist:* Have you heard the latest joke about the experimental physicist?

[Incongruency] *Stranger:* Perhaps I should warn you that I am an experimental physicist.

[Punchline] *Theoretical physicist:* Thanks for the warning, I'll tell it very slowly...

Anecdotes

An anecdote is a story that teaches a lesson, often with personal references. When anecdotes are told as jokes, they contain a funny twist (that's why they are called *funny stories*).

Language Play

Language play is another humorous verbal structure available to teachers. The following list of techniques is compiled from and illustrated by reference to Bryant et al. (1979, pp. 112-113), Hill (1988), and Wandersee (1982, p. 215).

Puns—"word play": A pun is a humorous statement that is designed to play on the multiple meanings of a word. The unusual or unexpected twist in meaning may be the result of the use or misuse of two words that sound similar but differ in meaning (homonyms), or of words that have similar meaning (synonyms), or by the mispronunciation of words. To illustrate:

Busting students (instead of bussing students).

Deaf penalty (instead of death penalty).

Did you hear the one about the psychiatrist who didn't get the job because he was too Jung? (instead of "young," a reference to Jung, the well-known psychiatrist).

Ironic definitions: Giving words an abstract meaning which goes beyond the standard dictionary definition. For example,

Deadwood is anyone in your department who is more senior than you are.

Using opposite, contradictory, impossible terms: Someone is a "successful failure," or a "rich pauper," someone who does not have a single "redeeming vice", or something that is a "sure guess."

Taking something to the absurd, causing an internal/logic clash. To illustrate:

> It usually takes more than three weeks to prepare a good impromptu speech. (Mark Twain).

> Let us be happy and live within our means, even if we have to borrow the money to do it with. (Artemus Ward).

> No one goes to the theater anymore...it's too crowded. (Artemus Ward).

Stating the obvious. To illustrate:

> Rich people have all the money.

> If you kill me, I'll never speak to you again.

> What color is the red bus?

> Question: Why did the chicken cross the road?

> Answer 1: To get to the other side.

Humorous riddle: An information-seeking question that does not seem to have a logical answer, and that provides a clever answer in a humorous punchline.

> Question: Why did the chicken cross the road?

> Answer 2: Because its mother told it to do so. Or,

> Answer 3: Because that's where the bus stop was.

Replacing, mixing, exchanging, or omitting words in an adage, saying, maxim, byword, metaphor, or the like. For example:

> A man said about the best years of his life that he was "drinking out of rose-colored glasses," building on the metaphor of "seeing the world through rose-colored glasses."

> About spending time on entertainment, which may be perceived by a faculty member as a waste of time: "A waste is a terrible thing to mind," which builds on the known adage, "A mind is a terrible thing to waste."

Jargon: Jargon is the specialized or technical language of a trade, profession, or class. Use of jargon can serve as an in-joke among group members who share a common vocabulary.

Taboo language: Saying the unspeakable.

Mistaken use of a word that sounds similar to the correct one. To illustrate (Hill, 1988, p. 66):

There was a man accused of bigotry who replied indignantly: I resemble that remark. [Intending: I resent that remark.]

Misuse of language that changes its meaning. To illustrate, the following are announcements written in English, collected by tourists in countries in which English is not the native language (taken from an unidentified file on the Internet):

At a Bangkok dry cleaner's: "Drop your trousers here for best results."

At a Rome laundry (similarly to the previous item): "Ladies, leave your clothes here and spend the afternoon having a good time."

At a tailor shop in Rhodes: "Order your summers suit. Because is big rush we will execute customers in strict rotation."

In a Copenhagen airline ticket office: "We take your bags and send them in all directions."

In a Paris hotel elevator: "Please leave your values at the front desk."

In a Japanese hotel: "You are invited to take advantage of the chambermaid."

Ironic processes. The following are several examples:

Murphy's Law and its results (Bloch, 1991):

If anything can go wrong, it will. [The basic law].

If you explain something so clearly that nobody can misunderstand, somebody will.

Only someone who understands something absolutely can explain it so no one else can understand it.

Any simple idea will be worded in the most complicated way.

It is a simple task to make things complex, but a complex task to make them simple.

Complex problems have simple, easy-to-understand wrong answers.

A good solution can be successfully applied to almost any problem.

If an experiment works, something has gone wrong.

If more than one person is responsible for a miscalculation, no one will be at fault.

Nothing is ever so bad that it can't get worse.

If anything fails, read the instructions.

There's never time to do it right, but there's always time to do it over.

The one time you come up with a great solution, somebody else has just solved the problem.

The person with the least expertise has the most opinions.

The Peter Principle:
In a hierarchy, every employee tends to rise to his level of incompetence.

And its corollaries:

In time, every post tends to be occupied by an employee who is incompetent to carry out his or her duties.

Work is accomplished by those employees who have not yet reached their level of incompetence.

Limerick: A nonsense poem of five anapestic lines.
Comic verse: A humorous poem that is metered and rhymed.
Humorous comment: A brief statement which has a humorous element.
Understatement: A statement that is disproportionally weak or moderate for the situation presented.

Nonverbal Humor

Nonverbal humor, mainly drawing or picture-based humor, can be presented on the board, in a handout, or on transparencies:
Cartoon: A drawing, often accompanied by captions or dialogue, depicting a humorous situation.
Caricature: A drawing, ludicrously exaggerating the properties of a person or thing.
Photon: A photograph accompanied by a humorous caption or dialogue statement.
Visual pun: A pun presented in cartoon format.

Combined Verbal and Nonverbal Humor

Teacher acting-based humor can include:
Impersonation: An imitation that exaggerates a person's most outstanding features, often for the purpose of ridicule.
Parody: Imitating a serious work for expression in a humorous way.
Satire: An attack on a person's follies and foibles using irony and sarcasm.
Monologue: An entertaining series of comic situations related by a single speaker.
Skit: A comic theatrical sketch.

General Categories of Humor That Can be Expressed Via Language, Drawing/Picture, or Teacher Acting

Nonsense: Humor based on illogical situations, actions that are absurd, or words that are meaningless.

Exaggeration: Magnifying (or reducing) humorous elements for comic effect.

Lack of skill or knowledge: Humor based on the ineptitude or naiveté of a character.

A violation of normal event order: Humor based on an improperly or an unusually arranged sequence of events.

Introduction of what belongs in one situation into another: Comic incongruity developed by transporting elements of one situation to a different one. To illustrate [from an unknown source in the Internet]:

> Why did G-D never receive tenure at the university? Because He had only one major publication, and it was in Hebrew, and it had no references, and it wasn't published in a refereed journal, and some even doubt He wrote it himself, and the scientific community has had a very rough time trying to replicate His experiment.

Reversal of a normal series of events: Events presented in reverse order for comic effect.

Hidden element: Humor based on a concealed comic element that is "seen" by the audience but not by the characters in the situation.

Masquerade: Humor that results when an element of a comic situation is disguised.

Small misfortune: Humor that results when a minor calamity of life befalls the character of a situation.

Phony advertisement: The modification of a bona fide advertisement for comic effect by alteration of words or visual images.

Reversed theory: The principles of an accepted theory are reversed and made to seem plausible.

Bogus experiment: A humorous account of an impossible experiment.

LEARNING TO USE HUMOR IN TEACHING

Many teachers would like to exhibit humor in their classes but feel constrained by the conviction they somehow lack the inborn gift for it, or that they "are not very funny people." Thus, for many teachers, humor seems incongruous with their own sense of identity and with their style of teaching. Hence, its use in teaching seems unlikely ever to be realized. However, one should not be unduly pessimistic about the prospect for change in this area. Because students so much appreciate an element of humor in their teachers, college teachers should make an effort to overcome any initial reluctance they may have to incorporate some humor into their teaching and come to view it as an important constituent of their repertoire of professional skills. Indeed, experts argue that it is possible to learn to use humor, if time and effort are invested.

In order for teachers to use humor in their lessons and process existing humor for this aim, they need to: (a) build a database of humorous items; (b) adjust particular items from this database to their particular needs; and (c) learn how to present humorous material to others. The practice section in this chapter includes a discussion of each of these three latter topics.

Developing and Maintaining a Database of Humorous Items

What should be the content of the database

The database should include contents of two types:

Collect a general library of humor. Collect episodes and learn from popular joke books, albums, and videotapes. Watch professionals and try to identify how they create humor. Your humor library should contain books on drama skills and public speaking as well as collections of jokes. Joke anthologies list thousands of witticisms and word plays.

Collect a specialized classroom humor library. Your humor library should be a personal collection of humorous items that will help you to get started as a joke teller, with humor tailored to your unique style. Find books which specialize in classroom humor or which list jokes about your particular subject area. Collect relevant humorous material of a variety of types: cartoons, puns, quotes, sayings, jokes, signs, and stories, among others.

What sources can you use for developing the database

Tap into many different sources to collect humorous items, related to the content of your database: newspapers, magazines, general humor books, the comic section of your newspaper, funny greeting cards in your local store, general humor/joke books, and anthologies at your local library or bookstore.

Record humorous occurrences in the classroom. Record and keep a list of funny things that happen in your classroom. When something humorous occurs, try to analyze why students laughed, filing incidents in categories relevant to your teaching situation. Similarly, when a joke fails, make a note of it and try to dissect what happened and how the joke might be improved in future retellings. Keep a record of what students laugh at among themselves, with other teachers, and so forth. To illustrate, the following are students' actual responses to exam questions as collected by their teachers:

- Bach was the most famous composer in the world, and so was Handel. Handel was half German, half Italian, and half English. He was very large.
- Beethoven wrote music even though he was deaf. He was so deaf he wrote loud music. He expired in 1827 and later died for this.
- Louis Pasteur discovered a cure for rabbis.
- Charles Darwin was a naturalist who wrote the "Organ of the Species."
- Madman Curie discovered the radio.
- Karl Marx was one of the Marx brothers.
-
- Get your students to collect relevant humorous material for you:
- Ask your students to produce original humor for a particular topic.
- Ask your students to keep their eyes open and collect appropriate related humor items.
- Start a humor board where students can post favorite cartoons with an award for the best cartoon of the week.

Ask your friends, peers, and TAs to collect humorous items for you that are related to your subject area and to the topics you teach.

Observe teachers who use humor effectively. Adapt their methods for use in your classroom.

How to organize and maintain a humor file

File the joke-material collected under indexes and cross-references.

Use a computerized database. This can greatly help you in filing and rapid retrieval.

Organize a list of standard joke structures. There are hundreds of stylized joke structures such as the "knock knock jokes," "light bulb jokes," "elephant jokes," "ten best ways to... ," or "good news bad news."

Organize a list of standard opening sentences that can serve for the setting part of a joke: Here are some sample standardized sentences you can use to suit your situation:

- My teachers used to say/do/make me do/...
- As my mother/grandma used to say/ Like I always say...
- And then there was the student who.../ That reminds me of (the student) who.../ This is like the student who...
- If you think that's funny, you should have seen...
- That reminds me of the time/ the story/ the joke/ the professor/ the student/...
- Did you hear the one about...
- That reminds me of a guy I knew...

- In an electrical engineering class one of the students asked... [This is the beginning of a joke told in a mechanical engineering class, whereas in an electrical engineering class the joke would start with "In a mechanical engineering class..."].
- Yesterday I met an electrical engineer who said... [again, this is a start of a joke in a mechanical engineering class.]

The last two starts can be adapted to any two competing groups of students or academic areas.

How to adapt humorous items to particular needs within the lesson plan

Select several items from your humor database and adapt them to the material you teach, as well as to the background and interests of your students. For example, as suggested above, the joke about the theoretical and experimental physicists can be adapted to any two rivaling or competing groups.

Look for famous quotes and sayings that can be modified for use in your teaching. To illustrate, the following is an adaptation of the "light bulb" joke to different professions (Devine & Cohen, 1992):

How many programmers does it take to change a light bulb?

- None, that's a hardware problem. Or

- Two, because one is sure to leave in the middle of the project.

How many supply-side economists does it take to screw-in a light bulb?

- None. And if the government would just leave it alone, it would screw itself in.

How many accountants does it take to change a light bulb?

- What kind of an answer do you need?

How many consulting engineers does it take to change a light bulb?

- One. That will be fifty dollars, please.

How many professors does it take to change a light bulb?

- Only one, but that's assuming he has enough graduate students to do the actual work.

How many survivors of nuclear war does it take to change a light bulb?

- So who needs light bulbs when you already glow in the dark? ["Black joke"]

Developing Skills for Using Humor in the Classroom

Developing skills for putting humorous items across in the classroom requires the investment of time and effort in observation and training. In principle, this is no different from learning any of the other teaching skills. The following are four ways to develop these particular skills.

How to use a variety of sources for learning to incorporate humor in teaching

Observe teachers who effectively use humor. Observe their lessons or lectures at professional conferences and record what causes their students to laugh. Adapt their methods for use in your classroom.

Learn from professional entertainers. When you watch humorous shows on TV or video, identify and write down what makes you and/or the audience laugh and what holds your interest—identify the comedian's mimicry, hand and body language, movement in space, variations in voice, and other nonverbal behaviors. Notice also the detail of their verbal presentation. Listen to recordings of comedians, obtain books on play techniques, or on public speaking, or which directly advise on how to use humor.

Study popular printed humor. Study published humor from the sources listed in your database. This will give you an idea about what others consider amusing.

Learn from humorous incidents in your own class. Study your records of humorous classroom occurrences, as listed in your database.

Build a library of techniques for creating humor. File all your records of the incidents described in the former sections.

How to train yourself in developing skills of using humor in class

Develop a humorous attitude. Because humor is mostly the result of a certain attitude, be spontaneously open to the unexpected, insane, silly, and ridiculous in situations constantly offered in the classroom.

Begin to think funny. Develop a comic vision, a comic outlook so that it becomes an integral and consistent part of teaching. If you look for humor, humor will find you.

How to plan ahead for using humor in class

Plan ahead where and when you'll use humor in your lesson, including the timing, gestures, and voice. Tailor the humorous items to the subject-matter before you start teaching; you may make prepared humor appear spontaneous to students. While you are planning the lesson, ask yourself when you might want to introduce a joke or anecdote that is relevant and that might reinforce the topics presented. Consider the points at which you are most likely to need to establish rapport, create interest, and maintain attention—the major benefits offered by the use of humor.

Start by using others' humor, and modify it to fit your situation—to make it relevant. Later you may create your own humor.

Choose a form/structure of humor that seems appropriate to your situation and that you will feel comfortable using. Screen the list of standard humorous structures in your database to identify appropriate forms.

Rewrite available jokes to fit your situation—to make them personal, relevant, challenging, and comprehensible to your students.

Practice your jokes. Joke telling, to be more effective, builds on the right choice and the right sequence of words. It is very important to be brief. Try writing a joke and rewriting it until the wording is as humorous as possible. Then memorize the joke but present it naturally. A good way to practice jokes is to tell them to a friend, spouse, or children. Open yourself up to criticism about how well you tell a story or joke. Still another way is microteaching—videotape yourself when you present the jokes and get feedback from several viewers. The more you practice, the better you will become at joke telling.

How to actually inject humor into teaching

Use a joke cue as a setup. Students may well need to be cued before you tell a joke. Make the sort of recognizable introduction that cues people to humorous material, as listed above, like "Did you hear the one about..."

Be concise. Jokes have the greatest impact when they are delivered with brevity. The information contained in the joke should be concise enough for students to be able to assimilate it quickly.

Construct in-group motifs. Every class has its own character. Class jokes should take advantage of the common experiences of the group. Having a humorous group mascot (which can be a person, place, or thing) provides a source of mirth that promotes group cohesion.

Create your own character—a funny persona. Teachers can take on the personality of a humorous character. To do this, the character must be different enough from the teacher in voice, gesture, and attitude to be recognizably unique. Then the teacher can cue students that he is acting out another character simply by changes of voice or by something more obvious like putting on a hat that tells students who that character is.

Tell funny stories as if they happened to you.

Find a "hook." A hook is the part of a phrase which is sure to get a laugh, for example, "I don't get any respect from you...."

Use a variety of types of humorous devices. Switch between jokes, anecdotes, puns, and so forth.

Act natural. Incorporate a joke into your lecture so that it appears to flow naturally, with good timing and natural pauses between phrases.

Be assertive. When you tell your joke, project confidence. Tell the joke from start to finish without pausing to find out if your students are amused. If no one laughs at the punchline, don't ask them if they got it.

Enliven your stories. Change your voice to suit the character in your story, use gestures, move about in the classroom.

Control your voice: Use clear speech, well articulated, at the right speed, volume, and pitch. Having a pleasant, resonant voice is an important quality of dynamic speaking, humorous or otherwise.

Laugh at yourself occasionally. This shows your sense of humor and your humanness.

Memorize some "safe" lines. These are to be used when a joke does not result in laughter, like "Should I pay somebody to laugh...?" Turn a story or pun that flops onto yourself.

Use humor in a variety of your activities in class: in test items, on the classroom bulletin board, in homework assignments, project outlines, and the course syllabus. However, do not slip into a routine. Part of the joy of humor is the fun of a comic moment which was totally unanticipated by the students.

Assign your students to use humor on topic-related tasks, either as a part of their homework or in the framework of group work during the lesson. The tasks can be: writing captions, puns, or humorous comments for cartoons; inventing the last lines for limericks; writing comic verses; drafting punchlines for jokes; and rewriting jokes and anecdotes. The use of humor tends to require higher level thinking skills, so that it actually challenges students to think.

Humor can be offensive and non-productive if used in the wrong way—it can hurt rather than help.

How not to use humor

Never lower a student's self-esteem through humor. Do not use humor at the expense of the students: do not belittle, ridicule, or mock them, or use other forms of "put-down." Never intentionally offend sensitivities. Avoid sexual, racial, or religious jokes.

The things to avoid are:

- Don't make fun of your students.
- Don't be negative.
- Don't use taboo language.
- Don't make light of serious issues (e.g., drinking, drugs, drunk driving, sex, religion, grades).
- Don't tell currently popular jokes.
- Don't put yourself down as a joke-teller.
- Avoid ambiguous messages.
- Don't explain a punchline.
- Don't use humor that is irrelevant to the topics you teach.

SUMMARY

Students like humor in teaching because they find it beneficial for their learning, supported by research. Humor serves psychological, social, and cognitive purposes. Humor is beneficial for student learning because it promotes: students' positive attitude toward, motivation for, and satisfaction with learning; student-teacher rapport; student attentiveness and interest; a positive class atmosphere; student involvement; class discussion and animation; individual and group task productivity; stimulation of students' creativity, ideas, and divergent thinking; students' willingness to take risks in the classroom; perceptions of the teacher as being confident and in control; reduced academic stress and anxiety; and reduced disruptive student behavior.

Humor can occur in a lesson in one of two forms: *spontaneous* or *planned*, and it should not be used too frequently. Many teachers would like to exhibit some humor in their classes, but feel constrained by a sense that humor is incongruous with their own identity and style of teaching. However, because students so much appreciate humor, college teachers should make an effort to overcome any initial reluctance they may have to incorporate at least some humor into their teaching and come to view it as an important constituent in their repertoire of professional skills. In order for teachers to incorporate humor in their lessons and process existing humor for this aim, they need to: (a) learn to know the main types of humor that can be used in the classroom; (b) build a database of humorous items; (c) adjust particular items from this database to their particular needs; and (d) learn how to present humorous material to others.

PART IV

ADDITIONAL TEACHING FUNCTIONS

Chapter 18

Planning the Course and the Lesson

A fundamental component of all teaching processes is planning the course and the lesson. Therefore, understanding of faculty's planning is important for improving teaching and learning (Lowther, Stark, Genthon, & Bentley, 1990).

PLANNING THE COURSE

Course planning includes making decisions about content, considering factors affecting teaching and learning processes, selecting strategies for engaging students with the content, and selecting ways to obtain feedback about student learning (Lowther et al., 1990). Dinham and Blake (1991) identified three categories of contextual influences that affect course planning by experienced university teachers: academic discipline, organizational environment, and educational realities. The *academic discipline* exerts the most central influence on course planning, but it interacts with the other factors. Within the *organizational environment*, teachers are strongly influenced by curriculum committees' design of the courses, by the courses' place in the university's general educational program, by resource availability, and by logistics. The *educational realities* include students' characteristics and expectations, and departmental educational policies and goals, among other factors. Teachers must consider all these contextual elements when planning a coherent course.

Considering the planning process, Thielens (1987) identified three key needs in designing material for a course or lesson: selecting; structuring, and simplifying.

Selecting the Course Content

Each discipline contains a vast body of knowledge, concepts, approaches, and ideas from which professors select what to teach and to what extent, at what level, depth, and with what orientation. The selection process is guided mainly by considerations related to the discipline and the students. Professors must select the disciplinary material which they perceive as the most central and significant, the key concepts, the desirable viewpoints and approaches, the most appropriate and representative examples, the level of depth and difficulty, the points to emphasize, and so forth. A major issue faculty face in selecting the disciplinary material is what new developments to incorporate into their teaching in order to show how the subject is evolving and growing. To keep their teaching up-to-date, they routinely collect material from new books or articles in journals, newspapers, and magazines, and from their own research. Besides the subject matter, teachers must keep their students in mind throughout the selection process. They should take students' background knowledge, aptitudes, and interests into consideration when designing the time and content allocation. They must also consider the applicability or relevance for students of each topic selected (ibid.).

A recent large-scale study of college teachers' planning of their courses (Stark, Forthcoming) has supported Thielens' findings. This survey revealed that content selection is the one step taken by almost all teachers in planning a course, and by one half of them as the first step. The three main considerations for selecting course content were to promote intellectual and personal development; learning of concepts and operations in the field; and vocational and/or skill development. Other major planning steps, taken by 60% or more of the respondents, were: taking students' characteristics and learning needs into consideration, establishing objectives based on students' background, and selecting materials and activities (ibid.).

Students clearly respond to their teachers' choice of lecture-based course material:

- The content provided a good overview of the subject matter.
- Material is interesting, challenging, relevant, and applicable to today.
- The course material is sometimes a little too hard, but overall this is a careful, thorough, comprehensive course.
- Takes a nice and different approach to the subject matter.
- Uses up-to-date material in the course.

- The texts and topics assigned were diverse in nature and scope, making the class interesting and holistic.

How to select the course content

Select the course content to adapt to students' needs. Course material should be interesting, challenging, up-to-date, relevant, and applicable to students; provide a thorough and comprehensive account of the subject matter; and offer a diversity of topics, approaches, and points of view.

Obtain general knowledge about the students who usually attend courses similar to yours. Identify their background knowledge, aptitudes and interests, needs, learning interests and expectations, learning styles, life experiences, and relevant knowledge.[80]

Define the course goals. Define the knowledge and skills you want your students to gain in the course. Include skills that are not directly related to the content of the course but that promote students' good functioning in the workplace and in society, for example, oral communication and writing skills, cooperation on assignment work, and analytical and critical thinking.[81]

Develop your own database for teaching your courses and keep it updated. Always keep the topics of your courses in the back of your mind so that you can collect and record related materials for future use whenever you read books, scientific articles, newspapers and magazines; whenever you watch a movie, a TV program, or a computer presentation; and whenever you hear or read riddles, anecdotes, or jokes. Arrange all these sources for effective storage and retrieval.

Build on your peers' knowledge that is related to your course content. Talk with colleagues who have taught courses of the type you teach. Get their ideas and advice on teaching these courses, ask them for their syllabi and other materials they have used in class or distributed to students.

Identify links between your course and other courses in the school/department. Identify the content of courses that serve as a prerequisite for your course and of those for which your course is a prerequisite, or that relate in some way to your course.

Limit the course content to the amount feasibly included within the time frame of your course, using the following considerations:

- **Avoid overloading the course with too many topics.** List all the topics that would fit your course objectives and make a reasonable estimation of how many of them can be fitted into the available time.

---

[80] See Chapter 12.
[81] See Chapter 1 for a list of the most common course goals.

- **Prioritize all your listed topics.** Select the ones that seem most essential and useful for the students, then first allocate class time for these topics. If there is time left, add the topics next in importance.
- **Assign other important topics to be studied outside the classroom.** After the previous selection, you may set aside certain materials for students' self-study rather than presenting them in class. You may also designate some material to be optionally studied by outstanding students or by those who show special interest in the course material.

Selecting the Textbook and Other Reading Materials

Selecting the textbook for the course is another major decision that affects the selection of course content (Stark, Forthcoming; Thielens, 1987). The following are representative of responses to a course textbook:

- The textbook was very good—a real life compelling and thorough case study—very informative.
- The book was excellent—gave a real conceptual framework for issues, and concrete examples.
- The textbook was a good overview.
- Assigned reading that is relevant to the work of a lawyer [a law student].
- Horrible textbook—makes the topics too simple and explains badly.
- For problem-solving , the book was much too ambiguous, it didn't give simple problems.
- The textbook seemed too cursory.
- The textbook was difficult to read and thus it was hard to distinguish what were important topics.

How to select the course textbook

Choose a textbook that is clear and informative, provides a conceptual framework for the topics of the course, and includes concrete examples. It should present the material in a thorough, non-superficial form and at an appropriate level for students.

Choose a textbook that agrees with your goals in teaching the course, and with your perception of content selection and of its structuring and organization.

Choose a textbook with the following characteristics: legibility (eye-friendly print), ease and clarity of reading (level not too low, i.e., sufficiently challenging), interest and relevance for students (e.g., relevant examples and applications), accuracy of content, currency of content, and reasonable cost.

Choose a variety of texts that are relevant to the profession, to enhance interest and expose students to a more integrated approach.

Organizing and Structuring the Course Content

The body of knowledge of any discipline is both too vast and too amorphous, and the connections among its parts too complex, for direct transmission to undergraduates. Students cannot be expected to organize this body of knowledge by themselves because they do not possess a conceptual overview of the course topics, nor do they have the necessary experience. It is, therefore, up to the professors to work out their own organization of the material selected so as to teach it according to a comprehensible structure, and to communicate this structure to the students. Often, devising this organization is a difficult task, closely resembling that of organizing a research report or a scientific article. It may mean going over much material that is not too challenging to the instructor and organizing it in a way that makes sense to him/her (Thielens, 1987).

What are the guiding principles in organizing the course material? A large-scale survey (Stark, Forthcoming) showed that college teachers' main preferences in organizing the course material are: to preserve the way that concepts of the field are traditionally organized (71% of respondents); to maintain the type of organization that best helps students learn (57%); to follow the organization of the knowledge as in the "real world" (49%); or to preserve the organization in which knowledge is created (33%). Additional organizing principles suggested by the teachers included: compliance with the course goals, use of the basic/core concepts as an organizing criterion, and embedding the content within a general framework.

How to organize the course content

Build a framework that serves as an infrastructure for laying out the concepts, notions, ideas and knowledge developed throughout the course.

Arrange the topics under a guiding idea, a unifying theory, a general context, a central theme, or a leading line of thought.

Allocate one extra lesson per semester. Allocate time for the course topics so that you have one lesson extra for unexpected issues or events, such as when you need to skip a class or are not able to cover an important topic in the time planned. Also set aside time for review sessions before the final exam.

Simplifying the Material—Adapting to Students

An academic discipline's body of knowledge (e.g., what is published in academic books and journals) will, on the whole, be too advanced or unfamiliar in nature for undergraduates to understand. Teachers must find ways to "translate" the material, that is, to simplify and adjust to a level that students can comprehend. This requires that the teacher be informed about students' background knowledge, aptitudes, and interests.[82] The simplification consists of translating technical terms to more familiar terms, converting abstractions into visual or concrete material, and otherwise reducing the difficulty level.[83] Finding the appropriate level of simplification is not an easy task. University teachers need to strike a balance between "going over the students' heads" versus "spoonfeeding" (Thielens, 1987). The teacher often finds it necessary to tailor the course to the different students with different student populations in class.[84]

After selecting the course content, organizing it and simplifying it, the teacher needs to design the course syllabus to be presented in the first lesson.

Designing the Course Syllabus

The syllabus has two main objectives: to provide a framework for the course content, and to clarify the course requirements and procedures. In essence, the syllabus may be perceived as a contract between the instructor and students, presenting the obligations of each of these parties to the other.

Which items are usually included in course syllabi and what is the frequency of their inclusion? A survey of college teachers (Stark, Forthcoming) found that:

– Items included in course syllabi *most often* are: basic course information, course calendar, information about texts and textbooks, information about discipline content, instructional methods or plans, and course requirements.
– Items included *sometimes* are: course goals and objectives, educational philosophy of the teacher, and rationale for course content.
– Items included *only seldom* are: learning resources and facilities, supplementary readings, and rationale behind arranging course content.

---

[82] See Chapter 12: Gaining knowledge of the Learners, Before Teaching.
[83] See Chapter 10: Simplifying the Material Presented.
[84] See Chapter 12: Adapting Teaching to Students in a "Very Heterogeneous" Class.

The syllabus contains four main components: basic information, course description, course policies, and timetable.

What basic information to include in the course syllabus

Information on the year, semester, or quarter, title of course and its number, full name and academic title of instructor(s) and TA(s), location and time of classes, labs, recitation sections.

Method of communication: office location and office hours of the instructor(s) and TA(s), office telephone and fax numbers, home phone number (optional), and email addresses (optional).

Prerequisites for the course (optional).

Learning materials: Titles of textbooks, supplementary readings (related and helpful books, articles), and other learning materials (e.g., computer software, relevant video cassettes, videotapes of lectures) for the course and for complementing the prerequisites of the course. Provide information about availability of these resources.

What course description information to include in the syllabus

The course goals: what the student will know and/or will be able to do upon completing the course.

The classroom format: lectures, discussions, student presentations, integration of technological tools, demos, section classes, guest lecturers, labs, among others.

The framework for the course content: list all the main topics of the course under headings and sub-headings. Arrange them in some logical structure and make this structure explicit to students. The main principles for arrangement are:

- Showing chronological/historical development.
- Going from theory to applications.
- Going from concrete to abstract.
- Maintaining the way concepts of the field are organized.
- using the way that best helps students understand.
- using the way the knowledge occurs in the "real world."

An excellent way to clarify the course framework is to present the topics graphically—giving a "roadmap" (flow chart, Venn diagram, timeline, hierarchical structure)[85].

---

[85] See Chapter 8: Providing a Conceptual Framework for the Course.

What course policies information to include in the syllabus

Policy regarding assigned reading, homework, and other course assignments; make-up policies (late or repeated submission, make-up exams).

Policy regarding testing and grading: number of tests, repeating a test, type of test, grading policies, and the weight of each test or assignment in the final grade.

Expectations of students: class participation, academic honesty, giving class presentations, attendance, punctuality, group work on assignments, and so forth.

Topics for homework (optional).

What timetable information to include in the course syllabus:

Dates of class meetings, of exams and quizzes, of other important events during the course, and due dates for submitting homework assignments.

Issues for each class meeting: the tentative topics, the required reading (provide page numbers so that students can plan their time), questions to consider or problems to solve, topics to prepare for discussion (optional).

The First Lesson in the Course

The first lesson is very important, as it is the lesson in which the teacher establishes relationships with the students and sets the framework for their learning. The three main components that should be addressed during the first lesson are: setting a positive environment, providing motivation for learning, and presenting the main information about the course.

How to set a positive environment for the course

Start by warmly greeting the students and inducing a pleasant classroom climate.

Communicate that you want the course to be good for them, that you care about their learning and that you will help and support them in their learning.

Suggest several techniques to help them learn or prepare for the course exams (e.g., learning in groups).

Obtain students' responses, address their concerns.

Encourage students to communicate with you, particularly when they face some problem in learning the course material. Invite them to use your office hours, to leave messages on your voice mail after office hours, and to send you email. Encourage them also to approach the course TAs during their office hours.

How to provide motivation for learning

Explain why it is important for students to learn in the course and what they will gain from doing so.

How to present the main information about the course

Go over the syllabus, section by section, with your students. Stop after each section and elaborate on its content. Provide a rationale for the main items in the syllabus.

Describe the course goals and elaborate on them, on what the student will know and will be able to do upon completion of the course.

Explain the framework for the course content, your reasons for selecting the particular course topics and for presenting them in the order you have chosen. Explain how this structure may contribute to achieving the course goals. Describe the unifying theory or line of thought. Show students a transparency with the list of the course's main topics, or better, with their graphic presentation.

Explain your choice of textbooks and of the other supplementary reading and learning materials. Explain how the readings relate to the course objectives and classroom activities.

Describe the prerequisites for the course and explain how to complement missing parts of the prerequisite knowledge.

Clarify all policy and timetable issues presented in the syllabus. Explain the rationale behind them.

PLANNING THE LESSON

Smith (1995, p. 15) found that in preparing their lessons, most faculty "concentrate on arranging the best material in the best package for the most effective transmission." However, there are other issues that teachers should attend to when planning a lesson. They should consider the same three components already identified with regard to course planning: selecting, structuring, and simplifying (Thielens, 1987). Although the lesson topics have already been selected at the course planning stage, the teacher still needs to decide what segments or aspects of the topic to present during the limited class time, and what to leave for students to complete through readings or homework assignments. Next, the teacher needs to plan how to organize the material for the lesson, and how to make it understandable, interesting, and challenging.

How to plan the lesson

Use the following stages:[86]

Define the content of the lesson within the framework of the course.

Limit the content to be presented or discussed during the lesson.

Organize and structure the lesson content.

Prepare teaching tools for the lesson—handouts, transparencies, computer presentations, demos, and so forth.

Decide on time allocation for the main topics. To save on lesson time, concentrate on the most important parts of the presentation and leave the rest for students to complement. For example, when solving a math problem, explain the solution method and steps of the solution in class and let students do the related calculations at home.

Plan the use of pedagogical principles of effective teaching throughout the lesson—make the lesson well-organized, clear, engaging, and so forth; pre-design the teaching methods to be used, the students' activities, and the homework to be assigned.

Prepare, in writing, a detailed lesson plan. You may use the forms in the Appendix. Prepare a written outline on paper or cards to take with you to the classroom and use throughout the lesson.

An essential aspect in planning the lesson is planning how to use the class time effectively.

EFFECTIVE USE OF CLASS TIME

Total classroom time is a fixed quantity. The teacher needs to effectively use this time to achieve all teaching objectives, as planned. Thus, the time of each lesson may be perceived as a limited resource that should be utilized in the most effective way to obtain optimal learning. Students need to feel that their time in class is not wasted, and that participating in class is cost-effective—that it promotes their learning and that it takes less time than self-learning, as expressed in these comments:

- He covers a lot during the lesson, and in a way that we understand.
- Thorough coverage, felt that I learned a lot.
- I felt comfortable in class and learned a great deal.

Alternatively:
- Covered only 50% in class of the material covered in exams.

Behaviors that Waste Class Time

- He stretches material of one lesson over a week or more.
- He should be concerned about rambling and going over the allotted time.
- He tells unfunny jokes and wastes our precious time.

These comments refer to teachers whom students perceive as wasting precious, limited class time. The following teacher behaviors lead to ineffective use of class time and should be avoided: going at too slow a pace, dwelling on unimportant topics, diverting from the main line of the content, coming unprepared to class, making errors, and conducting private discussions. These behaviors are described next, accompanied by enlightening students' comments.

Improper pace of instruction

- Shouldn't repeat each example ten times!
- Class discussions were often too slow and obvious.
- Classes sometimes get slowed down by the professor asking the class a lot of simple questions.
- Students are uncomfortable blurting out answers to obvious questions, so this slows things down.

> Adjust the pace of instruction to the particular student audience in class. Too slow a pace provokes boredom and impedes covering the overall curriculum of the course, whereas too fast a pace puts a strain on students' understanding. Avoid too many unnecessary repetitions, explanations of topics that students already understand, or overly long and detailed answers to students' questions.

Dwelling on unimportant topics or on too much use of teaching aids

- Shouldn't lecture 15 minutes on what she is going to teach in that lecture.
- I often felt that too much of the two hours was filled with watching clips.
- Good movies but took too much class time.

---

[86] You may use the layout in the Appendix—make copies and use it whenever planning a lesson.

Do not dedicate too much time to unimportant topics or to using teaching aids (demonstrations, presentation of movies or video clips) that do not add sufficiently to student understanding of the material.

Diversion from lesson objectives and topics, lack of focus

- This guy comes in with impromptu lectures and gets sidetracked faster than anyone I've seen before.
- This teacher is always dragged by students' questions and goes on tangents to residual topics that are very interesting but that do not belong to the material of the course.
- Some lectures were unfocused—irrelevant questions sidetracked the instructor.
- Lots of diversions in class.

Do not diverge to unplanned topics, even if they are very interesting. Do not present material that is irrelevant to the lesson or that is not crucial for understanding the topics. Avoid digressions in response to students' questions or for any other reason, unless there is a special justification for this diversion.

Coming unprepared, making errors

- Some professors come to class totally unprepared—didn't read the readings by themselves.
- Should be more prepared for class. He often gets lost in notation or in working out his examples during lectures.
- Sometimes more than half the lesson is wasted on arguing with students on small computational errors.

Always come to class very well prepared, with written notes, to avoid making errors in presentation of topics, in a development, in steps of a process, in solving a problem, and so forth. Solve fully and in advance, on paper, all problems that you plan to solve on the board in class; formulate everything you plan to put on the board; practice all demonstrations you plan to perform in class. Making errors or failing in demonstrations forces you to dedicate unnecessary time to explanations, corrections, and interpretations, that is, to wasting the lesson time.

Conducting private discussions in class

- Should conduct less irrelevant discussions with students.

When a student raises a question that is neither interesting to nor understood by most other students in class, do not direct your answer to that particular student, disregarding the other students in class. If the same student poses additional questions for clarification, beware not to develop a private dialogue with that student, while all other students switch off and do other things. This situation wastes the time of most students in class.

Cutting short the lesson duration

- She's always late for the class and fails to cover the course material.
- His lessons are always 30 minutes rather than 45!

Do not come late to class or end the lesson beforehand. In this way, you lose some of the precious limited contact time you have with students.

Improper allocation of time

- Should give more time to the principles and less to the secondary topics.
- I wish we had more time for discussion because the books were good.
- Should improve the pace: We dwelled on some topics and sped through others.
- He goes over both easy stuff and new difficult stuff at the same rate.
- She should put less emphasis on practice and more on theory.
- Could skip a lot of basic material and not dwell on it, cover more topics.
- Should cover less topics but more in depth.
- Should spend more time on the actual scientific significance of material.

One of the behaviors that strongly discriminated between clear and unclear university teachers was: "Distributes time adequately over topics" (Hines, 1982).

Plan the distribution of time for each topic to be presented in a lesson. Dedicate more time to more complex and difficult topics and go faster on easy ones. Distribute time appropriately between theory and practice.

Additional Ideas for Saving Class Time

How to plan saving class time

Prepare a detailed and accurate lesson plan with time allocation for the different topics. Include all didactic/pedagogic aspects of the material presentation and the time allocation for each topic.

Ensure that students have all prerequisites: Tell students in advance what material they will need to know in order to understand the next lesson. Guide them in how to obtain this knowledge by themselves[87]. In this way, you save

---

[87] See suggestions in Chapter 12

class time, avoiding many questions and misunderstandings due to lack of background knowledge.

Prepare clear and concise lesson notes and distribute them to students at the beginning of the lesson. These notes should reduce the amount of information that students need to write down and thus help your effective advancement in the material. For example, prepare a summary of the prerequisite knowledge for the lesson; copies of the transparencies you present during the lesson; a list of the topics, rules, formulas, and long developments that you rely on or develop during the lesson; copies of tables, graphs, or drawings that you plan to exhibit in class.

What to do right before the lesson starts to save class time

Come to the classroom before the students arrive. This enables you to get things started with a minimum of delay and confusion. Use the time until the lesson starts to talk with students informally and answer quick questions.

Check and verify proper learning conditions. Check out the learning conditions such as lighting, heating, that the board is not too shiny or too dark, and other noise interference. Erase the board if it is not clean enough and check if you have enough chalk to write with.

Check the availability and operational condition of technical equipment that you plan to use during the lesson such as a slide or overhead projector, or a videotape player. If you plan to use video, you should insert the cassette and run it to the point where you will begin its presentation.

Check all components of the demonstrations you plan to use—whether they are in place and if they work.

Write lesson essentials on the board—write everything that will help students follow the presentation, such as the outline of the lesson and key words, definitions, formulas, and so forth.

Draw on the board anything that may take a lot of your class time (if you have not prepared the drawings on transparencies).

Organize the notes you have prepared for class distribution.

Start the lesson exactly on time.

How to save class time during the lesson

Defer to after class all students' questions that are not fully relevant to the lesson topics, or that are out of the scope of the planned level of presenting these topics.

> Look at your notes often to ensure that you do not make errors and that you maintain the lesson plan and timing.

How to save class time at the lesson's end

> Summarize all lesson material in a succinct and effective form.
>
> Do not exceed the lesson time. End exactly on time.

SUMMARY

A fundamental component of all teaching processes is planning the course and the lesson.

Planning the course is influenced by three categories of contextual factors: disciplinary, educational, and organizational. Course planning includes making decisions about content, considering factors affecting the teaching and learning processes, selecting strategies for engaging students in the content, and selecting ways to obtain feedback about student learning. It consists of three key processes for designing the content: selecting, structuring, and simplifying. The content selection process is guided by the discipline, the students, and the textbook. A good textbook is clear, informative, thorough and at an appropriate level for the students. It provides a conceptual framework for the course and includes concrete examples. It suits the professor's goals in teaching the course, and with his/her perception of its content, structure, and organization. The body of knowledge of any discipline is both too vast and too amorphous, and the connections among its parts are too complex for direct transmission to undergraduates. Professors are compelled to organize the material selected in order to teach it according to a comprehensible structure. They must find ways to simplify and adjust the course material to a level that students can comprehend.

The course syllabus has two main objectives: to provide a framework for the course content, and to clarify the course requirements and procedures. The syllabus may be perceived as a contract between the instructor and students, presenting the obligations of each of these parties to the other. It includes basic information, the course description, course policies, and the timetable. In the first lesson of the course, the teacher establishes his/her relationships with the students and sets the framework for their learning.

Lesson planning consists of the same three components already identified with regard to course planning: selecting, structuring, and simplifying. A very important aspect of lesson planning is planning how to use class time effectively.

Effective use of class time. The time of each lesson is a limited resource that should be utilized in the most effective way for optimal learning. Teacher behaviors that lead to a waste of class time, resulting in boredom and impeding the instruction of the full course curriculum, include: using too many unnecessary repetitions; explaining topics that students already understand; giving overly lengthy and detailed answers to students' questions; going at too slow a pace; dwelling on unimportant topics; diverting from the main line of content; coming unprepared to class; making errors; and conducting private dialogues and discussions. Other causes for ineffective use of class time are cutting short the lesson duration and improper allocation of time over the lesson topics.

Chapter 19

Assessing Student Learning

THE ROLE OF STUDENT ASSESSMENT

The main theme of this book is teaching for effective learning. Effective learning occurs when learners feel challenged to work toward appropriately high goals (APA, 1997)[88]. Setting challenging goals and assessing the learner and learning progress toward achieving these goals are integral parts of the learning process.

We use diagnostic, process, and outcome assessment to provide important information for both the learner and teacher at all stages of the learning process. Appraisal of the learner's cognitive strengths and weaknesses, knowledge and skills, is important for the selection of instructional material of an optimal degree of difficulty. Ongoing assessment of the learner's understanding of the curricular material provides valuable feedback to both learners and teachers about their progress toward the learning goals. However, performance assessment can provide other sources of information about the attainment of learning outcomes (ibid.). The teacher should use performance assessment to evaluate students' understanding by examining their understanding performances (Perkins, 1992).

Testing and grading—the most common procedures for assessing students—are a source of immense anxiety for students. Because many students perceive grades as the bottom line of their learning in a course, the

---

[88] See Chapter 4: Principle 14.

course grade constitutes the main external motivator for studying. As can be seen from students' comments throughout this chapter, they feel very hurt and frustrated by testing and grading procedures that they perceive as unfair. On the other hand, many teachers feel deeply frustrated by the strong emphasis that students put on their grades as this emphasis communicates the notion that the only thing that interests students is how to obtain a good grade. Teachers deplore the question often asked by students of whether specific material is going to be on the test, and students' demonstration of lack of interest in case that the answer is "No."

In fact, students' interest in grades should not be seen in such a negative light. Grades do have a crucial effect on students' further progress. Good grades for an undergraduate degree are critical for admittance to graduate studies, particularly in competitive professional schools at prestigious universities. Good grades are also crucial for getting interesting, well-paid work positions in prestigious firms.

Student assessment is usually based on the evaluation of their tests and their homework assignments, as elaborated in the following sections.

TESTING

Testing directs students' study methods and aims and motivates them to invest time and effort in trying to understand and learn (Crooks, 1988). Students usually become very frustrated with tests they perceive as unfair:

- It is frustrating to study so much for an exam that left you so annoyed.

Test Design

Problematic Aspects of Test Design

The following comments illustrate several common problems characterizing university testing from the students' point of view:

Tests are too difficult

- The first midterm threw us off.
- Midterms are ridiculously hard.
- Exams were particularly difficult and way above the level of our understanding.

Tests do not fit the content or level of lectures or homework assignments

- His exams are killers and three times as difficult as the level of teaching and the homework problems.
- He gives easy lectures but hard exams that are impossible to pass simply by attending and understanding his lectures.
- His concept of what he had taught as exemplified by his tests was horrendously off base. Test only on what you teach!! Not random applications of what you have only hinted at.
- The exams were discouraging, our experience with respect to the content and the relevance of the material seemed questionable to a freshman.

Tests are badly composed

- If the means on the midterms are in the 30%-40% range, either the students are not learning or the test is not measuring our learning.
- The tests were quite incomprehensive. Should be longer with focus on larger number of concepts.
- Tests too long.
- Midterms were too easy and multiple choice isn't a good way to test students.

There is insufficient advance information about the test

- The TAs weren't able to give information about what the tests would be like or how they would be graded, because they themselves were not informed.

Types of Tests

There is a variety of types of tests. The main ones require writing an essay, solving problems, answering multiple-choice questions, responding to short-answer questions, and performing some tasks (e.g., computer lab or field work). Less common tasks are, for instance: discussing cases; presenting projects; participating in simulations; preparing portfolios or journals; analyzing video-clip presentations. By far the most common type of test consists of written performance in the classroom. Other methods include oral in-class performance, laboratory performance (including hands-on computer work), workplace performance, and take-home performance. Of all these types and methods, this chapter concentrates on the dominant form of test administration—those based on writing in the classroom. These can be sorted into "closed" multiple-choice tests versus "open" tests.

The type of test seems to affect students' learning strategies. In preparing for an essay- or problem-solving test, students use deep methods of thinking that are based on understanding and application of the material whereas in closed tests they use surface methods of studying, such as memorization (D'Ydewalle, Swerts, & de Corte, 1983). An additional shortcoming of closed tests is that they do not reflect performance in real professional life situations (Fredericksen, 1984). In selecting the type of test to be given, an important consideration is class size. Multiple choice tests take the most time to compose but the least time to score whereas essay tests take a short time to compose but a very long time to score. Short-answer tests are in-between in terms of time for design and scoring. Using these considerations, teachers tend to give multiple-choice tests to large classes, short-answer tests to medium-size classes, and essay tests to small classes. From the point of view of student learning, open tests are always preferable to closed ones. Even in large classes, it is important to add a few open-ended questions to multiple-choice tests, or to ask students to explain why their answer is correct, in order to make them study for understanding.

The majority of professors have never learned how to design a good and fair test. Thus, the following sections provide practical advice on this issue.

How to design/compose a test

List all objectives of the test material. List all topics, all main points, and all main concepts of the course curriculum. Weight each in proportion to its importance.

Compose questions that faithfully represent these objectives, reflecting their importance in your teaching throughout the term. Be sure to represent material you actually taught, if it differed from your planned curriculum. If you plan to use questions on material that you have not covered in class, be sure that you have guided students in attaining the relevant knowledge independently.

Do not use questions that are too general, trivial or surprising; or questions that concentrate on topics, points and concepts of relatively little importance. These types of questions raise students' anxiety and a sense of unfairness, and promote memorization of marginal issues.

Give questions of varying levels of difficulty and arrange them in order of difficulty, beginning with the easiest. Easy questions at the beginning of a test encourage students to continue. A good composition would include 40% easy questions that all students in the course can answer, 50% questions which require a higher level of understanding and thinking, and 10% challenging questions that only the best students can answer. This pattern enables only the excelling students to achieve the maximum score, but all students who have learned a sound amount of the course material can get a passing grade, and good students can still gain a good or very good grade (up to 90% of the maximal score). Thus, including items of varying levels of difficulty will ensure a good grade distribution.

Avoid questions that are more difficult or that require a higher level of thinking than those the students have experienced during the course—either in lectures, section classes, or homework. This advice relates to all questions except the challenging questions that account for 10% of the overall score—those designed to obtain the maximal score.

Compose questions that require a variety of thinking levels. Use Bloom's (1956) taxonomy of educational goals. He sorted the teaching objectives and cognitive levels invested in learning into six categories in increasing order of cognitive complexion: retention, understanding, application, analysis, synthesis, and evaluation. This categorization is useful in composing questions.

Include extra credit questions or enable optional selection from among the test items. This policy may reduce test anxiety.

Involve your students in the test design and get their feedback on your tests. You may use the following suggestions:

- **Ask students to submit possible questions for the test.** This will give you some sense of their expectations. You may adapt some of the questions submitted for use.
- **Ask students for feedback about the test.** Obtain this feedback anonymously, ask about questions that were either confusing or too difficult, the overall level of the exam, how representative it was of the course content and focus, and so forth. This feedback will guide you in future test construction.

How to handle technical aspects of test design

Formulate questions accurately and succinctly. You should make it very clear what students need to answer.

Fully answer all questions yourself on the test that you have composed, before giving it to the students.

Ask one or more of your peers or course TAs to go over the questions, answer them, and comment on their clarity and accuracy.

Design sufficient time for answering the test. The duration of a problem-solving test should be about three times longer than it took you to fully solve the test problems.

Include clear instructions on the test sheet itself as to the length of the test, use of auxiliary materials, length of answers, your expectations as to the nature of the answers, and so on.

Include (in the test sheet) the criteria and the main considerations for full/partial scoring of each item. For example, in a problem-solving test—would a correct method for solution be counted even if the student errs in computation? In an essay test, would originality and critical thinking be counted, or are students expected only to show knowledge?

Check the printed sheet for typos and other errors. Have other people (your TAs) make additional checks.

Include interesting, thought-provoking, or humorous items whenever possible.

Design the test sheet to be pleasant looking—eye-friendly. You may add humorous clip art to relax students.

Reducing test anxiety

Many students suffer from test anxiety. You should take care to reduce this type of anxiety by helping students prepare for the test. The following are a few suggestions in this direction.

How to reduce test anxiety before the test

Inform students at the beginning of the term—in the course syllabus and orally in the first lesson—about the number of tests/exams/quizzes, including their dates, content, and type.

Provide advance information about an upcoming test's type, content, and structure to guide students in their preparation for the test and to relieve their anxiety due to feelings of uncertainty. Inform students in advance about the place and time duration of the test; accurately delimit the material to be covered; suggest sources for learning beyond the textbook or handouts that you gave in the course; provide information about the number of items and the type of questions (open-ended/multiple-choice, difficulty levels, etc.); explain your expectations in answering open-ended questions—will you be looking for memorization? Knowledge? Application? Independent, critical, and original thinking? Also, give information about the scoring method of the items. Provide students with sample items that you gave in this course in previous years.

Arrange for a review session—a special class meeting before the test, to enable students to come up with questions regarding the material and the test procedure.

Arrange for students to have comfortable communication channels regarding the test with you and the course TAs. For example, organize group meetings in your office at certain times, and arrange for telephone or email connections. Announce that you will come to the place of the test one hour early to enable last-minute questions.

Guide students, particularly freshmen, on how to most effectively study for the test. Distribute a handout with suggestions about how to best prepare for the test, or with sample questions.

Distribute a handout with a summary of the material for the test—this should include the main points, main theorems/laws/rules/formulas included in the test material.

How to reduce test anxiety during the test

Repeat your guidance regarding the test: its time duration; your expectations regarding the open-ended questions as listed above, or as related to good organization and clarity of the answers. Briefly present the criteria for scoring the items.

Make sure that the questions are clear to the students. If you find that even a single student misunderstands a question, clarify its meaning to all students.

Maintain a relaxed atmosphere during the test. Visit the room where the test is administered frequently to answer students' questions. Avoid expressing anger or contempt as a response to questions that you judge as inappropriate or as not clever.

Take care to inform students several times about the time left for the test, for example, half an hour, and then again 15 minutes before the test ends.

How to provide test conditions that reduce anxiety

There are certain types of test conditions that work particularly well for reducing test anxiety:

Enable pair testing: Enable students to do the test in pairs: both members of the pair will get the same grade.

Enable open access to study material during the test. Enable students to use any book, class notes, a summary handout that you have distributed, and so forth.

Include familiar items in the test: Ask students in advance to suggest questions for the test and select one or more of these to be on the test. Alternatively, select one or more problems from assignments given in previous homework tasks.

Give a take-home test. Give a test that students can do in the security and confidence of their home environment. However, assign a limited time for returning the test forms.

If the test serves as a learning tool, for example, a mid-term test, it is important to give students detailed feedback on the test, with comments on wrong or less-than-perfect answers, to help them learn from their mistakes. Research indicates that giving only a grade contributes much less to learning than does giving feedback in the form of explanations—both general comments and those related to students' specific errors (Roberts & Park, 1984).

How to return graded tests

Before giving back the individual graded papers:

Discuss with the class the test items that showed to be the most problematic. Explain students' problems or misconceptions, the best ways for solution, and the grading criteria and reasons for deducting points. Also present some of the best or most interesting answers given.

Present the class distribution of grades (mean, standard deviation).

Enable students to ask general questions about the test and grading and invite interested students to talk to you after the lesson.

Distribute a handout with a sample of good answers for the different test items.

GRADING

- Professor needs to compensate for possible inconsistencies in grading styles of both graders.
- Grading needs to be more consistent for all students on homework and exams.
- The grading of examinations is often unfair. Many points are taken off when it is clear the problem is understood but a less than ideal approach is taken.

These comments illustrate students' frustration with grading procedures they perceive as unfair. Grading multiple-choice tests is simple and objective but, as explained above, this is the least recommended type of test. Grading of any other type of test is much less objective and reliable. That is, the grade for an essay question, a short open-ended question, or a solution to a problem may depend on the grader, on his/her mood or fatigue level when grading, or on the place of the particular solution sheet in the pile already graded. The first sheets graded may be scored differently than the later ones, and a sheet may be treated differently if it happens to come after several poor or extremely good sheets.

How to avoid inconsistencies in grading

Develop the criteria for scoring already during the stage of test composition. Then, when you get the test sheets, use your criteria to go over a small sample of sheets and modify the criteria on the basis of these students' answers.

Write down on paper the criteria for scoring. Include scores for partial answers, (e.g., for the correct approach in solving a problem despite incorrect calculations, for critical/original thinking, etc.).

When you go over the sample of answers for a particular question, identify which are excellent, very good, good, fair, and poor. Keep these answers as a model when you grade the rest of the sheets.

Maintain student anonymity while grading, particularly when you have institutional or departmental support for this procedure.

Grade all test sheets on each question separately. That is, grade all of them on the first question, then all of them on the second, etc.

In case of more than one grader, assign each only particular questions to grade on all test sheets. That is, on a four-item test, one grader evaluates only questions number 1 and 3, whereas the second evaluates questions number 2 and 4. Give each grader the criteria and model for grading that you have developed.

If more than one grader evaluates the same question for different students, train the graders on consistency in scoring. Assign all graders to evaluate the same test sheets of several students using the written criteria and model for grading that you have developed. Compare with the graders all the assessments of the same test sheet, and cooperatively sharpen the criteria.

In assigning the final grade you may summarize all grades for the different test items, but then you may also **add extra points** for the overall performance, on the basis of your impression from the overall test sheet.

Write comments on the test sheet whenever less than the full score is given for a question, to explain why the grade was reduced, so that if students later complain about unfair grading, the comments will help to support the grade that was given.

HOMEWORK ASSIGNMENTS

Assigning and assessing homework is a central part of teaching and plays a chief role in assessing student learning. There are many types of assignments: reading material that serves as a basis for the content presentation; reading material not covered in class yet included in a test; writing tasks such as short assignments submitted for each lesson, or term papers; submitting solutions to weekly problem sets; and working on independent projects. Several of these are discussed here.

Reading Assignments

Selecting and Assigning Readings

Positive comments:

- Readings were well chosen, up-to-date, and well suited to course topics.
- The material we read was incredibly fascinating and insightful.
- The readings were super interesting, with proper context.
- Enjoyed the variety, cross-cultural depth of the materials.

Negative comments:

- Some of the readings were too detailed for our purposes and seemed unnecessary.
- Some of the readings were rather dry and repetitive.
- Some assignments had only a few pages that were interesting and worth reading. I think we should cover a greater variety of works, but just sections of each.
- The readings were tedious and heavy on statistics.
- The readings were hard to relate to one another and to the class material.
- The bulk of reading is too dense for an introductory class. It's hard to grasp its total significance sometimes.
- He should cut the reading and give more time to students for thinking and applying the material.
- Reading material sometimes have problems because some cases are assigned without any type of context and you have to dive into a lot of extraneous material and to sort out what's relevant or irrelevant [a law student].
- The reading material was old and disorganized.

To summarize, these students whose statements are quoted perceive reading assignments as beneficial when the readings suit the course topics and are up-to-date, interesting, insightful, and deep. Non-beneficial readings are the opposite—they neither contribute to the course topics nor to student understanding and learning of the course material. They are unfocused, uninteresting or even boring, too old to be relevant, and do not fit students' prior knowledge and aptitude level. If the quantity of readings is too large for students to keep up with, reading comes at the expense of deep thinking and learning gains.

Additional problems with readings are the need to embed and incorporate them within the framework of the course and lesson[89], as shown these comments:

- The lessons fell behind the reading.
- I felt we read quite a few cases that were only peripheral and that were never discussed in class [a law student].
- Why has he assigned so much reading when we did not have time in class to discuss more than 50% of it?
- If you reduce the amount of reading, more people will read and we'll be able to follow the discussion better during the lesson.

The two last comments focus teachers who assign too many readings for a lesson. Therefore, they are unable to build upon or refer to all the readings in class, and most students cannot afford the time to read them all.

Maintaining Student Motivation to Read the Assigned Reading

To help students concentrate on the assigned reading as well as understand its main points and how they connect to the lesson topics, the teacher may provide several questions on the reading assignment to direct students' thinking, or even ask them to submit written answers and commentaries. This also makes students demonstrate "understanding performances."[90] To illustrate, on the sheet that listed the readings, an anthropology professor assigned her students to write a two-page "reading response" for each reading, answering specific questions on the key points of the material. In their course evaluation, her students highly appreciated these questions, feeling that they helped them integrate the readings with the lessons and promote their overall perception of the course material:

- I enjoyed answering the reading responses, it made me really think about the material and figure out how it fits with the overall themes and goals of the course.
- It's through the readings where we get a sense of continuity, how subjects hang together.
- It's very helpful to have weekly reading responses; it requires student to engage in the material and keep up with the reading.
- Reading responses motivated me to do assignments and focus on the reading.
- Reading responses were great as they forced us to think about the material before class.

---

[89] See discussion in Chapter 8.
[90] See Chapter 13.

However, caution should be taken to avoid some errors of the type criticized here:

- Reading responses were okay, but often dealt with the subject tangentially.
- At times questions were vague, not much explanation of what the answer to the reading response should be.
- Too time-consuming, took too much writing.

How to motivate unprepared students to do the reading

Clarify your expectations to students. Make your expectations about coming prepared to class clear to the students. If it is important for your lesson plan that students come prepared, you should insist on their doing the reading. However, this requires three conditions:

(a) Allow sufficient time for readings—preferably already allocated in the syllabus given during the first lesson of the term.

(b) Assign a feasible amount of readings that most students can cope with, given the available time.

(c) Assign only directly relevant readings that you will be able to build on or refer to in class.

Assign written tasks related to the readings. The written assignments can be "reading responses"—answering particular questions on key points, or a summary, outline, or list of main points concerning the set text for that lesson. Collect the assignments at the beginning of each class.

Give a short and easy quiz on the assigned reading at the beginning of each lesson or every few lessons. This may also serve to record class attendance.

Call on random students in class to answer questions about the reading. Be aware that this method may be threatening to students. Therefore, pose only simple/easy questions that verify that they have done the reading.

Ask students who have not done the reading to raise their hands, and give them a writing assignment on the reading that they should submit to you at the end of the class period, and dismiss them from class to do the assignment. Then check the remaining students by posing easy questions.

Allow students open access during tests only to those of their own written assignments that related to readings. Limit the open material to be used in tests to only those written assignments submitted in class. The assignments should be submitted on one page of a certain size, or even on a card. Stamp each summary and return it to the students some time before the test. Allow students to add information on this page or card, but not to add other pages/cards. Then, in the test, students are allowed to use only stamped pages or cards.

Problem-Solving Assignments

The following comments from students air good aspects as well as typical problems of problem-solving assignments.

Level of difficulty

- Homework problems were good, helped us to learn and were challenging but not impossible.
- Needed harder problem sets— the book's problems are too short and easy.
- Problems should be more comprehensive, that is, more problems, easy and hard.
- The first two sets were much harder than the last two.
- Homework problems were pretty frustrating because I didn't feel adequately prepared to do them, no TA or any other outside help was available, and the book wasn't really helpful as its approach was less mathematical than that of the instructor.
- It often happens that students get through the problem set not really understanding the material.

Integration with lecture

- Problems don't relate to lectures.
- Sometimes he doesn't cover the material in class that we need to do for the problem sets before the problem sets are due.

Technical aspects

- Many typos in problem sets; handwriting and notes not always clear.
- Problem sets are often too long and too much garbage is included.

How to design problem sets

Assign problems that fit the level of the students and the course requirements and that are well integrated with lectures.

Avoid technical problems in the printout of the problems.

Take care that each problem is based on knowledge students already have, mostly presented in class.

Give students guidance for solving the problems. Solve several sample problems during lecture and explain on this basis how to approach the problem, or assign your TAs to do this in practice lessons.

Writing Assignments

Written assignments have several purposes: to evaluate students' learning in the course, to promote students' writing skills, and to give them the opportunity to explore problems that are interesting and relevant for them.

How to design writing assignments—types of assignments
You may assign several types of writing assignments in your course.

A review/integration of research literature. In this writing assignment, students either all address a given topic, or they individually choose a topic of their own interest under the general headings of the course.

Reflection/log/journal on reading, observing, and thinking. The student should record his/her thoughts when doing the assigned reading, and when doing other activities related to the course.

An article on a study/research project. Ask students to conduct a simple study or work on a research project and to write it up like an article for a professional journal.

A letter. Assign students to write letters of different types: persuasive, argumentative, explanatory, critical, and so forth. The letters can be written as though addressed to policy or decision-makers, journal readers, professionals in the field, among others.

Building on an important article/book. Ask students to criticize the article/book, write a short summary or abstract, write an update based on related new findings since the publication of that article/book, write their reflections on the content, and so on.

Additional methods: Writing a case study, summarizing or commenting on a fieldwork experience, summarizing the readings for the course.

How to design writing assignments—instructions for assignments
Break down the process of writing a term paper into a series of easy steps, such as McKeachie (1994, p. 118) suggests:

1. Finding a topic

2. Gathering sources, data, or references

3. Developing an outline

4. Writing a first draft

5. Rewriting

You may, of course, use other steps that suit the particular writing assignment and course conditions.

The evaluation of written work is conducted to assess students' learning during the term, and to provide them with useful corrective feedback that will promote their writing skills.

How to evaluate students' writing

Design criteria for grading students' writing. It is important that the teacher develops an explicit detailed *set of grading criteria* which defines the qualities required in a paper to merit an "A," "B," "C," or so forth. You may take into considerations criteria such as originality, creativity, being up-to-date, persuasiveness, supporting evidence, clarity of writing, focus and well-definedness of the subject, organization, coherence of ideas presented, use of citations, quality of academic writing, and spelling, grammar, syntax, and style. This criteria set should be given to students to guide their work, and to graders to help them assign the grades objectively. The following is a good example of a checklist of grading criteria developed by Gary Lapree of Indiana University (1977, in McKeachie, 1994, pp. 126-7):

A. Content

1. Introduction

a. Is the topic novel and original?

b. Does the author state purpose, problem, or question to be considered?

c. How does the author convince the reader that the paper is worth reading?

d. Does the author present a preview of how the problem will be handled?

2. Body

a. How are the statements made warranted? Is there evidence that data collected have been analyzed and the literature reviewed? Are the assumptions logical?

b. Presentation of evidence

- Is contradictory evidence dealt with adequately?
- Are multiple sources considered if available?
- Is the evidence discussed relevant to the purpose stated?
- Is the argument plausible?
- Are the methods chosen for testing the argument convincing?

c. Suitability of paper's focus

- Is the problem chosen focused enough to be adequately covered in the space of the paper?
- Is the problem chosen too specific for the author's sources of information?

d. Background information

- Is enough information given to familiarize the reader with the problem?
- Is unimportant background material included?
- Is the presentation easy to follow and well organized?
- Does the author deal with the problem set up in the introduction?

3. Conclusion

a. Does the author summarize findings adequately?

b. Is the conclusion directly related to the questions asked in the introduction?

c. Does the author suggest areas where further work is needed?

B. Connections to class

1. Evidence that class materials have been read and understood

2. Application of lecture materials and assigned readings to paper

C. Form

1. Spelling

2. Grammar

3. Appropriate use of words: Does the writer use words incorrectly, awkwardly, or inappropriately?

4. Paragraph form: Are ideas presented in coherent order?

5. Footnotes and bibliography: are borrowed ideas and statements given credit?

6. Is the form of the footnotes and bibliography understandable and consistent?

7. Has the paper been proofread?

The assignments contribute to students' learning of the course material; therefore, students should do frequent assignments even if the teacher does not have the time to evaluate and grade them all. Teachers should find appropriate methods to reduce their evaluation load.

How to save faculty time in evaluating and grading student assignments

Limit the length of written assignments. There is no reason to think that long papers provide a better learning experience or better develop students' writing skills than short papers. On the contrary—writing succinct papers is usually more difficult than writing longer ones.

Assign students to submit work in groups. An accepted practice is that students work on projects in groups, and the grade on the project is given to all students in the group. This can also be used for any other type of assignment. Collaborative work contributes to students' learning of the course material[91].

Grade only a sample of student assignments. Select at random only a sample of students' work. Record the names of all students who submitted the work. If you give several assignments during the term, take care that you grade an assignment of each student at least once.

Grade only a part of the assignment, for all students. When the assignment consists of several parts, items, or problems, select at random only a few of these and grade them for all students. Give students a handout with solutions of the problems that you have not evaluated.

Record assignments without grading them. Collect students' papers or other assignments, skim them, record the names of the submitting students, write down for your own use some comments to discuss in class, and return the assignments to the students, ungraded.

Give only a pass/no pass grade to some of the assignments. This practice enables you to skim through students' work without the time-consuming process of grading them.

Arrange for peer feedback on student assignments. Ask students to work in pairs or small groups in class (or outside it), read each other's work, and for each member conduct a group discussion and critique on his/her work.

Initiate peer editing of students' papers. Ask your students to edit papers written by other students in class. Peer editing allows students to view their classmates as a valuable source of ideas, responses, and criticism. In addition to broadening the scope of student writing, peer editing may save time of faculty and TAs in evaluating papers. While they still must evaluate the final papers, faculty and TAs can teach students how to criticize the first, second, and third drafts of the papers. Before you allow your students to peer edit, you must model for them each step of the process. Discuss with them the criteria for evaluating student writing, demonstrate the types of comments you expect them to make on their peers' papers, give them written examples of positive and negative

---

[91] See Chapters 6, 7

criticism. Place students in small groups and have them mark sample papers and report their comments to the class. Then let each edit several papers. At the end of the peer-editing session, ask students to evaluate their experience with peer editing. Sharing positive and negative thoughts about the process will help to prepare them for the next peer editing session.

How to offer alternative tests and assignments for student assessment

Enable your students to be tested by different methods such as writing assignments, class presentations, empirical research, and other homework assignments.

Offer your students different options to fulfill the course requirements,[92] if you can afford the extra workload and if this does not obstruct the policy of your institution.

SUMMARY

Student assessment is usually based on evaluating their tests and their homework assignments.

Testing and grading are a source of immense anxiety for students. Many of them perceive the grade as the main result of their learning, and therefore the course grade is the main external motivator for their learning. Students feel very hurt and frustrated by testing and grading procedures they perceive as unfair. On the other hand, many college and university professors feel deeply frustrated by students' over-emphasis on their grades.

Common student complaints about tests are that they are too difficult, too much above the level of class presentations or of homework assignments, that they are badly composed, and that the students receive insufficient advanced information about the test. There are a variety of types of tests. We concentrated on written tests completed in the classroom: writing an essay, solving problems, answering multiple-choice questions, or responding to short-answer questions. The type of test strongly affects students' approach to studying. Closed tests (multiple-choice, with closed books) usually promote surface learning and the use of ineffective methods of memorizing, whereas open tests, such as essay-writing or problem-solving, promote deep studying based on understanding and application of the material.

---

[92] See illustration in Chapter 12, under "Adapting instruction to students in a 'very heterogeneous' class."

The chapter suggests ideas for composing tests that are fair and clear; for reducing test anxiety; for fair and objective grading; and for giving students constructive feedback on their test performance.

Assigning and assessing homework is a central part of teaching. There are many types of assignments—reading material for the lesson; reading material not covered in class but included in a test; writing assignments; submitting solutions to weekly problem sets; and working on independent projects.

PART V

PROMOTING TEACHING EFFECTIVENESS

Chapter 20: Improving Teaching for Effective
Learning

Chapter 20

Improving Teaching for Effective Learning

The quality of student learning in higher education should be improved and can be improved. How can it best be improved? ...The answer...lies in the connection between students' learning of particular content and the quality of our teaching of that content (Ramsden, 1992, p. 86).

TEACHING FOR EFFECTIVE LEARNING

As suggested throughout this book, college and university teaching should aim to achieve the broad educational goals of preparing students for their adult life, particularly for professional life in the 21st century. In additional to subject matter knowledge, professional success in this century requires original, imaginative, and non-routine thinking; the ability to engage in self-study, to solve problems, and to cooperate with others; and the flexibility to adjust to changing conditions.

Therefore, teaching should satisfy the 14 APA principles[93] for developing diverse students' skills in the cognitive and metacognitive domains, the motivational and affective domains, the developmental and social domains, and in taking individual differences into account.

To achieve this wide range of goals, teachers should involve students actively in their learning. They should encourage students to increase their effort and commitment to learning and to achieve high standards of comprehension; to strengthen their positive emotions; and to promote their

---

[93] See Chapter 4: What Makes Successful Learning? The APA Psychological Principles

personal responsibility for learning. Teachers should create a supportive and nurturing classroom environment that provides stability, trust, and care; increases learners' sense of belonging, self-respect, and self-acceptance; encourages social interactions and communication with others; and cultivates quality personal relationships in class. Teachers should also attend to individual differences by varying instructional methods and materials. These features pertain to the kind of multidimensional teaching that we should opt to provide to college and university students.

Altogether, we should aspire *to change teaching and learning from the transmission model to the transaction model; from teachers imparting knowledge to students constructing knowledge; from passive listening to active learning; from teacher-centered to student-centered perspectives; from teacher responsibility to student responsibility; from acquisition of knowledge to application, analysis, and critical thinking; and from assessment of factual recall to performance assessment and problem-solving* (Barnes, 1992).

However, many faculty members are unfamiliar with these ideas and continue to teach in ways that do not bring about beneficial and effective learning. In many college classrooms, teaching consists mainly of information-transmission, with the teacher being almost the sole speaker and students' role reduced to taking notes. These teachers tend to perceive students as passive vessels responsible only for absorbing the knowledge delivered.

The growing recognition of the need to make the desired changes in teaching has increased pressure on universities and colleges to transform their instructional practices. National education centers and associations now see it as their task to develop theory, disseminate information, and promote the use of instructional innovations. There is currently a growing tendency among institutions of higher education to invest substantial resources on faculty development programs that involve activities for the modification, if not revision of teaching (Lenze, 1996; Weimer & Lenze, 1991).

So, how can teaching be revised and improved? We first describe teaching strategies used by superior teachers, then present teachers' self-improvement activities, and conclude with institution-based instructional development activities.

STRATEGIES AND DIMENSIONS COMMONLY USED BY EXEMPLARY TEACHERS

An important guide in improving teaching is learning from the ways that exemplary teachers teach. In fact, a large proportion of the content of the previous chapters on teaching strategies is based on analysis of teaching methods of superior teachers. What do we know from research on their teaching?

> I can give you no rules [for effective teaching], for there are as many good ways of teaching as there are good teachers (Polya, 1957, p. 37).

> Teaching is a trade that has innumerable little tricks. Each good teacher has his pet devices and each good teacher is different from any other good teacher. Any efficient teaching device must be correlated somehow with the nature of the learning process (Polya, 1965, p. 102).

The notion revealed by these citations is that there is no single way to excel in teaching, but that teaching effectiveness is achieved through a variety of methods. Indeed, a study of four exemplary university teachers (Hativa, Barak, & Simhi, 1999) found that each of them excelled in at least two but not necessarily in all four main dimensions of effective teaching—organization, clarity, interest/engagement, and beneficial classroom climate—and that each used a different set of classroom strategies/techniques to achieve excellence along these dimensions. The authors concluded that no particular set of teaching dimensions or classroom strategies is mandatory for superior teaching, and that students do not expect perfect performance as a requisite for good teaching. That is, to become a superb teacher, one does not need to excel in all the main dimensions of effective teaching, nor to use all the classroom strategies known to be effective. Rather, every teacher achieves excellence in a different way, by excelling in a different set of teaching dimensions and strategies.

To concentrate on the main dimensions of teaching, Lowman (1996) summarized studies on this issue that were conducted using a variety of research methods. He defined only two main dimensions of effective teaching rather than the four suggested in this book. One dimension—classroom environment—is common to both sources; his second dimension—effective teaching—integrates the three other main dimensions identified in this book (organization, clarity, and interest). Lowman arrived at the same conclusion as the one by Hativa et al.:

> Exemplary college teachers, then, appear to be those who are highly proficient in either one of two fundamental sets of skills: the ability to offer presentations in clearly organized and interesting ways or to relate to students in ways that communicate positive regard and motivate them to work hard to meet academic challenges. All are probably at least completely competent in both sets of skills but outstanding in one or, occasionally, even both of them (Lowman, 1996, p. 38).

With regard to classroom strategies and techniques, Hativa et al. (1999) did identify a small set of strategies that were used by all four exemplary teachers studied. These strategies, all belonging to the main dimension of *clarity*, were: simplifying explanations, giving good examples and illustrations of the material, avoiding errors in presentation, speaking distinctly and clearly, and repeating and elaborating on difficult points. Several other strategies were used somewhat less frequently by all four teachers. These were: encouraging students to ask questions when they did not understand, answering well students' questions, and emphasizing important points.

Additional strategies that were frequently used by three of the four teachers, belonged to the dimensions: (a) *organization*—linking the lesson to the previous one and to the overall framework of the course, and dividing the lesson or the topic into subtopics or theses; (b) *interest/engagement*—motivating to study the material, presenting intellectual challenges, introducing diversity into the lesson, and activating students during the lesson, and (c) *positive classroom climate*—demonstrating care for students and their learning, behaving respectfully toward them, providing encouraging feedback, and being very accessible. All other strategies were used to a lower extent.

How to integrate effective teaching strategies into classroom instruction

Use the suggestions in this book to help you improve your teaching. **When reading this book, mark or record any new teaching strategy** that seems relevant and beneficial for use in your classes, and that fits your personality and your students.

Be aware that it is insufficient to simply decide to use a new teaching skill. It takes time to train oneself in using the skill and in implementing it effectively in teaching so that it positively affects student learning.

Do not work on all your weak points at once but rather try to gradually incorporate the desired strategies into your teaching. Start by using only one or two new strategies, and evaluate your success in applying them by reflecting on your performance with the help of student feedback. Then work on improving your performance of these skills. Only after you feel comfortable and confident in working with these strategies, when you are certain that you perform the new skills satisfactorily, should you add new ones and repeat the same process.

Work to develop your own personal style, methods, and strategies for effective teaching. Prepare a personalized list of teaching strategies that you know how to use in class and have it readily available when you prepare your lessons.

Incorporate into your lesson plan strategies for promoting effectiveness of presentation. When you plan your lesson, in addition to planning the material and examples, illustrations, demonstrations and so forth to be presented, ask yourself: how can I make the lesson organized? Clear? Interesting and engaging?

How can I create a classroom environment that is conducive to learning? You can use the strategies offered throughout the book to answer these questions.

Make copies of the forms for preparing a lesson provided in the Appendix and regularly use them in planning your lessons. They provide additional reminders on pedagogical aspects to incorporate into teaching.

SELF-IMPROVEMENT OF TEACHING

Chapter 1 suggests that university professors perceive the process by which they have learned to teach as based on three main sources: trial-and-error, self-evaluation, and student feedback. However, these sources, in fact, overlap substantially—trial-and-error is rooted in reflection on student feedback and on self-evaluation. A fourth important source for self-improvement of teaching can be peer evaluation and feedback.

Using Reflection and Modifying Own Thinking and Beliefs to Improve Teaching

Viewing teaching as a process of ongoing self-evaluation, inquiry, and reflection is an important ingredient of the perception of teaching as scholarly work (Shulman & Hutchings, 1997). Reflection uncovers reasons behind teachers' behavior and their sources. These revelations and the subsequent increased awareness may help teachers identify and eliminate points of professional ineffectiveness, whereas teachers' insufficient awareness of the sources of their actions poses a major threat to their practice (Argyris & Schon, 1974). Thus, by making teachers' implicit "theory in use" (or "theory in action") explicit, reflection may lead to improving practice.

When we reflect on our experience, our implicit theories become apparent, even transparent. Having been explicated, implicit theories and the behaviors they produce become part of what we can think about and experience directly. We are then able to use these theories productively, perhaps in combination with more formal theories. They become vehicles for improving our practice, rather than mere determinants of our reflexive behavior (Rando & Menges, 1991, p. 11).

Instructional development activities should encourage teachers to reflect on their assumptions and beliefs regarding teaching, learning, and students, and should lead teachers to revise these assumptions through critical self-reflection (Argyris & Schon, 1974; Cannon & Lonsdale, 1987; Cranton, 1994; Heller, 1982; Mezirow, 1991; Sherman, Armistead, Fowler, Barksdale, & Reif, 1987). However, I strongly argue that for refection on one's assumptions and own work to lead to the desired modifications in actual teaching, three conditions are imperative: that the teacher (a) is very familiar with current thinking about the goals and principles of good teaching, (b) is well familiar with classroom practices that can lead to the desired outcomes in student learning, and (c) is able to successfully implement the planned changes in his/her classroom instruction.

Without knowledge and acceptance of current thinking within the education community, a teacher may reflect on his/her assumptions and beliefs but not understand the need to change them. He/she may wish to improve on some teaching dimensions (e.g., clarity) but would not know what strategies to use, or may be aware of these strategies but fail to properly implement them in the classroom. Thus the first two conditions should serve as the foundations for reflection and the third for the successful modification of teaching following reflection.

Instructional development activities should therefore provide teachers with this knowledge. These activities should guide and support revision of teachers' perceptions and beliefs about teaching, learning, and students, as suggested above (Barnes, 1992). For example, faculty should change their view of teaching[94] from "covering the content" to "helping the students learn" (Travis, 1995), from transmitting information for students to absorb "to involving students actively in their own learning and to eliciting from them their best learning performance" (Cross, 1993, p. 12). Faculty should also modify their perception of good teaching from an aggregation of useful classroom techniques to a comprehensive logical model that is based on theory and research.[95] This view entails viewing themselves as responsible for the quality of their own teaching and for their students' learning. There is some research evidence on the crucial role of attempts to transform teachers' thinking and beliefs regarding teaching, learning, and students in improving instruction (Hativa, Forthcoming-a; Radloff, Forthcoming). However, these studies reveal the difficulties and consequent incomplete success in achieving the desired changes.

Using Self-Evaluation for Reflection

The main source for reflective practice is engagement in self-evaluation, much of which is done unconsciously. Because self-evaluation is self-generated, it is optimally meaningful to the teacher who can respond by making immediate adjustments (Fink, 1995).

---

[94] The existence of following beliefs among university teachers is discussed in Chapter 3: Thinking and Beliefs That Damage Teaching Effectiveness.

[95] See Introduction: Teaching as Scholarly Work.

How to use self-evaluation and reflection to improve teaching

Use diverse sources for reflection. You can reflect by thinking or writing in a journal on what happened in the lesson after each class that you teach; by viewing videotapes of your classes; by conducting classroom research[96]; and by obtaining feedback from other sources, primarily self-, students', and peer evaluation.

Learn from reflection. You can deduce from the reflection process which ones of your classroom behaviors are most beneficial for your students' learning and therefore should be used frequently and enhanced, and which behaviors are damaging and should be left out. Reflection can increase your knowledge of your students and identify their needs in learning and how they react to a variety of teaching situations. Reflection may also promote your knowledge of self—your awareness of your own values, dispositions, strengths, and weaknesses, and your educational philosophy, expectations from students, and goals in teaching.

Use written documents for reflection

- Complete the same (or slightly reworded) teaching evaluation questionnaire as your students.
- Fill out a self-composed questionnaire.
- Use written self-reports that document your teaching, such as students' daily journals. Integrate these reports into your teaching portfolio, as next explained.
-

Collect data for teaching portfolio, to be used for reflection

Prepare a portfolio that includes any material you feel might document your teaching in general and those revealing your teaching effectiveness in particular. Arrange them under four broad categories:

- The products of good teaching: examples of students' completed assignments (e.g., students' workbooks, logs, or reports of fieldwork) or of students' exam sheets along with their grades, and other indicators of their learning.
- Materials from your work, such as courses taught, documentation of high enrollment in elective courses, course materials, research on your teaching, instructional innovations, or course development.
- Information from others, particularly evidence of a variety of methods of teaching evaluation such as data from students' ratings of your teaching, and statements from peers and administrators who have observed your teaching.
- Statements of your teaching philosophy. Record your thinking about teaching and students, and your goals and strategies in teaching.

---

[96] See Angelo and Cross (1993) for ideas and guidance.

Using Peer Evaluation and Feedback for Reflection

Students are not able to evaluate all aspects of the teacher's work. For example, they cannot judge how updated the material presented is or how well selected the reading materials are. The best method to overcome this problem is obtaining peer evaluation and feedback. Peer evaluation is viewed as a comprehensive measure of teaching effectiveness and as a necessary supplement to student evaluation of teacher performance (Lichty & Peterson, 1979).

How to obtain peer evaluation feedback

Indirect evaluation. Present a short teaching segment to your peers and ask for their comments.

Direct evaluation. Ask your colleagues to observe one of your classes or videotapes of your classes and give you their feedback.

Pairing peers for mutual observations. Using paired peer observation you may learn both by observing how your partner handles problems as well as by getting advice on the basis of your partner's observations (McKeachie, 1994).

Integration of both student and peer evaluation techniques (Osborne, 1998). This procedure has three steps: preliminary meeting with a peer facilitator, in-class assessment session in which the facilitator engages students in focused discussion of teaching in your absence, and feedback and debriefing provided to you by the facilitator.

The feedback you receive via any of these methods should serve for reflection on teaching and for improving it. You may ask the same colleagues to repeat the procedure after awhile, in order to evaluate your progress.

Using Student Feedback to Improve Teaching

Good teaching and good learning are linked through the students' experiences of what we do. It follows that we cannot teach better unless we are able to see what we are doing from their point of view (Ramsden, 1992, p. 86).

Students are the direct consumers of teaching as they experience its effects on their learning firsthand. Because students have such a profound experience of teaching, teaching effectiveness should be judged primarily by students. Teachers can obtain feedback from students by doing classroom research in which they study their own teaching and their students' learning, by evaluating students' performance on the course assignments and tests, by interacting with students and interpreting their verbal and nonverbal behavior in and outside class, and by using group discussions. However, the main source for student feedback is their ratings of teachers.

How to obtain students' feedback from sources other than their teacher ratings

Obtain feedback from classroom research. You can involve students in diverse writing assignments designed to evaluate yourself, your teaching processes and methods, and students' own understanding and learning of the material presented (Angelo & Cross, 1993).[97]

Obtain feedback from testing. Student achievement on course tests is one of the two main indicators of effective teaching (the other being students' satisfaction from instruction) (Abrami, d'Apolonia, & Cohen, 1990). However, student achievement is not necessarily a valid measure of teaching effectiveness because mature students are able to learn by themselves. When they experience poor teaching and feel that they do not learn much during class time, they tend to compensate for this deficiency by investing extra time and effort in learning from other sources, such as textbooks, and by recruiting help from other people, such as peers or TAs.[98] To obtain a valid measure of how well students actually learn in your class, you should administer a short quiz at the end of the lesson on that particular lesson content, or use classroom research.

Obtain feedback from students' verbal and nonverbal behaviors. You should interact with students throughout the lesson and be sensitive and attentive to their verbal and nonverbal behaviors and identify when they face difficulties in understanding or feel bored.[99]

Obtain feedback from classroom group discussions. In this method, a peer or an instructional consultant visits one of your classes, divides students into groups, and asks each group to discuss the strengths and weaknesses in your teaching and to suggest changes. Then, each group reports to the class a summary of its conclusions. After class discussion, the consultant summarizes for you the feedback in writing.

Another method of group discussion, entitled "Quality Circles," has been adopted from the Japanese management system. In this method, you meet with students on a regular basis (e.g., once a week) to discuss how a course is going. In this setting, students give constructive criticism of teaching, and enable you to counter criticize and explain your teaching decisions. This method may help you

---

[97] Several illustrations for writing assignments, such as "interactive papers" and "minute papers," are presented in Chapter 12.

[98] See Chapter 2: Figure 2-2.

[99] See Chapter 12, Evaluating Student Understanding Continuously Throughout the Lesson, particularly Evaluating Students' Understanding Through Their Nonverbal Behavior.

with diversity issues, offer a mechanism for constructive criticism, and give students a sense of ownership in the classroom (Orts, 1997).

Because of the vast interest of faculty in student ratings of instruction, the following sections further elaborate on this issue.

Obtaining Feedback from Student Ratings— Reliability and Validity

Although student ratings of their teachers are the most significant input for reflection aimed to improve teaching, many faculty members have developed negative perceptions and beliefs, which are mostly myths,[100] about these ratings. In effect, faculty challenge the ratings' consistency, reliability, and validity. The ratings are reliable if, when taken repeatedly at different times during the course and even after its completion, the results are similar. The ratings are regarded as valid (in the regular perception of the ratings' validity) if they accurately reflect teaching effectiveness. However, because no single criterion of effective teaching is sufficient, evaluation of teaching effectiveness is difficult to validate from this perspective (Marsh & Dunkin, 1997). This book adopts a different interpretation of the validity of students' ratings of teachers. In this other view, students are seen as consumers of teaching, so that teacher evaluation is perceived as a measure of consumer satisfaction. From this perspective, the ratings are valid as long as they accurately reflect students' feelings, that is, as a measure of students' satisfaction with instruction.

There is a very extensive body of research literature—over 1,000 articles and books—on student ratings of teaching. The results regarding validity and reliability are very consistent (Marsh, 1984, p. 707):

...class-average student ratings are (a) multidimensional; (b) reliable and stable; (c) primarily a function of the instructor who teachers a course rather than the course that is taught; (d) relatively valid against a variety of indicators of effective teaching; (e) relatively unaffected by a variety of variables hypothesized as potential biases; and (f) seem to be useful by faculty as feedback about their teaching, by students for use in course selection, and by administrators for use in personnel decisions."

No major changes in research findings related to the ratings' reliability and validity have been identified since this summary was first published. That is, research has established the reliability and validity of student ratings.

Several studies examined the stability of teacher ratings taken in retrospect, after graduation. Marsh and Overall (1979) studied the ratings of the same students taken both at the end of a course and one year after graduation. Results showed that "individual student evaluations were

---

[100] See Chapter 3: Thinking and Beliefs That Damage Teaching Effectiveness. Refer to the beliefs listed as (c) and (d).

remarkably stable over time" (p. 139). This was true for both the global evaluation and the particular items of teacher-behavior dimensions. Marsh and Bailey (1993), analyzing repeated ratings of the same teachers in different courses over a 13-year period, found high consistency in the rating profile of the same teacher, in both graduate and undergraduate classes. A *ratings profile* illustrates the relative mean ratings of the different items for a teacher, or the rank order of all the items rated. Marsh and Bailey concluded that teachers had distinct profiles of strengths and weaknesses that were highly generalizable over time and across courses, taught at both graduate and undergraduate levels. Hativa and Raviv (1996) obtained similar results for physics (Figure 25-1) and chemistry (Figure 25-2) professors who had repeatedly taught the same course. Each was rated four times—at mid semester and at the end of the semester during two consecutive years, that is, by two different groups of students who took the same course. The findings showed that teachers' relative ratings by students on the main teaching dimensions (their ratings profiles) were stable over time. Even after an intervention to improve teaching took place in the chemistry department in the second year of the study increased the mean ratings of all the teachers in the department, the profiles were substantially preserved.

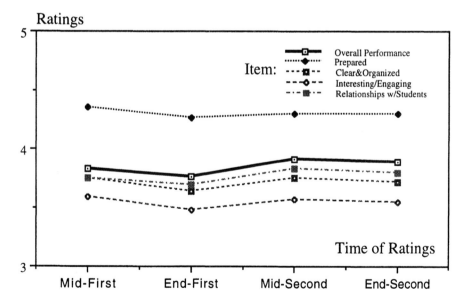

Figure 25-1: Combined Profile of Student Ratings for All (27) Professors in a Physics Department Who Taught Consecutively the Same Course, at Four Times (Middle and End of the Same Semester, During the First and Second Years of Study)

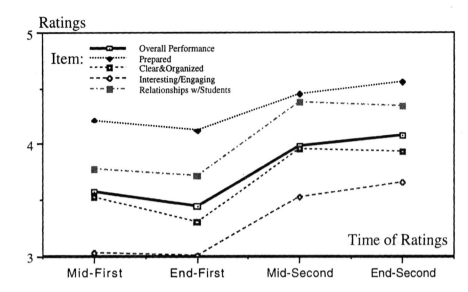

Figure 25-2: Combined Profile of Student Ratings for All (16) Professors in a Chemistry Department Who Taught Consecutively the Same Course, in Four Times (Middle and End of the Same Semester, During the First and Second Years of Study)

Using Feedback from Student Ratings to Improve Teaching

The large majority of teaching improvement activities is based on providing faculty with feedback based on students' written evaluations of instruction. The question remains, however, how effective is this feedback in improving teaching?

A summary of 22 studies on teachers who either received or did not receive this type of feedback during the first half of the term (Cohen, 1980) showed increased mean ratings at the end of the term for teachers who did receive the feedback, as compared with no increase for teachers who did not receive mid-term feedback. However, these results varied with the kind of feedback. Teachers who received mid-term feedback with no treatment improved only marginally whereas those whose feedback was augmented by personal consultation from experts, improved significantly. We may conclude that providing faculty with student ratings feedback in mid-term is helpful in improving instruction only if supported with some advice from an instructional expert. Similarly, there is no research supporting the contention that feedback received from students at the end of the term improves teaching unless it was augmented by some additional treatment, particularly personal consultation[101] (Lenze, 1996; Marsh, 1984; Rotem & Glasman, 1979; Weimer & Lenze, 1991). These results suggest that self-reflection based on students' feedback is insufficient, on average, for self-improvement of instruction and that additional instructional development activities conducted by experts are necessary for achieving this improvement.

USING INSTRUCTIONAL DEVELOPMENT ACTIVITIES TO IMPROVE TEACHING

Many faculty are unable to improve teaching on their own even if highly motivated, on the basis of reflection on their work using a variety of sources. These faculty should be able to acquire help through instructional development activities provided by their academic institution. Instructional development activities can take the form of workshops, instructional consultation, grants for instructional improvement, and print resources (Lenze, 1996; Weimer & Lenze, 1991). A survey of programs for instructional development in institutions of higher education in California (Berman & Weiler, 1987) identified the activities most commonly used in these institutions: awarding faculty grants, leaves, and sabbaticals; and conducting workshops, seminars, individualized consultation, peer mentoring, and evaluation of teaching. Consultation, workshops, and seminars were shown to be the most frequently used professional aids for college and university teachers.

Personal consultation. The consultant meets the client to discuss results of student ratings, or provide comments following the consultant's observations of the client's classes. The consultant and client may also watch together clips of the client's class videotapes and analyze the teacher behaviors. This procedure may be repeated several times during one or more terms, until the teacher achieves satisfactory results in terms of student ratings or in the consultant's judgment. Of all the different practices used in teaching development programs, personal consultation with an instructional expert was consistently found to be the most powerful methodology for the improvement of in-class teaching (Erickson & Erickson, 1979; Levinson-Rose & Menges, 1981; Ward, 1995; Weimer & Lenze, 1991; Wilson, 1986).

Workshops and seminars can take different forms. They usually provide not only theoretical knowledge but also enable participants to practice new teaching skills. An especially effective method is microteaching— videotaping actual or simulated teaching scenarios and having colleagues or experts provide beneficial feedback. Workshops and seminars also provide

---

[101] See also under the next headings.

faculty with the opportunity to talk with one another about their experiences in class (Weimer & Lenze, 1991).

To date, no clear or consistent research exists to support the benefits of workshops and seminars in improving instruction. This suggests that faculty may perceive some of these activities as failing to improve their teaching while others do succeed. It is feasible that treatments vary in their effectiveness. What, then, contributes to making an instructional development treatment effective?

Characteristics of Successful Instructional Development Programs

Successful workshops and seminars for teaching improvement—those that were most appreciated by faculty members—were shown to consist of activities that are *cost effective* for faculty *in terms of time, effort, and proven consequences*. They give participants *a sense of social support and increased communication*, and they encourage *autonomy, and personal initiative* (Eble & McKeachie, 1985; Joyce & Showers, 1980; Moses, 1985; Wilson, 1986).

These most successful instructional development programs were *carefully planned*, were neither too limited nor too broad, but offered a diversity of opportunities to *meet faculty needs*. They involved faculty and administration so that *faculty felt ownership of the program* while *broader institutional needs were also served*. These programs created a sense of increased *collegial support for investment in teaching*. They *stimulated faculty enthusiasm and participation*, had *high visibility on campus*, and provided *training to develop new skills*. As a result of these activities, there were tangible changes in courses, teaching strategies, subject matter competence, and curricula. This in turn increased interaction and communication between faculty and students in working toward common goals (ibid.).

Additional components of successful programs that were identified included offering faculty:
- Practical/pragmatic advice on specific issues, that is, prescriptive guidelines: do's and don'ts, and instructional strategies and skills.
- Familiarity with a variety of teaching methods accompanied by a discussion of their advantages and disadvantages and when to use them (i.e., general pedagogical knowledge).
- A sense of structure, purpose, and direction during the activity.
- A sense of learning something new and useful.
- A supportive climate in group sessions.

– *Active involvement during the sessions* (although some participants prefer to remain passive).
– *Theoretical background and justifications* for the suggested strategies (although some faculty members reject this aspect).
– An opportunity to discuss current work.
– *Feedback on individual teaching performance* in both simulated and real classroom settings.
– *Systematic feedback and continuous coaching* for the application of teaching skills and knowledge.

In addition to these components, successful instructional development programs should be adjusted to the context of teaching.

Taking the Context into Account in Improving Teaching

Ramsden (1992) suggested that activities for instructional development engage participants in ways that lead to contextualizing experiences of teaching rather than solely training them in general classroom teaching techniques. Thus, instructional development programs should relate to the subject domain or the department's culture (e.g., the department's norms and students' expectations) and should not ignore the notion that effective teaching is situation-specific (Abrami & d'Apollonia, 1990). Chapter 1 presents disciplinary differences in classroom dimensions of effective teaching. However, there are disciplinary differences in other aspects of teaching, such as those related to faculty thinking about teaching, learning, and students. Therefore, when working on improving teaching, contextual factors such as the institutional mission and the department's cultural milieu should be taken into account.

SUMMARY

In addition to promoting students' knowledge, college and university teaching should aim to achieve other broad educational goals of preparing students for their adult life, particularly for their professional life in the 21st century. Professional success requires original, imaginative, and non-routine thinking; the ability to self-study, solve problems, and cooperate with others; and flexibility in adjusting to changing conditions. Teaching should aim to promote meaningful learning and students' capacity to apply the new knowledge most effectively to a variety of new tasks and situations, and to develop students' achievements in cognitive, social, and affective domains.

The type of current teaching in many higher education classrooms does not bring about to the kind of learning that we consider as beneficial and effective.

The growing recognition in the importance of effective learning has increased pressure on universities and colleges to change their instructional practices. Faculty should be introduced to the new conceptions of teaching and learning and to new teaching modes and technologies, and learn to adapt to a student population that is much more diverse than it used to be.

Research findings indicate that there is no single way to excel in teaching, but that teaching effectiveness is achieved through a variety of ways and methods. However, to become a superb teacher, one needs to excel in some particular set of teaching dimensions and strategies that fit one's personality and context of teaching.

Self-improvement of teaching can be achieved by using reflection, modifying thinking and beliefs, self-evaluation, and peer and students' feedback. Student feedback can be achieved through classroom research, testing, students' verbal and nonverbal behaviors, classroom group discussions, and their ratings of teachers. These ratings were found in research to be reliable, valid, and consistent across courses and time of measurement. However, obtaining the results of students' evaluation of instruction either at the mid-term or at the end of the term is not helpful on average in improving instruction, as measured by student ratings. Only when augmented by additional treatments from instructional experts is this feedback beneficial in improving instruction.

The activities regularly used in instructional development programs in institutions of higher education are: awarding faculty grants, leaves, and sabbaticals; and conducting workshops, seminars, individualized consultation, peer mentoring, and evaluation of teaching. Consultation, workshops and seminars are the most frequently used of those activities. Of all the different practices used in instructional development programs, personal consultation with an instructional expert was consistently found to be the most powerful methodology.

The characteristics of successful workshops and seminars for teaching improvement—those most appreciated by faculty members—were shown to consist of activities that are cost effective for faculty in terms of time, effort, and proven consequences, that give participants a sense of social support and increased communication, and that encourage autonomy and personal initiative. They involved faculty and administration in leadership so as to created a sense of increased collegial support for the investment in teaching. They stimulated faculty enthusiasm and participation, had high visibility on campus, and provided training to develop new skills.

Appendix

Layout for Planning a Lesson

PLANNING THE CONTENT TO BE PRESENTED—THE LESSON OUTLINE

Break down the general lesson topic into clearly distinguishable main topics, then break down each main topic into sub-topics (Chapter 10). Break down the explanation or development of the topic into small steps. Arrange the lesson topics in a coherent logical sequence; organize the steps of presentation around central themes. Alternatively, they can be arranged to build up to a climax or to create suspense, surprise, and uncertainty. Plan the time allocation for each of the lesson topics and sub-topics.

Main Topics

a) _____

b) _____

c) _____

d) _____

e) _____

Subtopics

Main topic a): _____
Subtopics (include related notions, concepts, models, rules, key questions):
   1. _____

   _____

   2. _____

   _____

   3. _____

   _____

Main topic b): _____
Subtopics (include related notions, concepts, models, rules, key questions):
   1. _____

   _____

   2. _____

   _____

   3. _____

   _____

Main topic c): _____
Subtopics (include related notions, concepts, models, rules, key questions):
   1. _____

   _____

   2. _____

   _____

   3. _____

   _____

Main topic d): _____
Subtopics (include related notions, concepts, models, rules, key questions):
   1. _____

   _____

   2. _____

   _____

   3. _____

   _____

Main topic e): _____
Subtopics (include related notions, concepts, models, rules, key questions):
   1. _____

   _____

   2. _____

   _____

   3. _____

   _____

PLANNING PEDAGOGICAL ASPECTS OF THE PRESENTATION

Plan how to teach difficult topics in two or more cycles

Plan to start with or teach in parallel: a rough notion; a verbally simplified description; the core notion—the bottom line; a plan for action; a comparable familiar case: example, analogy, metaphor; a visual or intuitive interpretation—a picture, chart, graph, artifact, videotape presentation (Chapter 10). You may provide an "advance organizer"—a conceptual framework before teaching the topic (Chapter 8).

Inform students of the main points of the topic
Identify the most important points of the topics by repeating, summarizing, emphasizing/stressing (Chapter 10). Help students remember these points (Chapter 8).

Plan on looking back (upon completion of teaching the topic)

When you finish teaching the topic, sharpen its meaning by providing another example, analogy, metaphor, visual or intuitive interpretation; demonstrate applications; provide algorithms; review the steps; solve a related problem and help students apply it in alternative ways (Chapter 13).

Plan how to adjust instruction to your students

Plan how to compensate for missing prerequisite knowledge; treat expected difficulties; connect the material to their background knowledge; repeat, elaborate, pause, stimulate intuition and imagery.
Plan on how to keep track of the ongoing adjustment of instruction to students throughout the lesson. To do so, pose questions to identify understanding, give students short writing assignments that reflect understanding, and interpret their nonverbal behavior.

Plan how to avoid "noise"

Plan how to avoid those elements that reduce students' capacity for hearing and listening comprehension (e.g., "noise" in language, speech, regular noise), for seeing and visual comprehension (effective use of the blackboard, transparencies, or computer presentation), and for taking in, processing, and making sense of the information presented (avoid creating internal noise—Chapter 11).

Plan how to engage students and make the lesson interesting

Plan how to motivate students to study the particular topic (Chapter 14); dramatize; incorporate relevant anecdotes, analogies, examples, humor, and self-disclosure; present related cultural aspects of the academic domain and knowledge from other domains (Chapter 15).

Plan how to make students talk and listen, read and write, think, reflect, solve problems, guess, discover, and how to intellectually challenge them (Chapter 6). Plan how to make students participate in discussions (Chapter 5), and in group work, cooperative learning, role-playing, simulations, case-based learning, problem-based learning, or experiential learning (Chapter 7).

Plan how to demonstrate dramatic behavior, acting, nonverbal behaviors that attract attention, dynamism, and enthusiasm. Plan how to vary your behavior, mode of presentation and activities; plan the use of class demonstrations and visual aids (Chapter 15).

Plan how to create a pleasant classroom environment that is conducive to learning

Plan how to generate a positive emotional climate in class; use humor; promote interaction and rapport with students and among students; exhibit expectations for students' success in learning; and guide students in effective study methods (Chapter 16).

Plan how to use class time effectively (Chapter 18)

Plan what you will write or draw on the blackboard before the lesson starts, including the lesson outline and any information that you will use. Check the equipment, demonstrations, and teaching aids that you will use; ensure that these are all in place and working properly; prepare well-designed transparencies or computer presentations; prepare well-designed handouts related to the material presented, such as copies of the transparencies you plan to use during the lesson;

Organize the Lesson Presentation

Use three main lesson parts—introduction, body, and conclusion—and clearly identify them

Introduction

Provide the lesson outline. List the topics, subtopics, or objectives. Write these items on the leftmost or rightmost section on the board and leave them there throughout the lesson. Identify the connections among the various topics/objectives of the lesson (Chapter 8).

Make connections. Connect each topic presented as much as possible to topics presented in previous lessons, the general framework of the course and other courses in the school/department, the textbook, the assigned readings, the lab work, and the practice lessons (Chapter 8).

Link the topics to the previous lessons and to the general framework of the course and of the courses in the department. How are the lesson topics related to other topics already learned previously in the course? In previous courses? Where are they located within the framework of the courses in the school/department? (Chapter 8).

Motivate your students to learn the topics of the lesson (Chapter 14).

Start the lesson **in an interesting way**—with an attention-getter, or by creating expectations that something interesting is going happen (15).

Body

Mark/signal the start and end of each subtopic, **the move** from one topic or part of the lesson to another, and frequently inform students of the status within the lesson plan (Chapter 8).

Promote students' internal and external motivation to study the material, and promote their expectations for success (Chapter 14).

Repeat and elaborate difficult aspects of the topic, adjust the pace, support note-taking, use multiple representations, pause, stimulate intuition and imagination (Chapter 12).

Conclusion

Help students to remember the material presented in the lesson: Summarize, present comparison tables, repeat, emphasize main points (Chapter 8).

Conclude in an interesting way that will leave an impression (15).

Assign beneficial homework: readings with leading questions and problems (Chapter 23).

REFERENCES

Abrami, P. C., & d'Apollonia, S. (1990). The dimensionality of ratings and their use in personnel decisions. *New Directions for Teaching and Learning, 43*, 97-111.

Abrami, P. C., d'Apollonia, S., & Rosenfield, S. (1997). The dimensionality of student ratings of instruction: What we know and what we do not. In R. P. Perry & J. C. Smart (Eds.), *Effective teaching in higher education: Research and practice* (pp. 321-367). Bronx, New York: Agathon Press.

Abrami, P. C., d'Apolonia, S., & Cohen, P. A. (1990). Validity of student ratings of instruction: What we know and what we do not know. *Journal of Educational Psychology, 82*(2), 219-231.

Angelo, T. A., & Cross, P. K. (1993). *Classroom assessment techniques: A handbook for college teachers.* (2nd ed.). San Francisco: Jossey-Bass.

APA. (1997). *Learner-centered psychological principles.* Washington, DC: American Psychological Association.

Argyris, C., & Schon, D. A. (1974). *Theory in practice: Increasing professional effectiveness.* San Francisco: Jossey-Bass.

Ausubel, D. P. (1978). In defense of advance organizers: A reply to the critics. *Review of Educational Research, 48*(2), 251-257.

Baddeley, A. D. (1976). *The psychology of memory.* New York: Basic Books.

Bandura, A., & Cervone, D. (1986). Differential engagement of self-reactive influences in cognitive motivation. *Organizational Behavior & Human Decision Processes, 38*(1), 92-113.

Barnes, C. P. (1983). Questioning in college classrooms. In C. L. Ellner & C. P. Barnes (Eds.), *Studies of college teaching*. Lexington, MA: Lexington Books, D.C. Heath and Company.

Barnes, D. (1992). *From communication to curriculum*. Portsmouth, NH: Heinemann.

Barzun, J. (1945). *Teacher in America*. Boston: Little, Brown.

Bayless, O. L., & Moody, B. S. (1984). *The speech communication methods course in secondary teacher preparation*.

Becker, H. S., Geer, B., & Hughes, E. C. (1994). Definition of the situation: Faculty-student interaction. In K. A. Feldman & M. B. Paulsen (Eds.), *Teaching and learning in the college classroom* (pp. 439-450). Needham Heights, MA: Ginn Press.

Begle, E. G. (1979). *Critical variables in mathematics education: Findings from a survey of the empirical literature*. Washington: Mathematical Association of America.

Behr, A. L. (1988). Exploring the lecture method: An empirical study. *Studies in Higher Education, 13*(2), 189-199.

Belgard, M., Rosenshine, B., & Gage, N. L. (1971). Study I. Effectiveness in explaining: Evidence on its generality and correlation with pupil ratings. In I. Westbury & A. A. Bellack (Eds.), *Research into classroom processes: Recent developments and next steps* (pp. 182-191). New York: Teachers College Press.

Benz, C. R., & Blatt, S. J. (1994, April). *Faculty effectiveness as perceived by both students and faculty: A qualitative and quantitative study*. Paper presented at the annual meeting of the American Educational Research Association, New Orleans, LA.

Berliner, D. C. (1969). The effects of test-like events and note-taking on learning from lecture instruction (Doctoral dissertation, Stanford University, 1968). *Dissertation Abstracts International, 29*, 3864A.

Berman, J., & Skeff, K. M. (1988). Developing the motivation for improving university teaching. *Innovative Higher Education, 12*(2), 114-125.

Berman, P., & Weiler, D. (1987). *Exploring faculty development in California higher education. Volume I. Executive summary and conclusions* (88-18). Berkeley: California Postsecondary Education Commission.

Biggs, J. (1979). Individual differences in study processes and the quality of learning outcomes. *Higher Education, 8*(4), 381-394.

Blackburn, R. T., Boberg, Q., O'Connell, C., & Pellino, G. (1980). *Project for faculty development program evaluation: Final report*. Ann Arbor: Center for the Study of Higher Education. University of Michigan, Michigan.

Blackburn, R. T., Lawrence, J. H., Bieber, J. P., & Trautvetter, L. (1991). Faculty at work: Focus on teaching. *Research in Higher Education, 32*(4), 363-383.

Bloch, A. (1991). *The Complete Murphy's Law*. (Revised ed.). Los Angeles: Price Stern Sloan.

Bloom, B. (1956). *Taxonomy of educational objectives: Handbook 1—Cognitive domain*. New York: David McKay Co.

Boix, V. (1997). Of kinds of disciplines and kinds of understanding. *Phi Delta Kappan, 78*(5), 381-386.

Bolton, B., Bonge, D., & Marr, J. (1979). Ratings of instruction, examination performance, and subsequent enrollment in psychology courses. *Teaching of Psychology, 6*(2), 82-85.

Brophy, J. (1981). Teacher praise: A functional analysis. *Psychological Review, 88*(2), 93-134.

Brown, G. A. (1979). *Learning from lectures*. Nottingham: University of Nottingham.

Brown, G. A. (1980). *Explaining: Studies from their higher education complex* (Final report). Nottingham: SSRC, University of Nottingham.

Brown, G. A., & Atkins, M. (1988). *Effective teaching in higher education*. NY: Methuen.

Brown, G. A., & Daines, J. M. (1981). Can explaining be learnt? Some lecturers' views. *Higher Education, 10*(5), 573-580.

Bruner, J. S. (1960). *The process of education*. Cambridge, MA: Harvard University Press.

Bryant, J., Comisky, P. W., & Zillmann, D. (1979). Teachers' humor in the college classroom. *Communication Education, 28*(2), 110-118.

Bush, A. J., Kennedy, J. J., & Cruickshank, D. R. (1977). An empirical investigation of teacher clarity. *Journal of Teacher Education, 28*(2), 53-58.

Buzza, B. W. (1988). *Speech communication courses as basics in teacher preparation*.

Calderhead, J. (1983). *Research into teachers' and student teachers' cogitions: Exploring the nature of classroom practice*. Paper presented at the annual meeting of the American Educational Research Association, Montreal.

Calfee, R. (1986). *Those who can explain, teach...* (An unpublished manuscript). Stanford, CA: Stanford University.

Cannon, R. A., & Lonsdale, A. J. (1987). A "muddled array of models": Theoretical and organisational perspectives on change and development in higher education. *Higher Education, 16*(1), 21-32.

Cantor, J. A. (1995). *Experiential learning in higher education: Linking classroom and community* (7): ASHE-ERIC Higher Education Reports.

Carrier, C. A. (1981). Using student characteristics as the focal point for improving instruction. *Journal of Instructional Development, 4*(4), 31-35.

Cashin, W. E. (1990). Students do rate academic fields differently. *New Directions for Teaching and Learning, 43*, 113-121.

Cashin, W. E., & Downey, R. G. (1995). Disciplinary differences in what is taught and in students' perceptions of what they learn and of how they are taught. In N. Hativa & M. Marincovich (Eds.), *Disciplinary differences in teaching and learning: Implications for practice* (Vol. 64, pp. 81-92). San Francisco: Jossey-Bass.

Clabby, J. F., Jr. (1979). Humor as a preferred activity of the creative and humor as a facilitator of learning. *Psychology: A Quarterly Journal of Human Behavior, 16*(1), 5-12.

Claxton, C. S., & Murrell, P. H. (1987). *Learning styles: Implications for improving educational practices. ASHE-ERIC Higher Education Report No. 4* (ISBN-0-913317-39-X). Washington, DC: Association for the Study of Higher Education. ERIC Clearinghouse on Higher Education.

Cockburn, B., & Ross, A. (1980). *Why lecture? Teaching in higher education Series 2. Suggestions for the consideration of lecturers and others concerned with teaching in higher education.* Lancaster: Lancaster University (England), School of Education (ED 230-099).

Cohen, P. A. (1980). Effectiveness of student ratings of instruction: What we know and what we do not know. *Research in Higher Education, 13*(4), 321-341.

Cohen, P. A. (1990). Bringing research into practice. In M. Theall & J. Franklin (Eds.), *Student ratings of instruction: Issues for improving practice* (Vol. 43, pp. 123-132). San Francisco: Jossey-Bass.

Costin, F. (1972). Lecturing versus other methods of teaching: A review of research. *British Journal of Educational Technology, 3*(1), 4-31.

Cranton, P. (1994). Self-directed and transformative instructional development. *Journal of Higher Education, 65*(6), 726-744.

Crooks, T. J. (1988). The impact of classroom evaluation practices on students. *Review of Educational Research, 58*(4), 438-481.

Cross, P. K. (1977). Not can, but will college teaching be improved?, *New Directions for Higher Education* (Vol. 17, pp. 1-15). San Francisco: Jossey-Bass.

Cross, P. K. (1991). College teaching: What do we know about it? *Innovative Higher Education, 16*(1), 7-21.

Cross, P. K. (1993). On college teaching. *Journal of Engineering Education, 82*(1), 9-14.

Cruickshank, D. R. (1985). Applying research on teacher clarity. *Journal of Teacher Education, 36*(2), 44-48.

Cruickshank, D. R., & Kennedy, J. J. (1986). Teacher clarity. *Teaching and Teacher Education, 2*(1), 43-67.

Cruickshank, D. R., Myers, B., & Moenjak, T. (1975). *Statements of clear teacher behaviors provided by 1,009 students in grades 6-9* (Unpublished manuscript): The College of Education, The Ohio State University.

D'Ydewalle, G., Swerts, A., & de Corte, E. (1983). Study time and test performance as a function of test expectations. *Contemporary Educational Psychology, 8*(1), 55-67.

Darling, A. L., & Civikly, J. M. (1987). The effect of teacher humor on student perceptions of classroom communicative climate. *Journal of Classroom Interaction, 22*(1), 24-30.

deCharms, R. (1976). *Enhancing motivation: Change in the classroom.* New York: Irvington.

DeLozier, M. W. (1979). The teacher as performer: The art of selling students on learning. *Contemporary Education, 51*(1), 19-25.

Devine, B., & Cohen, J., E. (1992). *Absolute zero gravity.* New York.

Dick, R. C., & Robinson, B. M. (1994). Oral English Proficiency Requirements for ITAs in U.S. Colleges and Universities: An Issue in Speech Communication. *Journal of the Association for Communication Administration (JACA), 2,* 77-86.

Dinham, S. M., & Blake, V. M. (1991). *Influences on university teachers' course planning.* Paper presented at the annual meeting of the American Educational Research Association, Chicago.

Domino, G. (1968). Differential prediction of academic achievement in conforming and independent settings. *Journal of Educational Psychology, 59,* 256-260.

Domino, G. (1971). Interactive effects of achievement orientation and teaching style on academic achievement. *Journal of Educational Psychology, 62*(5), 427-431.

Donald, J. G. (2000). *Indicators of success: From concepts to classrooms.* Paper presented at the annual conference of the American Educational Research Association, New Orleans.

Duell, O. K., Lynch, D. J., Ellsworth, R., & Moore, C. A. (1992). Wait-Time in college classes taken by education majors. *Research in Higher Education, 33*(4), 483-495.

Dweck, C. S. (1989). *Motivation.* Hillsdale: Lawrence Erlbaum.

Eble, K. E., & McKeachie, W. J. (1985). *Improving undergraduate education through faculty development. an analysis of effective programs and practices.* San Francisco: Jossey-Bass.

Eccles, J. (1983). Expectancies, values, and achievement behaviors. In T. Spence (Ed.), *Achievement and achievement motives: Psychological and sociological approaches* (pp. 75-146). San Francisco: W. H. Freeman.

Eley, M. G., & Cameron, N. (1993). Proficiency in the explanation of procedures: a test of the intuitive understanding of teachers of undergraduate mathematics. *Higher Education, 26*(4), 355-386.

Emanuel, R. C., & Potter, W. J. (1992). Do students' style preferences differ by grade level, orientation toward college, and academic major? *Research in Higher Education, 33*(3), 395-414.

Entwistle, N. J. (1987). A model of the teaching-learning process. In J. T. E. Richardson, M. W. Eysenck, & W. D. Piper (Eds.), *Student learning: Research in education and cognitive psychology* (pp. 13-28). London: S.R.H.E./Open University Press.

Entwistle, N. J. (1990, May). *How students learn, and why they fail.* Paper presented at the Conference on Talent and Teaching, Bergen.

Entwistle, N. J., & Ramsden, P. (1982). *Understanding student learning.* NY: Nichols Publishing Company.

Entwistle, N. J., & Tait, H. (1990). Approaches to learning, evaluations of teaching, and preferences for contrasting academic environments. *Higher Education, 19*, 169-194.

Erickson, G. R., & Erickson, B. L. (1979). Improving college teaching: An evaluation of a teaching consultation procedure. *Journal of Higher Education, 50*(5), 670-683.

Evans, W. E., & Guymon, R. E. (1978, March). *Clarity of explanation: A powerful indicator of teacher effectiveness.* Paper presented at the annual meeting of the American Educational Research Association, Toronto, Canada.

Eylon, B., & Reif, F. (1979, April). *Effects of internal knowledge organization on task performance.* Paper presented at the annual meeting of the American Educational Research Association, San Francisco.

Fairhurst, M. A. (1981). Satisfactory explanations in the primary school. *Journal of Philosophy of Education, 15*(2), 205-214.

Feldman, K. A. (1976). The superior college teacher from the students' view. *Research in Higher Education, 5*(3), 243-288.

Feldman, K. A. (1978). Course characteristics and college students' ratings of their teachers: What we know and what we don't. *Research in Higher Education, 9*(3), 199-242.

Feldman, K. A. (1986). The perceived instructional effectiveness of college teachers as related to their personality and attitudinal characteristics: A review and synthesis of research. *Research in Higher Education, 24*(2), 139-213.

Feldman, K. A. (1989a). The association between student ratings of specific instructional dimensions and student achievement: refining and extending the synthesis of data from multisection validity studies. *Research in Higher Education, 30*(6), 583-645.

Feldman, K. A. (1989b). Instructional effectiveness of college teachers as judged by teachers themselves, current and former students, colleagues, administrators, and external (neutral) observers. *Research in Higher Education, 30*(2), 137-194.

Feldman, K. A. (1997). Identifying exemplary teachers and teaching: Evidence from student ratings. In R. P. Perry & J. C. Smart (Eds.), *Effective teaching in higher education: Research and practice* (pp. 368-395). New York: Agathon Press.

File, J. (1984). Student learning difficulties and teaching methods. *Studies in Higher Education, 9*, 191-194.

Fink, D. L. (1995). Evaluating your own teaching. In P. Selding (Ed.), *Developing new and junior faculty*. Bolton Mass.: Anker.

Fischbein, E. (1987). *Intuition in science and mathematics: An educational approach.* Dordrecht Holland: D. Reidel Publishing Co.

Ford, M. L. (1980, July). *Excellence in teaching: What does it really mean?* Paper presented at the International Conference on Improving University Teaching, Lausanne, Switzerland.

Fortune, J., Gage, N. L., & Shutes, R. (1966, March). *A study of the ability to explain.* Paper presented at the annual conference of the American Educational Research Association, Chicago.

Fox, D. (1983). Personal theories of teaching. *Studies in Higher Education, 8*(2), 151-163.

Franklin, J., & Theall, M. (1992). *Disciplinary differences: instructional goals and activities, measures of student performance, and student ratings of instruction.* Paper presented at the annual conference of the American Educational Research Association, San Francisco.

Fredericksen, N. (1984). The real test bias: Influences of testing on teaching and learning. *American Psychologist, 39*(3), 193-202.

Freedman, M., Brown, W., Ralph, N., Shukraft, R., Bloom, M., & Sanford, N. (1979). *Academic culture and faculty development.* Berkeley, CA.

Gaff, J. G. (1976). Overcoming faculty resistance, *New Directions for Higher Education* (Vol. 4, pp. 43-57). San Francisco: Jossey-Bass.

Gage, N. L. (Ed.). (1963). *Handbook of Research on Teaching.* Chicago: Rand McNally.

Gage, N. L. (1976). *Program on Teaching Effectiveness: A factorially designed experiment on teacher structuring, soliciting, and reacting* (Memorandum No. 147). Stanford: Stanford University, Center for Research and Development in Teaching.

Gage, N. L., Belgard, M., Dell, D., Hiller, J., Rosenshine, B., & Unruh, W. (1971). Explorations of the teacher's effectiveness in lecturing. In I. Westbury & A. A. Bellack (Eds.), *Research into classroom processes: Recent developments and next steps* (pp. 182-191). New York: Teachers College Press.

Gage, N. L., & Berliner, D. C. (1991). *Educational psychology.* (Fifth ed.). Boston: Houghton Mifflin Company.

Gage, N. L., & Berliner, D. C. (1998). *Educational psychology.* (Sixth ed.). Boston: Houghton Mifflin Company.

References

Gall, M. D. (1970). *The use of questions in teaching* (Report A70-9): Teacher Education Division Publication Series.

Gall, M. D., & Artero-Boname, M. T. (1995). Questioning. In T. W. Anderson (Ed.), *The International Encyclopedia of Teaching and Teacher Education* (pp. 242-248).

Gardner, H. (1993). *Multiple intelligences: the theory in practice.* New York: Basic books.

Gardner, H., & Boix, V. (1994). Teaching for understanding in the disciplines--and beyond. *Teachers College Record, 96*(2), 198-218.

Gibson, J. W. (1974). A re-examination of the first course in speech at U.S. colleges and universities. *Speech Teacher, 23*(3), 206-214.

Glassick, C. R., Huber, M. T., & Maeroff, G. I. (1997). *Scholarship assessed: Evaluation of the professoriate.* San Francisco: Jossey-Bass.

Goodman, R. M., Wade, S., & Zegar, D. (1974). Students without harness. *Journal of Higher Education, 45,* 197-210.

Gow, L., & Kember, D. (1993). Conceptions of teaching and their relationship to student learning. *British Journal of Educational Psychology, 63*(1), 20-33.

Graham, S., & Golan, S. (1991). Motivational influences on cognition: Task involvement, ego involvement, and depth of information processing. *Journal of Educational Psychology, 83*(2), 187-194.

Grossman, P. L. (1995). Teachers' knowledge. In W. Anderson (Ed.), *The International Encyclopedia of Teaching and Teacher Education* (2nd ed., pp. 20-24). New York: Pergamon.

Hartley, J., & Davies, I. K. (1976). Preinstructional strategies: The role of pretests, behavioral objectives, overviews and advance organizers. *Review of Educational Research, 46*(2), 239-265.

Hartley, J., & Davies, I. K. (1978). Note taking: A critical review. *Programmed learning and educational technology, 15*(3), 207-224.

Hativa, N. (1983). Factors in the organization and clarity of mathematics lessons (Doctoral dissertation, Stanford University, 1982). *Dissertation Abstracts International, 43,* 2583A.

Hativa, N. (1984). Good teaching of mathematics as perceived by undergraduate students. *International Journal of Mathematics Education in Science and Technology, 15*(5), 605-615.

Hativa, N. (1985). A study of the organization and clarity of mathematics lessons. *International Journal of Mathematics Education in Science and Technology, 16*(1), 89-99.

Hativa, N. (1993). Attitudes towards instruction of faculty in mathematics and the physical sciences: Discipline- and situation specific teaching patterns. *International Journal of Mathematical Education in Science and Technology, 24*(4), 579-593.

Hativa, N. (1995). The department-wide approach to improving faculty instruction in higher education: A qualitative evaluation. *Research in Higher Education, 36*(4), 377-413.

Hativa, N. (1997). *Teaching in a research university: Professors' conceptions, practices, and disciplinary differences* (An unpublished report). Tel Aviv: Tel Aviv University.

Hativa, N. (1998). Lack of clarity in university teaching: A case study. *Higher Education, 36*(3), 353-381.

Hativa, N. (1998-9). *1. Engaging Students: Actively engaging students; Getting students to think. 2. Getting Student Attention: Attention-getting teacher behavior; Attention-getting content. 3. Simplifying: Teaching in two cycles; Structuring and looking back. 4. Adapting to Students: Evaluating students' knowledge; Adjusting to students' diversity. 5. Classroom environment.* Bolton, MA: Anker Publishing Company Inc.

Hativa, N. (2000, April). *The tension between thinking and beliefs of professors and students regarding instruction.* Paper presented at the annual meeting of the American Educational Research Association, New Orelans.

Hativa, N. (Forthcoming). Becoming a better teacher: A case of changing the pedagogical knowledge and beliefs of law professors. In N. Hativa & P. Goodyear (Eds.), *Teacher thinking, beliefs and knowledge in higher education.* Dordrecht, Holland: Kluwer Academic Press.

Hativa, N., Barak, R., & Simhi, E. (1999, April). *Expert university teachers: Thinking, knowledge and practice regarding effective teaching behaviors.* Paper presented at the annual meeting of the American Educational Research Associaiton, Montreal.

Hativa, N., & Birenbaum, M. (2000). Who prefers what? Disciplinary differences in students' approaches to teaching and learning styles. *Research in Higher Education, 41*(2), 209-236.

Hativa, N., & Marincovich, M. (Eds.). (1995). *Disciplinary differences in teaching and learning: Implications for practice.* (Vol. 64). San Francisco: Jossey-Bass.

Hativa, N., & Raviv, A. (1993). Using a single score for summative evaluation by students. *Research in Higher Education, 34*(5), 625-646.

Hativa, N., & Raviv, A. (1996). University instructors' ratings profiles: Stability over time, and disciplinary differences. *Research in Higher Education, 37*(3), 341-365.

Heller, J. F. (1982). *Increasing faculty and administrative effectiveness.* San Francisco: Jossey Bass.

Hill, D. J. (1988). *Humor in the classroom: A handbook for teachers.* Springfield, Illinois: Charles C. Thomas.

Hiller, J. H., Fisher, G., A., & Kaess, W. A. (1969). A computer investigation of verbal characteristics of effective classroom lecturing. *American Educational Research Journal, 6*(4), 661-675.

Hines, C. V. (1982). A further investigation of teacher clarity: The observation of teacher clarity and the relationship between clarity and student achievement and satisfaction. (Doctoral dissertation, 1981). *Dissertation Abstracts International, 42,* 3122A.

Hines, C. V., Curickshank, D., & Kennedy, J. J. (1985). Teacher clarity and its relationship to student achievement and satisfaction. *American Educational Research Journal, 22*(1), 87-99.

Hirst, P. H. (1983). Educational theory. In P. H. Hirst (Ed.), *Educational theory and its foundation disciplines.* London: Routledge.

Holland, D. (1979). *An investigation of the generality of teacher clarity.* Unpublished doctoral dissertation, Memphis State University.

Horwood, R. H. (1988). Explanation and description in science teaching. *Science Education, 72*(1), 41-49.

Howard, R. (1989). Teaching science with metaphors. *School Science Review, 70,* 100-103.

Huh, K. C. (1986). The role of teacher logic and clarity in student achievement (Doctoral dissertation, Stanford University, 1986). *Dissertation Abstracts International, 47,* 472A.

Hutchings, P., & Wutzdorff, A. (1988). Experiential learning across the curriculum: Assumptions and principles. In P. Hutchings & A. Wutzdorff (Eds.), *Knowing and doing: Learning through experience.* San Francisco: Jossey-Bass.

Hyman, R. T. (1968). The concept of an ideal teacher-student relationship. In R. T. Hyman (Ed.), *Teaching: Vantage points for study* (pp. 175-185). New York: Lippingoatt.

Javidi, M., Downs, V. C., & Nussbaum, J. F. (1988). A comparative analysis of teachers' use of dramatic style behaviors at higher and secondary education levels. *Communication Education, 37*(4), 278-288.

Johnson, A. J. (1970). A preliminary investigation of the relationship between message organization and listener comprehension. *Central States Speech Journal, 21,* 104-107.

Johnson, D. W., & Johnson, R. T. (1995). Social psychological theories of teaching. In T. W. Anderson (Ed.), *The International Encyclopedia of Teaching and Teacher Education* (pp. 112-117).

Johnson, D. W., Johnson, R. T., & Smith, K. A. (1991). *Active learning: Cooperation in the college classroom.* Edina, Minn.: Interaction Book Company.

Jones, J. (1979). *Physics interface:* Higher Education Research Office, University of Auckland.

Jones, J. (1981). Students' models of university teaching. *Higher Education, 10*(5), 529-549.

Joyce, B., & Showers, B. (1980). Improving inservice training: The messages of research. *Educational Leadership, 37*(5), 379-385.

Kaplan, R. M., & Pascoe, G. C. (1977). Humorous lectures and humorous examples: Some effects upon comprehension and retention. *Journal of Educational Psychology, 69*(1), 61-65.

Karabenick, S. A., & Sharma, R. (1994). Perceived teacher support of student questioning in the college classroom: Its relation to student characteristics and role in the classroom questioning process. *Journal of Educational Psychology, 86*(1), 90-103.

Kelley, W. (1970). Speech instruction in California community colleges. *Speech Teacher, 19*(3), 211-224.

Kember, D. (1997). A reconceptualisation of the research into university academics' conceptions of teaching. *Learning and Instruction, 7*(3), 255-275.

Kember, D., & Gow, L. (1994). Orientations to teaching and their effect on the quality of student learning. *Journal of Higher Education, 65*(1), 58-74.

Kennedy, J. J., Cruickshank, D. R., Bush, A., & Myers, B. (1978). Additional investigations into the nature of teacher clarity. *Journal of Educational Research, 72*(2), 3-10.

Kerlinger, F. N. (1966). Attitudes toward education and perceptions of teacher characteristics: A Q study. *American Educational Research Journal., 3*, 159-168.

Kerlinger, F. N., & Pedhazur, E. J. (1968). Educational attitudes and perceptions of desirable traits of teachers. *American Educational Research Journal, 5*(4), 543-559.

Kinnear, J. (1994). *What science education really says about communication of science concepts.* (ED 372-455).

Kirsch, A. (1976, August). *Aspects of simplification in mathematics teaching.* Paper presented at the Third International Congress on Mathematical Education (ICME), Karlsruhe, Germany, published in the Proceedings, pp. 98-120.

Korobkin, D. (1988). Humor in the classroom: Considerations and strategies. *College Teaching, 36*(4), 154-158.

Kraft, R. G. (1990). Group-inquiry turns passive students active. In M. Weimer & R. A. Neff (Eds.), *Teaching college.* Madison, Wisconsin: Magna Publications, Inc.

Kreber, C. (2000). *Survey on the "scholarship of teaching",* [Internet]. Available: http://www.atl.ualberta.ca/evaluation/teach [2000,.

Kreber, C. (Forthcoming). Conceptualizing the Scholarship of Teaching and Identifying Unresolved Issues: The Framework for this Volume. *New Directions for Teaching and Learning.*

Land, M. L. (1981). Combined Effect of Two Teacher Clarity Variables on Student Achievement. *Journal of Experimental Education, 50*(1), 14-17.

Land, M. L., & Smith, L. R. (1979). Effect of a teacher clarity variable on student achievement. *Journal of Educational Research, 72*(4), 196-197.

Land, M. L., & Smith, L. R. (1981). College student ratings and teacher behavior: An experimental study. *Journal of Social Studies Research, 5*(1), 19-22.

Leinhardt, G. (1990). *Towards understanding instructional explanations* (CLIP-90-03). Pittsburgh: Center for the Study of Learning.

Lenze, L. F. (1996). *Instructional development: What works?* (Volume 2 No. 4). Washington, DC: National Education Association, Office of Higher Education, NEA Higher Education Research Center Update.

Lepper, M. R. (1985). Microcomputers in education: Motivational and social issues. *American Psychologist, 40*(1), 1-18.

Lepper, M. R., & Chabay, R. W. (1985). Computers and education? *Educational Psychologist, 20*(4), 217-230.

Levinson-Rose, J., & Menges, R. J. (1981). Improving college teaching: A critical review of research. *Review of Educational Research, 51*(3), 403-434.

Lichty, R. W., & Peterson, J. M. (1979). *Peer evaluations--A necessary part of evaluating teaching effectiveness* (ED175352).

Loftus, G. R., & Loftus, E. F. (1976). *Human memory: The processing of information.* Hillsdale, NJ: Lawrence Erlbaum.

Lowman, J. (1984). *Mastering the techniques of teaching.* San Francisco: Jossey-Bass.

Lowman, J. (1996). Characteristics of exemplary teachers. *New Directions for Teaching and Learning, 65*, 33-40.

Lowther, M. A., Stark, J. S., Genthon, M. L., & Bentley, R. J. (1990). Comparing introductory course planning among full-time and part-time faculty. *Research in Higher Education, 31*(6), 495-517.

Luiten, J., Ames, W., & Ackerson, G. (1980). A meta-analysis of the effects of advance organizers on learning and retention. *American Educational Research Journal, 17*, 211-218.

MacDonald, R. E. (1991). *A handbook of basic skills and strategies for beginning teachers: Facing the challenge of teaching in today's schools.*

Marsh, H. W. (1984). Students' college teaching: A critical review of research. *Journal of Educational Psychology, 76*(5), 707-754.

Marsh, H. W. (1987a). Reliability, stability and generalizability. *International Journal of Educational Research, 11*(3), 275-283.

Marsh, H. W. (1987b). Students' evaluations of university teaching: Research findings, methodological issues, and directions for future research. *International Journal of Educational Research, 11*(3), 253-388.

Marsh, H. W., & Bailey, M. (1993). Multidimensional Students' Evaluations of Teaching Effectiveness. *Journal of Higher Education, 64*(1), 1-18.

Marsh, H. W., & Dunkin, M. J. (1997). Students' evaluations of university teaching; A multidimensional perspective. In R. P. Perry & J. C. Smart (Eds.), *Effective teaching in higher education: Research and practice* (pp. 241-313). NY: Agathon Press.

Marsh, H. W., & Overall, J. U. (1979). Long--term stability of students' evaluations: a note on Feldman's "consistency and variability among college students in rating their teachers and courses. *Research in Higher Education, 10*(2), 139-147.

Marsh, H. W., & Overall, J. U. (1980). Validity of students' evaluations of teaching effectiveness: cognitive and affective criteria. *Journal of Educational Psychology, 72*(4), 468-475.

Marsh, H. W., & Roche, L. (1993). The use of students' evaluations and an individually structured intervention to enhance university teaching effectiveness. *American Educational Research Journal, 30*(1), 217-251.

Marton, F., & Säljö, R. (1976). On qualitative differences in learning II - Outcome as a function of the learner's conception of the task. *British Journal of Educational Psychology, 46*(1), 115-127.

McClelland, D. C. (1985). *Human motivation.* Glenview, Ill.: Scott, Foresman.

McKeachie, W. J. (1994). *Teaching tips: A guidebook for the beginning college teacher.* (9th ed.). Lexington, Massachusetts: D. C. Heath and Company.

McKeachie, W. J. (1999). *Teaching tips: Strategies, research, and theory for college and university teachers.* (10 ed.). Boston: Houghton Mifflin.

McKeachie, W. J., Pintrich, P. R., Lin, Y., & Smith, D. A. F. (1987). *Teaching and learning in the college classroom. A review of the research literature.* Ann Arbor: NCTIPTAL, The University of Michigan.

McLeish, J. (1968). *The lecture method.* (Vol. 1). Cambridge: Cambridge Institute of Education.

Menec, V. M., & Perry, R. P. (1995). Disciplinary differences in students' perceptions of success: Modifying misperceptions with attributional retraining. In N. Hativa & M. Marincovich (Eds.), *Disciplinary differences in teaching and learning: Implications for practice* (pp. 105-112). San Francisco: Jossey Bass.

Metcalf, K. K., & Cruickshank, D. R. (1991). Can teachers be trained to make clear presentations? *Journal of Educational Research, 85*(2), 107-116.

Meyer, B. J. F. (1975). *The organization of prose and its effects in memory.* Amsterdam: North Holland.

Meyers, C., & Jones, T. B. (1993). *Promoting active learning strategies for the college classroom.* San Francisco: Jossey-Bass.

Mezirow, J. (1991). *Transformative dimensions of adult learning.* San Francisco: Jossey-Bass.

Miltz, R. J. (1972). Development and evaluation of a manual for improving teachers' explanations (Doctoral dissertation, Stanford University, 1971). *Dissertation Abstracts International, 32,* 5474A. (University Microfilm No. 72-11,697).

Mogavero, D. T. (1979). It's confirmed: J-students like humor in the classroom. *Journalism Educator, 34*(1), 43-44.

Moses, I. (1985). Academic development units and the improvement of teaching. *Higher Education, 14*(1), 75-100.

Murray, H. G. (1983). Low-inference classroom teaching behaviors and student ratings of college teaching effectiveness. *Journal of Educational Psychology, 75*(1), 138-149.

Murray, H. G. (1997). *Classroom teaching behaviors and student instructional ratings: How do good teachers teach?* Paper presented at the annual meeting of the American Educational Research Association, Chicago, IL.

Murray, H. G., & Lawrence, C. (1980). Speech and drama training for lecturers as a mean of improving university teaching. *Research in Higher Education, 13*(1), 73-90.

Murray, H. G., & Renaud, R. D. (1995). Disciplinary differences in classroom teaching behaviors. In N. Hativa & M. Marincovich (Eds.), *Disciplinary differences in teaching and learning: Implications for practice.* San Francisco: Jossey Bass.

Murray, H. G., Rushton, P. J., & Paunonen, S. V. (1990). Teacher personality traits and student instructional ratings in six types of university courses. *Journal of Educational Psychology, 82*(2), 250-261.

Musella, D., & Rusch, R. (1968). Student opinion on college teaching. *Improving College and University Teaching, 16,* 1137-1140.

Myers, L., Jr. (1968). *Improving the quality of education by identifying effective television teachers. Final report* (ED 025-493): Syracuse University.

Needels, M. C. (1984). The role of logic in the teacher's facilitation of student achievement (Doctoral dissertation, Stanford University, 1984). *Dissertation Abstracts International, 45,* 791-792A.

Nunn, C. E. (1996). Discussion in the college classroom: Triangulating observational and survey results. *Journal of Higher Education, 67*(3), 243-266.

Orts, E. W. (1997). Quality Circles in Law Teaching. *Journal of Legal Education, 47*(3), 425-431.

Osborne, J. L. (1998). Integrating student and peer evaluation teaching. *College Teaching,* *46*(1), 36-38.

Pace, C. R. (1988). *Measuring the quality of college student experiences.* Los Angeles, CA: UCLA Center for the Study of Evaluation.

Pask, G. (1988). Learning strategies, teaching strategies and conceptual or learning style. In R. R. Schmeck (Ed.), *Learning styles and strategies* (pp. 83-100). NY: Plenum Press.

Patterson, M. (1983). *Nonverbal behavior: A functional perspective.* New York: Springer-Verlag.

Paulsen, M. B. (Forthcoming). The scholarship of teaching. *New Directions for Teaching and Learning.*

Perkins, D., & Swartz, R. (1992). The nine basics of teaching thinking. In A. L. Costa, J. L. Bellanca, & R. Fogarty (Eds.), *If minds matter: A foreword to the future* (Vol. II, pp. 53-69).

Perkins, D. N. (1992). Understanding performances. In D. N. Perkins (Ed.), *Smart schools: From training memories to educating minds* (pp. 75-79). New York: The Free Press.

Perkins, D. N. (1998). What is understanding. In M. S. Wiske (Ed.), *Teaching for understanding: A practical framework.* San Francisco: Jossey-Bass.

Perry, R. P., Hecher, F. J., Menec, V. H., & Weinberg, L. (1993). Enhancing achievement motivation and performance in college students: An attributional retraining perspective. *Research in Higher Education, 34*(6), 687-723.

Piaget, J. (1955). *The language and thought of the child* (M. Gavain, Trans.). New York: Meridan Books.

Pinney, R. H. (1970). Presentational behaviors related to success in teaching (Doctoral dissertation, Stanford University, 1969). *Dissertation Abstracts International, 30,* 5327-5328A. (University Microfilm No. 70-10,552).

Pintrich, P. R., Smith, D. A. F., Garcia, T., & McKeachie, W. J. (1991). *A manual for the use of the motivated strategies for learning questionnaire (MSLQ).* Ann Arbor, MI: National Center for Research to Improve Postsecondary Teaching and Learning.

Pohlmann, J. T. (1976). A description of effective college teaching in five disciplines as measured by student ratings. *Research in Higher Education, 4*(4), 335-346.

Pollio, H. R. (1984). *What students think about and do in college lecture classes* (Teaching-Learning Issues no 53): Learning Research Center, University of Tennessee.

Polya, G. (1957). *How to solve it?* (2nd ed.). Princeton, NJ: University Press.

Polya, G. (1965). *Mathematical discovery.* (Vol. II). New York: John Wiley & Sons, Inc.

Powell, J. P., & Andersen, L. W. (1985). Humour and teaching in higher education. *Studies in Higher Education, 10*(1), 79-90.

Quinn, J. W. (1994, January). *Teaching award recipients' perceptions of teaching award programs*. Paper presented at the Second AAHE Forum on Faculty Roles and Rewards, New Orleans.

Radloff, A. (Forthcoming). Learning to teach: Changes in technical college teachers' beliefs about learning and teaching over a two year teacher education program.

Ramsden, P. (1992). *Learning to teach in higher education*. London: Routledge.

Ramsden, P., & Entwistle, N. J. (1981). Effects of academic departments on students' approaches to studying. *British Journal of Educational Psychology, 51*(3), 368-383.

Rando, W. C., & Menges, R. J. (1991). How practice is shaped by personal theories. *New Directions for Teaching and Learning, 45*, 7-14.

Redfield, D. L., & Rousseau, E. W. (1981). A meta-analysis of experimental research on teacher questioning behavior. *Review of Educational Research, 51*(2), 237-245.

Riley, J. R., Ryan, B. F., & Lifshits, M. (1950). *The student looks at his teacher*. New Brunswick, NJ: Rutgers University Press.

Roberts, F. C., & Park, O.-C. (1984). Feedback strategies and cognitive style in computer-based instruction. *Journal of Instructional Psychology, 11*(2), 63-74.

Rochester, S. R. (1973). The significance of pauses in spontaneous speech. *Journal of Psycholinguistic Research, 2*(1), 51-81.

Rosenshine, B. (1986). Teaching Functions. In M. C. Wittrock (Ed.), *Handbook of Research on Teaching* (3rd ed., pp. 376-391). New York: MacMillan Publishing Company.

Rotem, A., & Glasman, N. S. (1979). On the effectiveness of students' evaluative feedback to university instructors. *Review of Educational Research, 49*(3), 497-511.

Rowe, M. B. (1974). Wait-time and rewards as instructional variables, their influences on language, logic and fate control. Part one--wait time. *Journal of research in Science Teaching, 11*(263-279).

Rowe, M. B. (1986). Wait times: Slowing down may be a way of speeding up. *Journal of Teacher Education, 37*(1), 43-50.

Rowe, M. B., & DeTure, L. (Eds.). (1975). *A summary of research in science education*. Columbus, Ohio: ERIC Information Analysis Center for Science, Mathematics, and Environmental Education.

Ruhl, K. L., Hughes, C. A., & Schloss, P. J. (1987). Using the pause procedure to enhance lecture recall. *Teacher Education and Special Education, 10*, 14-18.

Ryans, D. G. (1960). *Characteristics of teachers: Their description, comparison, and appraisal*. Washington, DC: American Council on Education.

Sallinen-Kuparinen, A. (1992). Teacher communicator style. *Communication Education, 41*(2), 153-166.

Salsibury, D. F. (1995, March 9). Gil Masters: Details key to success in teaching big classes. *Campus Report, Stanford University.*

Schmeck, R. R., Geisler-Brenstein, E., & Cercy, S. P. (1991). Self-concept and learning: The revised inventory of learning processes. *Educational Psychology, 11*(3-4), 343-362.

Sherman, T. M., Armistead, L. P., Fowler, F., Barksdale, M. A., & Reif, G. (1987). The quest for excellence in university teaching. *Journal of Higher Education, 48*(1), 66-84.

Shulman, L. S. (1986). Those who understand: Knowledge growth in teaching. *Educational Researcher, 15*(2), 4-14.

Shulman, L. S. (1987). Knowledge and teaching: Foundations of the new reform. *Harvard Educational Review, 57*(1), 1-22.

Shulman, L. S. (1997). *Communities of learners and communities of teachers.* Jerusalem: Mandel Institution.

Shulman, L. S. (1998). Course anatomy: The dissection and analysis of knowledge through teaching. In p. Hutchings (Ed.), *The Course Portfolio.* Washington, DC: American Association for Higher Education.

Shulman, L. S. (2000). From Minsk to Pinsk: Why a scholarship of teaching and learning? *The Journal of Scholarship of Teaching and Learning, 1*(1), 50-53.

Shulman, L. S., & Hutchings, P. (1997). *Fostering a scholarship of teaching and learning: The Carnegie Teaching Academy.* Menlo Park, California: The Carnegie Foundation for the Advancement of Teaching.

Shutes, R. (1970). Verbal behaviors and instructional effectiveness (Doctoral dissertation, Stanford University, 1969). *Dissertation Abstracts International, 30,* 3335A. (University Microfilm No. 70-01603).

Smart, J. C., & Ethington, C. A. (1995). Disciplinary and institutional differences in undergraduate education goals. In N. Hativa & M. Marincovich (Eds.), *Disciplinary Differences in Teaching and Learning: Implications for Practice* (pp. 49-58). San Francisco: Jossey-Bass.

Smith, L. R., & Land, M. L. (1980a). *Student perception of teacher clarity* (ERIC No. ED183105).

Smith, L. R., & Land, M. L. (1980b). Student perception of teacher clarity in mathematics. *Journal for Research in Mathematics Education, 11*(2), 137-147.

Smith, L. R., & Land, M. L. (1981). Low-inference verbal behaviors related to teacher clarity. *Journal of Classroom Interaction, 17*(1), 37-42.

Smith, R. A. (1995). Reflecting critically on our efforts to improve teaching and learning. In E. Neal (Ed.), *To improve the academy* (Vol. 16, pp. 5-25). Stillwater, Oklahoma: New Forums Press.

Smith, R. A. (Forthcoming). Expertise in teaching and in the schoarship of teaching. *New Directions for Teaching and Learning.*

Smith, R. A., & Geis, G. L. (1996). Professors as clients for instructional development. In L. Richlin (Ed.), *To improve the academy* (Vol. 15, pp. 129-153). Stillwater, OK: New Forums Press.

Smith, S. (1978). The identification of teaching behaviors descriptive of the construct: Clarity of presentation. (Doctoral dissertation, *Dissertation Abstracts International, 39(06)*, 3529A.

Snyder, S., Bushur, L., Hoeksema, P., Clark, S., & Snyder, J. (1991). *The effect of instructional clarity and concept structure on student achievement and perception.* Paper presented at the annual meeting of the American Educational Research Association, Chicago.

Spicer, C., & Basset, R. E. (1976). The effect of organization on learning from and informative message. *The Southern Speech Communication Journal, 41,* 290-299.

Stage, F. K., Muller, P. A., Kinzie, J., & Simmons, A. (1998). *Creating learning centered classrooms: What does learning theory have to say?*: ASHE-ERIC Higher Education Report Volume 26, No. 4. Washington, D.C: The George Washington University, Graduate School of Education and Human Development.

Stark, J. S. (Forthcoming). Planning introductory college courses: Content, context, and process. In N. Hativa & P. Goodyear (Eds.), *Teacher thinking, beliefs and knowledge in higher education.* Dordrecht, Holland: Kluwer Academic Press.

Stark, J. S., & Lattuca, L. R. (1994). Diversity among disciplines: The same goals for all? *New Directions for Higher Education, 84,* 71-86.

Stark, J. S., & Lowther, M. A. (1990). *Planning introductory college courses: Influences on faculty* (ED330277). Ann Arbor, MI: National Center for Research to Improve Postsecondary Teaching and Learning.

Stark, J. S., Lowther, M. A., Bentley, R. J., & Martens, G. G. (1990). Disciplinary differences in course planning. *Review of Higher Education, 13*(2), 141-165.

Svinicki, M. D., Hagen, A. S., & Meyer, D. K. (1996). Research on learning: A means to enhance instructional methods. In M. E. Weimer & R. E. Menges (Eds.), *Teaching on solid ground* (pp. 257-295). San Francisco: Jossey-Bass.

Sweller, J., & Cooper, G. A. (1985). The use of worked examples as a substitute for problem solving in learning algebra. *Cognition and Instruction, 2*(1), 59-89.

Tamborini, R., & Zillmann, D. (1981). College students' perception of lecturers using humor. *Perceptual and Motor Skills, 52*(2), 417-432.

Tetenbaum, T. J. (1975). The role of student needs and teacher orientations in student ratings of teachers. *American Educational Research Journal, 12*(4), 417-429.

Thielens, W., Jr. (1987). *The disciplines and undergraduate lecturing.* Paper presented at the annual meeting of the American Educational Research Association, Washington, DC.

Thompson, E. (1960). An experimental investigation of the relative effectiveness of organizational structure in oral communication. *Southern Speech Journal, 26,* 59-69.

Thompson, E. (1967). Some effects of message structure on listeners' comprehension. *Speech Monographs, 34,* 51-57.

Thorndyke, P. W. (1978). Knowledge transfer in learning from texts. In A. M. Lesgold, J. W. Pellegrino, S. D. Pokkema, & R. Glaser (Eds.), *Cognitive psychology and instruction.* NY: Plenum Press.

Tobin, K. (1987). The role of wait time in higher cognitive level learning. *Review of Educational Research, 57*(1), 69-95.

Travis, J. E. (1995). *Models for Improving College Teaching: A Faculty Resource* (6): ASHE-ERIC Higher Education Reports.

Treisman, P. U. (1983). *Improving the Performance of Minority Students in College-Level Mathematics.*

Treisman, P. U. (1985). *A study of the mathematics performance of black students at the University of California* (Unpublished manuscript). Berkeley: University of California.

Treisman, U. (1992). Studying Students Studying Calculus: A Look at the Lives of Minority Mathematics Students in College. *College Mathematics Journal, 23*(5), 362-372.

Vayda, A. P., McCay, B. J., & Eghenter, C. (1991). Concepts of process in social science explanations. *Philosophy of the Social Sciences, 21*(3), 318-331.

Wandersee, J. H. (1982). Humor as a teaching strategy. *American Biology Teacher, 44*(4), 212-218.

Ward, B. (1995). Improving teaching across the academy: Gleanings from research. In E. Neal (Ed.), *To improve the academy* (Vol. 14, pp. 27-42). Stillwater, Oklahoma: New Forums Press.

Warnock, P. (1989). Humor as a didactic tool in adult education. *Lifelong Learning, 12*(8), 22-24.

Weimer, M., & Lenze, F. L. (1991). Instructional interventions: A review of the literature on efforts to improve instruction. In J. C. Smart (Ed.), *Higher Education: Handbook of Theory and Research.* (Vol. 7, pp. 294-333). Bronx, NY: Agathon.

Weinstein, C. E., Zimmermann, S. A., & Palmer, D. R. (1985). College and university students' study skills in the USA: The LASSI. In G. d'Ydewalle (Ed.), *Cognition, information processing, and motivation* (pp. 703-726). Amsterdam: Elsevier Science Publishing.

Weisskopf, V. (1997). Points to ponder. *Readers Digest*(November), 194.

Wilkerson, L., & Feletti, G. (1989). Problem-based learning: One approach to increasing student participation. *New Directions for Teaching and Learning (The Department Chairperson's Role in Enhancing College Teaching), 37*, 51-60.

Williams, E. J. (1984). The short term stability of teacher clarity (Doctoral dissertation, 1983). *Dissertation Abstracts International, 44*, 3362A.

Williams, E. J. (1985). Research on teacher clarity. *Teacher Education Quarterly, 12*(3), 33-38.

Wilson, R. C. (1986). Improving faculty teaching: Effective use of student evaluations and consultants. *Journal of Higher Education, 57*(2), 196-211.

Wilson, S. M., Shulman, L. S., & Richert, A. E. (1987). '150 different ways' of knowing: Representations of knowledge in teaching. In J. Calderhead (Ed.), *Exploring teachers' thinking* (pp. 104-124). London: Cassell Educational Limited.

Wlodkowski, R. J. (1985). *Enhancing adult motivation to learn: A guide to improving instruction and increasing learner achievement.* San Francisco: Jossey-Bass.

Woolfolk, A. E., & Galloway, C. M. (1985). Nonverbal communication and the study of teaching. *Theory into Practice, 24*(1), 77-84.

Zeaks, S. J. (1989). Case studies in biology. *College Teaching, 37*(1), 33-35.

Zhu, X., & Simon, H. A. (1987). Learning mathematics from examples and by doing. *Cognition and Instruction, 4*(3), 137-166.

Ziv, A. (1976). Facilitating effects of humor on creativity. *Journal of Educational Psychology, 68*(3), 318-322.

Ziv, A. (1988). Teaching and learning with humor: Experiment and replication. *Journal of Experimental Education, 57*(1), 5-15.

NAME INDEX

SUBJECT INDEX

Revised Indexes

N. Hativa

Teaching for Effective Learning in Higher Education

0-7923-6662-X

NAME INDEX

SUBJECT INDEX

Printed in the United States
134267LV00002B/27/A

9 780792 368434